Rethinking Philosophy of Religion

Perspectives in Continental Philosophy
John D. Caputo, series editor

Rethinking
Philosophy of Religion

APPROACHES FROM
CONTINENTAL PHILOSOPHY

Edited by
PHILIP GOODCHILD

Fordham University Press
New York
2002

Copyright © 2002 by Fordham University Press

Perspectives in Continental Philosophy No. 29
ISSN 1089–3938

Library of Congress Cataloging-in-Publication Data

Rethinking philosophy of religion : approaches from
  continental philosophy / edited by Philip Goodchild.— 1st ed.
     p.   cm.—(Perspectives in continental
  philosophy ; no. 29)
  Includes bibliographical references and index.
  ISBN 0-8232-2206-3
  1. Religion—Philosophy—Congresses.   2.
Philosophy, European—Congresses.   I. Goodchild, Philip, 1965–
II. Series.
BL51 .R385   2002
210—dc21   2002006462

Printed in the United States of America
02   03   04   05   06   5   4   3   2   1
First Edition

CONTENTS

ACKNOWLEDGMENTS

Grateful acknowledgment is made for permission to reprint previously published material:

Chapter 2: John D. Caputo, "The Poetics of the Impossible and the Kingdom of God" was previously published in Graham Ward, ed., *The Blackwell Companion to Postmodern Theology* (Oxford: Blackwell, 2001).

All the chapters published here, except chapter 1, were prepared as papers for the conference entitled "Continental Philosophy of Religion," 18–21 July 2000, hosted by the Department of Religion and Ethics, St. Martin's College, Lancaster, UK. I gratefully acknowledge sponsorship of this conference by the British Academy.

Rethinking Philosophy of Religion

1

Continental Philosophy of Religion: An Introduction

Philip Goodchild

> Criticism of religion is the premise of all criticism.
>
> KARL MARX

WHAT IS a Continental philosophy of religion?[1] Philosophy of religion, in English-speaking countries, has a clear and distinct identity, and has been enjoying a resurgence: it focuses largely on the truth-claims, rationality, and coherence of religious propositions, and particularly those of "classical theism."[2] Yet for those who work in the traditions of philosophy derived from Germany and France, the problems, tasks, concepts, reasoning, and

---

[1] This is the topic of the call for papers that announced a conference on "Continental Philosophy of Religion" at St. Martin's College, Lancaster, UK, in July 2000. All the other essays in this volume were prepared for the conference. Some further essays prepared for the conference, locating thought in relation to religion, gender, tradition, culture and politics, are collected in Philip Goodchild, ed., *Difference in Philosophy of Religion* (Aldershot: Ashgate Publications, 2002).

[2] Although few are bold enough to define "philosophy of religion," Charles Taliaferro lists a number of questions that help identify it in a contemporary sense, in *Contemporary Philosophy of Religion* (Oxford: Blackwell, 1998), 4–5. An alternative approach, taken by Brian Davies, is to present "what would commonly be taken as standard examples of it" (*Philosophy of Religion: A Guide and Anthology,* Oxford: Oxford University Press, 2000, preface). There is a strong coherence in the field, demonstrated by the overlap of topics in the abundance of excellent, recently published textbooks and anthologies. Even Gary E. Kessler, who wishes to transform philosophy of religion to take a more global approach, understands it as concerned with "fundamental" questions and, thus, reproduces a diverse and thought-provoking anthology under the usual chapter headings (*Philosophy of Religion: Toward a Global Perspective,* Belmont, Calif.: Wadsworth, 1999).

cultural location are markedly different from this identity. When even the individual terms of the phrase "Continental philosophy of religion" are highly contestable, can this title designate any determinate field? In spite of its weaknesses, this phrase functions as a useful identity marker to bring together some of those who feel it is time to rethink the discipline of philosophy of religion. Beneath this title, therefore, it is possible to sketch the shape of an emerging body of work in continuity with elements of a long historical tradition.

In the first place, modern reason was constructed through a critique of religious thought and practice, and many of the defining arguments and motivations of the Continental tradition have been inherited from the emergence of modern philosophy of religion as a purely rational discipline. In order to uncover the tasks and problems of a Continental philosophy of religion, I have therefore returned to its historical emergence to highlight concerns that are not always at the forefront of analytic philosophy of religion.

In the second place, Continental philosophy has transformed philosophical reflection through a critique of reason itself. The completion of this second phase of critical modernity reopens the possibility of discovering religion already inside the limits of reason itself.

In the third place, contemporary thinkers are beginning to respond in diverse ways to the possibilities and opportunities afforded by this new critical circumstance. In what follows, then, I shall discuss the emergence of modern philosophy of religion and the critique of reason in Continental thought insofar as it has led to a "return to religion," and introduce the essays included in this volume.

THE EMERGENCE OF PHILOSOPHY OF RELIGION

(a) From "Authority" to "Reason"

Philosophy of religion emerged alongside, and indeed contributed to, the emergence of modernity itself.[3] Its origins are in-

---

[3] Of course, the key concepts of classical theism, the use of rational argument in philosophical theology, and the debates about the respective provinces of

separable from its historical context: all intellectuals in the seventeenth and eighteenth centuries in northern and western Europe were acutely conscious of how religious divisions were used by political leaders to extend their influence by persecution and making war. The conflicts between competing denominations raised questions about religious authority. For, as Lord Herbert of Cherbury, who may perhaps be regarded as the father of modern philosophy of religion, observed in *De veritate* (1624), arguments from authority may be used to establish a false religion just as easily as a true one. Then dissension demanded epistemology: Herbert attempted to establish "the fundamental principles of religion by means of universal wisdom."[4]

The disputes that raged over "religion" were disputes over liturgical forms of worship, sources of authority, church institutional structure, and articles of faith; only when these were brought before rational reflection did religion become treated as a genus containing several species. While it was unlikely that reason could determine the "outward" forms of worship, it could determine the principles and practice that the "ceremonial practices" and "formularies of belief" could imitate.[5]

Given the extent of the dissension, Herbert suggested that revelation could only be believed if it were proved beyond any doubt that it had indeed taken place, that it was given by God, had been

---

faith and reason have much longer histories, and contemporary philosophy of religion draws heavily on these. It may be regarded as anachronistic, however, to call such earlier endeavors philosophy of religion, both because the phrase did not come into frequent use until Hegel's lectures on the topic and because the reasoning, motivation, and intellectual context were quite different. In particular, prior to modernity there was little separation of an autonomous "reason" from the created and ordered cosmos that it understood.

[4] See Peter Gay, ed., *Deism: An Anthology* (Princeton: D. Van Nostrand, 1968), 31. "Religion," at this time, no longer had the medieval sense of the "state of life bound by monastic vows," but retained some of its sense of "true religion," derived from Augustine's *De vera religione* as "worship of the one true God," while being significantly augmented by the popularity of Calvin's *Institutes of the Christian Religion*, describing the correct form of faith and worship. See Wilfred Cantwell Smith, *The Meaning and End of Religion* (London: SPCK, 1978), 29, 36; for a fuller account, see Peter Harrison, *"Religion" and the Religions in the English Enlightenment* (Cambridge: Cambridge University Press, 1990).

[5] See G. W. Leibniz, *Theodicy: Essays on the Goodness of God and the Freedom of Man and the Origin of Evil,* trans. E. M. Huggard (London: Routledge and Kegan Paul, 1951), 49.

accurately reported, and concerned later ages.[6] Variations of this
key argument were repeated by the radical thinkers who contributed to the creation of the modern secular state, such as Thomas
Hobbes,[7] John Locke,[8] and Thomas Paine.[9] For by contrast to
revelation in scriptural or ecclesiastical authority, the scientific
methods of Francis Bacon, Galileo Galilei, and René Descartes
suggested a method for reaching a secure foundation for human
knowledge on which all could agree. Although the analogy between science and religion was weak, since evidence and experiment were lacking in religion, a rational foundation for religion
promised a possible cure for dissension.

Moreover, since the miraculous, the supernatural, and the historically particular relied on dubious testimony, universal foun-
dations for religion were sought from reason itself. Herbert
attempted to identify Common Notions, innate religious ideas
deriving directly from God, as a universal basis for religion. Prior
to Descartes, Herbert elevated introspection above authority and
tradition as the new standard of truth.[10] Locke's persuasive dismissal of these, and the innate ideas of the Cartesians and Cambridge Platonists, further shifted the ground for rational inquiry
into religion: the incipience of cognition was reduced to a tabula
rasa, eliminating the authority of tradition as well as innate ideas.
Adding this to the critique of Aristotelian teleology by Bacon,
Descartes, Blaise Pascal, Benedict de Spinoza, and Isaac Newton, then the full heritage of Augustinian illumination, through
which religious knowledge had been authenticated by its own

---

[6] Gay, *Deism*, 43.

[7] "None can know [the scriptures] are God's word (though all true Christians
beleeve it), but those to whom God himself hath revealed it supernaturally."
Thomas Hobbes, *Leviathan,* ed. Richard Tuck (Cambridge: Cambridge University Press, 1996), ch. 33, 267.

[8] "Without such a *revelation* [direct from God of the authenticity of scrip-
ture], the believing or not believing that proposition or book to be of divine
authority can never be matter of *faith*, but matter of reason, and such as I must
come to an assent to only by the use of my reason." John Locke, *An Essay
Concerning Human Understanding,* vol. 2, ed. John W. Yolton (London: J. M.
Dent, 1964), 284.

[9] "It is revelation to the first person only, and *hearsay* to every other person,
and consequently they are not obliged to believe it." Thomas Paine, *The Age of
Reason* (Amherst, N.Y.: Prometheus Books, 1984), 10.

[10] Harrison, *"Religion" and the Religions in the English Enlightenment,* 67.

truth, was broken in favor of clear and distinct ideas within the subject. All knowledge, even with respect to religion, had to be reconstructed by the processes of reason, and by each individual.

It is important to note the confluence of theologico-political concerns that fed this rational inquiry into religion. While Herbert wished to overcome dissension, Leibniz aimed to publish "such knowledge of God as is needed to awaken piety and to foster virtue."[11] The particular danger Leibniz wished to guard against was a conception of God as a despotic power or will, making arbitrary choices of whom to save, without being guided by reason, for such a conception was "unfit to make men good and charitable through the imitation of God."[12] Leibniz sought reasons to explain Protestant doctrine not only to "plead the cause of God," but also to foster true piety, based on reasons and insight, which "consists in principles and practice."[13] This emphasis on reason motivated by piety had the effect of undermining the mystifications of authority based on emphasizing the divine will.

Locke's "Letter on Toleration" had a similar effect in undermining the role of authority in religion. Although his specific target was the judicial power of the "magistrate" over religion, he did not regard religious belief to be subject to political influence. For "to believe this or that to be true does not depend upon our will";[14] instead, it is only "light and evidence that can work a change in men's opinions."[15] Use of judicial power leads to the artificial pretense of religion, which is by no means salvific.[16] Moreover, the church does not have authority to determine orthodoxy, for each church is orthodox to itself; indeed, the church is more likely to be influenced by state power than the state influenced by the church.[17]

Thus no one could pass on responsibility for his or her salva-

---

[11] Leibniz, *Theodicy,* 63.
[12] Ibid., 59–60.
[13] Ibid., 49.
[14] John Locke, "Letter on Toleration," in *The Locke Reader,* ed. John W. Yolton (Cambridge: Cambridge University Press, 1977), 269.
[15] Ibid., 247.
[16] Ibid., 260.
[17] Ibid., 259.

tion to another,[18] and since the princes of the world were as divided over religious opinions as they were over secular interests, many would not receive salvation by following their prince.[19] At the center of Locke's thought and faith was the role of the individual conscience before God: it was this that would determine one's eternal destiny.[20]

Finally, we may note another concern motivating the use of reason to shape religion. This is to unmask the "pretence of religion" that "serves as a cloke to covetousness, rapine and ambition."[21] For religion has been used to justify immorality not only by the corrupt princes, but also by the greatest of theologians: one need only think of Thomas Aquinas's rationalization of loving heretics by torture for the sake of their immortal souls,[22] or Gregory of Nyssa's and Martin Luther's unspeakable declamations of unrestrained hatred against the Jews. Theological orthodoxy was no guarantee of virtue and piety; indeed, it was often a hindrance. Spinoza diagnosed the essence of popular religion as "respect for ecclesiastics," leading to the corruption of the church by avarice and ambition. The result was the hypocrisy whereby those who preached love, joy, peace, temperance, and charity to all measured the strength of their faith by their bitter hatred toward each other.[23] It was reason that could bring such hypocrisy to light.

It is important to recognize that such a confluence of theologico-political concerns—the overcoming of dissension, the fostering of true piety, the liberation of religion from political interference, and the exposure of the undermining of ecclesiastical authority by avarice and ambition—contributed to the rational exploration of religion in the seventeenth and eighteenth centuries, and not an abstract love of a disembodied reason for the sake of its own purity. The philosophers who engaged with religion in this period must be regarded as a small minority of

---

[18] Ibid., 246.
[19] Ibid., 247.
[20] Ibid., 273.
[21] Ibid., 267.
[22] Thomas Aquinas, *Summa Theologica* part II, question XI, article IV.
[23] Benedict de Spinoza, *A Theologico-Political Treatise,* trans. R. H. M. Elwes (New York: Dover Publications, 1951), 6.

intellectuals and entrepreneurs inspired by the advances of science, agricultural and industrial technology, overseas exploration, trade, and conquest, to take control over their own fortune and destiny.[24] Whatever their political and religious views, this minority was pitched against the vested interests of church, state, and aristocracy on the one hand, and against the religious enthusiasms of puritans and pietists on the other, while divorced from the uneducated rural masses. They were apostles of "truth," missionaries inspired by their patron saints and pioneers: Bacon, Newton, and Locke.

One should note as well that the enthusiasts for reason were also engaged in their own political project: this beleaguered yet confident minority built its autonomy, self-mastery, and future hegemony by distinguishing the "light" of reason from anything that limited its power. Rational men set themselves above the "superstitious," women, children, "savages," "Orientals," "mystics," and the insane. It was among such a minority in the eighteenth century that arose the scandal of deist natural religion in England, the anticlericalism of the *philosophes* in France, and Wolffian rational metaphysics in Germany.

Although contemporary philosophy of religion may carry forward the heritage of these eighteenth-century debates, it carries little of their theologico-political concerns.[25] Those whose prime concern is to argue that holding religious beliefs is not irrational, and who wish to be readmitted to the community of rational people or even to departments of philosophy, subsequent to the demise of the verificationist challenge of logical positivism, ostensibly have a very different set of theologico-political interests. In particular, the contemporary requirement that philosophy of religion make no presuppositions about religious truth[26]— however rarely fulfilled in practice by those who set out to rationalize or defend a position—is often an attempt to pass as members of a hegemonic rational community, rather than an at-

---

[24] See Peter Gay, *The Enlightenment: The Science of Freedom* (New York: W. W. Norton, 1969), 6–7.

[25] Unless one suspects it of maintaining the hegemony of a rational Western elite.

[26] See, for example, Roger Trigg, *Rationality and Religion* (Oxford: Blackwell, 1998), 4.

tempt to purify passions, counteract dominant interests, expose hypocrisy, or discover "true religion" or "true piety." It is often used as an attempt to justify religious beliefs that have their origin in the very conceptions of authority and revelation that the early modern philosophers were attempting to exclude from reason.

(b) From "God" to "Religion"

The principal common thread linking contemporary philosophy of religion to seventeenth- and eighteenth-century debates is rational argumentation about the existence and nature of God. Yet the fundamental motivation of the philosophers of the latter half of the eighteenth century was the political demand for the right to question everything, rather than the assertion that all could be known or mastered by rationality.[27] The skeptical contributions of David Hume and Immanuel Kant have been widely, although not universally, regarded as eliminating any possibility of absolute certainty about the existence of God—a certainty sufficient to base one's eternal destiny upon. Nevertheless, the influence of these two thinkers is decisive for the philosophy of religion for at least two additional reasons. First, as Peter Gay quips, "the Enlightenment was not an Age of Reason but a Revolt against Rationalism."[28] In the philosophy of Hume we find the culmination of the later Enlightenment's doubt about the powers of reason—especially in regard to the passions. For Hume, "Reason is, and ought only to be the slave of the passions, and can never pretend to any other office than to serve and obey them."[29] One development is to use reason to negotiate between competing passions and interests, in a utilitarian philosophy allied to a free market; another development is the critique of ideology, the concealment of interests.

Hume's skeptical line is partially incorporated into the philos-

---

[27] Peter Gay, *The Enlightenment: An Interpretation,* vol. 1, *The Rise of Modern Paganism* (London: Weidenfeld and Nicholson, 1970), 141.

[28] Gay, *The Enlightenment,* vol. 1, 141.

[29] David Hume, *Treatise of Human Nature* (Oxford: Clarendon Press, 1988), 415.

ophy of Kant, where we find a systematic critique of the extension of reason beyond its proper limits in experience: most famously, Kant aimed to deny possible knowledge of God in order to make room for practical faith.[30] Both Hume's and Kant's gestures, as we shall see, have been repeated in Continental philosophy of religion. Then these two philosophers do not simply enter a rational debate in order to argue that God's existence cannot be proved; more significantly, *they question the whole framework of the debate* by questioning confidence in the empirical and rational epistemologies used to decide the issue. They demonstrate how reason is used to produce its own illusions. This remains their principal challenge to contemporary debates concerning rational theism—a challenge that is only too rarely addressed.

Second, there is a further legacy of their work that remains perhaps more significant still. For Hume and Kant, abandoning rational reflection on God, turn their attention instead to *religion*: the relationship of humanity to God.[31] This anthropological turn toward an object of study that seemed available for rational investigation bore more promise of progress toward the allied goals of serving the common good rather than party spirit,[32] of removing private interest from religious pretension,[33] of removing dissension by discovering a universal maxim of practical reason,[34] and of enhancing true piety.[35] For where propositions concerning God would seem to be true or false independently of the status

---

[30] Immanuel Kant, *Critique of Pure Reason,* trans. Norman Kemp Smith (Basingstoke: Macmillan, 1933), 29. This antimetaphysical stance is not original to Kant: one may find precursors of it in Condillac, Locke, Pascal, Montaigne, and even Sextus Empiricus.

[31] James Collins's important study, *The Emergence of Philosophy of Religion* (New Haven: Yale University Press, 1967), focuses on the significance of this shift.

[32] Collins, *The Emergence of Philosophy of Religion,* 372.

[33] Thus Kant divided all religions into those that were attempts to win favor and those that were moral religions of good life-conduct (i.e. Christianity). Immanuel Kant, *Religion within the Limits of Reason Alone,* trans. Theodore M. Greene and Hoyt H. Hudson (New York: Harper Torchbooks, 1960), 47.

[34] Immanuel Kant, *Critique of Practical Reason,* in *The Philosophy of Immanuel Kant,* ed. and trans. Lewis White Beck (New York: Garland Publishing, 1976), 142.

[35] Ibid., 190.

of those who assert them,[36] thus justifying an artificial bracketing of theologico-political concerns, "religion" is not merely a matter of purely rational concern, but is shaped by imagination and passion, involving the whole person.

Moreover—and this point is crucial—even a rational discourse on "true religion" may involve the motivations, obligations, passions, and piety of the thinker. By shifting the rational postulation of God to the sphere of practical reason, Kant takes this point precisely into account. Moreover, G. W. F. Hegel founded "philosophy of religion" as a discipline in his famous lectures of this title by bringing to self-consciousness this synthesis of religion and reason in his concept of "spirit."

Where Hume's *Dialogues Concerning Natural Religion* explored the foundation of religion in reason, his *Natural History of Religion* explored the origin of religion in nature.[37] Hume postulated the temporal origin of religion in hopes and fears, and in self-interested flattery of the gods. Such motives remained in "popular religion"; thus Hume was able to raise suspicious questions about the actual religions of his day. In particular he condemned those who "still seek the divine favour, not by virtue and good morals, which alone can be acceptable to a perfect being, but either by frivolous observances, by intemperate zeal, by rapturous extasies, or by the belief of mysterious and absurd opinions."[38] Such motives of self-interest may be concealed by being overlain with superstition: "What so pure as some of the morals, included in some theological systems? What so corrupt as some of the practices, to which these systems give rise?"[39] Then the philosophy of religion that follows from Hume may evaluate religious beliefs according to their motivations, as re-

---

[36] This is a general assumption of contemporary philosophy of religion; I raise a question about it because of the hermeneutic issue of whether the concept of the God of classical theism can be effectively translated across cultures, and whether its meaning is always consistent, based as it is on culturally relative concepts such as "spiritual," "incorporeal," "good," "eternal," "infinite," power, and knowledge; further questions arise from the theological issue of whether God is appropriately described as a "being" who may be an object of propositions.

[37] David Hume, *The Natural History of Religion,* ed. A. Wayne Colver (Oxford: Clarendon Press, 1976), 25.

[38] Hume, *Natural History of Religion,* 87.

[39] Ibid., 95.

vealed in the practices to which such beliefs give rise. Philosophy of religion becomes a diagnosis of self-deceptions, as in Karl Marx, Friedrich Nietzsche, and Sigmund Freud.[40]

Kant was even more explicit about his opposition to interests: "true *enlightenment*" lay in the capacity to distinguish between true religion, the practical principles that could be recognized as unconditionally necessary and thus as divine commands,[41] and "fetishism," which deemed a statutory faith of laws and observances as pleasing to God.[42]

The fundamental religious illusion, according to Kant's pietism (which, as we will see, cannot be sustained), is to take a means, a set of prescribed duties from revealed religion that properly aim at a recognition of moral obligations, as an end in themselves for the service of God. Religions of "cult" seek merely divine favor. Kant's philosophy is relentlessly anticlerical (and supersessionist): those who take revealed faith to precede rational religion transform service of the church into domination of its members.[43] The result is that there are no special duties in true religion over and above those of morality. Instead, all that is required is "the religious temper in all our actions done in conformity with duty":[44] "Religion is conscientiousness."[45]

Indeed, although Kant postulates the existence of God in *Religion within the Limits of Reason Alone* in order to reconcile moral duty (the purposiveness of freedom) with the outcome of happiness (the purposiveness of nature),[46] such a postulation is admitted as being purely practical in his posthumously published writings: It was "the necessity of acting in such a way as if I stood under . . . the knowledge of all my duties as divine commands; hence the *existence* of such a being is not postulated in this formula, which would be self-contradictory."[47] The religious

---

[40] See Merold Westphal, *Suspicion and Faith: The Religious Uses of Modern Atheism* (New York: Fordham University Press, 1998), 26–29.

[41] Kant, *Religion within the Limits of Reason Alone*, 156, 142.

[42] Ibid., 167.

[43] Ibid., 153.

[44] Ibid., 142.

[45] Immanuel Kant, *Opus Postumum*, ed. Eckhart Förster (Cambridge: Cambridge University Press, 1993), 248.

[46] Kant, *Religion within the Limits of Reason Alone*, 3–5.

[47] Kant, *Opus Postumum*, 200.

relation to God is no longer concerned directly with belief in propositions, but enters the province of transcendental practical philosophy.

This redirection of philosophy of religion opens up a number of lines of inquiry. In the first place, Kant grounded reason within the subject. Those approaches to the study of religion that emphasize religious propositions, a phenomenology of religious experience, or even a science of religion, rely upon the privileging of Cartesian or empiricist concepts of truth as clear and distinct ideas, whether or not grounded in sense experience. "Truth" may be grounded in the subject here, but "reason" is not: they do not attain to transcendental philosophy, which concerns the synthesis of a priori ideas. In particular the fact of self-deception, grounded in an unwarranted linking of ideas, cannot be fully taken into account and corrected within the subject as well as the object of inquiry. Such traditions, insofar as they eliminate the consideration of interests from reason, cannot distinguish between justification and rationalization—particularly in regard to self-interest or clerical claims to authority. Thus one direction for philosophy of religion, explored by Hegel and Ludwig Feuerbach, is the self-correction of religion as a progress toward self-consciousness.

Secondly, locating religion in the practical sphere as a "temper" or as "conscientiousness" does not reduce it to morality, but opens the possibility of an exploration of "truth as subjectivity" that will be explored by Kierkegaard. For Kant, religion is not simply obedience to moral duties, but treating such duties as if they were divine commands.[48] This opens up the question of the subjective relation to such duties. Furthermore, within the practical sphere, the "truth" about religion may be discovered by a moral evaluation of its practical consequences. Thus an exploration of the practices and functions of religion, such as that suggested by Marx, is a further consequence of this approach to religion.

In the third place, religion becomes a relationship between humanity and God in which the God-pole is not available for rational scrutiny.[49] Nevertheless, the philosopher of religion is part of

---

[48] Kant, *Religion within the Limits of Reason Alone*, 142.
[49] See Collins, *The Emergence of Philosophy of Religion*, 9.

the human-pole of that relationship; there is a reflexivity by which the subject is also part of the object of study. Kant himself attempted a reconciliation of these two sides of the subject in the concept of the "categorical imperative," which is objectively universal and subjectively a duty. Admittedly, there is a circularity here, for this imperative is conditioned by autonomous reasoning, the very practice that it is intended to constitute. The unconditioned cannot be located within reason without contradiction. Then two directions for inquiry emerge subsequent to Kant: on the one hand, the formulations of negative theology become appropriate for articulation of this unconditioned. On the other hand, in the practical sphere, reasoning remains a practice: philosophy is a "way of life," a quest for wisdom or true piety, which includes the very religion that it purports to study as its own mode of conscientiousness. Kant's pietist religion returns in his postulation of the will that alone admits of being described as "good." Philosophy of religion is also an inquiry into the religion of philosophy. Reason becomes a process of reform and purification of religion and philosophy.

(c) From Rationalization to Exploration

To conclude this historical survey, we may extract a number of tasks that emerge for the discipline of philosophy of religion:

- To critically examine claims of authority and certainty made within existing religious traditions.
- To articulate the principles, reasons, and ideals governing religious thought and practice, so as to correct arbitrary or complacent thoughts and practices.
- To diagnose structures of domination and oppression within religious traditions, and to liberate people from such powers.
- To diagnose self-deception and hypocrisy within religious traditions, particularly by contrasting discourse and practice.
- To explore illusions internal to reason, and their links with passions and interests in a diagnosis of self-deceptions.
- To enact a self-correction of religion in a progress toward self-consciousness.
- To explore the subjective relation to religious principles.
- To locate the unconditioned in the practical sphere, perhaps drawing on the apophatic formulations of negative theology.

- To incorporate religion as a "way of life" into the practical sphere of reason itself.

In general, philosophy of religion may aim to enhance conscientiousness within all forms of thought and practice, by enhancing awareness of their roles and functions within economies of goods, violence, knowledge, power, desire, and spirituality. As such, philosophy of religion becomes a precondition of all other fields of study. One may remark how rarely such tasks are pursued as a coherent whole in the contemporary study of religion.

"CONTINENTAL" PHILOSOPHY

These tasks may first of all be pursued against a modern "religion" of the sovereignty of reason—as epitomized by Kant's own attempt to set religion within the limits of reason alone. "Continental philosophy" is a phrase commonly used in the English-speaking world to describe a tradition of thought deriving from Kant, Hegel, Marx, Nietzsche, and Freud, especially as mediated through Martin Heidegger and the Parisian thinkers of the 1960s and 1970s, or the Frankfurt school of critical theory. In this critique of reason on behalf of reason, many features of the Enlightenment heritage have been subjected to radical questioning. In particular, the emancipatory potential of reason has been suspected of bringing a further cultural hegemony: its supposed grounds in universal human nature have been exposed as particular cultural and gendered practices. For reason is not simply a set of timeless syllogisms; it is also a temporal process selecting problems, premises, and concepts. Where the logical linking of atomic propositions may lead to skepticism, a transcendental reasoning, based on synthesis rather than analysis, turns attention to such problems, premises, and concepts.

As soon as such a transcendental philosophy was located in practical reasoning, then the practical self-positing of the subject, the source of transcendental synthesis, became infected with its own practice of self-positing. In short, in Fichte's successors, Schelling and Hegel, we find the self-consciousnessness and transcendental reasoning of the subject located in history. In their recent successors, the subject is located in language, tradition, culture, and gender. The result is that all syllogistic reasoning becomes circular and applicable only within a given perspective where its assumptions can be taken for granted: the very conclusion for which one argues has contributed, through a particular location of the subject in history, language, tradition, religion, culture, and gender, to the selection of problems, premises, and concepts.

Such premises are only "valid" and meaningful, only have currency, within a particular location; if translated outside that location, then the outsider is presented with the stark alternative of affirmation or denial, neither of which may seem satisfactory for questions of interpretation. At any rate, the framework of the dominant discourse is given by the one who asserts premises; the other as other is rendered imperceptible and reduced to silence. All meaning has currency within a community; the recognition of meaning reinforces both that meaning and the coherence of the community against others.

Thus the empiricist banishment of all evidence apart from that of the senses is a willful self-blinding to the role of community and tradition in shaping problems, premises, concepts, and reasoning.[50] It is an attempt to render the thought of those outside the community and tradition irrelevant, by a process of self-deception whereby it appears that one is only reasoning from sense-experience alone, denying the heritage of problems, premises, and concepts. Similarly, in transcendental philosophy, it can appear that there is a "self-creation (autocracy)" of ideas into a complete system of the objects of pure reason.[51] The linear flow of reasoning and the atemporal creation of ideas do not correspond to the complex interdependence of thoughts in the course of history and society.

One consequence is that the "outer" components of religion—its traditions, worship, liturgy, narratives, and practices—have a greater role in shaping the complex interdependence of thoughts than does reasoning from principles. Then emphasizing the role of these "statutory duties" may not only "cloak the self-interest"

---

[50] See Charles Taylor, *Sources of the Self: The Making of Modern Identity* (Cambridge: Cambridge University Press, 1989).

[51] Kant, *Opus Postumum*, 249–50.

of those with authority in religion; in particular, these duties may be indispensable to a broader conception of reason that is not merely logical or transcendental, but embedded in a way of life.

This is not to deny the continuing role of authority and power concealed within traditions; the situation is deeply ambivalent. If, in Western modernity, the theologico-political hegemony has reversed, so that secular reason has taken on the dominant role, then an emancipatory critique may attempt to remove the hegemony of a purely secular reason. Two courses of action may result: on the one hand, we have a route back into theology, no longer restrained by the Kantian bounds of reason alone, but disciplined by its own autonomous critique. Such a theology can only remain critical when it applies its criticism to itself as well as to secular reason, and when it effectively fulfills all the necessary tasks detailed above, including addressing the original modern problem of "religious diversity." On the other hand, one may follow the trajectory of Continental philosophy that welcomes difference.

(a) Heidegger: The Question of Orientation in Thought

Continental philosophy cannot be identified with a cultural perspectivism. Its overall effect is not to negate and constrain, or to delimit to a particular cultural location, but to add dimensions and perspectives, to show what is there in determinate and located acts of human thought. Its critique of reason is constructive. This is evident above all in the work of Heidegger, who explored basic assumptions about the meaning of knowledge, truth, and being. In technological reason, the dominant form of reason in twentieth-century Europe, Heidegger finds being determined as desire for mastery.[52] Once being is determined in this way, then the rational subject will comport itself toward all other beings in such a way that they only offer themselves for thought insofar as they may be incorporated within one's own projects. There is a preontological comprehension of beings as objects

---

[52] The question of whether this is a satisfactory interpretation of Nietzsche can be put aside for the moment; suffice it to say that a more subtle reading of this concept is given by Gilles Deleuze, *Nietzsche and Philosophy* (London: Athlone, 1983).

"We are to do nothing but wait."[60] It is even possible to keep open to the mystery hidden in technology, the mystery of the oblivion of being.[61] "Philosophy means to be addressed by Being itself.[62]

(b) Levinas: Orientation Toward the Other

If so, this "address" has been given in several different ways. Four critical responses to Heidegger may illustrate what is at stake in a Continental philosophy of religion by exploring the inherited orientations of our thinking.[63] Emmanuel Levinas recognized that although the philosophical project aimed to suppress multiplicity and violence—violence coming from opposition[64]—it necessarily had recourse to violence by thinking the whole in a totality, as is done in both ontotheology and the thinking of being.

Levinas drew attention to the violence implicit in all our intentional thinking—whether epistemological or ontological—which reduces the other to our own fundamental categories.[65] Instead, he explored the construction of meaning in a new way, not from what is said, from postulations and premises, but from speaking itself, insofar as speaking is already a relation to the other.[66] In this new meaning, "to signify is to signify the one *for* the other,"[67] where "for" is the way in which a relationship with the

---

[60] Martin Heidegger, *Discourse on Thinking,* trans. John M. Anderson and E. Hans Freund (New York: Harper and Row, 1966), 62.

[61] Ibid., 55.

[62] Heidegger, *Parmenides,* 120.

[63] This selection is somewhat arbitrary; one might also have included Julia Kristeva, Michel Foucault, Theodor Adorno, or Ernst Bloch, for example. I have omitted them on the grounds that although they make religion a frequent object of analysis, they do not have quite such an influence over the writings collected here as a whole. Kristeva and Bloch are dealt with in individual essays; Foucault and Adorno are notable absences.

[64] Emmanuel Levinas, *Basic Philosophical Writings,* eds. Adriaan T. Peperzak, Simon Critchley, and Robert Bernasconi (Bloomington: Indiana University Press, 1996), 13.

[65] Emmanuel Levinas, *Totality and Infinity,* trans. Alphonso Lingis (Dordrecht, The Netherlands: Kluwer, 1991).

[66] Emmanuel Levinas, *Otherwise Than Being or Beyond Essence,* trans. Alphonso Lingis (Dordrecht, The Netherlands: Kluwer, 1991).

[67] Emmanuel Levinas, *God, Death, and Time,* trans. Bettina Bergo (Stanford: Stanford University Press, 2000), 138.

other eventuates.[68] Signification is thus a substitution for the other, a responsibility that interrupts my relation to myself, since the relation to the other is involved in my relation to myself. Levinas writes: "This tie to the other, which does not reduce itself to the representation of the Other but rather to his invocation, where invocation is not preceded by comprehension, we call *religion*. It is prayer."[69]

Levinas, here, does not need to speak about God or the sacred; he accepts the ethical resonance of the word, with its Kantian echoes.[70] Levinas differs from Kant, however, in placing the emphasis not on the individual conscience and its relation to its duties, but on the relation to an actual other person. Obligation derives from the other who faces me, not from within. Religion is born through the other, prior to emotions, voices, or religious experiences,[71] in the trauma that consists in being subjected to the need of my neighbor. Levinas does not hesitate to speak of God, and the desire for the Good beyond being, where this is understood through the idea of the infinite as a surplus over all intentionality.[72] This idea of the infinite is ungraspable and unthinkable; it can never be assumed, but is more "like the state of the soul in which the bewildered subject immediately finds himself again within his own immanence."[73] Where Heidegger made attentiveness central to philosophy, Levinas redirects that attentiveness as originating in responsibility for the other.

(c) Derrida: Orientation Toward Justice

Similarly, where Levinas exposed the violence of our thematizations and postulations, Jacques Derrida exposed how ineffective they are within their own epistemological frame of reference. The philosophical logos posits a determined meaning, a content of thought, as present to and understood by the thinker. Yet Derrida explores how this "metaphysics of presence" effaces the

---

[68] Ibid., 157.
[69] Levinas, *Basic Philosophical Writings*, 7.
[70] Ibid., 8.
[71] Ibid., 143.
[72] Levinas, *Basic Philosophical Writings*, 19.
[73] Levinas, *God, Death, and Time*, 220.

conditions of its own possibility. For in language, words do not bring their referents with them. According to Ferdinand de Saussure's linguistics, if the relation between a sign and its meaning is arbitrary, then meaning is never present absolutely with the sign. It is produced by a differential system of signs, and thus deferred. Philosophy, insofar as it is committed to thinking in terms of meaning, has no access to the differential system—the "text" or "context"—by which meaning is produced. Thus Derrida contrasts the philosophical logos, where the speaker is present and determines meaning, with "arche-writing" or *différance,* the differential play of signs that constitutes language and makes philosophical discourse possible: "*Différance* is not only irreducible to any ontological or theological—ontotheological—reappropriation, but as the very opening of the space in which ontotheology—philosophy—produces its system and history, it includes ontotheology, inscribing it and exceeding it without return."[74]

Derrida is concerned here not with the contents of thought or its structure, but with the way in which the materiality of the sign introduces spacing and temporalization into the production of meaning, both in the deferral of presence and in the very production of meaning as a system of signs. Deconstruction thus launches a program of research into the determinate contexts, the determinate system of signs, for each particular positing of presence. Each transcendent concept or value has no determinate meaning in itself; its meaning is only constructed from the system of signs that it claims to transcend. Yet no system will be complete.

Thus it is not only the case that everyday religious propositions may be irreligious by claiming to master the divine within thought, not only the case that they may be violent by reducing persons to objects of intentions, but their claims to possess a determinate meaning may be founded on a dissimulation, a closure, a forgetfulness, in that saying what one means is impossible, for what one means is always different from what one has said, always deferred.

---

[74] Jacques Derrida, *Margins of Philosophy,* trans. Alan Bass (Brighton, England: Harvester, 1992), 6.

Such suspicion may appear to leave little grounds for faith: nothing remains that is solid. Yet it repeats the Kantian gesture of denying theoretical knowledge in order to make room for faith. Derrida deconstructs the naïve contrast between "Religion, on the one side, and on the other, Reason, Enlightenment, Science, Criticism (Marxist Criticism, Nietzschean Genealogy, Freudian Psychoanalysis, and their heritage)."[75] Instead, knowledge is interpenetrated with the "sacred"—that which is to be kept unscathed, immune from questioning—primarily in the sacredness of the metaphysics of presence. Then philosophy has to make use of the concepts of religion, especially the sacred and faith, in order to describe its own condition of "original bereavement or emptying of language and experience."[76]

Drawing on his deconstructive reading of Marx, as well on the influence of Levinas, Derrida has also salvaged the concept of the messianic: "This would be opening to the future or to the coming of the other as the advent of justice, but without horizon of expectation and without prophetic prefiguration. The coming of the other can only emerge as a singular event when no anticipation *sees it coming,* when the other and death—and radical evil—can come as a surprise at any moment."[77]

What remains undeconstructible, for Derrida, is a certain formal messianism, an emancipatory promise, which is a pure structure lacking content: a regulative idea of justice.[78] It is precisely the experience of faith in regard to this abstract messianism that allows for the possibility of a universal discourse on religion:[79] a philosophy of religion.

(d) Irigaray: Orientation Toward Becoming

Luce Irigaray, although she has worked within and developed the philosophical frameworks of Heidegger, Levinas, and Derrida

[75] Jacques Derrida, "Faith and Knowledge: The Two Sources of 'Religion' at the Limits of Reason Alone," in *Religion,* eds. Jacques Derrida and Gianni Vattimo (Cambridge: Polity Press, 1998), 5.

[76] Hent de Vries, *Philosophy and the Turn to Religion* (Baltimore: Johns Hopkins University Press, 1999), 9.

[77] Derrida, "Faith and Knowledge," 17.

[78] Jacques Derrida, *Spectres of Marx: The State of the Debt, the Work of Mourning, and the New International,* trans. Peggy Kamuf (London: Routledge, 1994), 59.

[79] Derrida, "Faith and Knowledge," 18.

with regard to sexual difference,[80] offers a distinctive approach
to the return of the religious. In her early work, she explored not
simply a system of signs, but a "cultural imaginary," a system
of images constructed as if by a play of mirrors where the logic
is primarily "specular" or "scopic": the dominant metaphors are
those of sight and gaze. In the Lacanian system of psychoanalysis in which she trained, the crucial event is the mirror-stage
whereby identity is acquired through self-reflection in a mirror,
seeing oneself as others see one. Such an identity is a precondition of locating oneself within the discourse of others, of identifying with one's name, in the symbolic order of language. For
Lacan, such a symbolic order is structured around the "Name-
of-the-Father," a transcendental signifier or God. Irigaray places
more emphasis on the gaze: one is given an identity by being
located in the divine gaze. The crucial point is that this identity
is external: "We look at ourselves in the mirror to *please someone,* rarely to interrogate the state of our body or our own spirit,
rarely for ourselves and in search of our own becoming. The
mirror almost always serves to reduce us to a pure exteriority—of a very particular kind."[81]

Irigaray finds the same self-reflective logic at work in Western
philosophy: the incorporeal image, itself reflecting masculinity
and culture, is privileged over the images of woman, body, and
nature that serve as its support.[82] A crucial stage is achieved with
Descartes, however, when the mirror is taken back into the subject, whose self-reflection constitutes his own ground and his
freedom over the world he surveys.[83] This serves as a basis for
autonomy apart from the cosmological order guaranteed by the
sight of God.

It is clear that the Judeo-Christian God, for Irigaray, is the
foundation of identity for men, which leaves women without an

[80] See Tina Chanter, *Ethics of Eros* (London: Routledge, 1995).
[81] Luce Irigaray, "Divine Women," *Sexes and Genealogies,* trans. Gillian C.
Gill (New York: Columbia University Press, 1993), 65.
[82] Luce Irigaray, *Speculum of the Other Woman,* trans. Gillian C. Gill (Ithaca:
Cornell University Press, 1985).
[83] See the discussion by Ellen T. Armour, *Deconstruction, Feminist Theology,
and the Problem of Difference: Subverting the Race/Gender Divide* (Chicago:
University of Chicago Press, 1999), 113.

identity of their own; it is used by men to oppress women.[84] If Irigaray follows Feuerbach in seeing such a God as a projection of the cultural imaginary, she also follows the Feuerbachian reversal: seeing it as having possibilities for women. Her pivotal essay, "Divine Women," picks up on Feuerbach's declaration that "God is the mirror for man," to point out that woman has no mirror to become woman.[85] What Irigaray does not quite say is that women should postulate a female God as a mirror to become woman; indeed, she criticizes the mirror here as offering a superficial image, freezing becoming.[86] Such an image, of course, would have all the attendant problems of positing a perfect, ideal woman, privileging some over others.[87] Irigaray tries to guard against this danger: "In order to *become,* we need some shadowy perception of achievement; not a fixed objective, not a One postulated to be immutable but rather a cohesion and a horizon that assures us the passage between past and future. . . . A *female* god is still to come."[88]

It is easy to miss Irigaray's typical mimesis of Feuerbach in this passage, which subverts his logic as well as his intention just as much as Marx does in his appropriation of Feuerbach. For the specular logic of projection is no longer in operation: we no longer have a model, but a horizon, a principle of synthesis, "an objective-subjective place or path whereby the self could be coalesced in space and time."[89] The "goal" that Irigaray appears to posit is merely a condition of becoming, a synthesis of space and time, replacing Heidegger's *Dasein* with becoming; it must be incarnated,[90] not held up as a transcendent image.

Irigaray admits that to have a goal is essentially a religious move (according to Feuerbach): "Only the religious, within and without us, is fundamental enough to allow us to discover, affirm, achieve certain *ends.*"[91] Yet God, for Irigaray, is merely the

---

[84] Irigaray, *Sexes and Genealogies, v.*
[85] Ibid., 67.
[86] Ibid., 65.
[87] See Ellen Armour, *Deconstruction, Feminist Theology, and the Problem of Difference,* 132.
[88] Irigaray, *Sexes and Genealogies,* 67.
[89] Ibid.
[90] Ibid., 71.
[91] Ibid., 67.

rational condition of freedom, a principle of synthesis, for God conceives and loves himself.[92] Irigaray, therefore, offers a return to the cultural imaginary of mythology, for the sake of becoming, as a version of religion without religion: "Only the divine offers us freedom—enjoins it upon us. Only a God constitutes a rallying point for us that can let us free—nothing else. These words are but a statement of *reason*. So far it requires no faith other than the faith in the possibility of our autonomy, our salvation, of a love that would not just redeem but glorify us in full self-awareness."[93]

Where man's autonomy has been achieved by the specular relation of self-reflection, which itself neglects its own material conditions, Irigaray seeks women's autonomy through a self-relation that is not founded on neglect of its mediation. For that mediation can be the religious relation of love of God, as a will, a temporal synthesis, a medium of becoming: "Love of God has nothing moral in and of itself. It merely shows the way. It is the incentive for a more perfect becoming. It marks the horizon between the more past and the more future, the more passive and the more active—permanent and always in tension. God forces us to do nothing except *become*."[94]

(e) Deleuze: Orientation by Immanent Life

A fourth figure who haunts this collection is Gilles Deleuze. Deleuze gave no encouragement to a "return of the religious." Even the "death of God" is of no consequence.[95] Deleuze is not interested in endlessly going over the history of philosophy. Becoming does not happen like that. Deleuze follows Heidegger's critique of ontotheology in refusing to subject being to any transcendent figure of the One, whether as the Whole or the Subject (or even as a tradition). For to do so is to place a transcendent plane of organization over being: an organization of essences that transcends existing individuals.

---

[92] Ibid., 68.

[93] Ibid., 68.

[94] Ibid., 68.

[95] Gilles Deleuze and Félix Guattari, *Anti-Oedipus,* trans. Robert Hurley, Mark Seem, and Helen R. Lane (London: Athlone, 1994), 107.

The crucial shift is once more from epistemology to ethics: it is a shift from regarding thought as a representation to regarding it as a production of the real;[96] it is a question of whether metaphysics poses problems of meaning or use.[97] The distinction is present in Marx, Bergson, and Nietzsche: it is a question of whether life is determined by consciousness, or consciousness by life. Critique, then, has no need to trace thought back to absent origins or dissimulations, for nothing can be recovered by these means.

Instead, the aim of critical philosophy, on a plane of immanence, is to make connections, disjunctions and conjunctions with what is outside philosophy—life, nature, history, art—that will enable the creation of concepts. Against the reductionism of cultural relativism, Deleuze defines philosophy as "the creation of concepts,"[98] where concepts are neither true nor false. The utility of a concept resides solely in the problems with which it enables us to engage, and the new ways it creates for us to think. Philosophy invents modes of existence or possibilities of life.[99]

There are no transcendent criteria for judging such modes of existence. Evaluations themselves are modes of existence on a plane of immanence:[100] "[T]here are never any criteria other than the tenor of existence, the intensification of life."[101] Deleuze adopts Spinoza's immanent philosophy, but abandons Spinoza's God in favor of a singular life manifested in events and singularities: "Very young children, for example, all resemble each other and have barely any individuality; but they have singularities, a smile, a gesture, a grimace—events which are not subjective characteristics. They are traversed by an immanent life that is pure power and even beatitude through the sufferings and weaknesses."[102]

Deleuze does not abandon Spinoza's concepts of beatitude and

---

[96] Ibid., 55.

[97] Ibid., 109.

[98] Gilles Deleuze and Félix Guattari, *What Is Philosophy?* trans. Graham Burchell and Hugh Tomlinson (London: Verso, 1994), 5.

[99] Ibid., 72.

[100] Deleuze, *Nietzsche and Philosophy*, 1.

[101] Deleuze and Guattari, *What Is Philosophy?*, 74.

[102] Gilles Deleuze, "Immanence: A Life . . ." *Theory, Culture, and Society* 14, no. 2 (1997): 5.

power: "A life is the immanence of immanence, absolute immanence: it is sheer power, utter beatitude."[103] Here there is no religious relation to God; and yet there is a relation to the immanent
life, power, beatitude and joy that constitutes our essence. Philosophy has no other aim than the intensification of this life, even
though such life is often too great to bear.

Deleuze, therefore, steps outside the cultural heritage of Western philosophy and theology by producing a life as the outside
of this tradition, where philosophy confronts chaos.[104] Deleuze
does not appear to offer us a philosophy of religion. He does,
however, affirm the exploration of the modes of existence of
those who are religious, who believe in God, by Pascal and
Kierkegaard, for example;[105] he even recommends a faith as believing in this world, as it is. Religion, then, like art and science,
affords the possibility for philosophy to create concepts or modes
of existence, in a philosophy of religion.

On the other hand, our bond to immanent life bears all the
hallmarks of a "religion without religion," or rather, a religion
without God, transcendence, or even conscientiousness—a
purely critical or philosophical religion that retains creativity,
power, and beatitude without substance.[106]

In conclusion, although Continental philosophy does not have
a separate discipline entitled "philosophy of religion"—any
more than it divides other domains of philosophy into compart-
ments—the concerns of the founders of philosophy of religion
are still present. There are concerns to diagnose self-deception,
to unmask structures of power, to expose unwarranted and unau-
thorized faith, and to raise awareness of the unthought dimensions within thought. When reason is taken to task for its
theological heritage, the criticism of religion remains the premise
of all criticism.

But this is so in a dual sense: for the religious, in a purely
conceptual sense abstracted from all existing religious traditions,

---

[103] Ibid., 4.

[104] Deleuze and Guattari, *What Is Philosophy?*, 218.

[105] Ibid., 73–74.

[106] For a fuller exploration of the religious potential of Deleuze's thought, see
my book *Gilles Deleuze and the Question of Philosophy* (Madison, N.J.: Fair-
leigh Dickinson University Press, 1996).

returns as the condition of possibility for critique. A meditation
on the essence of this religion of philosophy, in order to purify it
from the contaminations of domination within existing religious
traditions, becomes an essential part of conforming the religion
of philosophy to true piety.

CONTINENTAL PHILOSOPHY OF RELIGION

If there has been another generational shift in the work presented
here, then it is perhaps that the contemporary inheritors of this
tradition are generally less concerned with the fate of critical
philosophy than with the fate of critical religion. Indeed, in the
study of religions, many of the problems explored in Continental
philosophy receive an exemplary manifestation: problems of
unity of identity or tradition; problems of language and translation; problems of understanding an other; problems of comprehending the ineffable or the transcendent; problems of uniting
multiplicity into generic unity; problems of separating violence,
power, and authority; problems of reform and self-critique; problems of determining and living out a good way of life; problems
of practical social reform and transformation. Communication
between these two fields can only be enriching for both.

An initial point to note is that if religious strategies are invoked
for the purpose of critical thought, then the "religion" of philosophy may have little more unity than the historical religions. Each
critical strategy is affected by the religious strategy of its practitioners. This is, once more, not to collapse into a cultural relativism or arbitrary decisionism, giving critique a purely local
authority—this strategy, invoked all too frequently in postmodernity or postmodern theology as an excuse to make an arbitrary
decision for or against one particular theology, is not reasonable.
For each critical point made against religious traditions, or the
tradition of reason, from whatever perspective, still stands unless
it requires absolute certainty of its own ground.

Then critique will stand at some distance from historical traditions. Yet critique, once situated, can no longer claim to be comprehensive, decisive, and definitive; there may be more in
religion than has been dreamed of in some philosophies. The

multiplying of perspectives neither undermines certainty nor detracts from critical knowledge; it adds further dimensions to critical knowledge without ever approaching a final limit. The task of critique continues as urgently as before; lacking pretensions of comprehensiveness, it becomes more comprehensive.

(a) Ruptures in the Boundaries of Reason

Similarly, true religious thought and practice can no longer be assumed to spring from principles, reasons, and ideals. Indeed, it may call these into question. Thus John Caputo juxtaposes the prophetic gospel of the Kingdom of God to the philosophical principles of being, reason, order, possibility, presence, sense, and meaning—which collectively determine what is possible. The Kingdom of God as the coming of justice is *the* impossible, in that it does not submit to the laws of possibility, of being, or of reason; it breaks into our familiar world, shattering our horizon of expectations. In this essay, then, Caputo does not turn to philosophical argument, but to a poetics of the impossible, a logic with passion and imagination, that is a prophetic, transformative, and salvific supplement to philosophy.

Caputo's aim is not romantic irrationalism, but to allow the prophetic message of the Kingdom, whose boundary is defined by the paradox that the outsiders are in and the insiders are out—a paradox that undermines all claims to authority of this message—to "sit down at table" with deconstruction, which effects a comparable reversal of boundaries. The result is that deconstruction is structured like a prophetic religion, insofar as it interrupts the business of the world; similarly, deconstructibility is the principal requirement for rendering things pliable for the Kingdom of God. Knowledge and faith become complementary.

If Caputo presents a classic formulation of the confrontation of philosophy and religion subsequent to deconstruction, Matthew Halteman shows how such a confrontation can come about. Continental philosophy of religion is shaped by three recurrent motifs: first, Continental thought is concerned to set limits to reason; second, once the limits of speculative analysis have been recognized, then the practical turn followed by Kant and his successors yields a nondogmatic faith, a thematization of religion into a logic of concepts abstracted from practical experience.

This latter is in turn subjected to critical scrutiny, with the result that Kant's categorical imperative is replaced at the limits of reason by something that presents itself as unpresentable. This is the logic that Derrida explores in his discussion of responsibility: a concept of practical reason that threatens to invert itself into irresponsibility if it is replaced by speculatively specified duties that can be discharged. The experience of responsibility before singular and contingent others gives us all an infinite, and thus religious, responsibility toward an infinite and impossible justice.

The result of Kant's practical turn is that reason itself is only reasonable when it is also ethical. Then a critique of "good conscience" in ethics is at the same time a critique of certainty in epistemology: certainty is no longer desirable, for it excludes sensitivity to that which has not yet been comprehended. Donna Jowett, building on Levinas, Derrida, and the Freudian analyst Melanie Klein, provides such a critique of good conscience, in its complacency of excluding claims from without and drives from within. This is, at the same time, a critique of grounding reason within the sphere of mastery of the subject, for the subject is already called into question. Then bad conscience is not indulgent self-accusation, but a pathos of responsibility and a susceptibility to being affected by what is exterior to us.

As Derrida shows, such responsibility can never be completed in a good conscience, for by being responsible to one, one necessarily sacrifices all the potential responsibilities to others in a way that is not justifiable. The critical distance maintained here from both historical religions and the tradition of pure reason is effected by bad conscience. Just as dissension among competing traditions provoked epistemology, it continues to provoke bad conscience.

Bettina Bergo then continues to examine the significance of this anxious responsibility for philosophy by means of a comparison between Levinas and Kierkegaard. Both note that our relation to excess, to freedom, and to evil change the nature of secular inquiry: for they are temporal relations that involve transcendence, a transcendence that is there before a subject chooses it. Moods such as anxiety and earnestness may give the mode of approach of the religious: they are not generated by the subject, but come to pass prior to distinctions of subject and object. Then there is no collapse of philosophy into religion here, for religious insights are appropriated for their existential meaning. Religion returns as a mood, a mode of approach, as a precondition of ethics that cannot be reduced to existing paradigms of practical reason.

As a result, Continental philosophy of religion cannot be said to give primacy either to faith, as unreasoning trust in authority, or to suspicion, which attempts to account for itself. If philosophy is inscribed in an intersubjective and anthropological field, where reason emerges from human relations and emotions, then the complicity of founding a community on shared trust is no more absolute than the suspicion with which one treats strangers. A new social order of justice as the basis of reason may emerge when the dominant moods or modes of approach to reason include responsibility, anxiety, and expectation.

The final essay in this section, by Gary Banham, raises questions concerning the appropriation of Derrida's celebration of the messianic. For, showing how this emerges from a conception of temporality involving an eschatology that Derrida had previously criticized in Heidegger, evil emerges from the same structure and chance as the messianic. In the "return of the religious," then, what is there to prevent our exposure to the worst? Banham presents three alternatives: a more rigorous philosophical thinking, as in Heidegger; or a revolutionary appropriation of religion, as in Walter Benjamin; or a strategic "mixing" that must partake of the worst in order to discern its arrival, as in Derrida.

The problem of evil—not the problem of theodicy, but the problem of the return of evil into philosophy via religion—remains a vital, unsolved problem in Continental philosophy of religion. It exposes to critical questioning a dominant consensus deriving from Levinas and Derrida.

(b) Locating Reason in Culture and Gender

Grace Jantzen introduces another strand into Continental philosophy of religion: she draws heavily from Levinas and Derrida, but her overall approach has been inspired more directly by Irigaray's project of becoming divine.[107] In this essay, however, she uses the work of Julia Kristeva to explore the change of a thinking subject from a fulcrum of reason to a loving subject. She questions the narrow model of rationality and philosophy at the heart of secular modernity, which has split itself off from the passions as well as the cathartic power of religious themes.

This splitting is conducted by a process of *abjection,* whereby one separates oneself as far as possible from objects that remind us of death, that do not conform to rigid boundaries between what is inside and outside. Objects of investigation are rendered inert, mechanical and lifeless, thus leading to a secularized world; at the same time, the abject, which threatens to undermine rational domination, become lifelike in their fluidity. Death has a central place in the symbolic order of the Western tradition as an overcoming of the gendered, bodily relation to this world; nevertheless, as part of the symbolic order, it has no fixed essence but a gendered social construction.

For certain objects are abject because they are threatening not to all, but to the masculinist, disembodied, rational subject. Such a subject is caught in ambivalence, for it must constitute its own body as a secure, solid object dominating abject female bodies, while it must itself also be mastered. By contrast, to start from natality rather than mortality enables an affirmation of the condition of being composite, between identities, as in pregnancy. As a result, religion may affirm separation as a creative part of becoming loving subjects, and not as death work requiring mourning.

Pamela Anderson's overall approach is shaped by Irigaray's method of mimesis.[108] This allows her, by contrast to Jantzen, to seek to build bridges between Continental and analytic philosophy, drawing on a discussion between A. W. Moore and Derrida that is concerned with the role of the ineffable. She thus takes issue with Jantzen over the supposed ambivalence toward death, limits, and the infinite that is part of masculinist philosophy,

---

[107] See Grace M. Jantzen, *Becoming Divine: Towards a Feminist Philosophy of Religion* (Manchester: Manchester University Press, 1998).

[108] Pamela Sue Anderson, *A Feminist Philosophy of Religion* (Oxford: Blackwell, 1998).

treating it as a contradiction in Jantzen's own account. Drawing attention to ineffable "know-how," rather than "knowing-that," a distinction that cuts across the Continental/analytic divide, Anderson finds a rich complexity of associations between gender and the infinite.

On the one hand, there is a masculinist urge for infinity as a refusal to accept boundaries, and a corresponding quest for infinite knowledge. Yet there is an ancient value hierarchy that associates the infinite with matter and the female. On the other hand, the urge to express the ineffable may shape practical knowledge as productive know-how, as in the case of women's ineffable knowledge of knowing how to be finite. Then the religious is not simply reduced to the practical, but becomes a condition of the practical when it is shown rather than said. Reflection on the ineffable may be both enabling and corrupting; it requires further critical reflection.

(c) Locating Reason in Theology and Spirituality

A third major approach to the field is presented by Graham Ward, as a theological challenge to Continental philosophy of religion. Recognizing the political and ethical danger of the undecidable as that which undermines resistance, Ward offers a theological account as a supplement to Continental philosophy of religion. For poststructuralist thought engages with alterity, with an ineffable site exceeding speculative investigation; but it does not keep silent, or equivocate. It aims to establish a relation, to speak about one thing while at the same time speaking about something else, and such a relation bears the structure of analogy. This is exemplified in the analogy between the face of God and the face of the other in Levinas's work, and in Derrida's transposition of Levinas's discourse on the name of God to a discourse by analogy on human names. Now, these analogies border on equivocation, for although they establish a transcendent horizon under which the analogy is able to carry, they refuse to give any content to the horizon. Yet horizon it remains, for in the poststructuralist thought of relation, it is not simply a figure of speech that is examined, but relation as such: thus Ward is able to explore the cosmology implied by such uses of analogy. In Levinas, he finds a world composed of strangers, betrayals, absences, and with-drawals. In Derrida's structural messianism, deprived of every determinate content, he finds a regulative use of analogy, similar to Kant's; yet it is undecidable whether this analogy is regulative or constitutive, and consequently it is undecidable whether any-one has ever acted justly.

Derrida's cosmology is sketched in his metaphorics, in which at times "rafts of illumination travel like star ships through the folds of a dark infinity," and at other times a utopic scene of universal reconciliation is announced. Then Ward's challenge is pragmatic: endless ambiguity and infinite responsibility are more difficult ethical and political commitments than market ideolo-gies, fundamentalisms, or instrumental reason. By contrast, a theological supplement can offer transformative practices of hope that stall the paralysis of action suggested by enduring the undecidable.

Jonathan Ellsworth continues to argue for the need of Conti-nental philosophy of religion to draw on historical religious tradi-tions. In particular, he explores the role of apophaticism in recent Continental thought as a means of avoiding metaphysics, of con-struing the relation between the finite and the infinite, and of speaking of deconstruction and the other. Such conceptual work is carried out without paying attention to the conditions of the subject; in its original formulation, however, apophaticism was accompanied by askêsis.

For it was believed that forms of askêsis, or spiritual discipline, could bring a new receptivity to philosophical insight, truth, and experience. Then thinking apophatically becomes an exercise, a way of life, and not simply the resolution of a conceptual *aporia*. Ellsworth argues for a much broader sense of philosophy as a way of life, involving disciplinary practices following Pierre Hadot and Michel Foucault.

Gregory Sadler questions how a philosophy that claims to speak for none, or only for the other, can appear to speak for all. He recalls how the relationship between philosophy and theology was negotiated in the philosophy of action of Maurice Blondel, and maintains that Blondel engaged with many of the same themes as recent Continental philosophy, and specifically Der-rida. But this philosophy-theology relationship also provided a systematic treatment of the relation between these themes and the specific historical traditions, practices, and institutions of the Roman Catholic Church. Blondel gave an immanent analysis of dominant philosophical positions to show that they were insufficient on their own terms: he provided a general critique of hypostatization and the practices that maintain it, contrasting it with an orientation of the subject toward God.

The ultimate limits of philosophy must be sketched by philosophy itself, where it discovers, as in Derrida's work, that autonomy is grounded in heteronomy. Yet if philosophy, at its own limits, draws once more on the religious, then what is the status of the historical institutions that have mediated the religious? If philosophy welcomes the other, then why not the voices and concerns of those who are engaged in the tradition? Sadler suggests that in particular it is the practice—liturgical, spiritual, and social—of those engaged in the Catholic tradition that the most subtle philosophers may lack.

(d) Religion inside the Limits of Reason Itself

Edith Wyschogrod takes a very different approach from the preceding essays: she applies the deconstructive strategies of Continental philosophy of religion to the current vogue of understanding the human person through genetics. Through a careful analysis, she shows how conceptions of the gene as a disembodied individual, surviving death, and conceptions of artificial life, whereby thought patterns may survive the body if transferred to computer, are both haunted by Neoplatonic conceptions of the soul based on number. The common factor is that number is both the measure and the being that is measured; as a soul, it is both a being and a measure. Then there is a return of the religious in the most materialistic of contemporary worldviews, manifested in hopes for immortality, or a heaven in silico. Philosophy of religion here is used to read the dominant beliefs and ideas of the present, attending to what has been thought in the past as presaging what is to come. Remaining faithful to deconstructive strategies, Wyschogrod refuses to give a moral condemnation of this phenomenon, noting instead its ambivalence.

The remaining essays in the book distance themselves in varying ways from this emerging debate. Clayton Crockett does so, surprisingly, by means of a return to Kant. Where the Levinasian and Derridean approaches concentrate on the presentation of the unpresentable, and the theological responses aim to return the site of the unpresentable to cosmology, spiritual discipline, and historical tradition, Crockett undercuts this debate by taking the Kantian aporia of the sublime away from the infinite or the other, as well as away from the mastery of the subject. Following Deleuze's reading of Kant's analytic of the sublime, he finds a depth dimension underlying modern reason that is figured in the notion of the sublime. He situates religion in relation to Kant, not as a source of knowledge or a regulation of practice, but as a "fold" such as that found in the experience of the sublime. Crockett is concerned here not with the "mathematical sublime," the self-interruption of reason explored by Derrida, but with a "baroque" sublime, the folding of the faculties back onto each other in a discordant accord. In Kant's architectonics, this folding of the faculties generates the higher forms of knowledge, desire, and feeling; it is also found in the reflexive act of thinking, a folding of thought back upon itself. Deleuze himself performs such a fold when he suggests that belief should be reformulated to become belief in this world, as it is—for in our intolerable daily banality, we need reasons to restore our link with the world.

(e) Reason within the Limits of Religion Itself

Wayne Hudson, drawing primarily on the tradition of critical theory rather than poststructuralism, moves completely beyond the terrain of any of the preceding contributions. For insofar as the preceding approaches to philosophy of religion are structured around Kantian aporias in reason, they merely demonstrate the limitations of the reason that is being practiced. He recommends following Schelling's development of the history of philosophy following Kant, in which a "negative philosophy" of pure reason is grounded within a positive philosophy that takes seriously human freedom, not simply as an adjunct to duty, but as the source itself of reason and metaphysics. The result is a thoroughgoing historicization of reason, in which current questions and debates are the product of the contingent social facts of history.

Schelling's vision of a philosophical religion, which is both philosophy and religion and comprehends all the stages of history—mythological, revelational, and rational—can be taken up again today. Hudson modifies it by drawing on Ernst Bloch, who retained hope and imagination as the afterlife of a religion that is no longer believed in. It becomes possible to replace Kantian aporias with historically positive data: the forms of hope and critique found in actual religious traditions and current new religious movements may be more effective than the radical and obscure critiques enacted by philosophers. Unreason is accepted as a real state of affairs that will not be reformed by ideal judgments. Then Hudson calls for a historical sociology of reason, a location of the subject inside nature, and a clarification of the nature of human freedom. Taking up the emancipatory task of philosophy of religion, he asks how we may determine the future.

Finally, my own contribution poses a similar challenge to the heritage of Kantian philosophy through the work of Henri Bergson. Conscious of the political task of philosophy of religion, I try to separate the inspiration in religion that makes for social cohesion from the social forms that make for division. This requires a rethinking of the possibilities of reason as a way of linking ideas. Returning to Bergson as a common source for Levinas and Deleuze, and their philosophies of transcendence and immanence, I attempt to recover a mode of reasoning that is not simply practical or empirical, but ritual, aimed at directing attention to the sources of experience. Bergson's emphasis on the category of memory introduces the mediation of a virtual past into every present encounter or association—even the association of ideas. Every practice of association exhibits the habit of distributing a certain degree of honor to the characters of the virtual past: the ancestors, spirits, or gods who have an interest in the events of the present. In contrast to Bergson himself, this requires a revalorization of the cultic elements of actual religions, rather than their dismissal by reason.

In practice, in spite of the fact that ritual is by no means static, capitalist distribution is more effective as an instrument of social cohesion than is ritual, even if such cohesion is still limited. Then the moral and political task of practical reason is to introduce the categories of dynamic religion into the framework of capitalist distribution in order to seize creative technical power for moral ends.

PROSPECTS FOR PHILOSOPHY OF RELIGION

Philosophy of religion stands at the threshold of an extraordinary transformation and emancipation. This is not simply a matter of taking into account other modes of the religious life apart from the belief in classical theism; nor is it simply a matter of introducing gender-specific and culturally specific perspectives into the practice of a reason applied to the truth-claims, rationality, and coherence of religious propositions. For—as has long been suspected and feared—it is sufficient to raise a few critical questions about the status of reason for the whole edifice to become completely transformed.

Philosophy of religion must remain a critical discourse on the beliefs and practices of actual existing religious traditions. Beliefs included in and associated with classical theism may remain a part of that. Yet to reduce religious life to propositional form, where it may subjected to interrogation and analysis, is an objectification of religious life that has more to do with the patterns of reason that have emerged in modern Western thought than it does with historical traditions—until they adopt such a framework for their own self-reflection. For a fuller critique, however, the resources of contemporary approaches to the study of religion will yield a richer picture than such objectifications.

At the same time, the conception of reason may itself be transformed. Continental philosophy has already achieved this by opening thought onto its social preconditions, its psychological motivations, its gendered and embodied locations, its strategies of domination and violence, its passions, its symbolic structures, its fundamental presuppositions, its ethical responsibilities, its incompletions, its aspirations, its creative becomings, and its religious modes. Let me repeat: All of this takes nothing away from reason; it merely adds further dimensions. It is the latter stage, the embedding of reason within broader religious projects, that makes reason fully critical.

Such a discipline remains a philosophy of religion: it remains philosophy, for it proceeds by creating concepts to add further dimensions to the practice of reason. It remains a philosophy of religion, for it creates concepts of religion, each differing according to the particular philosophical discourse, strategy, or system involved. That such concepts of religion are a creation of a particular, localized, Western tradition of thought that stands in a critical relation to existing religious traditions is no objection. The aim is no longer to categorize, comprehend, encompass, and master other traditions of thought as "the religions"; the aim is to learn from them, as well as to critically examine them.

Yet there remains much work to be done, for it is evident that critical reason does not have sufficient power to contest dominant ideologies and fundamentalisms. If anything, critical reason has less emancipatory power than it had in the seventeenth and eighteenth centuries, for its enemies have grown stronger. Philosophy of religion, drawing its resources for the reformulation of reason from powerful religious traditions, may be well placed to take up the vanguard of critical thought in the coming century.

Unlikely as this suggestion sounds, the essays collected here offer seeds of hope. Much requires further clarification:

- What relations can be forged between a philosophy of religion and actual religious traditions, including their theologies?
- What can be salvaged from religious traditions, without succumbing to domination and oppression? What is lost in the process of abstraction and salvaging from religious traditions?
- How might one produce a transformation of subjectivity from purely rational to ethical subjectivity?
- How does one open oneself to the other, yet guard against the incoming of evil?
- How might one situate a philosophy of responsibility in relation to a philosophy of desire?
- What resources are available in current religious movements and esoteric traditions for social and political critique and emancipation?
- How may one incorporate social, ethical, and spiritual awareness into the construction of reason?
- Finally, and most important, what are our most pressing theologico-political problems today?[109]

---

[109] I would like to acknowledge with gratitude comments received on a draft of this introduction from Bettina Bergo, Pamela Sue Anderson, and the reader for Fordham University Press.

1
Ruptures in the
Boundaries of Reason

2

The Poetics of the Impossible and the Kingdom of God

John D. Caputo

A Poetics of the Impossible

THE KINGDOM OF GOD abides by a certain logic, but it is a divine logic. From the point of view of the world, which is its antagonist, what goes on in the Kingdom looks mad and even impossible. Still, it can be said in defense of the Kingdom that it is not simply impossible but rather, let us say, *the* impossible. We might even speak of the logic of the impossible, on the perfectly logical assumption that with God, all things are possible (Luke 1:37), including the maddest and most impossible. But beyond any possible logic, even a logic of the impossible, I prefer to speak of a poetics of the impossible. By a poetics I mean a constellation of strategies, arguments, tropes, paradigms, and metaphors, a style and a tone, as well as a grammar and a vocabulary, all of which, collectively, like a great army on the move, are aimed at making a point.

We might say that a poetics is a logic with a heart, not a simple or bare bones logic but a logic with pathos, with a passion and desire, with an imagination and a flare, a mad logic, perhaps a patho-logic, but one that is healing and salvific. A poetics of the impossible describes the movements of a desire beyond desire, a desire beyond reason and what is reasonably possible, a desire to know what we cannot know, or to love what we dare not love, like a beggar in love with a princess, whose desire is not extinguished but fired *by* the impossibility of his plight. For our hearts are burning with a desire to go where we cannot go, praying and weeping for what eye has not seen nor ear heard, hoping against hope (Rom. 4:18). To desire what is merely possible, to curb our passion so that it remains confined by the parameters of a carefully calculated probability—what would that amount to if not a lover without passion, who is, according to Johannes Climacus, a "mediocre fellow"?[1]

This poetics has cultivated an ear for parable and paradox and a taste not for measure or moderation but for excess and going beyond, for the hyperbolic, for the odd system of accounting—the "aneconomy"—in the Kingdom. The way things are counted in the Kingdom confounds the calculations of the world. If your brother offends you seven times a day, you should forgive him, and that still holds even if he offends you seven times seventy, which seems excessive. If one sheep among a hundred is lost and then found, there is more rejoicing over that one than over the ninety-nine, which is an unaccountably odd way to count, since there is more profit in the ninety-nine and the one is not worth the risk to the ninety-nine, as any cost accountant who knows how to calculate risks can assure us.

In the Kingdom there is an odd predilection for reversals: the last shall be first, sinners are preferred to the righteous, the stranger is the neighbor, the insiders are out. That makes for the astonishing hospitality portrayed in the story of the wedding banquet in which the guests are casual passers by who are dragged in off the street, while the invited guests snub the host. That seems like an excessively mad party, which would stretch the imagination even of a Lewis Carroll. In general, in the Kingdom the general rule is the rule of the unruly, the possibility of the impossible.

The poetics of the impossible does not spring from a taste for heady rhetoric or from impish authors with no head for logic. On the contrary, it is a discourse with a deadly serious concern, a prophetic concern to contradict the world, to confound its calculations, and to interdict its hardness of heart, its cold-blooded logic and heartless economics. When St. Paul says that God chose the foolish and weak things of the world to shame the wise

---

[1] Søren Kierkegaard, *Kierkegaard's Works,* vol. 7, *Philosophical Fragments,* eds. and trans. H. Hong and E. Hong (Princeton: Princeton University Press, 1985), 37.

and strong, and that God chose the nothings and nobodies *(ta me onta)* to reduce to nothing the things that boast of being and presence *(ta onta),* he was confronting the world head-on, trying to shock and startle and antagonize the world with the way things happen in the Kingdom (1 Cor. 1:27–29).

For the Kingdom comes to contest the economy of the world, to loosen the grip of its merciless rationality. The world keeps rigorous books. Nothing is for free, and nobody gets off scot-free. Everything is for sale, everything has a price, nothing is sacred. The world will stop at nothing to get even, to even a score, or to come out ahead; the world is pomp and power and ruthless reckoning. In the world, offenders are made to pay for their offenses and every investor expects a return; every equation is balanced and every bill is paid, in one way or another, with blood or money.

The poetics of the Kingdom is prophetic—a diction of contradiction and interdiction—that "calls for" *(prophetein)* the rule of God, calls for things to happen in God's way, not the world's. The discourse of the Kingdom gets in the world's face, which is a costly business, for the world keeps strict accounts and knows how to make its critics pay. If anyone comes into the world and confronts the world, the world will receive him not, which usually means it will cost him dearly, maybe everything, which is not a good investment.

It is this prophetic passion, which contradicts the world, that explains why the discourse of the Kingdom takes such a contrarian form, why it is so unyielding, so full of poetic perversity. The poetics of the Kingdom moves about in the distance between logic and passion, truth and justice, concepts and desire, strategizing and praying, astute points and mad stories, for it can never be merely the one or the other, can never occupy a spot that is simply exterior to one or the other.

The whole idea is to speak out in the name of justice, in the name of God, and to call for the coming of the Kingdom, to pray and weep for the coming of justice. For the Kingdom comes to interrupt the business as usual of the world, to put the world in question, to bring the world up short. To proclaim the coming of the Kingdom of God is to deny that the world is all in all, to resist enclosure by the horizon of the world, to refuse the totalizing grip of the world, and to insist that the merciless calculations that obtain in the world are not the last word. For the horizon of the world is set by the calculable, the sensible, the possible, the reasonable, the sound investment. In the world, we are made to pay for everything. The world is nobody's fool.

GOD'S OWN GOOD TIME

The Kingdom of God is not a place but a time, the time when God rules rather than the world. The rule of God contests the powers and principalities of the world, what Luke calls the *exousiai* (Luke 12:11), which is a suggestive expression meaning the "powers that be," the powers that have prestige and presence and all the weightiness of being *(ousia)*. The reign of God challenges the rule of the men of means, the men of substance, and the pomp of this world, by exposing them to the power and sovereignty of God. For there is no ousia and no exousia except from God (Rom.13:1).[2] The rule of God resists the way things are done in the world and rejects the order of rank, the *arche,* that is installed in the world. The Kingdom is neither another world beyond this one, nor another time outside time, but rather the time of God's rule in the world, another way to be in time and to be in the world. It is the rule of a certain time, God's own good time, as opposed to the time-keeping that goes on in the world, for in the Kingdom time is God's, not ours.

When we pray, we pray for the Kingdom to come, asking that life become a time when God rules, that time be kept by God, as opposed to the way it is kept in the world. Time is one of the keys to the Kingdom, a sign or a clue that we are moving freely and easily with the rhythms of the Kingdom, rather than being sucked into the vortex of the ways of the world. In the Kingdom, time is like God's pulse, God's echo, God's orchestration, whereas in the world, time is money. In the Kingdom, time is the music that God plays in our ears. Its fortes and pianissimos must

---

[2] Although, pace Paul, who is being an excessively good Roman citizen in this text, it seems to me to follow from this point that the ruling government is precisely *not* to be confused with something invested with divine power.

be sorted out from all the background noise coming from the world. If no one has seen God and lived, we just might be able to hear God playing sweetly in time, and dance to God's own good time.

The world's time has been faithfully recorded by the philosophers, where it is said to keep a steady beat, to maintain the steady tick-tock of now succeeding now, in a succession so regular that Husserl called it a "form" and was even able to draw a diagram of it.[3] The razor-thin source point of the "now phase" is thickened by the now that has just lapsed and the now just about to come. Now phases flow smoothly from the future into the present, enjoying their fleeting moment in the sun of the present, only to flow off just as smoothly into the past, where they assume their inalterable place. Everything is tightly organized and regularized around the rule of retention and protention, memory and expectation, past-present and future-present, which is the basis of all the prudent long-range planning and careful record-keeping that goes on in the world. The time of the world is the sort you can count, the time that you can count on, the sort upon which economics depends. It is regular and reliable enough for us to calculate equivalences and fair exchanges, and to do a close cost analysis.

But time in the Kingdom is decidedly different. The steady beat of ousia's presence in the world fades before a more ephemeral openness to and dependence upon God's daily provision. Behold the lilies of the field, the day-lilies: they are not worrying about anything, for today is God's day, today is in God's hands, and God will provide. Give us this day our daily *(epiousios)* bread, the bread we need for today. For the cares of today are enough to worry about, and we should not even worry about them. "Ousiology" gives way to "epiousiology" *(epiousios),* which means the rule of God over the quotidian *(quotidie)* day-to-day time of the fleeting day-lily. The steady reliability of substance and of people of substance, the ousia and exousia of this world, gives way to a more fragile, lily-like, insubstantial, transient *un*-self-sufficiency.

---

[3] Edmund Husserl, *On the Phenomenology of the Consciousness of Internal Time, 1893–1917,* trans. John Barnett Brough (Dordrecht, The Netherlands: Kluwer Academic Publishers, 1991), 237–38.

The world stands there on its own, in all its pomp and worldly adornment, boasting of its *Selbstständigkeit,* self-standing, self-sufficiency; it is as if the world thinks itself able to put up a kind of ousiological resistance to God or to declare its independence of God. But the towering lordship of the world is laid low by the lilies of the field, who neither sow nor reap, while God keeps watch over their every need. In the Kingdom time yields to God's sway, becoming entirely transparent to God, alive to God, responsive to God, who watches over each day, each moment, from moment to moment, sustaining each moment. For God has counted every moment, just as he has counted every tear and every hair on our heads (Luke 12:7; Matt. 10:30).

When God rules, when time is a tune played by God, the results are generally unruly. The expectations and assumptions, the patterns and regularities, the rules and regulations that are built up in economic time are ruptured. The steady beat of the time of presence, which measures the regular rhythms of ousia, gives way to epiousiological initiative, innovation, and surprise. The regularities of kinetics succumb to the marvelous metamorphoses of "metanoetics"—from *metanoia,* to be of a new mind and heart—where things are given over to transformation and transfiguration. What is is what is *given*—what have you that you have not been given? Even so, what is ever so given that it cannot be forgiven, so thoroughly done that it cannot be undone or pardoned? Even as, in the Kingdom, the unforgiving past can be forgiven, so the future is held open in messianic expectation for the coming of the unforeseeable.

WITH GOD ALL THINGS ARE POSSIBLE

In the eleventh century, Peter Damian argued that God's power was so great and extended so far that, were it good to do so, God could actually alter the past and make it to be that what had happened in the past did *not* happen. Damian did not make this point as part of a machismo effort to prove that our God is mightier than your God, but as an argument about forgiveness. God's power to forgive sin was such that God could, were it good to do so, make it to be that the sinner had not sinned, that the sinner was not only forgiven but rendered innocent.[4]

The good is so much better and more powerful than being, so much beyond being, that the good takes the stuff right out of being and ousia and can even trump the difference between being and nonbeing. Things, being, ousia, presence, sense, and nonsense, indeed even the seemingly almighty principle of noncontradiction itself, all fade fast before the exousia of God, the power and benignity of God, who alone is almighty, who alone is good. These much-honored philosophical principles, these "princes and principalities" of the philosophers, are no match for God's power and goodness. As a result, in the Kingdom, when God rules, things take on an astonishing alterability, unpredictability, revisability, and contingency, the likes of which are not dreamed of by the philosophers.

I must confess my doubts about whether Damian can make stick the argument about the alterability of the past. For over and above the puzzling question of the sheer coherence of this suggestion, it seems to me that were God to annul the past offense, God would thereby also annul forgiveness, inasmuch as there would then be nothing to forgive. Forgiveness requires that the past offense be forgiven, not annulled, that it be left standing even as it is *somehow* lifted, lest it become blind fate and inalterable destiny.

But if I have my doubts about its logic, I am very much attached to the poetics of Damian's sometimes very technical argument. For Damian has dared to push the poetics of *the* impossible that is astir in forgiveness about as far as one can go. Like Angelus Silesius, he dares to go where you cannot go. Damian is one of the great theoreticians of the impossible, and this because he has a keen sense for the difference between the world's time and the time in which God rules. Like Kierkegaard

---

[4] See Damian's *De divina omnipotentia* in *Die Briefe des Petrus Damiani,* ed. Kurt Reindel (Munich: Monumenta Germaniae Historica, 1983–93), 4 vols., vol. 3, Brief 119, 341–84. For the English translation, see Peter Damian, *Letters,* 4 vols., trans. Owen J. Blum, *The Fathers of the Church* (Washington, D.C.: Catholic University of America Press, 1989–98), vol. 4, Letter 119, 344–86. For an excellent commentary in English, see Irven M. Resnick, *Divine Power and Possibility in St. Peter Damian's De Divina Omnipotentia* (Leiden, The Netherlands and New York: Brill, 1992).

and like Levinas later on, he is a philosopher with a biblical ear, with an ear tuned to the divine rhythms. All like him have noticed the idiosyncratic character of forgiven time.[5] Like them, he actually has two good ears, thanks be to God: one for the poetics of God's rule and the other for a good argument. He has two anti-Tertullian ears, one for Athens and another for Jerusalem. Two ears are better than one, and they make it easier to write with both hands; monauralism will only get you halfway.

Damian thinks of time metanoetically, regarding each moment as a new creation in which the past lapses in order to let life begin anew, which means to make all things new, which is a basic idea in the Kingdom. That idea also makes its way into Descartes, of whom we are accustomed to think as the father of rationalism, but to whom Levinas has lent a very biblical ear. This evangelic or metanoetic time is exemplarily realized in "forgiven time," in the time of forgiving, which requires a second chance, a turned-back clock, a "gift" of time and of a new birth, in which all things are made new, which is what it means to be saved. In a similar spirit, although the letter of their texts are very different, early in his career, Levinas spoke of repairing the irreparable:[6]

> Time, which is a condition of our existence, is above all a condition that is irreparable. The *fait accompli* . . . forever evades man's control, but weighs heavily on his destiny. . . . Remorse—that painful expression of a radical powerlessness to redeem the irreparable—heralds the repentance that generates the pardon that redeems. . . . Time loses its very irreversibility.

To have the time of a grievous mistake *back*—is that not our desire beyond desire, our hope against hope? If that is not possible, if the impossible is not possible, if we cannot repair the irreparable, "how then can we live?" as the great prophet of turning around *(Teshuvah)* asks (Ezek. 33:10).

---

[5] Johannes Climacus also noted the paradoxical character of forgiven time, its "retroactive power to annul the past," as a thought that faith spends a lifetime trying to realize, while the Hegelians claim to go further. See Kierkegaard, *Philosophical Fragments*, 77; and *Kierkegaard's Works*, vol. 12, 1, *Concluding Unscientific Postscript to "Philosophical Fragments,"* eds. and trans. H. Hong and E. Hong (Princeton: Princeton University Press, 1992), 224.

[6] Emmanuel Levinas, "Reflections on Hitlerism," trans. Sean Hand, *Critical Inquiry* 17 (Autumn 1990): 65.

Damian believed that God's power to make all things new meant that time no less than space could offer no real resistance to God, that the ousia of this world was no match for the exousia of God, even as the philosophers who offered resistance to theology were fuel for the flames (Damian was a little rough around the edges when it came to dissenters). Damian affirmed the central biblical motifs of *creation* and *recreation,* of making all things to begin with and then of making all things new, that is, making them again, in a divine repetition, for every yes yearns for repetition. There cannot be one yes, for every yes insists on saying yes again. God made the world, yes, and then he saw that it was good, yes, and so God kept on making it, yes, yes, and even after God rested from creating, the workweek of the created world went on, which required his constant attention.

The Greeks, by contrast, had a very different and worldly experience of time. For Damian, time had a radical contingency and revisability, which even extended to the contingency of the past. The past was hollowed out for Damian by the goodness and omnipotence of God, who just might be of a mind and a heart to alter it. For the Greeks, on the other hand, the very idea of the divine meant the rule of the unchanging and immortal, which is what they meant by the divine. The Greeks divided everything into unchanging being and changing being, immortals above and mortals below, and they bent their knees above all to the things that could not be otherwise, which were alone truly divine, and about which there was alone true *episteme.*

For the Greeks to love things divine was to prize the necessary, immobile, and universal over the contingent, changing, and singular, exactly the opposite of the way things happen in the Kingdom of God. Like all men of good sense, the Greeks, who kept an eye out for how things happen in general and for the most part, would have preferred the ninety-nine to the one, the general rule to the unruly oddity, which should be cast away. Hence, the ideal way to think about God for the Greeks was to imagine God traveling in a circle while thinking endlessly and only of himself, quite heedless of and impassive about us bleeding mortals down below. Whereas in the Kingdom, God has counted every tear and every hair on our heads, and God grieves and suffers with us through our every crisis.

The Greeks constantly recommended that changing things strive after and seek to be as unchanging as their humble circumstances permit, instead of acknowledging that the infinite elasticity and contingency of things is a sign of the gods. The Greeks were scandalized by the idea that being would come from nonbeing, that knowledge could come from ignorance, that any business at all could be transacted between nonbeing and being, two parties that must be rigorously prevented from making contact with each other. They wanted to subordinate the changing things that just happened to a thing *(symbebekos)* to what that thing steadily and permanently was (ousia). Necessity ruled in all things, which is what they would have meant by the "Kingdom" of what they called *theos,* had anyone coined such an expression among them. Which nobody did.

That is why forgiveness, which requires much humility, holds a pride of place in the Kingdom of God, and that is why the poetics of Damian's project is so interesting and un-Greek. Forgiveness is an impossible attempt to do something impossible, to repair the irreparable, to make the sinner new, to say to the sinner, "it never happened!" Even and especially if it did. Forgiveness is a sign of our love of the impossible. For the impossible is just what we love. Love will not put up with the idea that the impossible is off limits, or rather, the impossible is the only thing that can fire love to the limit. Otherwise the lover would be a mediocre fellow who has carefully counted the coins in his pocket, carefully calculated what can and cannot be, who is never surprised or overtaken by the advent of the astonishing. The impossible is what sets our hearts afire, what we are driven by. Love begins *by* the impossible. Forgiveness is a blow struck by the good against being and necessity, a *reductio ad nihilum,* which reduces the being of an offense to a certain nonbeing, which continues and extends the work of creation by leading the offender from nonbeing into being, into metanoia.

The dead rise from their graves, the lame are made straight, a virgin gives birth, bodies pass through hard surfaces or are sustained on water, seas are parted, walls are brought down by trumpets. Wonders never cease. It is, all in all, a very unruly and anarchic world, but still it is a very edifying and holy chaos, a sacred anarchy, a hier-an-archy that ought to make the established hierarchy nervous. In the Kingdom, things do not seem to be made of the stiff stuff of Greek ousia, but seem to have a wondrous pliability and plasticity that would have left the Greeks themselves wondering, even though the Greeks were supposed to be famous for their wonder.

RAISING HOLY HELL

On the whole, the Kingdom confounds the philosophers, who are accustomed to arrange things according to the principles of being, reason, order, possibility, presence, sense, and meaning, an intimidating parade of luminaries enjoying pride of place in philosophy, the men of means and of substance (Col. 1:16), the princes and principalities of philosophy, who sit at the head of philosophy's table. To that is opposed a Kingdom that is foolishness, a joke, a Kingdom *ironice,* where the last are the first, the weak are strong, the out are in, the crooked are straight, the nobodies and nothings are preferred, and the blind and the lame take the lead.

A veritable anarchic Kingdom, a Kingdom whose arche is whatever is an-arche, without princely and principial authority. The Kingdom marches to its own drummer, has its own beat and its own laws of space and bodily permeability, the key to which (the key to the Kingdom), shows up in its own very nonstandard time and its own sense of what is possible and impossible. That is why, exceeding any Greek sense of wonder, the texts of the Kingdom read—if we may adapt a suggestion coming from Gilles Deleuze—like a veritable *Alice in Wonderland,* packed with stories of the most astonishing transformations and transfigurations, of paradoxes and aporias, of wedding feasts as mad as any hatter's party, of eventualities that confound the time of the philosophers, who do not have nearly as good a time.

If the truth be told—and this is my hypothesis, for which I fully expect to be made to pay—what comes about when the Kingdom comes looks and sounds like what contemporary French philosophers call an event *(événement).* We could say of the Kingdom what Deleuze says of Alice: to understand it requires "a category of very special things: events, pure events."[7] The coming of the Kingdom is an out-coming, from the Latin *evenire,* the coming out or bursting out of something we did not see coming, something unforeseen, singular, irregular. Alternatively, the event is also what Derrida calls *l'invention de l'autre,* the in-coming *(invenire)* of something "wholly other," the breaking into our familiar world of something completely amazing, which shatters our horizon of expectations.

In the military, when someone shouts "incoming," the sensible thing to do is head for cover lest we be blown to kingdom come. This outburst or out-coming shatters our horizons of expectation. Otherwise nothing is happening, nothing much, nothing new; creation is grinding to a stop, and the yes is losing the strength to repeat itself, to come again. The "event" is something that does not seem possible, that for which no mundane horizon of possibility or foreseeability is able to prepare us. To wait for the event is to expect to be surprised and overtaken, to prepare for something for which you cannot be prepared, which is like knowing in advance that the Kingdom will come like a thief in the night.

I am, in short, in imitation of the one who dined with sinners, allowing the Kingdom to sit down at the table with deconstruction and other disreputable French types. I am, to the great scandal of deconstructors and the Christian Right alike, contending that the way the Kingdom contests the mundane powers that pretend to be and to have presence goes hand in hand with the notorious critique of the "metaphysics of presence" (ousia) in deconstruction. I am aligning the opposition of the Kingdom to the world in the Scriptures with the opposition of the gift, which is *the* impossible, to economy in deconstruction. I am aligning the coming of the Kingdom with the in-coming of the *tout autre* or the out-coming of the event in deconstruction. I am arguing that in the Kingdom and in deconstruction, we have to do with two different versions of the poetics of the impossible. I am not trying to reduce the one to the other, by any means, because they are importantly different, but to open the lines of communication

---

[7] Gilles Deleuze, *The Logic of Sense,* trans. Mark Lester with Charles Stivale, ed. Constantin V. Boundas (New York: Columbia University Press, 1990), 1.

between them and to show the good news that they bear to each other.

In a poetics of the impossible things are highly deconstructible, but being deconstructible is not as bad as it sounds. In fact, my contention is that it is good news and arises in the wake of *the* good news. For something is deconstructible only if it has been constructed to begin with, which is why deconstruction comes along in the wake of a theology of creation, and why its critique of the metaphysics of presence springs from a frame of mind that keeps an eye out for the idols of presence. Deconstructibility is the condition of the event. Otherwise things would be nailed down too tightly, and ousia would cling too tightly to ousia. That is what inflamed the desire of Parmenides, whose idea of a good time was an airtight perfectly spherical solid, which is, if you let yourself think about it, an exceedingly odd ideal to hold close to your heart. For anything new or surprising to eventuate, for anything strange or amazing to happen, which is what we long for and desire, pray and weep for, things must be deconstructible.

So far from being the enemy of faith and religion, far from being the last nail in the coffin prepared for the death of God, the deconstructibility of things is one of the hallmarks of the Kingdom of God, one of the first things to come about when the Kingdom comes, one of the first things to happen when God rules, one of the things we are praying for when we pray for the Kingdom to come, when we pray and weep, *viens, oui, oui.* Deconstructibility is the principal thing we need for things to open up and be pliable to the rule of God, when time is God's rather than the timeless now of a rock-solid, well-rounded sphere, which was the first form ousia assumed when it came into the world.

It is astonishing to me that anyone who reads the Scriptures faithfully and who is in love with the idea of the Kingdom of God would also fall in love with ousiology or with Neoplatonic hyperousiology, with essentialism or hyperessentialism, or with Greco-Roman "natural law" theories with which ousiology often keeps company. True, nature has its laws. But God, who is the author of nature, is the law of these laws, the exousia that trumps all worldly ousia, which is why in the Scriptural stories God will, from time to time, beg leave to set those laws on their head. That interruptibility, that deconstructibility in the name of justice is what we *mean* by the Kingdom.

If, in the world, God's glory is shown in the regular course that nature follows, which is an idea that even philosophers can follow, then the rule of God is made still more manifest in the Kingdom stories by the interruptions and contraventions of nature's regular course. In the Kingdom, things happen a lot more like the way things fall out in deconstruction (whose least bad definition, Derrida says, is an "experience of *the* impossible")[8] than they do in classical metaphysical theology, which, as Johannes de Silentio quips, "sits all rouged and powdered in the window and . . . offers its charms to philosophy,"[9] to philosophy's love of necessity, order, presence, essence, regularity, and stability.

I do not know how to cushion this blow, either for the learned despisers of religion or for the learned despisers of deconstruction, for both of whom this good news signals an exceedingly bad turn of events: deconstruction, in my view, is *structured like a religion* and makes use of religious structures. For Derrida can say, no less than St. Augustine, *inquietum est cor nostrum,* our hearts are restless and driven by desire, a desire beyond desire, a desire for the impossible. For by the impossible Derrida does not mean just any wild or crazy eventuality, however bizarre, mean, or violent. The event begins *by* the impossible, is moved and driven by a desire for the gift beyond economy, for the justice beyond the law, for the hospitality beyond proprietorship, for forgiveness beyond getting even, for the coming of the *tout autre* beyond the coming of the same, for what Levinas, picking up on an ancient tradition, called the excess of the good beyond being, which is a lovely idea that lovers of the Kingdom can use, if one drops the Neoplatonic metaphysics, which has next to nothing to do with the Kingdom and would have left Jesus of Nazareth dumbfounded.

---

[8] For a more carefully elaborated and documented implementation of the claim that deconstruction lends itself to a religious interpretation, see my book *The Prayers and Tears of Jacques Derrida: Religion without Religion* (Bloomington: Indiana University Press, 1997).

[9] Søren Kierkegaard, *Kierkegaard's Works,* vol. 6, *"Fear and Trembling" and "Repetition,"* eds. and trans. H. Hong and E. Hong (Princeton: Princeton University Press, 1983), 32.

The event is driven by a desire for the Messiah to come, a Messiah who will contradict the smug complacency and the pomp of the present, a Messiah who will confront the world and the way things are done in the time of the world. So if, on the one hand, the Kingdom is the sphere where God rules, and if, on the other hand, deconstruction means the rule of the gift, of the good, of justice, of hospitality and forgiveness, then it seems to me that the two of them, deconstruction and the Kingdom of God, should get along famously, even if they have their differences, and even if their respective staff and campaign workers do not trust each other.

I am not proposing to put the New Testament on the same footing as *Alice in Wonderland,* even though I think the lovers of the Kingdom have something to learn from Deleuze's love of Lewis Carroll in the *Logic of Sense.* I am only doing my duty, to keep time and space holy, and to protect them both from idolatry by saying that they are God's, that in the Kingdom space and time are the scene of God's rule. But if—and we have this on the highest authority (exousia)—the Kingdom of God is within us, then what I am saying bears upon the transformability of our lives, having to do with the most powerful and transfiguring figures of self-transformation, in which we and all things are made new. The idea behind the poetics of the impossible is metanoetic and transformative, prophetic and salvific, creative and recreative. It is to repair the irreparable, transforming the face of the earth, always beginning by the impossible, by a breathtaking transformation ex nihilo, which, according to the Greeks, is impossible.

I stick to my hypothesis with devilish persistency, with unrelenting itchiness, and without the least compunction, trying to make life difficult both for the learned despisers of religion and the learned despisers of deconstruction, who are, alas, a learned legion. This is risky business and unlikely to win a large following. For the self-appointed Defenders of the Good have always been scandalized by the way the Kingdom consorts with sinners (or deconstructors), whom they denounce as a devilish lot, even as the Deconstructors of the Transcendental Signified have worked themselves into an unholy heat about religion, which

they regularly denounce as the slave revolt in morals or as piti-
able people longing for their mommies.

The Kingdom ought to be as hospitable as possible, in the
spirit of that impossible story about a very strange wedding feast,
a veritable hatter's party, where the distinction between who is
in and who is out in the Kingdom starts to look a little mad. I am
very interested in the question of the borders of the Kingdom, its
inside and outside and its politics, a question that also spills into
other important questions about the borders that divide the "religions of the Book," or the borders between orthodoxy and het-
erodoxy, between the community and the excommunicated,
between theism and atheism, theology and atheology, and, in
general, between religion and what has been called in a devil-
ishly delicious phrase "religion without religion."

Are there rigorous walls around the Kingdom? Do they have
border patrols there? Do they have a problem with illegal immi-
grants? Who is in and who is out? Is anyone there who rightly
passes for an atheist? The guidance we get from the story is that
the insiders are out, and the outsiders are in. That, I readily agree,
is perfectly mad—it makes perfect sense or non-sense, is in perfect compliance with the poetics of the impossible, with the sort
of goings-on you come to expect when the Kingdom comes.

For, according to my hypothesis, the rule of God is a bit unruly, and the Kingdom has the look of a holy or sacred anarchy
where, truth to tell, it seems like all hell has broken loose.

Holy hell, that is.

3

Toward a "Continental" Philosophy of Religion: Derrida, Responsibility, and "Nondogmatic" Faith

Matthew C. Halteman

FROM ITS INCEPTION in Kant's strivings to imagine a "religion within the limits of reason alone," the Continental tradition has maintained a strict division of labor between theological and philosophical reflection on religion. Many of its most influential thinkers have argued, moreover, that theological inquiry is secondary to the more fundamental philosophical task of elucidating a conceptual logic of "the religious," the universal structure that underlies all particular faith traditions.

In what follows, I examine this Continental legacy in the context of Jacques Derrida's recent work on the concept of responsibility. First I discuss three guiding themes (the limits of speculative analysis, the idea of nondogmatic religion, and the importance of "the other") that characterize the Continental tradition's general orientation toward philosophy of religion, as well as Derrida's approach to the concept of responsibility. I turn next to elucidating Derrida's account of this concept as developed in two recent texts, "Force of Law: The Mystical Foundation of Authority"[1] and *The Gift of Death.*[2] Finally, I conclude with a discussion of the uses and limits of this account for reli-

---

[1] "Force of Law: The Mystical Foundation of Authority," trans. Mary Quaintance, in *Deconstruction and the Possibility of Justice,* ed. Drucilla Cornell (New York: Routledge, 1992).

[2] *The Gift of Death,* trans. David Willis (Chicago: University of Chicago Press, 1995).

gious (and theological) reflection, as well as for the task of articulating a contemporary Continental philosophy of religion.

I

In generalizing the problems and tasks of Continental reflection on religion, it will be helpful to start with a provisional sketch of what goes on in the contemporary analytic mainstream. Broadly speaking, current Anglo-American philosophy of religion is concerned with providing reasoned accounts for or against religious belief (both in general and in particular religious traditions). Accordingly, the central debates in this field tend to surround problems that threaten the rational defensibility of such belief, such as evil (Is it reconcilable with the existence of God?),[3] freewill (Is it compatible with God's knowledge of the future?),[4] faith in divine revelation (Is it rational? How does it affect our epistemic faculties?),[5] religious knowledge (Is it comparable to scientific knowledge? What is its relationship to theology?).[6]

While Continental philosophers of religion also entertain these kinds of questions, their tradition has historically placed a special emphasis on a more foundational, transcendental question: "What is religion and how is it possible?" Or, more specifically: "What are the conceptual conditions that render our faith lives meaningful?" The Kantian tone of these questions is obvious, as is the tension between the epistemological and critical tasks set forth in them. On the one hand, there is the task of tightening reason's grasp on religion by taking an inventory of its concep-

---

[3] See *The Problem of Evil,* eds. Marilyn Adams and Robert Adams (Oxford: Oxford University Press, 1990); and *The Problem of Evil, Selected Readings,* ed. Michael Peterson (Notre Dame: Notre Dame University Press, 1992).

[4] See *God, Foreknowledge and Freedom,* ed. John Martin Fischer (Stanford: Stanford University Press, 1989); and Tom Flint, *Divine Providence: The Molinist Account* (Ithaca: Cornell University Press, 1998).

[5] See Alvin Plantinga, *Warranted Christian Belief* (Oxford: Oxford University Press, 2000); and Nicholas Wolterstorff, "Are We Entitled?" in *Divine Discourse* (Cambridge: Cambridge University Press, 1995).

[6] See William Alston, "On Knowing That We Know: The Application to Religious Knowledge," in *Christian Perspectives on Religious Knowledge,* eds. C. Stephen Evans and Merold Westphal (Grand Rapids, Mich.: Eerdmans Publishing Company, 1993), 15–39.

tual preconditions. On the other, there is the task of reining in reason's tendency to deduce more than it should from its conceptual resources.

The animating force of Kant's project, of course, is the question of how to discipline speculative reason's false confidence in its ability to adjudicate matters of faith. For though reason provides us with problematic concepts of numinous things like God and freedom, we lack any intuition of them that would yield bona fide knowledge. Our only recourse, then, is to acknowledge the limits of speculative analysis and turn to an account of the practical necessity of the problematic concepts at issue. The result, for Kant, is "Natural Religion," the pure practical "hypothesis of all religion" that "gives weight to all our concepts of virtue and uprightness."[7]

Though this Kantian emphasis on the limits of speculative analysis (and the resulting importance of practical reason) has taken various and often conflicting forms, its continuing influence on the tradition has been pervasive.[8] We find a variation on this theme articulated quite elegantly, for example, in the following excerpt from Hegel's famous "Tübingen Essay":

Let the theologians squabble all they like over what belongs to objective religion, over its dogmas and their precise determination: the fact is that every religion is based on a few fundamental principles which, although set forth in the different religions in varying degrees of purity, however modified or adulterated, are nonetheless the basis of all the faith and hope that religion is capable of offering us. When I speak of religion here, I am abstracting completely from all scientific (or rather metaphysical) knowledge of God, as well as from the relationship of the world and ourselves to him, etc.; such knowledge, the province of discursive understand-

---

[7] Immanuel Kant, *Lectures on Philosophical Theology,* trans. Allen W. Wood and Gertrude M. Clark (Ithaca: Cornell University Press, 1978), 26.

[8] I do not mean to suggest, of course, that Kant is the Continental tradition's only (or seminal) archive on the issue of speculative reason's limits with respect to religious reflection. On the contrary, this insight is already alive and well in modern philosophy in the work of Leibniz and Lessing, among others. The significance of Kant here is primarily heuristic. Since his work on these issues is widely known among philosophers in all traditions (pervasively so among Continental philosophers), and since my purpose here is to give a provisional and accessible overview, Kant's work is a compelling touchstone.

ing, is theology and no longer religion. And I classify as religious only such knowledge of God and immortality as is responsive to the demands of practical reason and connected with it in a readily discernible way.[9]

Similar approaches to religious reflection are apparent, more-over, in Husserl's unpublished manuscripts on "the problem of God,"[10] Kierkegaard's account of the "leap-of-faith" and the "becoming subjective" of religious experience,[11] Heidegger's critique of "ontotheology" and his insistence on the hiddenness of the origins of being,[12] Levinas's attempt to show that religious ethics (not ontology) is first philosophy,[13] and, of course, Derrida's account of responsibility (as we shall directly observe). What all these accounts share, despite their profound differences and complexities, is a commitment to articulating what Derrida has called a "nondogmatic doublet" of religious faith,[14] that is, a

---

[9] See G. W. F. Hegel, "The Tübingen Essay," in *Three Essays, 1793–1795,* trans. Peter Fuss and John Dobbins (Notre Dame: University of Notre Dame Press, 1984), 35.

[10] See Louis Dupré, "Husserl's Thought on God and Faith," in *Philosophy and Phenomenological Research* 29 (1968): 201–15. Says Dupré: "[For Husserl, t]heoretical reason can never justify the proposition that life is wholly meaningful. Yet, the acceptance of this proposition is necessarily postulated by man's ethical striving. Religious faith alone then provides the foundation of morality. Husserl's interpretation is obviously influenced by Kant's theory of the postulates of practical reason, to which he refers repeatedly," 213.

[11] See Søren Kierkegaard (Johannes Climacus), *Concluding Unscientific Postscript to Philosophical Fragments,* vol. 1, trans. Howard V. Hong and Edna H. Hong (Princeton: Princeton University Press, 1992), 72–188.

[12] See, among other places, Martin Heidegger, *An Introduction to Metaphysics,* trans. Ralph Manheim (New Haven: Yale University Press, 1959), 6–10.

[13] See Emmanuel Levinas, *Totality and Infinity,* trans. Alphonso Lingis (Pittsburgh: Duquesne University Press, 1969), 42–52. Two other short texts that are particularly relevant here (as well as to Derrida's account of responsibility in *The Gift of Death*) are Levinas's discussion of the "messianic/messianism" distinction in *Ethics and Infinity, Conversations with Philippe Nemo,* trans. Richard Cohen (Pittsburgh: Duquesne University Press, 1985), 113–24; and "God and Philosophy," in Levinas, *Of God Who Comes to Mind,* trans. Bettina Bergo (Stanford: Stanford University Press, 1998), 55–78.

[14] Derrida puts the point as follows: "[A] certain Kant and a certain Hegel, Kierkegaard of course, and, I might even dare to say for provocative effect, Heidegger also, belong to this tradition that consists of proposing a nondogmatic doublet of dogma, a philosophical and metaphysical doublet, in any case a thinking that 'repeats' the possibility of religion without religion." Derrida, *The Gift of Death,* 49.

thematization of religion into a logic of concepts (for example, infinite love, responsibility, sin and salvation, repentance and sacrifice) that can be abstracted from practical experience and studied independently of the specific content of particular religious traditions.[15]

Though an adequate account of the evolution of this Continental approach to religious reflection would require a much lengthier treatment, one productive way to understand the general trajectory of the tradition since Kant is in terms of an increasing awareness of the "unpresentability" of the other. In the simplest terms, the other is what religious reflection encounters (or would seem to encounter) at the limits of its power. For Kant, the other is the noumenon, the regulative ideal that chastens speculative reason, but is accessible as a necessary postulate of practical reason.[16] For Hegel, the other is reason's as-yet-unfulfilled awareness of itself, the *telos* that all particular historical traditions anticipate and latently contain.[17] For these two modern Continentals, then, the other, though initially a barrier, is eventually ren-

---

[15] Examples of the attempt to think this nondogmatic doublet abound in the work of all of the above. Two particularly instructive examples are: (1) Heidegger's analysis of Dasein's ontological tendency toward "falling" (as a conceptual precondition of any account of sin), in *Being and Time,* trans. John Macquarrie and Edward Robinson (New York: Harper and Row, 1962), 224; and (2) Levinas's analysis of "recurrence" (as a conceptual precondition of any account of responsibility or "finite freedom") in *Otherwise Than Being or Beyond Essence,* trans. Alphonso Lingis (Dordrecht, The Netherlands: Kluwer Academic Publishers, 1991), 102–29. Heidegger's assessment of the nondogmatic status of his account of falling is especially illuminating: "[O]ur existential-ontological Interpretation makes no ontical assertion about the 'corruption of human Nature,' not because the necessary evidence is lacking, but because the problematic of this Interpretation is prior to any assertion about corruption or incorruption. . . . [W]e have not decided whether man is 'drunk with sin' . . . or whether he finds himself in . . . the *status gratiae.* But in so far as any faith or 'world view,' makes any such assertions . . . it must come back to the . . . structures which we have set forth, provided that its assertions are to make a claim to *conceptual* understanding," 224.

[16] See Immanuel Kant, *Critique of Pure Reason,* trans. Norman Kemp Smith (New York: St. Martin's Press, 1965), 24–25, 29, 377, 379–80, 382–83, 526–27, 530–31, 617, 637 ff.; and *Critique of Practical Reason,* trans. Lewis White Beck (New York: Macmillan, 1993), 116–55 ("Dialectic of Pure Practical Reason"), especially 141 ff.

[17] See G. W. F. Hegel, *Phenomenology of Spirit,* trans. A. V. Miller (Oxford: Oxford University Press, 1977), 14–22, 479–93 (sections 25–37, especially 27, 28, 29, and 37; and "Absolute Knowing," sections 788–808).

dered presentable in the necessary postulates of practical reason, and in reason's necessary fulfillment of its telos, respectively.

In the work of many contemporary Continentals, by contrast, we find an increasing sensitivity to the profound difficulty (and risk) of attempting to present the other.[18] For these philosophers, thinking at the limits of reason is not an experience of inevitable deliverance beyond speculation, but one of *impasse* or *aporia,* an experience of the other as an absolute limit that not only defies presentation, but presents itself (paradoxically) as unpresentable.[19] To clarify the consequences of this heightened sense of the other's unpresentability for religious reflection (and for the attempt to think nondogmatic faith), let us turn directly to Derrida.

II

Until the late 1980s, thinking through deconstruction's import for philosophy of religion demanded serious reading between the

---

[18] Jean-François Lyotard has famously identified this sensitivity as the essence of the postmodern condition: "[T]he postmodern would be that which, in the modern, puts forward the unpresentable in presentation itself; that which denies itself the solace of good forms, the consensus of a taste which would make it possible to share collectively the nostalgia for the unattainable; that which searches for new presentations, not in order to enjoy them but in order to impart a stronger sense of the unpresentable" (*The Postmodern Condition: A Report on Knowledge,* trans. Geoff Bennington and Brian Massumi, Minneapolis: University of Minnesota Press, 1984, 81). The tone of ethical urgency here is consonant, as we shall see, with Derrida's account of responsibility.

[19] This difficult notion of an "unpresentability that presents itself as such" is an ancient legacy in Western philosophy that has its roots in Plato's discussion of *epekeina tes ousias* and in Plotinus's appropriation of this notion in the *Enneads,* his discourse on "The One (Beyond-Being)." More recently, variations on this theme have enjoyed a renaissance in late- and post-Husserlian (hermeneutic) phenomenology, most notably in Heidegger's 1927 account of Dasein's presentation to itself as a "basis for its own nullity" (*Being and Time,* 326 ff, section 58); Edmund Husserl's 1931 discussion of the "alter-ego" in the fifth of the *Cartesian Meditations* (trans. Dorion Cairns, Dordrecht, The Netherlands: Kluwer, 1991), 89 ff.; Merleau-Ponty's treatment of "the flesh" ("The Intertwining-The Chiasm," in *Signs,* Evanston, Ill.: Northwestern University Press, 1960); Levinas's account of "the face" (*Totality and Infinity),* 187 ff.; Jean-Luc Nancy's discussion of "literary communism" (*The Inoperative Community,* trans. Peter Connor et al., Minneapolis: University of Minnesota Press, 1991), 71–81; Jean-Luc Marion's account of "the present and the gift" (*God without Being,* trans. Thomas Carlson, Chicago: University of Chi-

lines. Though Derrida claims in retrospect that a commitment to responsibility before the other has been the animus of his work from the beginning, later texts like "Force of Law," *The Gift of Death, Politics of Friendship,*[20] and, most recently, "Faith and Knowledge"[21] take up the ethical and religious significance of this commitment more explicitly than ever before. Of these four texts, "Force of Law" and *The Gift of Death* together provide an excellent framework for understanding: (1) how deconstruction is related to the idea of infinite responsibility; and (2) why this responsibility is conceived as involving a "religious" commitment to the other.

Derrida's first concern in "Force of Law" is to establish an explicit link between deconstruction and the demand for infinite responsibility before an infinite idea of justice.[22] The essay begins, ironically enough, with a discussion of deconstruction's apparent reticence regarding the issue of justice. The temptation, Derrida admits, is to view deconstruction's alleged silence on matters of ethics and justice as an abdication of responsibility in the perceived absence of an unshakable standard of judgment. He insists, however, that this obliqueness regarding justice is a not a sign of indifference but one of deference, an indication of deconstruction's sensitivity to the fact that one cannot thematize or objectify justice without immediately betraying it.[23] Deconstruction has deferred speaking directly of justice, Derrida ex-

---

cago Press, 1991), 161–82; and, as we shall see directly, Derrida's account of "responsibility."

[20] Jacques Derrida, *Politics of Friendship,* trans. George Collins (London: Verso, 1997).

[21] Jacques Derrida, "Faith and Knowledge: The Two Sources of 'Religion' at the Limits of Reason Alone," in *Religion,* eds. Jacques Derrida and Gianni Vattimo (Stanford: Stanford University Press, 1998). This volume includes five other essays by leading Continental philosophers, including Gianni Vattimo's "The Trace of the Trace"; Eugenio Trias's "Thinking Religion: The Symbol and the Sacred"; and Vincenzo Vittiello's "Desert Ethos, Abandonment: Towards a Topology of the Religious." As its essay titles indicate, the volume is an excellent primer on the problem of nondogmatic faith.

[22] The text of "Force of Law" is divided evenly into two more or less self-contained parts; part 1 consists of Derrida's central argument for associating justice with deconstruction (1–28); part 2 gives a related but supplementary reading of Walter Benjamin's *Zur Kritik der Gewalt* (29–63). I will focus exclusively on part 1.

[23] Derrida, "Force of Law," 10.

plains, out of respect for "a possibility of justice that cannot be rendered present in any law."[24] The problem with conceiving justice in terms of law, he continues, is that the authority of law is ultimately unjustifiable: law derives its authority from enforceability, enforceability is made possible by force, and force is essentially self-authorizing in that it founds the very standard that legitimates judgment, that is, law. In short, since every law has self-authorizing violence at its origin, no law can serve as the standard of justification for any other.[25] Thus, since there is no clear criterion for distinguishing the arbitrary violence that founds law from the allegedly justified violence that enforces it, the justice of law is never fully just.

It follows, Derrida argues, that law is essentially deconstructible, for insofar as law is constructed on unfounded and therefore "infinitely transformable textual strata," it is always open to interpretation and revision. So, while law is a poor substitute for justice, the fact that it is open to revision is actually good news, given the many injustices that arise in legislating and upholding laws. In fact, Derrida maintains, this curious serendipity concealed in the structure of law is nothing less than a paradox through which the possibility of justice can be glimpsed. For it is precisely in the possibility of deconstruction opened by the deconstructible structure of law that the infinite demand of justice resides. If we experience justice at all, Derrida maintains, it is only in the interval of indecision that separates the revision of one unjust law from its recalculation into another. The experience of justice, then, is an "experience of the impossible," insofar as the demands of justice are infinite and our resources for realizing these demands are finite and deconstructible. What this "experience of the impossible" impresses upon us, Derrida claims, is a sense of infinite responsibility before an infinite idea of justice: "This 'idea of justice' seems to be irreducible in its affirmative character, in its demand of gift without exchange, without circulation, without recognition or gratitude, without economic circularity, without calculation and without rules, without reason and without rationality."[26]

---

[24] Ibid., 5–6.
[25] Ibid., 13.
[26] Ibid., 25.

Derrida is adamant, of course, that the incalculability of justice is by no means an alibi for inaction. It is in the name of this incalculable justice, rather, that deconstruction must constantly calculate, disrupt, and reevaluate the dominant network of concepts that determines the possibilities and the limits, the inclusions and the exclusions, of present discourse.[27] More specifically, Derrida continues, this vigilance against unjust exclusion must take shape as "a responsibility before the very concept of responsibility that regulates the justice and appropriateness of our behavior, of our theoretical, practical, and ethico-political decisions."[28] In other words, Derrida is suggesting that one of our most pressing responsibilities is to continually reevaluate the common-sense notions of what it means to be responsible that discipline our everyday decisions.[29] Derrida's worry here is that our common conceptions of responsibility are all too often irresponsible, in that they demand far too little of us and give us a false sense of duty discharged. Thus, at the very moment that deconstruction's interrogation of the present boundaries of responsibility appears to be a move toward irresponsibility, it is in fact a hyperbolic raising of the stakes of responsibility that is nothing short of what Derrida calls "a mad desire" for justice.[30]

It is precisely this concept of a responsibility that verges on madness that Derrida will associate with the religious in *The Gift of Death*. His task in this text is to reinscribe within the concept of responsibility a chain of conceptual associations (secrecy, irresponsibility, irrationality, madness) that the concept's Platonic and Christian heritages have respectively subordinated and repressed. Derrida's primary vehicle for accomplishing this task is a reading of Kierkegaard's interpretation in *Fear and Trembling* of the famous Biblical story of Abraham and the binding of Isaac. By juxtaposing Kierkegaard's account of religious responsibility with Levinas's religious ethics (two divergent nondog-

---

[27] Ibid., 19–20.

[28] Ibid., 20.

[29] This responsibility before the concept of responsibility itself is what obligates Derrida (in *The Gift of Death*) to revisit past philosophers' "nondogmatic doublets of dogma," in search of their inevitable conceptual exclusions and betrayals in presenting the unpresentable.

[30] Derrida, "Force of Law," 25.

matic doublets of dogma), Derrida hopes to convince us that Abraham's radical responsibility before God parallels that of each person before every other.

His point of departure in *The Gift of Death* is an essay from Jan Patočka's *Heretical Essays on the Philosophy of History,* in which Patočka gives a genealogical account of responsibility that locates this concept as a uniquely Christian, indeed uniquely European, invention.[31] Derrida situates Patočka within a tradition that problematizes religion by "proposing a nondogmatic doublet of dogma, a philosophical and metaphysical doublet, in any case a thinking that 'repeats' the possibility of religion without religion."[32] Though Derrida is interested in exploring the logic of the nondogmatic doublet (as we have already noted), he criticizes Patočka's particular version of this logic for its complicity with the Christian-Hegelian insistence on synthesis, the guarantee that every sacrifice will be reborn in a higher unity.[33]

In search of a nondogmatic doublet that comprehends a responsibility beyond the promise of synthesis, Derrida turns to the account in *Fear and Trembling* of God's unspeakable demand of Abraham. He explicates Abraham's responsibility before God in terms of two central concepts: the secret and the sacrifice (or gift of death). First, Abraham's responsibility binds him to a double secret: he must proceed without knowing why God has so charged him, and he must avoid disclosing his charge to Sarah and (most of all) to Isaac. That Abraham undertakes his obligation in secret is crucial not only because the secret is too horrible to be told or believed, but also because telling it would immediately deliver him from the singularity that binds him to God.

Paradoxically, then, the ethical demand of responsibility to his family is for Abraham a *temptation to irresponsibility,* an inviting consolation that would dissolve his singularity and bring him back into the friendly company of society. To remain faithful to his responsibility before God, Abraham must renounce his filial

---

[31] Specifically, "La Civilisation technique est-elle une civilisation de déclin, et pourquoi?" in *Essais herétiques sur la philosophie de l'histoire,* trans. Erika Abrams (Lagrasse, France: Verdier, 1981).

[32] Derrida, *The Gift of Death,* 49.

[33] See John D. Caputo, *The Prayers and Tears of Jacques Derrida* (Bloomington: Indiana University Press, 1997), 193.

and civic duties in favor of sacrificing his beloved son, thereby becoming the most hated among men: a deceiver, a murderer, an infanticide. In this act of madness, Derrida explains, Abraham suffers the paradox of responsibility: he is at once the most moral and the most immoral, the most responsible precisely because he is absolutely irresponsible.[34]

The improbability of Abraham's dilemma is undoubtedly its most impressive feature. Yet, as we have been warned, Derrida's intention is to make the scandal universal, to get us to believe that every single one of us offers the gift of death every single day. As we have seen, Kierkegaard conceptualizes the religious in terms of an absolute and singular responsibility before a wholly other God. In so doing, Derrida claims, he has shown (on a purely formal level) that the concepts of alterity and singularity (and the aporias that accompany them) constitute the very concepts of responsibility and decision that inform our everyday dealings with others. Since this conceptual contamination makes it extremely difficult (if not impossible) to locate a determinate boundary between religious and ethical responsibility, it would seem that Kierkegaard has left the door ajar to the Levinasian possibility that "ethics is also the order of and respect for absolute singularity, and not only that of the generality or of the repetition of the same."[35]

Thus, the nondogmatic doublet (or moral of morality) that Derrida solicits from Kierkegaard (by way of Levinas) is that every other is wholly other and that, as a result, *all* responsibility has the structure of sacrifice: "As soon as I enter into a relation with the other . . . I know that I can respond only by sacrificing ethics, that is, by sacrificing whatever obliges me to also respond, in the same way, in the same instant, to all the others."[36] The impossible conclusion of this nondogmatic doublet, in short, is that *all* the commitments and decisions that bind one to various persons and communities must finally remain (like Abraham's hyperethical sacrifice) unjustifiable.[37] Accordingly, Derrida argues, the act of undertaking one's daily responsibilities (notwithstanding their

---

[34] Ibid., 72.
[35] Derrida, *The Gift of Death*, 84.
[36] Ibid., 68.
[37] Ibid., 71.

unjustifiability) is akin, at least structurally and conceptually, to the radical act of faith undertaken by Abraham on Mount Moriah.

III

Given the fact that improbability, impossibility, and unjustifiability are the distinguishing features of Derrida's nondogmatic faith, it is easy enough to see how his account might appear, prima facie, to be of questionable importance for religious reflection. It remains, then, to examine the relevance of Derrida's account for philosophy of religion in general, as well as for the specific task of articulating a contemporary Continental philosophy of religion. The prospects for adequately addressing this remainder are significantly complicated, however, by the proliferating diversity of discourses on religion made available through our increasingly global exchange of ideas. For better or for worse, the discourses of religious anthropology, comparative religion, and philosophical theology—among others, and each in multiple traditions—coexist side by side in the conference proceedings, journals, and anthologies that make up the professional literature of philosophy of religion. Though these various discourses are frequently at odds, the beauty of Derrida's work, I want to suggest, is in the facility with which he moves between them, juxtaposing their methodologies, exposing their conceptual limits, and hybridizing their conclusions.

A brief topical survey of *The Gift of Death* alone is sufficient to illustrate the versatility and fecundity of Derrida's engagements across the wide spectrum of philosophical discourses on religion. In chapters 1 and 2, for example, he offers a genealogy of the concept of responsibility in Western religious thinking that doubles (quite ingeniously) as an interrogation of the genealogical method itself. Interlacing his own account with that of Patočka, Derrida takes such great care to bear witness to the contextual assumptions and conceptual exclusions that perforate Patočka's narrative, that one can scarcely avoid the conclusion that Derrida's own is similarly vulnerable.[38] In chapter 3, this

---

[38] Ibid., 1–52.

double narrative narrows seamlessly into a comparative confrontation of the "religions of the book" on the site of Mount Moriah. At stake, along with Isaac, are the conflicting (yet, as Derrida persuades, oddly complementary) offerings of Kierkegaard's radical Christianity and Levinas's Jewish humanism; bearing witness on the margins is a third party: Islam.[39] In chapter 4, finally, Derrida employs the hybrid doublet solicited from Kierkegaard and Levinas as the hermeneutic principle for a jarring reading of the gospel of Matthew, one that acutely reveals the inevitable risks of conceptual reversal hidden in our philosophical theologies.[40] The picture that emerges from this brief survey is that Derrida's account of responsibility has an important critical employment within the discourses on religion it inhabits. In John Caputo's words, "it put[s] us on the alert to the way things can turn around and reverse themselves, by a secret operation, so that they produce effects diametrically opposed to what they intend."[41]

This "vigilance about reversibility," moreover, can be as relevant to our religious and moral lives as it is to our academic discourses. Caputo invites us, for instance, to approach Derrida's work as a kind of devotional exercise for author and reader alike, an extended commentary, if you will, on Saint Augustine's prayerful question "What do I love when I love my God?" In Caputo's view, Derrida's commentary evidences a passion for God that calls everything into question, thus "making utter nonsense of the Heideggerian dogma that faith in God puts questioning to sleep."[42] From this standpoint, then, Derrida's nondogmatic faith can nurture and deepen our own prayerful questioning of the responsibilities that bind us to our particular faith traditions.

A second, complementary approach is to understand this vigilance (as both Caputo and Derrida do) as a critique of "good conscience," an interrogation of the complacency that can besiege us when we allow ourselves to believe that our faith lives are in good order and our duties are discharged. On this reading,

<hr>

[39] Ibid., 53–81, especially 64, 79–81.
[40] Ibid., 82–115, especially 109.
[41] Caputo, *The Prayers and Tears of Jacques Derrida,* 220.
[42] Ibid., xxii.

deconstruction's call to responsibility can awaken us to the "deeply historical and textual character of [our] sacred scriptures" and to "the contingency of the dogmatic formulations" we espouse. These awakenings, moreover, can heighten our awareness of the multiplicity of traditions within our broader narratives, as well as increase our sensitivity to the minority voices within this multiplicity.[43]

As useful as this account of responsibility is in its critical and devotional capacities, one might still have reservations as to whether these broadly regulative employments constitute a genuinely positive contribution to the field. We philosophize about religion, after all, not simply to humble ourselves, but to better understand our commitments and to help us decide which courses of belief and action they demand of us. One might wonder, then, whether the ideal of hyperbolic responsibility is sufficiently action-guiding to aid (and not hinder!) us in pursuing these important, practical goals. In his aptly titled article "Much Obliged," for example, David Wood argues that Derrida runs the risk of "de-actualizing" our obligations in a way that comes dangerously close to idolatry.[44] Says Wood:

> My concern is that Derrida is de-actualizing obligation, that he is giving no privilege to those obligations, precisely that we have not willed, but that we find ourselves in, to those we have voluntarily acquired, to those expectations we have allowed others to have of us. And the thought that there are no fixed boundaries here does not mean that there are none. Hospitality would self-destruct if it were "infinite." Is not Derrida giving voice here to a kind of hyperbolic expansion of obligation that it would be quite as appro-

---

[43] John D. Caputo, "The Good News about Alterity: Derrida and Theology," in *Faith and Philosophy* 10, no. 4 (1993): 453–70 (see citation, 467). Merold Westphal endorses a similar version of this reading in his review of "Force of Law" entitled "Derrida As Natural Law Theorist," *International Philosophical Quarterly* 34 (June 1994): 247–52.

[44] David Wood, "Much Obliged," *Philosophy Today* 41 (Spring 1997): 135–40. Despite the concerns expressed in "Much Obliged," Wood remains sympathetic to the idea that Derrida's account is a useful challenge to complacency and good conscience. In a more recent article, in fact, he argues that Derrida's account can help us to "appropriate the risks and opportunities" of "open[ing] ourselves to the sufferings of others, to the pressures and exigencies of the world." See Wood, "Notes Towards a Deconstructive Phenomenology," *Journal of the British Society for Phenomenology* 30 (1999): 97–105.

priate to consider as an identification with God rather than a response to God in or as the singular other, the other as other?[45]

Wood notes, further, that it is obviously possible to take a non-complacent stand on the wider grief and suffering of others without being in "bondage" to an ideal of obligation that renders one's situated responsibilities unjustifiable. Such bondage, in Wood's view, is not only excessive to the task of staving off good conscience (one can surely be convinced both that one's immediate responsibilities are justified and that there is always more to be done), but also runs the risk of lapsing into a mechanism for avoiding "bad" good conscience, a kind of deconstructive messianic complex that verges on just the sort of good conscience it sets out to prophesy against.

Though Wood's concerns about the practical hazards of espousing hyperbolic responsibility are certainly warranted, they are perhaps less worrisome in view of the broader Continental context within which (and to which) Derrida addresses his account. Perhaps the most distinguishing feature of this context, especially when juxtaposed with the contemporary Anglo-American scene, is its seemingly inexhaustible *memory;* without exception, the important problems and debates in contemporary Continental philosophy have long and tortuous histories. It is exceedingly difficult, therefore, to do justice to the work of a philosopher in this tradition without understanding the relationship of her work to its broader sources. In our specific case, I would like to affirm both that the dangers Wood discusses are indeed imminent, and that they are nonetheless worth risking in view of the leverage that Derrida's account can give us over certain untimely exclusions in contemporary Continental reflection on religion. More concretely, I want to argue that the hyperbolic aspects of Derrida's account speak prophetically against the trend toward marginalizing the sacred that has held sway in Continental philosophy until comparatively recently.

Before elaborating on this claim, it will be useful to review our progress so far. We began with an examination of three closely linked, broadly Kantian themes that characterize, or so

---

[45] Wood, "Much Obliged," 136–37.

I argued, the Continental tradition's general orientation toward philosophy of religion (these are the limits of speculative analysis, the idea of nondogmatic faith, and the increasing unpresentability of the other). We moved on to a discussion of Derrida's appropriation of these themes in his account of responsibility, an account that, as we have just seen, shows significant promise for critically assessing the uses and limits of our various philosophical discourses on religion. What is as yet missing, as Wood's concerns have reminded us, is a narrative of the exclusions standardized into these themes by Continental reflection leading up to Derrida, a narrative that would enable us to put the hyperbolic aspects of Derrida's account into better perspective, and to assess their positive significance within the tradition.

To be sure, there are many complicated stories one could tell as to how and why philosophical discourses on religious experience of the sacred have been marginalized in the Continental tradition. One intriguing possibility (given what we've seen so far) is to understand this trend as the legacy of what I'll call Kant's "mixed message" to Continental reflection on religion. In the simplest terms, Kant's approach to religion is characterized by a tension between the "faith-saving" and "emancipatory" aims of his project. On the one hand, his concern is to ward off the religious skeptic, or, more famously, "to deny knowledge in order to make room for faith."[46] This move is necessitated, in Kant's view, by the threats posed to religion and morality in materialism, fatalism, and atheism, dogmatic speculative positions that he saw as becoming increasingly emboldened by modern science.[47] To Kant's mind, the "inestimable benefit" of his critical strategy is that "all objections to morality and religion will be forever silenced, and this in Socratic fashion, namely, by the clearest proof of the ignorance of the objectors."[48] In this faith-saving mode, then, Kant's aim is to defend religion and morality by demonstrating the inability of speculative reason ever to disprove the articles of faith upon which they depend.

On the other hand, however, Kant is also concerned to hold

[46] Kant, *Critique of Pure Reason,* 29.
[47] Ibid., 32.
[48] Ibid., 30.

in check the equally "injurious" flights of metaphysical fancy represented in religious "fanaticism" and "superstition."[49] He is quite unwilling, in fact, as we have seen, to grant reflection on religion any credence whatsoever beyond the presuppositions of natural religion, the minimum practical requirements sufficient to ground morality. In this respect, Kant's aim is emancipatory: he is concerned, as Foucault notes in commenting on "What Is Enlightenment?" to deliver reason from the "state of immaturity" to which it resigns itself when "a book takes the place of understanding" or "a spiritual director takes the place of conscience."[50]

The upshot of this mixed message, in my reading, is that Kant left little room for the development of a philosophical discourse on religious experience of the sacred.[51] Simply put, the possibility of a genuine encounter with exteriority through religious faith is a priori foreclosed, insofar as religion's proper employment extends only as far as the practical necessity to ground the moral sense within. In the wake of *Kritik* (to which all must submit), then, there are two acceptable attitudes that philosophers can take toward religion: they can strive to account for its significance practically or, in any case, without appeal to any genuine experience of exteriority; and they can strive to liberate existing faith narratives from any residual precritical tendencies toward fanati-

[49] Ibid., 32.

[50] Michel Foucault, "What Is Enlightenment?" trans. Catherine Porter, in *The Foucault Reader*, ed. Paul Rabinow (New York: Pantheon Books, 1984), 32–50, citation p. 34.

[51] One might protest here that Kant's discussions of beauty and the sublime in the *Critique of Judgment* (New York: Macmillan, 1951) invite creative appropriation toward discourses on religious experience of the sacred. The fact remains, however, that the aesthetic pleasure and edification that follow upon experiences of the beautiful or the sublime are, for Kant, yet again, merely reminders (manufactured by an a priori faculty of judgment) of the moral sense within; they are not the effects of an encounter with, or a bearing-witness to, a sacred exteriority. See xviii–xx (J. H. Bernard's introduction); and 37 ff. Compare, for example, Kant's description of the agitation (not fear) characteristic of an experience of the sublime, with Derrida's account in *The Gift of Death* of fear and trembling before the sacred. Says Kant (my emphasis): "This estimation of ourselves loses nothing through the fact that *we must regard ourselves as safe in order to feel this inspiring satisfaction* and that hence, as *there is no seriousness in the danger*, there might also (as might seem to be the case) just as little seriousness in the sublimity of our spiritual faculty."

cism and superstition (for example, the temptations to dwell on any one "revelation," or to let "God" bear the weight of one's speculative endeavors).

From this vantage point, we can provisionally understand the evolution of Continental reflection on religion (after Kant) in terms of a double movement produced by the dialectic of these two attitudes. Hegel, for instance, exhibits both attitudes in spades, distilling religion into a logic of practical concepts and reducing its history to a series of increasingly enlightened stages on reason's journey toward absolute self-awareness. Though Nietzsche, Marx, and Freud unequivocally reject Hegel's absolutist confidence in reason, their respective philological, anthropological, and psychological critiques of religion are not unlike Hegel's: each attempts to save the appearances of religion within the limits of reason alone, and liberate thinking, in so doing, from heretofore hidden obstacles. So it goes, of course, with Heidegger's critique of ontotheology, in which even Nietzsche stands accused of making a veiled appeal to transcendence beyond the limits of possible experience.

On a straightforward reading, this provisional history indicates an increasing suspicion as to the philosophical significance of religious faith in any form, practical or otherwise. It would seem, perhaps, that the emancipatory trajectory of Kant's project ultimately culminates in our liberation from the very faith-saving intuition that gave it rise. Least of all, one might suspect, could we hope to find traces in this history of the necessity for a different kind of faith altogether, a faith beyond practical faith, a faith through which an encounter with radical exteriority would be possible, if unthinkable.

But such traces are just what Derrida finds. His realization about this history, in fact, is that the idea of emancipation betrays at its limit a clandestine dependence on an idea of infinite justice. This latter idea, as we have seen, presupposes, in turn, the possibility of a profound and dangerous faith,[52] indeed, a faith through

---

[52] It is clear enough in "Force of Law" that Derrida's interest in the link between emancipation and the faith implicit to the "messianic structure of language" is motivated by his concern to ground the "motif of emancipation" in something other than justification, the inadequate ground imported into ethics from modern epistemology. In "Remarks on Deconstruction and Pragmatism,"

which an experience of the sacred can be glimpsed, if not fully undergone. The logic of reversal at work here is familiar: just when it appears that emancipation requires an abandonment of faith, we must undertake faith, more radically than ever before, in the name of emancipation.[53] The fundamental insight here, ironically, is as profoundly Kantian in structure as it is Levinasian in content. In order to check the natural tendency of our discourses to overreach their limits, we must deny knowledge to make room for faith, albeit a hyperbolic faith that Kant could never have countenanced.

Make no mistake, however, that Derrida does not submit this faith as a guarantee that the sacred exists, or that communion with it is possible. He takes great pains, on the contrary, to distinguish the *singular* experience of the sacred (made possible across an unbridgeable distance by hyperbolic faith) from the *subsuming* experience of the sacred (conceived in terms of proximity to an actual presence). This latter interpretation of the sacred, of course, is one that Derrida stands resolutely against. Following Nietzsche, Heidegger, and Bataille (among others), he understands this interpretation (and its history) as betraying a naïve desire for immanence that suspends earnest truth-seeking and, when frustrated, inevitably gives way to nihilism.[54]

Derrida is still more explicit about the necessity in ethics to link emancipation to faith, and about his ongoing commitment to emancipation: "There is no language without the performative dimension of the promise. Even if I say that 'I don't believe in truth' or whatever, the minute I open my mouth there is a 'believe me' at work. Even when I lie, and perhaps especially when I lie, there is a 'believe me' in play. And this 'I promise you that I am speaking the truth' is a messianic a priori, a promise which, even if it is not kept . . . takes place and *qua* promise is messianic. And from this point of view, I do not see how one can pose the question of ethics if one renounces the motifs of emancipation and the messianic. Emancipation is once again a vast question today and I must say that I have no tolerance for those who—deconstructionist or not—are ironical with regard to the grand discourse of emancipation. This attitude has always distressed and irritated me. I do not want to renounce this discourse." See *Deconstruction and Pragmatism,* ed. Chantal Mouffe (London: Routledge, 1996), 83.

[53] Derrida's account here, as we have seen in both "Force of Law" and *The Gift of Death,* is intimately related to Levinas's derivation of finite freedom from the infinite responsibility assumed in "recurrence to oneself." See Levinas, *Otherwise Than Being or Beyond Essence,* 99–129.

[54] See, for example, in Martin Heidegger, *Contributions to Philosophy,* trans. Parvis Emad and Kenneth Maly (Bloomington: Indiana University Press, 1999),

On the other hand, notwithstanding his assent to the importance of combating this latter sense of the sacred, Derrida does not conclude (as Foucault, Habermas, Nancy, and Rorty sometimes seem to)[55] that the failure of the sacred in this latter sense necessitates our abandonment of the sacred in *every* sense. Indeed, Derrida is as concerned about the risks of reducing the sacred to the finite as he is about those of subsuming the finite in the sacred. In particular, he is acutely aware that contemporary philosophy's disenchantment with religious faith is perhaps as naïve about its conceptual debts to the sacred as the tradition of ontotheology allegedly is about the limitations of finite discourse.[56]

It is this vigilance over the relationship of mutual dependence between the finite and the sacred that constitutes Derrida's timely contribution to the tradition,[57] and that characterizes much of the most interesting work recently undertaken in Continental philos-

---

97–98; and in Georges Bataille, *Theory of Religion,* trans. Robert Hurley (New York: Zone Books, 1992), 92–93.

[55] See, for example, Jean-Luc Nancy in *The Inoperative Community,* 34–35: "Yet just as we must not think that community is 'lost,' so it would be foolish to comment upon and to deplore the 'loss' of the sacred only then to advocate its return as a remedy for the evils of our society (something Bataille never did, following in this Nietzsche's most profound exigency—nor did Benjamin, nor Heidegger nor Blanchot, in spite of certain appearances to the contrary here and there). What has disappeared from the sacred—and this means finally *all* of the sacred, engulfed in the 'immense failure'—reveals rather that community itself now occupies the place of the sacred. For the sacred—the separated, the set apart—no longer proves to be the haunting idea of an unattainable communion, but is rather made up of nothing other than the sharing of community."

[56] Nowhere is Derrida more explicit on this point than in "Faith and Knowledge: The Two Sources of 'Religion' at the Limits of Reason Alone," 65: "The law of this untimeliness interrupts and makes history, it undoes all contemporaneity and opens the very space of faith. It designates disenchantment as the very resource of the religious. The first and the last. Nothing seems therefore more uncertain, more difficult to sustain, nothing seems here or there more imprudent than a self-assured discourse on the age of disenchantment, the era of secularization, the time of laicization, etc."

[57] In addition to the accounts of this relationship he offers in "Force of Law" and *The Gift of Death,* Derrida outlines yet another such account (in "Faith and Knowledge," 62) in terms of the concept of bearing witness. Says Derrida, "the experience of witnessing situates a convergence of these two sources: the *unscathed* (the safe, the sacred or the saintly) and the *fiduciary* (trustworthiness, fidelity, credit, belief or faith, 'good faith' implied in the worst 'bad faith'). . . . The act of faith demanded in bearing witness exceeds, through its structure, all intuition and all proof, all knowledge. Even the slightest testimony concerning

ophy of religion. For Derrida, Caputo, and Jean-Luc Marion (to name only a few),[58] the pressing questions for reflection on religion concern the possibility and the content of this finite experience of the sacred. Is it a purely "negative" encounter? Is it accessible, in glimpses, to phenomenology? Is it reconcilable with any (perhaps all) of the historic messianisms? Is it simply an epiphenomenon of the play of our finite discourses, or does it indicate, if only provisionally, a "there is" or an "I am" beyond those discourses? In his submission of and to these questions, Jacques Derrida has gifted Continental reflection on religion beyond calculation.

---

the most plausible, ordinary, or everyday thing cannot do otherwise: it must still appeal to faith as would a miracle."

[58] We have already discussed Derrida and Caputo in some detail. On Marion, see *God without Being*; "Sketch of a Phenomenological Concept of Gift," in *Postmodern Philosophy and Christian Thought*, ed. Merold Westphal (Bloomington: Indiana University Press, 1999), 122–43; and "In the Name: How to Avoid Speaking of 'Negative Theology,'" in *God, the Gift, and Post-modernism*, ed. John D. Caputo (Bloomington: Indiana University Press, 1999).

4

Ethical Experience: *Mauvaise Conscience* and Necessary Sadness

Donna Jowett

INTRODUCTION

Is CONSCIENCE the "voice of God within," or is it, as both Nietzsche and Freud would see it, the internalized authority of our culture and family? I have put this question baldly and naïvely; my intention is only to gesture toward the different camps or traditions that have framed themselves on either side of the question. And today such a question has a slightly old-fashioned appearance; it is built on a series of binary oppositions and it further fortifies and extends them in anticipating, if not forcing, the terms of mutual exclusion it presumes. My aim in this paper is not, however, to deconstruct the question, but to explore the experience of what Levinas calls *mauvaise conscience,* which is echoed in Derrida's *Aporias* and *The Gift of Death* as the "scandal of good conscience."[1] For both thinkers, ethical responsibility to the other opens us to a certain sorrow, a sorrow that is not only endured but also affirmed.

But what does it mean to "affirm" such sadness? The insistent emphasis throughout Levinas's work is on our openness or vulnerability to exteriority, and hence to the other and to infinity. For many of Levinas's readers, he brings relief and an antidote to nearly four hundred years of subject-centered philosophy. However, in order to think about what it means to affirm sadness

---

[1] Jacques Derrida, *Aporias,* trans. Thomas Dutoit (Stanford: Stanford University Press, 1993), 19.

or mauvaise conscience, we cannot entirely forego the dimension of interiority. Despite the hermeneutic of suspicion that broadly characterizes the psychoanalytic position on the origins of conscience, psychoanalysis offers certain insights into the capacity to experience sadness. Freud and, most particularly, Melanie Klein explore the interiority of our experiences of an exteriority it is not our lot to command or control.

There is, of course, an intellectual abyss between two such disparate thinkers as Levinas and Klein, or between the traditions that draw Levinas and Derrida together when it comes to conscience as juxtaposed to psychoanalytic and especially Kleinian "concretist" treatment of the individual psyche. Without trying to reconcile the differences between philosophical and psychoanalytic discourses, I will use each to explore exterior and interior dimensions of conscience. As it sometimes happens, an immense abyss can also turn out to be narrow, and I hope to show that something like this is the case when it comes to appreciating ethical pathos. Beyond this, ethical pathos may indicate that religious emotion is present even when religion or God is officially absent. And if this is the case, then we may in turn be brought a step closer to currently developing Continental thought concerning "religion without religion."

Philosophical Pathos

Levinas and, more recently, Derrida have spoken compellingly about the absolutely nonformulaic character of ethics. As an encounter with the other in which I am, precisely, *open* to the claim of the other, there can be no rules for managing such ethical experience. "Otherwise," as Derrida has observed, "one would unfold a program and conduct oneself, at best, like 'smart' missiles."[2] To demand a rule, a guarantee, or even subjective certainty as preconditions for recognizing responsibility is, Derrida argues, a substitution of technique for responsibility. The mere application of a rule or the subsumption of a case to the general-

---

[2] Jacques Derrida, *Points,* ed. and trans. Elizabeth Weber (Stanford: Stanford University Press, 1995), 359.

ity of a given law actually manages to *irresponsibilize* our decisions and our singular responsibility for them.

According to Levinas, ethics is possible only starting from me, which means that it is my affair, my responsibility, that is, a matter of my response to an other.[3] It is not a matter of figuring out what is owed to me, or what rules should be invoked to control the behavior of others. To calculate in this way may be an inevitable aspect of governing or managing, but it has nothing to do with ethics as my responsibility to and for an other. I am in a masterful rather than an ethical space if what I am concerned about is what the other should do for me, or even how others should behave toward each other. In Levinas's view, ethics is always my going toward the other, the tug or tear in my complacency, experienced through the ambivalent magnetism and obsessiveness of the other's claim on me.

This is indeed how many of us recognize experience that we call ethical; we find ourselves unable to do or carry out what we simply want. We are faced with a troubling question; an other contests or interrupts our normal and unreflective commitment to our own being. Active affirmation of being is, as Levinas sees it, particularly characteristic of modernity, where the strength and strain of being maintains the powers of the rational sovereign subject.[4] Ethical experience means a pause, an arrest, a difference in our own project of being through the impingement of an other.

To speak in this way is, however, somewhat misleading. It sounds as if a discrete and unethical "I" goes about its individual business until its monadic existence bumps into an other's. Upon this encounter such an I must then decide what to do, how to behave, as if both sociality and ethics were a rational addition to the consciousness of an already fully developed I. This outlook is deeply ingrained in the tradition of Enlightenment philosophy, which continues to influence modern conceptions of ethics and politics. We can recognize in Kant's exemplary modern approach to ethics the solidity of an autonomous, self-legislating "man of reason" who is rationally equipped to recognize the moral law of

---

[3] Emmanuel Levinas, *The Levinas Reader,* ed. Seán Hand (Oxford: Basil Blackwell, 1989), 80.

[4] Ibid., 78.

which he is also the author, and to act on it with an untroubled conscience.

Yet Kant's insistence on the supreme power of reason also sounds a note of anxiety, an anxiety that is defended against when Kant implausibly extends the powers of rational sovereignty over any experience of the sublime that we mistakenly attribute to exterior nature. "Sublimity . . . does not reside in anything in nature, but only in our mind insofar as we can become conscious that we are superior to nature."[5]

Through Levinas's ethical optics, the Enlightenment and the modernist approach to ethics appear to serve the purpose of "disappearing" the very space of the other, and hence of ethics, of ensuring that we will not have any experiences of which we are not the master/author. But we should note that even for Kant, exteriority is what is first experienced; the rational self is deduced as a presupposition of experience, but this self is subsequently accorded priority in Kant's thinking. Phenomenologically speaking, is it not actually the case that ethical relationship is what we come from, and not what we—sooner or later in light—are dragged into? Is it not instead that our departure in and from ethical relationship is what humanizes us? On this view, it is partaking in ethical relationship from point zero that humanizes us, and this does not come as an option.[6]

We do not have an option about this because we do not start out in the world from a position of self-sufficiency. Our becoming more fully human begins and proceeds through our vulnerability to others. There can be no consciousness of individuality outside of or prior to a relationship to an other. So, to return to the misleading modernist language above and correct it: we are always (Levinas would say "primordially") interrupted by an other; there is no time prior to the time of the other, no space in which my being is entirely my own. Ethics is then not something late upon the scene, something that needs to be argued for; it is a fissure in what would otherwise be my enclosed being. I can

---

[5] Immanuel Kant, *Kant Selections,* ed. Lewis White Beck (New York: Macmillan Publishing Company, 1988), 379.

[6] Arne Johan Vetlesen, "Worlds Apart? Habermas and Levinas," *Philosophy and Social Criticism* 23 (1997): 7.

desire this fissure, since without it I am truly forsaken, cut off, not able to be human, not able to be a self.

Levinas often paraphrases a sentence from Dostoyevsky's *The Brothers Karamazov* to illustrate what he means by the ethical symmetry of the relationship to the other: "We are all responsible for everyone else—but I am more responsible than all the others." In other words, I can demand of myself what I do not have the right to demand of others. If ethics is relentlessly and exigently a matter of my responsibility, then I will never reach a point of equilibrium, of restful conscience in relation to the other. The virtue that would be its own reward—if such a thing is to amount to anything other than smugness—brings about a heightening of my openness to and responsibility for the other. My "reward" is the opposite of that promised by optimistic Enlightenment philosophy: as I become more responsible, I increasingly suffer from bad conscience.

The "scandal of good conscience" must, according to Derrida, be avoided at all costs: "Not only good conscience as the grimace of an indulgent vulgarity, but quite simply the assured form of self-consciousness: good conscience as subjective certainty is incompatible with the absolute risk that every promise, every engagement, and every responsible decision—if there are such—must run."[7]

A good conscience would be at one with normative social convention; it would suspect nothing better than what is. Good conscience would be satisfied—both with itself and with the given reality; nothing would cut across it. It might well be conscious of responsibilities, but only so as to be done with them. For Levinas, responsibility goes beyond whatever acts may or may not have been committed: it is a "guiltless responsibility, whereby I am none the less open to an accusation of which no alibi, spatial or temporal, could clear me."[8] No matter what I do, no matter how "good" I am, the other—the neighbor or the stranger, the widow and the orphan—are already there and already in need. What Levinas calls mauvaise conscience is the register of the need of and fear for the stranger or neighbor, for whom I can

[7] Derrida, *Aporias,* 19.
[8] Levinas, *The Levinas Reader,* 83.

only always be late upon the scene. Levinas's guiltless responsibility could not be sustained by a good conscience; such an accusation could only register as a persecuting element, something to be speedily ejected from consciousness. Since this ejection includes the source of the persecuting element (the other who solicits my response), the inability to tolerate mauvaise conscience is connected to neglect and persecution of the other.

Levinas's mauvaise conscience emerges as an essential aspect of experience that precedes (in the sense of having priority over) the organization of our egos and interests. In our most basic orientation, we are without recourse to the excuses and entitlements that cognitively produce the scandal of the good conscience, the unafflicted conscience, freely devoted to its own being and interests, yet lonely, in restless search of an exterior stimulant from which it has mistakenly sealed itself away. It is a fact that we *can* turn away from the other; it may be that we are affected and afflicted in ways that make us scramble to assert or defend our own entitlement to being.

If this is not to add up to combativeness and war—which Levinas clearly recognizes it can—then we cannot let go of that initial and never-vanquished uncertainty concerning our right to be. As Levinas says, ethically speaking, "One comes not into the world but into question."[9] Letting the question stand, perpetually, gives us more than what we ask for and more than we can ever successfully answer; it gives mauvaise conscience and the capacity "to fear injustice more than death, to prefer to suffer than to commit injustice, and to prefer that which justifies being over that which assures it."[10]

In Levinas's description of ethical experience, we are radically vulnerable to being affected, so much so that we are "hostages" in our relation to the other. Mauvaise conscience is both affliction and opening; it is the register of the other, the wound in self-involved being for which we can only be thankful, because through it we experience more than what is already and only within us. Risk and bad conscience constitute the very possibility of ethical encounter, which is, for Levinas, the "royal road" to the other.

---

[9] Ibid., 81.
[10] Ibid., 82.

But who would not prefer a good conscience to a bad one? Racked, as Levinas describes it, by an ever-growing anguish for all the violence and murder my existing might generate, in spite of its conscious and intentional innocence, how can I be expected to live my life? It is not "reasonable" to expect people to live with some concern for ethics if they can never be sure of getting things right. And, in a sense that is not intended by such a complaint, Levinas would say this is correct: ethical opening is not reasonable, it does not shape itself to the contours and limits of any rational ethics within which we could comfortably live.

If this were the case, then we would cease to be claimed, haunted, and open to the ethical itself; in getting it right we would announce the end of ethical wakefulness. Here the reassurance or guarantee of being guiltless will also serve to foreclose precisely on those experiences in which we are called to ethical responsibility. We will have rules to live by and some sense that with these rules we can sleep well at night. On this point, Levinas and Nietzsche are very close: "Blessed are the sleepy ones, for they shall soon drop off." [11] A good conscience, dreamless sleep, and rules to live by: this is the triumph of technique over responsibility. Here we wake only so that we might sleep well. The certainty we long for and the reason we use to purchase it betray their commitment to unconsciousness, to a fading of life, to what Freud referred to as the Nirvana Principle or, more provocatively, the Death Instinct. [12]

As the following section on psychoanalytic pathos intends to show, Freud's evocative reflections of the affirmation of our vulnerability to and attachment to exteriority are heightened in Melanie Klein's treatment of the interiority of what she calls the "depressive position." Even while they speak another language, Freud and—perhaps most surprisingly—Klein draw near to the ground from which Levinas emphasized the radical character of our ethical relation to the other.

---

[11] Friedrich Nietzsche, "Thus Spoke Zarathustra," *The Portable Nietzsche,* ed. Walter Kaufmann (New York: Viking Press, 1954), 142.

[12] Sigmund Freud, "Beyond the Pleasure Principle," *The Pelican Freud Library,* vol. 11 (London: Penguin, 1984), 269–338.

PSYCHOANALYTIC PATHOS

From Freud's psychoanalytic perspective, some special aspects of mental life come into view when we consider individual lives in their contexts of vulnerability and transience. Freud helps to shed light on the question of how we can come to prefer war with a good conscience to the ambivalent gift of Levinas's mauvaise conscience.

To the extent that Freud was a product of Enlightenment optimism about science and reason, he saw psychoanalysis as a means to understand and master more of our hidden emotional lives. To the extent that he drew his inspiration from the ancient, especially Greek and biblical, narratives of Western civilization, Freud never believed we could escape suffering grievously from life.

Given that change, transience, and ultimately loss are inevitable aspects of life, Freud suggests that mourning is necessary to the capacity for experience itself. He explores this in a somewhat philosophical mood in a short paper entitled "On Transience."[13] During a walk through the hills in springtime, just before the outbreak of the First World War, Freud finds that one of his companions is unable to appreciate the beauty around him. This companion, a poet, states that all that he would otherwise have loved and admired was ruined and shorn of its worth by the transience that was its doom. The aching despondency of the poet and his rebellion against the fact of impermanence are understood by Freud as the mind's revolt against mourning, a revolt that represents a denial of the experiences of love and separation. Loss and separation are painful, tragic experiences; defenses against them may succeed in burying the pain, but this suppression takes its toll in depriving us of access to experience itself. Freud tends to see life as a tragic affair, but he thinks that in mourning we affirm the value, meaning, and importance of something exterior and sustaining to our lives that may not be ours to keep or control.

---

[13] Sigmund Freud, "On Transience," *Standard Edition of the Complete Psychological Works,* ed. and trans. James Strachey (London: Hogarth Press, 1957), 305–7.

What Freud means by the Death Instinct is the desire to avoid being affected by experience, to feel as little as possible, to achieve an inner state of equilibrium. Freud's companion on his walk, the poet, has not achieved equilibrium, since Freud describes him as given over to despondency, but he has managed to eliminate joy and gratitude. In "Mourning and Melancholia," Freud makes a distinction between our need to mourn the loss or absence of someone we love, and melancholia (today we would call it depression), which he describes as a revolt against the reality of loss. While mourning expresses or affirms our openness to exteriority, melancholia represents a rejection of it, or a withdrawal designed to protect ourselves against exteriority.[14]

Melanie Klein, the analyst whose theories caused considerable controversy in the British Psychoanalytic Society in the 1940s and '50s, made the struggle to achieve what she called the depressive position the central problem to be surmounted in development.[15] Her terminology is somewhat confusing, for the depressive position is not one in which we are clinically depressed, but in which we recognize that we are capable of harming or hurting people through our own anger and aggression. With the achievement of the depressive position, we understand that the people we love are the same ones who sometimes arouse our anger and hate—that is, we do not permanently split our world into idealized "good" objects and vilified "bad" objects. Klein believes that a split of exterior objects or people into all good or all bad is paralleled by a split of love and hate in the ego; in this way, the frightening aspects of both inner and outer experience can be isolated and controlled.

In Klein's view, the mature expression of the depressive position is characterized by two notable features: a recognition that good and bad can be complexly interwoven, and a desire to make reparation for the damage we may have wished upon whatever we have experienced as hateful. Klein describes a process in which psychic reality becomes "increasingly poignant," in which our fear for ourselves becomes fear for others.[16]

---

[14] Freud, "Mourning and Melancholia," *The Pelican Freud Library,* vol. 11, 247–68.

[15] Melanie Klein, *Envy and Gratitude and Other Works, 1946–63* (New York: Delacorte Press, 1975).

[16] Ibid., 73.

From Klein's observation of infants and analyses of young children, she concluded that we have all, at least in fantasy, been torturers and murderers. It is understandable that we erect defenses against these experiences, projecting our own aggression outward, while at the same time we try to keep the overwhelming experiences of love and hate separate. But these defenses depend upon and require the maintenance of a fragmented world of inner and outer experience. Psychological and moral maturity depend, for Klein, on the same haunting ground as does Levinas's mauvaise conscience: "fear for all the violence and murder my existing might generate, in spite of its conscious and intentional innocence." Levinas's "extreme" concern for the other "whom I have already oppressed or starved, or driven out into a third world," can be seen through the psychoanalytic perspective of Klein as a desire to make reparation.[17]

Freud never accepted the prominence Klein gave to the depressive position in psychological development. Klein maintained, however, that she had done nothing but follow in Freud's footsteps in his hypothesis of the Death Instinct and in his treatment of loss, separation, and the defenses constructed against them. Freud may or may not be entirely correct when he sardonically observes that "most of our sentimentalists, friends of humanity and protectors of animals have been evolved from little sadists and animal-tormentors," but he is serious.[18] From a psychoanalytic perspective, good conscience is not so much a scandal as an illusion.

Given the brevity and suffering that characterize human existence, as well as our own capacity for aggression and hate, one might wonder why both Freud and Klein do not give way to despair. It is important to note that they do not, that melancholia or withdrawal are viewed as defenses. Both Freudian and Kleinian variants of psychoanalysis advocate an ongoing engagement with and openness to the world, no matter how disappointing it can sometimes be, for it is this same world in which we experience love and gratitude.

---

[17] Levinas, *The Levinas Reader,* 82.
[18] Freud, "Thoughts for the Times on War and Death," *The Pelican Freud Library,* vol. 14, 69.

What makes this possible is a capacity to mourn, to feel a sadness that affirms the value of what we have loved without being able to control, and a desire to make reparation for what we may have injured, even if only in fantasy. Bad conscience and sadness are not only indicators of psychological health, they are the emotions that accompany the experience of ethics. Our capacity to register and endure them is connected to the reparative efforts and gestures through which we affirm responsibility to and for others. The interior aspect of mauvaise conscience is not, in this view, stuck only with itself and condemned to solipsistic reverie and indulgent self-accusation; nor can it cynically be reduced to the mere internalization of culture and ideology. It is connected to the pathos of responsibility and our susceptibility to being affected by what is exterior to us.

THE PATHOS OF RESPONSIBILITY

Levinas argues for "ethics as first philosophy" in a deliberate effort to displace from prominence certain aspects of Greek thought. According to Levinas, the Greek roots of Western philosophy display a trajectory toward a transcendental utopia harnessed to and by reason. The emphasis on this trajectory may well be due to the Enlightenment fixation with reason, refracted backward onto Greek thought so that Greek concern with the nonrational is diminished or ignored. According to Levinas, this "elevated" concept of reason rises "like a fantastic sun that makes the opacity of creatures transparent. . . . Henceforth, nothing can absorb or reflect this light which abolishes even the interiority of beings."[19]

Levinas's concern is with the way that salvific traditions displace the significance of ethical fidelity without reward. Goodness is no longer good if it is guaranteed reward, recompense, repayment. The only way in which being good preserves its distance and difference from, say, putting money in the bank occurs—and this is never fully achieved within being—when we are "good for nothing," or good for no reason.

---

[19] Levinas, *The Levinas Reader,* 253.

If it seems unlikely or even impossible to be concerned with goodness for no reason, this may have less to do with ethical experience than it does with the crudity of the categories we employ in order to think about that experience. Levinas argues that there is more in experience than can be exhausted by cognitive, thematizing consciousness. This experience has "always already" happened before consciousness or philosophy catch up with it; it is the originary situation that makes it possible to have even the idea of ethics. "It is through the condition of being hostage that there can be in the world pity, compassion, pardon and proximity—even the little there is, even the simple, 'After you, sir.' The unconditionality of being hostage is not the limit case of solidarity, but the condition for all solidarity."[20]

This would be the infinitely binding solidarity of responsibility enacted as reparation for my unavoidable sacrifice of one for an other. The need to make reparation is inexhaustible, because there can be no final "accounting" that would pass by way of reference to a general rule to legitimize my ethical attention to one thing and not another. It is not possible to achieve a state or condition of solidarity, of responsibility and answerability such that I could be rid of my bad conscience, my sadness, which are also the conditions of my love. The more vigorously and sincerely I appeal to "responsibility," the worse my dilemma becomes. This is understood by Derrida as connected to an aporia at the heart of responsibility.

> I can respond only to the one . . . that is, to the other, by sacrificing that one to the other. I am responsible to any one (that is to say to any other) only by failing in my responsibilities to all the others, to the ethical or political generality. And I can never justify this sacrifice, I must always hold my peace about it. Whether I want to or not, I can never justify the fact that I prefer or sacrifice any one (any other) to the other.[21]

Absolute responsibility "declines the autobiography that is always auto-justification, *egodicee.*"[22] In Derrida's view, it is not

---

[20] Emmanuel Levinas, *Otherwise Than Being or Beyond Essence,* trans. Alphonso Lingis (The Hague: Martinus Nijhoff Publishers, 1981), 117.

[21] Jacques Derrida, *The Gift of Death,* trans. David Wills (Chicago: Chicago University Press, 1995), 70–71.

[22] Ibid., 62.

that we have no responsibility toward ethical or political generality—we do have such responsibilities—but that there is no pure
equilibrium, no perfect commensurability between our responsibility to the general and to the particular. Whenever a language,
set of practices or belief system causes it to appear that we are
not in this bind, we move further away from responsibility, which
is the condition of being hostage, of being caught in this very
bind. I can free myself only by abandoning responsibility itself;
I can "save" myself and restore my good conscience only by
betraying conscience itself.

Ethical responsibility means I must live with the fact that my
actions remain always and also irresponsible; they never accede
to or fully accomplish responsibility. Whatever I might say to
make it appear that my responsibilities have been fulfilled only
betrays my real interest in no longer being held responsible. Even
if I have evolved from the "little sadist and animal-tormentor" I
may once have been, I still, daily, sacrifice one to an other, that
is, I prefer my loved ones over others, the dog or cat I keep and
care for over those in the pound; the hungry that I feed over
those whose hunger I ignore. Derrida's point is that any rational
calculus employed to justify these sacrifices causes them to disappear, and it is only through their hold on me that I remain
responsible and open to ethical experience itself. It is in this context that Derrida, in the *Gift of Death,* interprets the biblical story
of Abraham and Isaac on Mount Moriah.

Abraham has little to say for himself in the Genesis narrative;
he explains to no one that God has asked him to sacrifice Isaac,
and he says nothing to Isaac after the voice of God tells him not
to harm the boy, but to look to the ram caught in the thicket.
While traditionally Abraham's faith has been seen as the compelling point of this story, Derrida sees it as posing the irresolvable
dilemma of responsibility. In being responsiblê to God, Abraham
"fails" in, or sacrifices his responsibility to any human ethics.
Derrida interprets Abraham's silence as his acceptance of responsibility for this sacrifice.

There is nothing Abraham can possibly say to ameliorate the
awesome and terrible nature of the sacrifice he was about to
make. There is nothing than can ever erase what Isaac endured
while Abraham bound him and then raised his knife over him.

We might be inclined at this point to think: But this is a biblical narrative, and Abraham cannot apologize to Isaac without questioning God; as an exemplar of faith this is something Abraham cannot do, but our own situation is neither so dramatic nor extreme; it is permissible for us to make excuses. Derrida's point is simply that our excuses excuse us from responsibility itself, which is always awesome and terrible because it always involves sacrifice. Derrida asks if this is not exactly what is replayed, every day at every hour, in our ethical lives. Whenever we choose the general over the particular, the particular over the general, any one over any other, we find ourselves already and perpetually living on Mount Moriah again, Moriah, the site of responsibility for what we sacrifice in order to be responsible to the one or to the other.

The pathos and poignancy of psychic and ethical experience is something my fully conscious "I" would never choose for itself. But I can only be thankful that it does not wait my choosing. It is because I *am* caught in this bind, open and vulnerable to exteriority and bound ineluctably to the other, as well as to the others whom I sacrifice in order to go on being so bound, that my efforts at escape can, with effort and against the grain of any defensive rational calculus, be recognized as defense, cruelty, and forsakenness.

5

Anxious Responsibility and Responsible Anxiety: Kierkegaard and Levinas on Ethics and Religion

Bettina Bergo

IN RECENT YEARS two thinkers, Derrida and Levinas, have contributed decisively to shaping the concept of radical responsibility, both before the human other and what has been called the divine. Within the parameters of philosophy of religion, if we would understand the way in which the concept of responsibility opens new avenues of thinking about the meaning of of human justice, then we must come to terms with what Derrida and Levinas have recently argued. Furthermore, both men's thought—preeminently and explicitly that of Derrida—is as if haunted by the work of Kierkegaard.

One caveat is in order. The notion of responsibility, as radical and original with regard to human intersubjectivity and subjectivity itself, might be read starting from different figures—such as Benjamin and Celan, to name two; or indeed Jean-Luc Nancy—and with a different outcome. But that is not the question at stake here; and I would even maintain that, although some have credited Levinas with the now well-known "return of the religious" *(retour du religieux),* there is possible a secular or nonmetaphysical reading of Levinas; indeed, it is done with great seriousness by Derrida himself.

However, Levinas's thought has also inspired philosophies that combine aspects of religious ethics and questions of justice. This is as much evident on the Jewish side as it is on the Protestant and Roman Catholic sides.[1] That said, the return of the religious is a phenomenon that could have no single instigator because it has itself taken so many forms, from a defense of "theophany" in Marion, to the rereading of Cohen and Rosenzweig, to the exploration of the identity and meaning of Paul as apostle and as Jew, to the assertion by intellectuals such as Vattimo that Catholicism was always present in their thinking. The phenomenon is broad-based and proceeds from a host of interests and toward different ends.

This question of the return of the religious opens onto the question of the fate of contemporary philosophy. For his part, Kierkegaard maintains a philosophical rigor as he challenges the idealism of his time. Still, he is from the first less troubled by the challenge of remaining in philosophy than Levinas is, but this is due to several things: first, Kierkegaard's use of pseudonymy; second, his employment of irony; third, and most important, the insistence that philosophical questions must be inscribed within a field—that of faith or man's religious life—that exceeds philosophy in capacity for truth, and belongs to a qualitatively different order than philosophy.

Note that Kierkegaard can argue this because the philosophy against which he is doing battle, above all, is Hegelianism and, more generally, speculative system building. He writes, in *The Concept of Anxiety,* "Every human life is religiously designed. To want to deny this confuses everything and cancels the concepts of individuality, race, and immortality. . . . To explain how my religious existence comes into relation with and expresses itself in my outward existence, that is the task."[2] For this last reason, Kierkegaard will say of his *Concept of Anxiety* that it is "a psychologically orientating deliberation" on sin, or evil. It is, therefore, not philosophy or metaphysics *eo ipso,* and it permits

---

[1] With Alain Finkielkraut on the Jewish side, Paul Ricoeur and Marc Faessler on the Protestant side, and Jean-Luc Marion on the Catholic side. Levinas's concepts of alterity, responsibility, Saying, sincerity, and prophetism have also been used by theorists of human rights, two of whom are African Catholic clerics.

[2] Søren Kierkegaard, *The Concept of Anxiety: A Simple Psychologically Orienting Deliberation on the Dogmatic Issue of Hereditary Sin,* trans. Reidar Thomte and Albert B. Anderson (Princeton: Princeton University Press, 1980), 105.

itself an access to Christian "dogmatics" that philosophy could not allow: the presupposition of human evil as trans-temporally present, *and* as affecting each person individually as well. Therefore, Kierkegaard is not concerned here that the ethical questions he approaches belong to a philosophy synonymous with secular, rational inquiry. His is a critique of the possibilities and limits of psychology in the wake of evil and freedom.

That position, which I am highlighting here in its independence from certain norms of philosophical inquiry (secularity, rationality, deduction or consistent description), is one that Levinas approximates in his work after *Totality and Infinity,* notably in his *Otherwise Than Being or Beyond Essence.*[3] *Totality and Infinity* developed an ethics that displaced metaphysics as first philosophy. It did so by showing the intersubjective origin of our notion of transcendence, and of reason itself. *Otherwise Than Being* explored the subjective experience of investiture by a force (or alterity) that it could not integrate in the synthesis of everyday consciousness.

This subjective experience is thematizable as experience only if we accept two suppositions: first, that the expression of suffering and redemption by the prophets *signifies* preeminently as an experience of investiture by alterity, and opens to the creation and preservation of a community constituted in ethical service to a principle of difference, a wholly other that commands. Second, that sensibility—in its moments of exasperation—as vulnerability, obsession, expiation, has a significance rooted in the excessiveness of sensible "experience." This excess is indeterminate, its symptom is suffering, but one ought to avoid saying too much about it or romanticizing it, lest it become either a conceptual moment in a prescriptive ethics or an aesthetics of suffering or sacrifice. Thus, in the late Levinas, prophetism mobilizes figures of speech that denote an excess in the experience of self-consciousness, before consciousness consolidates itself. This opens us to the other person in an original way—generally in a peaceful

[3] Emmanuel Levinas, *Totality and Infinity: An Essay on Exteriority,* trans. Alphonso Lingis (Pittsburgh: Duquesne University Press, 1969), first published in French in 1961; *Otherwise Than Being or Beyond Essence,* trans. Alphonso Lingis (Dordrecht, The Netherlands, and Boston: Kluwer Academic Publishers, 1974), first published in 1972.

way, and it explains the possibility of the unexpected act of generosity. By 1972 Levinas, like Kierkegaard, had stepped beyond philosophy. And he was not the only one in the second and third generations of phenomenologists to do so. This brings me to the question of phenomenology's destiny.

Why does phenomenology venture out of philosophy whenever it is interested in something more than Husserlian exegesis? If we hold aside Heidegger's destruction of the tradition of metaphysics by the recollection of its forgotten ground (which arguably amounted to its closure), we still confront thinkers like Max Scheler who attempted to extend phenomenology into a philosophy of values. We encounter Husserl's assistant, Edith Stein, who ultimately turned phenomenological analysis to a reading of Thomist systematics. But more recently we note Levinas, we note the later Merleau-Ponty, who sought to step beyond logics of "consciousness" toward a thinking in which the thinker was intricated in its thought: the Merleau-Ponty of the chiasmatic logic.

We also find the recent works of Marion taking donation out of ontology. Indeed, Marion uses phenomenology and ontology to read the Kant of the third *Critique* against the Kant of the first.[4] To what end? To show that theophany is not an event that belongs prima facie to a Thomist or Augustinian metaphysics: theophany, like the gaze of the human other, belongs to an interpretative phenomenology that has no recourse to metaphysics. Given these moves by the second and third generations, phenomenology appears, for better or for worse, to open both beyond its own epistemological boundaries *and* beyond philosophy.

Is this the mere structural repetition of the fate of German idealism after Kant, such that figures like Hegel attempted to bring the gains of the second *Critique*—notably the intuition of freedom and the ideal of the reconciliation—into the domain of objective logic itself? Figures like Schleiermacher and Kierkegaard now turned attention to the missing wealth of a logic of existence, in its particularity and its dependence vis-à-vis an alterity

---

[4] Marion argues that Kant's first *Critique*'s epistemological analyses failed to account adequately for a host of instances in which the given, or donation, overwhelmed either the immanent structures of intuition or those of conceptuality, within the schematism.

that it could not subsume in thought. Is the age and aftermath of phenomenology the repetition, in the twentieth century, of the drama of idealism?

It may well be this—but if so, then we must keep in mind that the Kant of the third *Critique* resembles the later Husserl, inasmuch as both men were stepping outside of the epistemological systems they elaborated in earlier works.[5] Thus the seeds of a hermeneutical and historical turn in phenomenology, like the seeds of some of existentialism's precursors, were already sown in phenomenology and idealism themselves. In both cases we may speak of an impetus to get past the limitations they establish, and this is possible, thanks to certain ambiguities like the Husserlian notion of horizon that evolves into that of open horizon*s* in the later works.

The question that concerns me here touches on the figures of Levinas and Kierkegaard, both in their relation to phenomenology and idealism and in relation to the question of responsibility, which is also the question of the relationship of their thought to ethics. For if responsibility is the paradoxical prereflective yet describable, and theorizable, possibility of our spontaneously being-for-another *within being itself* (although according to a temporality different from being's time), then ethics, as a vertical, unchosen commitment to the other, is both constitutive of all discourse (including traditional first philosophy) and a promise entailing neither prescription nor a *telos,* whether eudaimonistic or functional. And so Levinas's ethics is both inside and outside of philosophy; that is its radicality. Indeed, Levinas calls his thinking "ethics" in the original sense I just described, but he also calls it "religion" in *Totality and Infinity* (p. 40), playing on the sense of a prereflective human bond.

Kierkegaard has a more ambivalent relationship to ethics. A systematic ethics explains too much for him: its principle of the

---

[5] The Husserl of the third volume of the *Ideas* and of the "Origin of Geometry" is a historicized Husserl; one who comes nigh to abandoning the transcendental subjectivity he markedly set forward in the first volume of the *Ideas.* Merleau-Ponty shows clearly how Husserl transformed his project toward the end of his writing career; and third *Critique* Kantianism has been called "Kant stepping outside of Kant" (Claude Imbert, lecture course at Johns Hopkins University, Fall 1997).

good proposes to integrate human acts and interiority to such a point that even sacrifice is amenable to rationality. We find this evaluation of ethics in *Fear and Trembling*. In *The Concept of Anxiety,* the problems of evil, moral suffering, and turpitude are necessarily of interest to ethics, but neither ethics nor psychology can explain how and when evil arises. I suspect Levinas would agree with this formulation. He is certainly convinced, as Kierkegaard is, that evil is found in both historical societies and individuals. Think of his remark in *Totality and Infinity:* "There exists a tyranny of the universal and of the impersonal, an order that is inhuman though distinct from the brutish. Against it man affirms himself as an irreducible singularity. . . . aspiring to the religious order where the recognition of the individual concerns him in his singularity."[6]

But whatever the outcome of his aspirations, man is caught, as perpetrator and victim, in the judgment of history: "The virile judgment of history," of "pure reason" is cruel, for Levinas. In Kierkegaard's words, the judgment of history can be sin, having become reflective over its own history. Against this, what Levinas calls the "invisible," or the wrong done to another who is reduced to a statistic, must be made visible through speech. This is what bearing witness is—in its most extreme formulation, bearing witness, as the subjectivity that apologizes or proclaims the unseen wrong, gives voice to the "judgment of God."[7] What else would the notion of God represent, at least understood as a god of history, than the vision that perceives from a point from which all are equally seen? Since this is not ontology, the judgment of God can only be taken up and ventured as a risk.

Thus in *Totality and Infinity,* Levinas approaches the concept of sin from the perspective of history, and from that of him who endures others' sins unseen and unhelped. Kierkegaard approaches sin from the perspective of the one whose sin has come to pass like a leap into a void. Later, in *Otherwise Than Being,* Levinas turns in this direction as well, developing concepts like *recurrence, obsession, persecution, expiation, and Saying.* These represent the moments of the vertigo of the other as a force within me, as a memory whose onset I cannot recall.

---

[6] Levinas, *Totality and Infinity,* 242.
[7] Ibid., 244.

As the making visible of evil, the so-called judgment of God is a *figure* in *Totality and Infinity,* but God operates as the principle of alterity or the absolute other that gives rise to our pronouncing the word *God,* as Levinas put it in "God and Philosophy." But if we proceed to reduce this God to another *being,* then we diminish the alterity of humans! And we approach Levinas in Christian fashion, or from a pre-Maimonidean Jewish framework. Instead, the other is a principle, and alterity is a reality, but they are not beings. "The future . . . comes to me across an absolute interval whose other shore the Other absolutely other— *though he may be my son*—is alone capable of marking."[8] The point is not that the other is human or divine or some synthesis of each, it is that what we *call* divine, and what we *call* the particular person, is other: unknowable in her fullness, unanticipatable, unbanishable in her call. Alterity becomes the principle of ethical life in a time that is punctuated by the gesture Levinas called the judgment of God.

This Continental ethics has little in common with what the Anglo-American tradition calls ethics, because it gets behind theoretical foundationalism to what might be called a transcendental anthropology. In recent years, it has been both attacked and defended within Continental debates. These debates engage two questions of interest to me here: First, if we bracket those ethics of virtue that blend the ethical and the aesthetical vision of a beautiful life in a community, then is an ethics "without philosophy" possible? Second, can an ethics be developed without the assumption of an extratemporal ideal or perspective, whether this be the perspective of the ideal discursive community, or the universal agent, or the ideal of a reconciliation of duty and happiness, or the idealized calculus of happiness, or the other who affects me despite my rational judgment even in the wake of history's vicissitudes?

My second question about possibility is related to the first: Is there an ethics without a *belief* in *a* good, and, if this good is pragmatic and processual in character, then is there implicit in it a metaphysical assumption about subjects and their capacities? In a sense, the two questions turn around the relationship be-

---

[8] Ibid., 283.

tween ethics and so-called religion. We will see that Kierkegaard and Levinas address these two questions in a similar way.

Badiou has answered the questions recently in his *L'Éthique*.[9] Yes, there is an ethics without an ideal conception of the good; yes, emphatically, we can conceive our ethics without including a transcendental presupposition. To that end we find in his work a scathing attack on Levinas and his "human rights" epigones. I quote Badiou at length to allow him the fullness of his argument.

> Levinas proposes a whole series of phenomenological themes in which the originality of the Other is experienced, at the heart of which is found that of the face, of the singular and "in person" donation of the Other through his carnal epiphany, which is not the trial of a mimetic recognition (the Other as my "similar," *identical* to me), but on the contrary that starting from which I feel myself ethically as if "destined" *[voué]* to the Other qua appearing, and subordinated in my being to this vocation.

In this way, says Badiou, "ethics is for Levinas, *the new name of thought,* which has tipped its 'logical' containment (in the principle of identity) toward its prophetic submission to the Law of founding alterity."[10] In other words, Athens has tipped toward Jerusalem. Badiou continues:

> The capital—but also superficial—objection one could make to ethics (in Levinas's sense) is the following: what is it that *shows* the originality of my de-votion *[dé-vouement]* to the Other? . . . We require . . . the explicitation of the axioms underlying the thinking that *decide* such an orientation. . . . The difficulty, which is also the application point of such axioms, can be stated this way: the ethical primacy of the Other over the Same demands that the experience of alterity be ontologically 'guaranteed' as an experience of a distance, or an essential non-identity, whose *crossing* is the ethical experience itself. But nothing in the simple phenomenology of the other person *[autrui]* contains such a guarantee. And this, simply because it is certain that the finitude of appearing of the other person *can* be invested as resemblance, or as imitation,

---

[9] Alain Badiou, *L'Éthique: Essai sur la conscience du mal* (Paris: Hatier, 1993). Recently translated into English by Peter Hallward, *Ethics: An Essay on the Understanding of Evil* (London and New York: Verso, 2001). I translate from the French.

[10] Badiou, *L'Éthique,* 20.

and thus lead us back to the logic of the Same. The other person always resembles me too much for the hypothesis of an originary opening to his alterity to be *necessary*.[11]

The crux of Badiou's critique, therefore, is dual: he presupposes being as the only game, or scene, thinkable, and he focuses on necessity *versus* possibility—two themes of extreme concern to Levinas and Kierkegaard, to which I will return. It is not clear, in any case, that ethics ought to be a domain in which ethical ties, ethical behavior, or ethical sentiment are governed by an axiom, that is, by logical necessity. Nevertheless, Badiou argues that Levinas's possible absolute other cannot produce an ethical philosophy per se.

> In truth, there is no philosophy of Levinas. It is no longer even a philosophy 'servant' to theology: it is philosophy (in the Greek sense of the word) *annulled* by theology, which moreover is not a theo-logy (a nomination still too Greek, and which supposes an approach to the divine by way of the identity and predicates of God), but, precisely, an ethics. . . . Taken out of its Greek usage (where ethics is clearly subordinated to the theoretical), and taken in general, Levinas's ethics is a category of pious discourse.[12]

Badiou insists upon this for a good reason. The West is well pleased to call for the rights of the other person, provided that that other accept as his/her own the principal tenets of the Western rights credo. This credo masks important practical abuses in France, argues Badiou. As such, its repetition serves a host of interests, not the least of which are conservative. Asks Badiou, have we come so far with the other that we've no difficulty in recognizing the same?

His argument against Levinas could be directed to Kierkegaard as well. An ethics that lacks a logical guarantee of the transcendence of the other, which in Kierkegaard's schema implies his "faith" and "earnestness," becomes a pious discourse grounded on the supposition of transcendence, or the *possibility* of a call or leap that is *qualitatively* different from all other events. Now, Kierkegaard's *Concept of Anxiety* eludes this charge by calling

---

[11] Ibid.
[12] Badiou, *L'Éthique*, 22–23.

itself a work of psychology and ethics. It reflects upon the psychology of anxiety and sin, and on the supplement afforded by dogmatics for the significance of a sin that is hereditary. Nevertheless, the logic of the work depends upon three crucial, quasi-philosophical notions: inwardness, earnestness—which resembles Levinas's concept of sincerity synonymous with the Saying—and faith. Kierkegaard's central presupposition is "pious" and yet better than pious: it states that human life is "religiously designed," and that human particularity shows this religious vocation *precisely through sin as humanly inevitable, but which can be avoided in particular instances provided one has inwardness.*[13]

My purpose is not to argue, against Badiou, that Levinas's thought is in no sense tied to piety. But there is piety whose end lies in the service of a God believed by faith, and there is piety that influences but does not conclude philosophical arguments concerning good and evil. This claim walks a thin line. It asks in essence: Are there insights from a religious tradition that can be appropriated for their existential meaning, without thereby returning to that religion's dogma?

---

[13] The point of interest to me is this: that the ethical happens at all, given war and the continuous competition of commerce, suggests that generosity and goodness have nothing of the bestial to them, and also nothing of the will that we find in Nietzsche, or that in Spinoza, or the desire for recognition in Hegel—all of which resume the essence of humans. Perhaps it is a "moral sentiment" based upon a certain empathy, in which case it is the proper of Scottish moralists *and* Husserl alike; but Levinas shows that this sentiment often takes the form of a pang of conscience or even the distraction of a call that we would like to be rid of; so the possibility that it be something other than the above options leaves Levinas's "moment" open.

As to Kierkegaard, the argument works in such a way that none of us can deny that we understand wrongs and wrongdoing, even if it is up to us to define what these mean personally. From there, the notion of the demonic leaves faith as the only option of courage in being, since both unbelief and superstition will be shown to be two sides of the same coin, made up of passivity and activity. Actively believing in forces invisible to us, superstition holds us demonically and passively in our anxiety about the eternal by placing hope in something more like fate; actively denying that there is a divine, unbelief holds us passively in our anxiety about the good (which is Kierkegaard's definition of the demonic). Again, it comes down to allowing ourselves to be tried by the possibility of our own capacity, our being-able-to-do-x, which is the heart of anxiety, and which opens onto the leap of sin or onto a deeper understanding of what it means to be tried by possibility rather than determined by necessity.

This is precisely what both Kierkegaard and Levinas attempt to do. Levinas does it through a discourse expressly nondogmatic. And if we find parallels between his Talmudic readings and his philosophy, then we should point to the spirit of Hermann Cohen's essays on the "ethics of Judaism," in which it is no longer clear whether ethics is in service to religion or religion in service to ethics. Despite this fluidity, many have urged a crypto-religiosity beneath any argument for the movement between religion and ethics.

Their claim is founded upon the idea that any religious inspiration behind an ethical scheme taints the ethical claims with ideology. But does this then mean that Kant's categorical imperative has rationalized the Christian golden rule, while reading it through the ideology of pietism? To argue this suggests a naïveté about ideology. Moreover, it sets up a distinction between those discursivities that qualify as ideological, those that employ rationality toward ideological ends, and those that ideally escape ideology. But what escapes ideology—and unless we deny that every significant text has an imaginary dimension, whether this be utopian or paranoid or narcissistic—we must ask where piety begins and ends. We must ask what the relationship is between ideology, piety, and the imaginary in a work of ethics. Badiou's own ethics posits a pursuit of truths and operates under the imperative *Continuez* ("continue")! But if we ask: continue for the sake of whom, for the sake of what? are we forcing an ideological supposition, disguised as the desire for grounding, back into Badiou's work? How shall we avoid the questions *for what* and *for whom,* recognizing that they are also philosophical questions?

Let me resume and go on. My purpose is to muddy Badiou's claims about piety and ethics, using Kierkegaard's discussion of anxiety and Levinas's exploration of responsibility. Before doing so, I emphasize the most significant difference pervading their work, without which their *rapprochement* will be forced: faith is a central concept in Christianity, and for Kierkegaard, but above all for Protestantism with its emphasis on grace. Faith concerns belief in the incarnation of God, and it concerns a commitment to the promise of redemption and resurrection. Such a faith is not central to Judaism. Fidelity to the revealed law—oral and written—is central, however, and this law has a long tradition of rational interpretation, which underscores its ethical reason for being. This interpretation takes different forms in Jewish thinkers, from Saadia and Maimonides to Hermann Cohen. The ethical core of the law is precisely why it was revealed to humans, and that which allows humans to escape the reign of bestiality: it makes possible the human being to assume the position of "shepherds of Being."

Thus, for Levinas, who was influenced by the rationalist rabbinics of Lithuania, it is not that ethics is a dimension of piety; piety is meaningful only if it is ethical from the outset. For Kierkegaard, it is not that ethics is a dimension of piety, either, it is that the meaning of anxiety, inwardness, earnestness, and faith are misunderstood by ethics, which takes them as spiritual modes of a search that reason can undertake with greater transparency. Yet Kierkegaard argues that anxiety, inwardness, and earnestness are the preconditions *in possibility* for an ethical selfhood that unfolds neither in self-prescription (Kant) nor in the aestheticization of a life (in narcissism). Anxiety, inwardness, and faith are the preconditions for self-opening.[14] They constitute an original disposition or personality.

In this personality, "Earnestness . . . is the *acquired originality of disposition,* its originality preserved in the responsibility of freedom." Earnestness alone is what makes it possible for us to repeat our tasks; earnestness makes Kierkegaard's famous concept of repetition possible, and repetition, taken in the sense of doing the same act again and again—if this is possible—is the only form of eternity available to humans. In the human sphere, repetition is infinity, to speak like Levinas. Repetition is what Levinas designates by his "recurrence" of responsibility. Moreover, like Levinas's recurrence of responsibility, Kierkegaard's "inwardness" is not conquered by the will and has nothing to do

---

[14] Kierkegaard writes: "If [we] now turn back and pursue [Rosenkranz's] definition of 'feeling' as the spirit's immediate unity of its sentience [*Seelenhaftigkeit* = 'soulfulness'] and its consciousness, and recall that in the definition of *Seelenhaftigkeit* account has been taken of the unity with the immediate determinants of nature, then by taking all this together, [we have] the conception of a concrete personality." He adds that this is the best of possible human dispositions: "[E]arnestness is a higher as well as the deepest expression for what disposition is." Kierkegaard, *The Concept of Anxiety,* 148–49.

with idealism's self-consciousness or the "pure subject."[15] It is a movement that begins in the state of anxiety. It is the precondition of ethics, just as an unchosen responsibility and later a tormenting sense of remorse and obsession are the preconditions of ethical generosity in Levinas. Let us now look more closely at the parallels and differences between their thought.

LEVINAS AND KIERKEGAARD ON ETHICS

Having pointed to the most significant difference between Levinas and Kierkegaard, namely the difference of fidelity to law and faith in incarnation, in Jewish and Christian thought, I would suggest that three intuitions unite their thought: one is logical, the second is temporal and existential, the third is psychological and phenomenological.

Both thinkers break with logics built on sufficient reason and identity, and argue that quality cannot be reduced to quantity. Both men establish qualitatively different levels of being and transcendence (Levinas's being and better-than-being; Kierkegaard's leap), which cross each other chiasmatically but cannot be reduced to each other. These levels are what characterize existence in its *human* form. Now, the peculiarly human form of existing is to surpass its worldly existence in three ways: (1) in committing conscious acts of wrong (Kierkegaard's "sin"); (2) in opening oneself to a sociality of generosity; (3) in hollowing out or deepening one's interiority by removing limits to it (whether these are stated in philosophical discourse or experienced in the care we exert in our lives). This human form of existing is made possible by the supposed duality of immanence and transcendence characteristic of human "being."

The second intuition uniting Levinas and Kierkegaard pertains to temporality and existentialism: both thinkers attach distinct temporalities to modes of experience; they show that existence is understood through different moods, which form distinct layers. Transcendence in Levinas and Kierkegaard is not something from which one returns; it has the distinctive temporality of the

---

[15] Kierkegaard, *The Concept of Anxiety,* 151.

interruption. For Levinas, transcendence is interruption by the *other person* whose approach fills my perceptual and cognitive consciousness: I am for-that-other in a split second. In Kierkegaard's *Concept of Anxiety,* transcendence is a leap from anxiety about one's possibilities, into an act: sin. The definitive quality of transcendence is in each case its temporality: it is sudden, it is already past when we become aware of it. Only a temporality that could not be reduced to the countable and the accountable could be said to be different from subjective duration and objective chronometry.

As this other temporality, transcendence is immeasurable, and so irreducible to any determination of quantity. But this brings up a genetic problem in both philosophies: how did this leap, or this moment, come to be? The answer is that it did not; it was already there before an "I" discovered it. This is the famous deformalization of time in Levinas, which he calls, in *Totality and Infinity,* the "posteriority of the anterior."[16] It is found in Kierkegaard as well, worked out in regard to sin as the cumulative acts of the entire human race *and* as the choice each one of us enters for reasons that are inexplicable to logic or metaphysics. Both thinkers therefore deploy a paradoxical temporality following the same chiasmatic logic that we saw in their separation of being and better-than-being, or being and the transcendence of sin.

Third, each philosopher seeks a proto-subjectivity beneath the self-positing and self-synthesizing consciousness of idealism and Husserlian phenomenology. In Levinas, as we know, the subject is fissured: an irreducible and alien dimension always already inhabits it; we become aware of this through modes of being and their accompanying moods, like the mode of division against itself signaled by remorse and trouble. Writes Levinas: "The psyche is the form of a peculiar dephasing, a loosening up or unclamping of identity: the same prevented from coinciding with itself, at odds, torn up from its rest, between sleep and insomnia, panting, shivering."[17] Levinas's psyche, or, as he puts it, "this prior psyche, which is signifyingness par excellence," is also

---

[16] Levinas, *Totality and Infinity,* 54.
[17] Levinas, *Otherwise Than Being or Beyond Essence,* 68.

"sensibility when phenomenologically reduced." It is prior to the sensible subject sensing its objects; it is, rather, the active meaningfulness of sense or "animation."[18]

But as meaning and the root of the act of signifying, it is like Kierkegaard's anxiety. What is anxiety for Kierkegaard? Although *The Concept of Anxiety* influenced Heidegger considerably, anxiety for Kierkegaard is *not* one of those privileged moods through which our notions of nothingness come to us and with it, our notion of being qua being. Anxiety for Kierkegaard is, rather, the "sign" and mood of spirit. What he calls spirit is the nonspatial, nonlogical site—the mode—in or by which body and mind are united in a human being. Spirit is, in a sense, close to intelligence; not intellect but a holistic sort of perceptual and sentient intelligence, and a capacity to make a certain leap or to "sober up" within existence, as Levinas puts it. It is, therefore, as Levinas claimed of ethics, "an optics": the condition of a precise way of perceiving.[19] So "it is the power of intelligence and its preponderance that in the indifference of the spirit neutralize both the erotic and the moral relation to the erotic," that is, to sin.[20]

Now, spirit, in Levinasian terms, would be dis-inter-*ested*ness, a momentary but recurring stance outside of any commitment to physical *being* and political history. However, in Kierkegaard spirit has a historical evolution *and* an individual one. In both the historical and the individual cases, the more developed spirit is, the greater the human capacity for that vertigo before its own possibilities, which Kierkegaard calls "anxiety." He puts it beautifully:

Anxiety may be compared with dizziness. He whose eye happens to look down into the yawning abyss becomes dizzy. But what is the reason for this? It is just as much in his own eye as in the abyss, for suppose he had not looked down. Hence anxiety is the

---

[18] Ibid., 69.

[19] Kierkegaard, *The Concept of Anxiety,* 69. Writes Kierkegaard: "As soon as [spirit] is posited not merely as that which constitutes the synthesis [of sentient body and cognitive psyche] but as spirit, the erotic [the pure bodily experience] comes to an end. The highest pagan expression for this is that the erotic is the comic."

[20] Kierkegaard, *The Concept of Anxiety,* 69.

dizziness of freedom, which emerges when the spirit wants to posit the synthesis and freedom looks down into its own *possibility*, laying hold of finiteness to support itself. Freedom succumbs in this dizziness.[21]

This anxiety, which is a mood not unlike the horror experienced by Levinas's insomniac before the indeterminate positivity of being, characterizes with spirit the proto-subject, the self in Levinasian terms, before the indeterminate being and its accompanying possibilities. It is impossible, for Kierkegaard, to say unequivocally whether this belongs to being or to the subject: dizziness is as much in the eye as it is in the abyss. As a mood it is prior to distinctions of subject and object, and Kierkegaard adds that it is the "middle term" between human possibility and actuality; a middle term that *pervades* both possibility and actuality.

Anxiety preconditions the transcendence of the leap into evil, just as it constitutes the trial of human possibility itself and can be used otherwise than to plunge into sin. Here, Kierkegaard is Schellingian and presages Heidegger, but he gives us an insight into Levinas's thought, in which anxiety grips us *both* before the "there is," before the positive presence of being, *and* as the trace of the other who has fissured my consciousness before I was aware of it happening. As Kierkegaard writes in what is a very Levinasian sentence:

> Just as the relation of anxiety to its object, to something that is nothing . . . is altogether ambiguous, so also the transition that is to be made from innocence to guilt will be so dialectical that it can be seen that the explanation is what it must be, psychological. But he who becomes guilty through anxiety is indeed innocent, *for it was not he himself but anxiety, a foreign power,* that laid hold of him.[22]

Anxiety is likened to a foreign power much the way that the other, absolutely other yet immanent in me, functions for Levinas as a foreign power over the will, "like an inversion of the *conatus* of *esse.*"[23] These "powers" and this blurring of the bor-

---

[21] Ibid., 61 (emphasis added).
[22] Ibid., 43.
[23] Levinas, *Otherwise Than Being or Beyond Essence,* 75.

ders between subject and self, subject and other, subject and being, constitute the proto-subjectivity that lies beneath our cognition of sensible moments in Levinas and Kierkegaard alike.

Thus, the Kierkegaardian schema can be summarized as follows. We approach sin in order to approach questions of ethics and faith. At the heart of ethics is the question of evil, which is, for Kierkegaard and Levinas both, the question that is prior to the question concerning being.[24] The question of evil is also, for both men, one approach to the meaning and possibility of transcendence and alterity.[25] This is because sin appears first as humans' "other," the counter nature that was nevertheless a possibility open to them. Why it was possible, and why sin gets chosen are more difficult questions. Psychology can begin to answer them, provided we accept the claim from Christian dogmatics that each human being can and will sin, and that the history of the human race is a history of an accumulating reflection on acts of sinfulness it commits.

Psychology can answer the question of why sin is possible by examining the state of mind that precedes sin: anxiety. As we have seen, anxiety exists in various intensities, according as human possibilities get focused upon conscious ends of good or evil. But anxiety is found in all human beings because of their more or less developed sense of being-able-to-do. At the extreme, anxiety can by itself give rise to the sense that one is guilty of something, of x, or that one has *already* transgressed. Kierkegaard illustrates this using the notion of the concupiscent gaze of the other, who constitutes me in anxiety and shame: *as though I had already desired that other!* Here, without glimpsing all the implications of his move, Kierkegaard gives us a Levinasian face to face, in which the self contains both self and the other *in* the self—even if that other is simply his/her desiring gaze and makes no appeal for help. Shame suggests, in any case, a sense of guilt assumed in advance; its temporal form is the

---

[24] Compare these remarks made by Levinas in his essay "Transcendence and Evil" (in Emmanuel Levinas, *De Dieu qui vient à l'idée* (Paris: J. Vrin, 1986, 201): "The ontological difference is preceded by the difference between good and evil." See my English translation, *Of God Who Comes to Mind* (Stanford: Stanford University Press, 1998).

[25] Levinas, *Of God Who Comes to Mind,* 198.

posteriority of anteriority, and shame and guilt weaken the self, which ultimately may take a leap into sin.

Psychology cannot explain the nature of the leap itself. It can simply trace the stages and states that lead, temporally and quantitatively, to the leap. However, the notion of a leap introduces the existential distinction of quality into the quantitative accumulation of everyday time, words, and deeds. Kierkegaard insists that this distinction cannot be found in logic, where the qualitative is the result of quantities of quantitative modifications. If the qualitative change that is sin is merely quantitative, then the individual is mechanistically determined in time and by the events in her/his life. Yet that would destroy the meaning of sin as evil, since sin occurs for each individual in gratuitous *possibility,* that is, in the temptation of one's *own* possibility, which is to be able to do x, y, ad infinitum.

Kierkegaard's leap into sin is thus a transcendence from which one does not return. One sins, one is henceforth guilty, and each person individually brings sinfulness into the world through her sins. Now, the sins that receive Kierkegaard's attention are sins of concupiscence, probably because of the significance of eros in constituting humans as historical, generational beings (which expresses humans' discontinuous mode of infinity).[26]

How one responds to anxiety and what its principal objects are determines the sort of personality one develops. Kierkegaard speaks of a personality caught up in the state of the "demonic."[27] This is a state in which freedom, entangled with itself in anxiety, slowly turns into non-freedom and obsession. The visible symptoms of the demonic are enumerated like a hodgepodge of psychoanalysis and more literary troubles: "in hypochondria, in capriciousness; it manifests itself in the highest passions";[28] and

---

[26] Indeed, Kierkegaard hardly mentions any other form of sin than the sexual-sensuous. Perhaps if he did so, the leap that is so clear in the passage to carnal knowledge would be obscured, and the notion of sin would be problematized by attempts to find the reasons behind these other acts. Still, the temptation of Abraham to kill Isaac would have resulted in a leap had Abraham been allowed to act; yet Abraham did not sink under the weight of anxiety precisely because he believed he would receive everything back. So faith redirects anxiety and teaches us the meaning of trial by the possible.

[27] Kierkegaard, *The Concept of Anxiety,* 118–46.

[28] Ibid., 124.

elsewhere again, in "a hypersensibility and a hyperirritability, neurasthenia, hysteria, hypochondria, etc."[29]

These symptoms accompany and are heightened by the principal phenomenon of the demonic: the refusal to speak and to open oneself to the other, which is Kierkegaard's concept of "inclosing reserve."[30] As such, no life is wholly without the demonic, which proves to be whatever limits the human being face-to-face with the other. The state arises in one of two possible sorts of anxiety: anxiety before the good, and anxiety before evil. It is not difficult to imagine what or why anxiety is found before evil: the apprehension of harm or of sin is its content. But as a human being shuts itself off in cynicism, skepticism, or some emotional state like envy, it shows an increasing anxiety about the good, about love and the other transcendence that expresses itself in "confession," such as Levinas's apology. Inclosing reserve thus desiccates freedom as possibility; it is anti-sociality, a negative ethic of sociality par excellence. States Kierkegaard:

> The utmost extreme in this sphere is what is commonly called bestial perdition. In this state, the demonic manifests itself in saying, as did the demoniac in the New Testament with regard to salvation: *ti emoi kai soi* (what have I to do with you)? Therefore it shuns every contact. . . . Therefore [also], from such a demoniac is quite commonly heard a reply that expresses all the horror of this state: Leave me alone in my wretchedness.[31]

We cannot fail to be impressed by Kierkegaard's exploration, underrepresented in Levinas, of anti-sociality arising from anxiety. But note two significant Levinasian themes in Kierkegaard: first, that such a refusal of the other is possible. Was it not Levinas who, in speaking of the face, said that it is the only thing that "I can wish to kill?" In *Totality and Infinity,* the interpellative power of the face *opens* a subject *up,* but it may also produce a decision to turn away. The gnawing remorse that Levinas calls substitution, which comes to pass in the diachrony or peculiar temporality of being-for-the-other, may remain with us even if we do turn away from the other. If it does remain, it certainly

---

[29] Ibid., 136–37.
[30] Ibid., 123ff.
[31] Ibid., 137.

will not diminish our wretchedness. For it is a singular circularity that has it that the one who locks himself up within himself can simultaneously feel unworthy of help in getting out.

The second Levinasian theme here is language. Early in *The Concept of Anxiety,* Kierkegaard argues that it is inconceivable that man could have invented language by himself. Thus Kierkegaard writes on the Biblical story of Adam, father of hereditary sin:

> Here we must remember what was said about the prohibition [of the tree] and the word of judgment. . . . The imperfection in the narrative—i.e., how it could have occurred to anyone to say to Adam what he essentially could not understand [because he did not yet know good and evil]—is eliminated if we bear in mind that *the speaker is language,* and also that it is Adam himself that speaks.[32]

Precisely so: in freedom, and in any trial of possibility, the speaker *is* language; language is immanence, the "voice of conscience." But we need not follow Heidegger reading Kierkegaard here and insist upon maintaining a dichotomy between the inner and the outer. In his note to that page, Kierkegaard adds: "But this much is certain, that it will not do to represent man himself as the inventor of language."[33] It is readily admissible that man would not invent language *on his own, in his pastoral soliloquizing.* And Kierkegaard is not interested in so ontologizing and moralizing the difficult notion of "God" that God now becomes a father speaking to Adam.

What Kierkegaard grasps, notwithstanding, is Levinas's insight that language is speaking-to, it is responding-to. This supposes that the origin of language would be the *entre-nous,* as Levinas puts it. Further, insofar as language is response and responsibility *to,* it is so when we are able to stay clear of the Kierkegaardian inclosing reserve or psychoanalytical narcissism. For Kierkegaard and for Levinas, then, what saves us from inclosing reserve is "the word."[34] Kierkegaard does not mean, here, Jesus *stricto sensu;* he would rather say, I suspect, that

---

[32] Ibid., 47 (emphasis added).
[33] Ibid.
[34] Ibid., 124.

Jesus is called the Word because he operated as an interpellator, opening those who listened to him; or again, that in interrupting our reflexive anxiety over the good, Jesus and the prophets generally extended humans' possibility of escaping from inclosing reserve. That would be the ethical-psychological reading of Jesus as the Word.

Kierkegaard writes: "Language, the word, is precisely what saves, what saves the individual from the empty abstraction of inclosing reserve. . . . For language does indeed imply *communication.*"[35] Moreover, if Levinas's self, interpellated by a force that is both within and without him, *responds* without first choosing to do so, in sincerity, then Kierkegaard also glimpses that the linguistic response is not sufficient: the proper tone and modality of the response must be specified to understand the difference between the response of responsibility and the mechanical responses of everyday temporality, whatever their resemblances. Kierkegaard will take pains to show how the notion of salvation is expressed in the everyday by "disclosure";[36] and disclosure itself requires a measure of what he calls inwardness.

This "most concrete content [where *concrete* means "real"] that consciousness can have, is consciousness of itself. . . . *not the pure self-consciousness,* but the self-consciousness that is so concrete that no author . . . has ever been able to describe [it]." This inwardness "is action" and "cannot be something completed for contemplation."[37] But if inwardness is action and self-consciousness is not pure self-consciousness, then Kierkegaard is reaching toward what is prior to the Fichtean posited "I" of formal freedom; and he is deliberately blurring the notion of action and passivity—something he does throughout the work. Why should this paradoxical consciousness of self—for which Kierkegaard clearly could not come up with a more distinct category to help himself here—not be likened to Levinas's "sincerity" of the Saying? Recall what this means in the section "Responsibility for the Other," in *Otherwise Than Being:*

> But if time is to show an ambiguity of being and the otherwise than being, [then] its temporalization is to be conceived not as

---

[35] Ibid. (emphasis added).
[36] Ibid., 127.
[37] Ibid., 143.

essence, but as saying. . . . A linear regressive movement, a retrospective back along the temporal series toward a very remote past,
would *never* be able to reach the absolutely diachronous pre-origi-
nal which cannot be recuperated by memory and history. . . . The
relationship with such a past . . . is included in the *extraordinary
and everyday* event of my responsibility for the faults or the misfortune of others.[38]

And again, on sincerity and the Saying:

Sincerity is not an attribute of saying; it is saying that realizes
sincerity. It is inseparable from giving. . . . Sincerity undoes the
alienation which saying undergoes in the said. . . . Is not a saluta-
tion the giving of a sign signifying this very giving, this recognition of a debt? Sincerity in which signification signifies, in which
one is exposed without holding back to the other, in which the one
approaches the other, is . . . [a] fission of the ultimate substantiality
of the ego.[39]

The Levinasian emphasis on intersubjectivity goes under-dis-
cussed by Kierkegaard, whose "path" is more solitary. Viewed
in light of intersubjectivity, then, Levinas's "sincerity" and
Kierkegaard's "inwardness" and "disclosure" resemble each
other. In a sense, Kierkegaard's claim that the word suspends
anxiety (over the good) is echoed in Levinas's chapter on "Substitution," where obsession and persecution open into a Saying
that is not tragic, but comparable to "laughter through my tears."
Now, if earnestness is how Kierkegaard characterizes the self
that is prior to any formal, reflective subjectivity or ego, then
sincerity is Levinas's notion of earnestness. And although
Kierkegaard does not underscore the fissure in the proto-subject,
anxiety, as the "middle category" between possibility and actuality, serves as a *site* comparable to Levinas's situation of being
fissured.

It should not be forgotten, here, that one of the most difficult
questions of *Otherwise Than Being* asks how we can hold on to
the idea of the other as externality (that does not appear the way
that an object does) *and* internality, or "transcendence within

---

[38] Levinas, *Otherwise Than Being or Beyond Essence,* 9–10 (emphasis
added).
[39] Ibid., 143–44.

immanence." But we must hold on to both, and when we do, we may choose to speak of an inter-space, or a middle category like Kierkegaard's anxiety and the trial of the possible that it offers us.

Language thus arises as a giving of signs; not as sign-indices, or deicticals, but as giving, which Kierkegaard calls disclosure but also "accounting and judgment."[40] Together, and like Levinas's sincerity before the other, these are "modes of eternalizing earnestness"[41] (read: sincerity) that are neither abstract nor metaphysical, because they complete the process of the communication all the way into the Levinasian moment of the third party, who brings the demand for justice with him. Accounting and judgment also suggest the sense of being accounted and judged *by* another. These moments have a purgative effect on anxiety, and they modify everyday temporality.

Writes Kierkegaard: "Precisely because the accounting and the judgment are essential, what is essential will have the effect of a Lethe on whatever is unessential. . . . The soul has not been essentially present in the drolleries of life, in its accidental circumstances . . . hence all this vanishes except for the soul that was essentially in this."[42] This hollowing out, the burning up of the inessential occurs in the face of the other as well, for this too is a moment of apology, accounting, and judgment. For Kierkegaard, this kenosis and its aftermath allow humans the little eternity we can glimpse: the possibility of repetition.

For Levinas, something like repetition occurs prior to our conscious pursuit of it. Something like repetition comes to pass, unchosen, in "recurrence"—for before the other, responsibility comes to pass, it flickers. I do not choose it, and I can reject it. But Levinas argues that it increases in the measure that it is assumed, and this is a heightening of Kierkegaard's notion of repetition. Thus recurrence is the spontaneous fact of responsibility in everyday life, a fact whose temporality is so condensed that its descriptions have recourse to the agonistic and exalted language of the prophets. If repetition is the opening of eternity

---

[40] Kierkegaard, *The Concept of Anxiety,* 153.
[41] Ibid., 149.
[42] Ibid., 154.

within the present, then recurrence is similarly the opening of eternity, the eternity of transcendence in immanence this time, in the compact moment of interruption by the other.

CONCLUSION

If I have come close to making Kierkegaard into Levinas's direct precursor, that was not my intention. Their works, their readers, and their interlocutors (imaginary and real) are generally not the same. On the one hand, Kierkegaard owes a debt to Schellingian and Hegelian idealism for his concepts of the abyss of freedom and for "spirit." Levinas's conceptual debt is to Husserl, Bergson, and Heidegger's hermeneutic ontology.

Nevertheless, they come to the same question as if from two different sides: Kierkegaard approaches the question of sin and evil via the psychology of anxiety and faith. Levinas approaches the question of evil in light of the wrong done to the other, a wrong that is not seen by history but by the one who bears witness. A host of reasons, many quite obvious, can be evinced for this. The absence of original, and certainly "hereditary," sin in Judaism is one such reason. Nevertheless, Levinas and Kierkegaard both deem evil to be a qualitative difference in being. In reviewing Philippe Nemo's book on Job, Levinas calls evil the "excess" that leads us past all logics of the quantity.

> Quite remarkably, that which is purely quantitative in the notion of excess is shown in the guise of a qualitative content characteristic of the malignity of evil. . . . In the appearing of evil, in its original phenomenality, in its *quality,* there is a announced a *modality* or a manner: the not-finding-a-place, the refusal of any accommodation with . . . a counter-nature, . . . the disturbing and foreign in itself. *And in this sense transcendence!*[43]

Leaving aside these remarkable resonances, here, with Kierkegaard's central distinction between quality and quantity, leaving aside the question of the counter nature that Kierkegaard approaches in his concept of the demonic and its monadic inclosing reserve, note that both men discern one sense of transcendence

---

[43] Levinas, "Transcendence and Evil," in *Of God Who Comes to Mind,* 128.

in evil itself. This is possible in each case, if *we allow the anxiety of an evil done to us,* in this case done to Job, *to constitute an interpellation, a call.* Just as in Kierkegaard's logic, inclosing reserve threatens Job. Indeed, inclosing reserve and any tendency to a counter-natural demonism are modes of evil different from Job's plight, but they are such that he could easily have sunk into them in anxiety. These now are broken open by a call in the midst of suffering, and by the recognition of the good in the trial that caused the suffering of anxiety.

In the case of Job, as Levinas puts it, "a first 'intentionality' of transcendence: someone is searching for me. A God who causes pain, but God as a You *[Toi]*."[44] This is precisely the movement of faith in Kierkegaard. In *The Concept of Anxiety,* it is what he calls the trial by possibility. This is ethical and religious at once, because the domains overlap at the categories of evil and, if you will, modes of atonement and redemption. But ethics traditionally conceived gives us essentially three manners for grounding or deriving responsibility: either a practico-aesthetic manner (Aristotelian *phronesis*); or a law as the form in which freedom recognizes itself bound and enabled (Kant); or, finally, a calculus for determining the contribution of responsibility to general happiness. This leaves open the question of the rise, the incipience of responsibility such as Levinas conceives it (even Kant's freedom must first recognize itself in the moral law). So responsibility remains problematic in ethics. Something similar is true for evil. As Kierkegaard points out:

> Sin belongs in ethics, and the mood that corresponds to its conception is ethical earnestness or, more correctly, earnestness. . . . Ethics does not overcome sin metaphysically, for it knows . . . that sin has endurance; it does not flee sin esthetically or mourn over it esthetically, for it abrogates sin; it does not become psychologically absorbed in it, for it knows that sin is not a state. But there is also a difficulty about sin having a place in ethics.[45]

The difficulty is adjudicating the meaning of wrongs, and so too that of culpability, in light of the different possible norms held outside the arena in which the wrong is committed. Kierkegaard

---

[44] Ibid., 130.
[45] Kierkegaard, *The Concept of Anxiety,* 181–82.

argues that dogmatics "explains hereditary sin *by presupposing it.*"[46] In short, dogmatics too has a problem with sin, but it is not that of sin's place, it is the recognition that evil occurs to us and is done by us beyond the categories of freedom and determination, prior and posterior. No explanation is really afforded by presupposing something, but a certain commitment to what we might call "the real" is made in this way.

Like Kierkegaard, Levinas assumes that the ontological difference is preceded by the ethical difference.[47] Like Kierkegaard, Levinas agrees that ethical questions are intelligible in their proper mood. He writes: "Husserlian phenomenology has opened new possibilities. It affirms the rigorous solidarity of everything intelligible and the psychic modalities *by* which and *in* which the intelligible is thought: not just any meaning is accessible to any thought."[48] If we take the question of mood seriously, then a path of communication between so-called religion and ethics can be understood in terms of one *mode* of approach: earnestness, or the sincerity of the Saying.

This may not sound so "religious"—after all, where is the master signifier, the distance of transcendence crossable only by faith, where is the dogma in this religion? A suspicious intelligence might suspect such postulates beneath all the talk about moods and modes of thoughts in their limited accessibility. But mood concerns the meaning of inwardness, or obsession, and that much broader meaning of belief that accompanies our adherence to any ethical and ideological system, consciously or unconsciously. Mood concerns belief as the argumentative and descriptive impetus to conclusions that cannot be logically verified, and I would argue that this forms the core of ethics and values theory. We see this core in the elegant *failures* of recent ethical systems, for example, the failure to define the good (G. E. Moore), the failure to remain under Rawls's "veil of ignorance," and the failure to maintain consistent adherence to a regulative ideal.

Badiou's argument that Levinas requires the *logical axiom* of absolute alterity in order to maintain human alterity states (as

---

[46] Ibid., 182.
[47] Levinas, "Transcendence and Evil," in *Of God Who Comes to Mind,* 130.
[48] Ibid., 124 (translation modified).

Derrida did already in 1967) that Levinas's thought relies on the supposition of a *Deus absconditus*. Against Kierkegaard, I argue that the axiom Badiou would criticize is that "human life is religiously designed," even more so than Kierkegaard's presupposition that the historical and individual fact of evil is necessary. In the case of Levinas, the notion of absolute alterity is both operative and largely unverifiable, because it is an axiom. But Levinas's axiom changes in *Otherwise Than Being*, although Badiou is not interested in that work. There, absolute alterity is meaningless as a logical category, unless we derive *it* from our immanence and our interactions with others. In other words, first-person responsibility "verifies"—if verification is always possible and desirable—the *efficacy* of what Levinas calls absolute alterity, not the other way around.

In *Otherwise Than Being*, it is human speech that verifies, at the level of enactment, not logic, the alterity of the human other. Speech verifies this alterity in the form of an answer or account given to another *and* in the form of the sincerity of the response. Is this sufficient verification to allow us to assert that there is a circle, rather than a linear deduction, between the (logical) concept of absolute alterity and the enacted unique response to the other? I am not sure, because there is always the risk of magical thinking, when one speaks of the power over me of something that affects me before I can think about it. However, I contest that in its pure form, Levinas's thought is philosophy *consumed* by religion.

Insofar as religion is present in Levinas's later thought, it is present in a form purified of any traditional metaphysical notions of transcendence. It is religion become ethics and, as such, it reminds us of Hermann Cohen's ideal of Judaism as religion of reason, running parallel to Kant's project. That does not mean that Levinas's readers are not free to reintroduce religious notions. Indeed, anyone is free to remind us that religion is never far from a thinking that asks, What must I do? For whom? In the name of whom or what?

In *The Concept of Anxiety*, the postulate of the religious design of human life implies something we are now familiar with, thanks to psychoanalysis, genealogy, and critical theory: reason's limitation in making the human being transparent to himself. The novelty of this notion is clear. For Levinas, it is "that the *appearance* of rationality . . . [has] powers of mystification [that] dissimulate themselves to the point that the art of logic cannot suffice to its demystification."[49]

For Kierkegaard, writing as a psychologist, the religious design assumes that the category of possibility exceeds the binaries of freedom and necessity. Guilt, not necessity, is the contrary of freedom for Kierkegaard.[50] Guilt arises with anxiety in the wake of the experience of the possible as being-able-to-do. Guilt accompanies anxiety as "freedom tangled up in itself." So the expansion of the experience of the possible, and with it anxiety about good or evil, takes the place of traditional notions of freedom. In so doing, Kierkegaard's experience of the possible becomes a trial and a *kind* of modalized comprehension, a comprehension through moods. What I comprehend is that I belong to my history as much as to my personal choices, and that I *can* flee my anxiety in a host of ways. Some flights will lead me to commit a wrong; others will commit me to the self-inclosure of despair. But the possible, as a trial, directs me to seriousness about myself and my condition: that is the sense of the concept of earnestness.

Faith enters Kierkegaard's schema last, as belief in the good, in God, within the disposition of earnestness. I would argue that this schema of the possible admits a religious and a secular reading. It is not necessary here to hypostatize or reify divinity or eternity to grasp that anxiety before what is possible to me *can* be a call to seriousness. Indeed, Badiou misses the rethinking of ethics in Levinas and Kierkegaard when he focuses solely upon the axioms on which their thought is based.[51]

My point is this: the movement between religion and ethics in both Kierkegaard and Levinas enables us to rethink ethics as a summons and a call, before it is a prescription or a calculus. The

---

[49] Ibid., 18.

[50] Kierkegaard, *The Concept of Anxiety,* 108.

[51] Of course, he does so in order to maintain that we still require an ethics without metaphysical axioms—which he seems to take to be equivalent to axioms that require an engagement of belief. We require an ethics without metaphysical axioms, it seems, so that philosophy, as a logos, is not robbed of all content by a pious discourse. No need to argue here that piety takes more forms in recent ideologies than it did in historical religions.

axiom underlying the summons may be absolute alterity, but it may well be that the source of the summons is undecidable, and it may well be that it is a human other who is like and unlike me. In any case it is "verified" in conscience and practice, in simple and courageous instances. But that does not necessitate the devastation of philosophy by piety.

6

Derrida, the Messianic, and Eschatology

Gary Banham

THE PREDOMINANT RECEPTION of *Specters of Marx* has been to view it as a work in which Derrida reveals an unexpected receptivity to the notion of the messianic. That this understanding of the work is at best partial is what I wish to make clear, through setting out the kind of use Derrida is making of the notion of the messianic. In one of the most frequently cited passages from the work, Derrida refers to an "ascesis" that strips the messianic hope of all Biblical forms, and he adds that this "denuding" is done in view of:

> responding to that which must be absolute hospitality, the "yes" to the *arrivant(e)*, the "come" to the future that cannot be anticipated—which must not be the "anything whatsoever" that harbors behind it those too familiar ghosts, the very ones we must practice recognizing. Open, waiting for the event *as* justice, this hospitality is absolute only if it keeps watch over its own universality. The messianic, including its revolutionary forms (and the messianic is always revolutionary, it has to be), would be urgency, imminence but, irreducible paradox, a waiting without horizon of expectation.[1]

In other places within the text of *Specters,* Derrida connects the thought of the messianic to the work of Benjamin, and, in an important footnote to chapter 2, he cites extensively from Benjamin's "Theses on the Philosophy of History." It would thus seem reasonable to suppose that *Specters of Marx* is a work sin-

---

[1] Jacques Derrida, *Specters of Marx: The State of the Debt, the Work of Mourning, and the New International,* trans. P. Kamuf (London and New York: Routledge, 1994 [1993]), 168.

gularly close in inspiration to Benjamin and in particular to his thought of the messianic.

That matters cannot really be this simple, however, is confirmed if we turn from *Specters of Marx* to a work that is often cited in its pages, Derrida's essay "Force of Law: 'The Mystical Foundation of Authority.'"[2] In this other text, Derrida undertakes an extensive reading of Benjamin's early essay "Critique of Violence," and, in the context of some concluding remarks that present an extremely controversial hypothesis about the work, he states: "This text, like many others by Benjamin, is still too Heideggerian, too messianico-marxist or archeo-eschatological for me."[3] Leaving aside for a moment the reference to Heidegger in this citation, it is immediately noteworthy that Benjamin is faulted for his messianic and eschatological thought here, when it appeared that it was precisely these attributes of his work that were inspirational for *Specters of Marx*.

How should the relation between "Force of Law" and *Specters of Marx* be understood, and what accounts for the difference there appears to exist between them in the reception of Benjamin's messianic thought? This is the question that I hope to address, through making clear the nature of the reference to the messianic and the nod to Benjamin given in *Specters of Marx,* and then underlining the unity between these treatments and those provided of both Benjamin and the thought of the messianic in "Force of Law."

HAUNTOLOGY, ESCHATOLOGY, AND THE MESSIANIC IN *SPECTERS OF MARX*

Returning to the earlier citation from *Specters,* the first matter of importance is that Derrida makes clear he is performing a kind of *epoche* of the thought of the messianic, in reducing it to its formal trait of a promise "without horizon of expectation,"

---

[2] Jacques Derrida, "Force of Law: The Mystical Foundation of Authority," trans. M. Quaintance, in D. Cornell, M. Rosenfeld, and D. G. Carlson, eds., *Deconstruction and the Possibility of Justice* (London and New York: Routledge, 1992).

[3] Derrida, "Force of Law," 62.

which will thus involve no reference to Biblical forms. Once reduced to this formal structure, we are left with a promise that has a double relation to temporality: this promise is to be conceived of as involving both urgency and a waiting that has no determinate outcome. Both the urgency and the waiting relate to the future but, again inscribing a double relation to temporality, also involve an irreducible finitude.

This latter is inscribed by Derrida in the following way: "Some, and I do not exclude myself, will find this despairing 'messianism' has a curious taste, a taste of death."[4] At once urgent and involving incessant waiting, futural and radically connected to absolute finitude, this temporality of the messianic seems to require a relation to the history of thought about time, and, hence, to require thinking in response to Heidegger as much as to Benjamin.

The reference to Heidegger in *Specters of Marx* is to the essay of 1946 "The Anaximander Fragment,"[5] an essay already visited by Derrida as early as 1968 in the classic piece "Différance."[6] It will be worth attending to the distinction and the closeness between the two references Derrida makes to this writing of Heidegger's. In *Specters of Marx,* Derrida reaches for this text to remind us of the translation Heidegger proposes of the word *dīk,* normally translated as "justice." Heidegger determines it instead as order and contrasts with it the term *adikia* as involving disorder. More pertinently to the reason for the reference, however, is that Heidegger states that when adikia rules, then "something is out of joint." But what? That which is present in its presencing, or, as Heidegger writes:

> To presencing as such jointure must belong, thus creating the possibility of its being out of joint. What is present is that which lingers awhile. The while occurs essentially as the transitional arrival in departure: the while comes to presence between approach and withdrawal. Between this twofold absence the presencing of all

---

[4] Derrida, *Specters of Marx,* 169.

[5] Martin Heidegger, "The Anaximander Fragment," in Heidegger, *Early Greek Thinking,* trans. D. F. Krell and F. A. Capuzzi (San Francisco and London: Harper and Row, 1975).

[6] Jacques Derrida, "Differance," in Derrida, *Margins of Philosophy,* trans. A. Bass (Brighton: Harvester Press, 1982 [1968]).

that lingers occurs. In this "between" whatever lingers awhile is joined. This "between" is the jointure in accordance with which whatever lingers awhile is joined, from its emergence here to its departure away from here.[7]

The notion of time is revealed here to be a joining, a connection between approach and withdrawal that makes presencing possible in the spacing of absence. Time as experienced comes to be in the lack of presence; this lack makes possible fulfillment in a time we call ours, but since time's joining is predicated on a disjoining, time in its presencing also makes possible for us a lack of connection, a failure to relate the time gone to the time to come, and, thus, a disorder in order. To which Heidegger adds that what lingers awhile "gives jointure."

> Giving is not only giving-away; originally, giving has the sense of acceding or giving-to. Such giving lets something belong to another which properly belongs to him. What belongs to that which is present is the jointure of its while, which it articulates in its approach or withdrawal.[8]

Since the giving of time is the jointure of the while in the possibility of presencing, there is, beyond the understanding of dīk as justice, a sense to the fundamental experience of temporality of a due order. Having unraveled this much from Heidegger's treatise, let us now return to the question put to it by Derrida in *Specters of Marx.*

While Derrida insists on retaining the sense of dīk as justice, his question to Heidegger turns not fortuitously precisely on the problem of how time has here been determined as the primary possibility of presencing. Not, however, to deny the necessity inscribed within the thought of the disjointure, but rather beyond the possibility of presencing to precisely rescue the urgency of the demand to relate to disjoining in a time we call ours:

> The necessary disjointure, the de-totalizing condition of justice, is here that of the present—and by the same token the very condition of the present and of the presence of the present. This is where deconstruction would always begin to take shape as the thinking

---

[7] Heidegger, "The Anaximander Fragment," 41.
[8] Ibid., 43.

of the gift and of undeconstructible justice, the undeconstructible condition of any deconstruction, to be sure, but a condition that is itself *in deconstruction* and remains, and must remain (this is the injunction) in the disjointure of the *Un-Fug*.[9]

Redetermining dīk as justice, the necessity that lies at the heart of the disjoining that connects intimately the possibility of time to its impossibility, allows for the ever-so-slight trembling within time that allows and enforces the deconstruction of deconstruction in the opening to the other. The ethics hereby revealed to be *of* deconstruction are also *in* deconstruction. Remaining in the present, rather than thinking the presencing of the present as Heidegger would, the radicality of deconstruction would turn on this urgency, an urgency that inevitably signals long waiting.

The coming of the other as that which we open to in remaining in the present urgency of the Un-Fug involves an arrival of advent thought in its adventicity, under what "we have nicknamed here without knowing the messianic,"[10] and which remains an ineffaceable mark of inheritance, should this involve ethical relations at all. This necessarily also involves an openness to evil of precisely the type that it might well be thought that Heidegger never allowed, and thus opened himself to in a different register: "To be 'out of joint,' whether it be present Being or present time, can do harm and do evil, it is no doubt the very possibility of evil. But without the opening of this possibility, there remains, beyond good and evil, only the necessity of the worst."[11]

This attentiveness to the evil that emerges from out of and because of the opening of jointure to disjointure is what motivates Derrida's invention of the term *hauntology*. Whereas Heideggerian thought of being involves the thought of presencing as determinative of time, Derridean thought turns on the trace within each present of the futural memory of finitude as that

---

[9] Derrida, *Specters of Marx,* 28.

[10] Ibid., 28.

[11] Derrida, *Specters of Marx,* 29. See also Gary Banham, "Mourning Satan," in G. Banham and C. Blake, eds., *Evil Spirits: Nihilism and the Fate of Modernity* (Manchester: Manchester University Press, 2000), for an account of the evil caused by forgetting evil. Since this problematic of evil is also directly treated by Heidegger in his reading of Schelling, it is of some note that this essay of Heidegger's has not as yet been treated to an extensive response by Derrida.

which makes possible the other's coming. This distinction permits the reference to the "nickname" of the Messiah in the notion of a time that is not (and this is precisely what is quoted from Benjamin's "Theses on the Philosophy of History") "homogeneous, empty time."

Before turning to the relationship between Derrida and Benjamin in more detail, however, it is first necessary to complete the account of Derrida's relation to Heidegger's treatise "The Anaximander Fragment" by turning to Derrida's classic 1968 essay "Différance."

HEIDEGGERIAN HOPE AND DERRIDEAN AFFIRMATION

In the 1968 essay, Derrida turns to reading "The Anaximander Fragment" in order to address the question about the essence of the present. In doing so, he turns to a part of the essay that is slightly later than the passages discussed in *Specters of Marx*. Re-citing part of this section, we discover the following to be said:

> Presencing itself unnoticeably becomes something present. Represented in the manner of something present, it is elevated above whatever else is present and so becomes the highest being present. As soon as presencing is named it is represented as some present being. Ultimately, presencing as such is not distinguished from what is present: it is taken merely as the most universal or the highest of present beings, thereby becoming one among such beings. The essence of presencing, and with it the distinction between presencing and what is present, remains forgotten. *The oblivion of Being is oblivion of the distinction between Being and beings.*[12]

When presencing comes to language, it does so in the vein of representation. Representation conveys presences rather than presencing, so the coming to representation of presencing is its oblivion as highest presence. The oblivion of presencing in the representation of the present is connected to another cardinal dis-

---

[12] Heidegger, "The Anaximander Fragment," 50.

tinction being lost: the difference between Being and beings. But while the distinction between presencing and the present is lost in forgetting the relation between Being and beings, the oblivion of Being belongs to "the self-veiling essence of Being" and does so in such an essential manner that the dawn of the destiny of Being "rises as the unveiling of what is present in its presencing."[13]

So while the self-oblivion of Being ensures the collapse of the ontological difference as part of the essence of this difference, the distinction between presencing and the present is unveiled in a forgetting of itself. Through this movement, ontotheology is constituted as an orientation to God as the highest presence.

Derrida's responses to these statements in 1968 turn on his thought of the trace. Heidegger stated that "even the early trace" of the distinction between presencing and the present is obliterated when presencing is conceived of as highest presence. In the process of rethinking Heidegger's terms, Derrida simply insists upon this word *trace*. If trace is conceived of as a simulacrum of a present that dislocates itself, then: "[T]he present becomes the sign of the sign, the trace of the trace. It is no longer what every reference refers to in the last analysis. It becomes a function in a structure of generalized reference. It is a trace, and a trace of the erasure of the trace."[14]

Following the clear sense of Heidegger's own account, we now, however, lose what he seemed to wish to keep: a primary reference to presencing as possibility of time. In its place, we have time thought from the impossibility of the present. This impossibility consists in the inability of the present to maintain itself as a presence and to be constituted as that which traces its own erasure. The loss of the presence of the present is the thought of the present itself. This ensures that while erasure is integral to time (and hence to experience), this erasure does not render time unavailable, but makes us aware of it in our finitude as a horizon that lacks boundary.

In a part of "The Anaximander Fragment" that Derrida does not cite either in 1968 or in 1993, Heidegger spoke of how the

---

[13] Ibid.
[14] Derrida, "Differance," 24.

history of Being is gathered in the departure of Being from us. He added that: "The gathering in this departure, as the gathering *(logos)* at the outermost point *(eskhaton)* of its essence hitherto, is the eschatology of Being. As something fateful, Being is itself inherently eschatological."[15] While Heidegger immediately makes clear that this eschatology is not a regional discipline of theology or philosophy, but is to be thought within the history of Being, he still concludes that within this eschatology, as with any other, there is an essential relation to futurity, a relation that is also inherently connected to the past. Thus he states: "If we think within the eschatology of Being, then we must someday anticipate the former dawn in the dawn still to come; today we must learn to ponder this former dawn through what is imminent."[16]

In the recovery of the thought of Being, then, there would be opened an essential futurity. Reconverted into Derrida's terms, it is precisely the eschatology of Heidegger that needs to be questioned. In the final section of the essay on differance, Derrida refers to a Heideggerian hope that he connects to nostalgia for a proper name. Derrida then contrasts this nostalgia for a name that would truly name with an affirmation of that which is beyond all such nostalgia, a commitment to the injunction that emerges from the Un-Fug as that which allows a messianic thought that is not eschatological.

The move beyond Heidegger from within his text follows the pattern of the trace. That which Heidegger wished to cast into oblivion, or to forget, is the primary productivity of forgetting, the oblivion that makes present the present in its absence. The temporality of the messianic epoche would promise itself as that which opens without an archeological structure, but with an essential connection to the futurity of the past as that which makes impossible the present. The difference between Heidegger and Derrida here is small, but it touches the sense of why Derrida is also at once close to and far from Benjamin—as we will discover the same points of connection and disconnection there as apply to the relation between Derrida and Heidegger.

---

[15] Heidegger, "The Anaximander Fragment," 18.
[16] Ibid.

DERRIDA'S DOUBLE RESPONSE TO BENJAMIN

The relation to Benjamin in *Specters of Marx* is surprisingly allusive when it comes to the point of trying to unfold the points of connection and disconnection here. In chapter 2, Derrida refers to Benjamin as enabling us to rethink the relation between weakness and strength precisely in the thought of a *"weak* messianic force," which historical materialism is said to inherit. The footnote that follows this reference makes clear that the filiation between Derrida and Benjamin turns precisely on the latter's thought of a temporality that is heterogeneous, disjointed, and futural. Rapidly condensing the reading of Benjamin's "Theses," we immediately remember the closing sentence of them when, after contrasting the time of soothsaying prophecy with that of Jewish remembrance, Benjamin concludes that the reason why the future is not "homogeneous, empty time" for the Jews is because "every second of time was the strait gate through which the Messiah might enter."[17]

Going back slightly, Benjamin stated the revolutionary potential of the notion of the messianic as "the sign" of a happening, or "a revolutionary chance in the fight for the oppressed past." But how does this chance for the past form the possibility of a revolutionary future? The historical materialist "takes cognizance of it in order to blast a specific life out of the era or a specific work out of the lifework. . . . The nourishing fruit of the historically understood contains time as a precious but tasteless seed."[18] The return to the past as a model for the future was indicated to be the model of revolutionary remembrance in the fourteenth thesis's reference to the French Revolution's recovery of Republican Rome.[19] A past time recovered in the urgency of the present inaugurates a revolutionary relation to the future.

---

[17] Walter Benjamin, "Theses on the Philosophy of History," in Benjamin, *Illuminations,* trans. H. Zohn (London and Sydney: Pimlico, 1970 [1940]), 255.

[18] Ibid., 254.

[19] This fourteenth thesis of Benjamin's is worth contrasting with the opening of Karl Marx, *The Eighteenth Brumaire of Louis Bonaparte,* in K. Marx and F. Engels, *Selected Works in One Volume,* trans. unattributed (Moscow, London, and New York: Lawrence and Wishart, 1968 [1852]). See Derrida's extensive discussion of this latter text precisely from the standpoint of its attempt to avoid spectrality in *Specters of Marx,* 107 n. 19.

The messianic is again related to as a "sign" and through the structure of the present, which latter "comprises the entire history of mankind in an enormous abridgement," and in which "the time of the now" is shot through with chips "of Messianic time." This form of present is not a Heideggerian presencing, but, in its urgency and through its structural relation to a futural energy based on a past remembrance, is part of the constellation of that which Derrida declared "undeconstructible."

If this is so, however, why is it that in his reading of Benjamin's "Critique of Violence" in the essay oft-cited in *Specters of Marx*, "Force of Law," Derrida aligns Benjamin with Heidegger, and, in this alignment, marks an essential divergence from him? Benjamin's early essay "Critique of Violence" (1921) contains a set of cardinal distinctions. In this piece, Benjamin responds with urgency to the political situation of Weimar Germany, and, in doing so, reflects on those who in response either to the First World War or to the Bolshevik Revolution have been driven to question the relationship between law and violence. In the process, Benjamin argues for a conception of law as, in its essence, mythical. Law comes to peoples from without, in the sense that legislation does not cover the cases it applies to, the space for exception always being a matter for sovereign decision, and the criminal, hence, a victim of the nature of power's violence. Law creates crime, as according to Saint Paul, it institutes sin. The freedom that would involve a relation to divinity beyond fate would allow for Benjamin the chance of justice.

These contrasts are then set out in a crucial passage: "If mythic violence is lawmaking, divine violence is law-destroying; if the former sets boundaries, the latter boundlessly destroys them; if mythic violence brings at once guilt and retribution, divine power only expiates; if the former threatens, the latter strikes; if the former is bloody, the latter is lethal without spilling blood."[20] The power of these contrasts resides in the firm relation built here between law and vengeance, the divine and a destruction that liberates. The reference to divine violence is connected with

---

[20] Walter Benjamin, "Critique of Violence," trans. E. Jephcott, in W. Benjamin, *Selected Works,* vol. 1, *1913–1926* (Cambridge, Mass., and London: Belknap Press, 1996 [1921]), 249–50.

an orientation toward Judaism, the reference to mythic violence a clear statement about the Greeks, as is made clear by Benjamin's citation of Greek myths in this text.

Connected to these distinctions is a clear revolutionary politics when Benjamin refers to the occasional breaking of the rule of myth in the present age, and he adds that "revolutionary violence, the highest manifestation of unalloyed violence by man, is possible." This possibility, the openness to which Benjamin wishes to make clear in his incessant critique of the mythic, is a relation to the future through the past sense of a Judaism that is here left very general in form.

Derrida connects the whole of the argumentation underlying this essay point by point with that we have found in "The Anaximander Fragment." In both texts, representational language is taken to be a sign of a fall. This fall is treated explicitly by Benjamin in connection with the critique of parliaments, and, hence, political representation is connected to representational language. Finally, the founding distinction between lawmaking violence and law-sustaining violence is revealed to be unstable in the course of Benjamin's exposition, and to be connected to an instability between mythic and divine that mirrors Heidegger's statement that the oblivion of Being relates to the replacement of presencing by presence. But unlike in the reading of Heidegger, where the motifs of futurity are released from the erasure of metaphysics, this reading of Benjamin consigns the latter to an eschatology that our reading of Heidegger has already given us reasons to suspect.

But is this text of Benjamin's youth so clearly aligned with the motifs of Heidegger and so far removed from the "Theses on the Philosophy of History," as Derrida suggests? There would be many reasons to doubt this. The relation to divine violence is given in a present that, in its urgency and imminence of expectation, forces us to utilize the structural notion of the messianic as Derrida has given it, and as Benjamin transmits it with force later. Connected to this sign of the messianic is a displacement of law. In recognizing law as filled with the power of vengeance, a "turning" is made possible for one who resides within the Un-Fug. Finally, the notion of the "divine" here utilized by Benjamin draws not on ontotheology, but is, instead, a figure in the same way as the messianic is later determined to be.

Why, then, does Derrida's 1989 response to Benjamin necessarily align the latter with Heidegger, when his 1993 address seems to promise a means of separating Benjamin from Heidegger, and even of setting Benjamin against Heidegger? The differences of strategy between the pieces may well be connected to Derrida's redetermination of dīk as justice, even in the wake of Heidegger's well-known reservations about just such a translation. Underlying the difference between divine and mythic violence in Benjamin's "Critique of Violence" is a distinction between law and justice. Law is set against justice as that which is established in the realm of fate, and which can only be understood through the guise of myth. If justice, by contrast, is that which opens the futural relation to the divine, then can it be a coincidence that Derrida should use this same distinction between justice and law, even in interpreting the text by Heidegger that would seem to disallow this move?

Between 1989 and 1993, it would appear that Derrida, having begun by aligning Benjamin with Heidegger, comes to separate them and reunite them in mixing the terminology of their essays. This remixing, which makes possible the understanding of the temporality of the messianic as just, may well, thus, involve a lack of justice to Benjamin, and it is noticeable that in his reading of "Critique of Violence," Derrida states of the last part of this work that his reading cannot claim "to do it justice."[21]

Beyond the opposition between Derrida and Benjamin, and suggesting that the reasons for this opposition are grounded in a blockage between them that goes under the name of Heidegger, we can conclude with what remains to be thought on the basis of this threefold encounter. If, as becomes clear from Derrida's reading of "The Anaximander Fragment," evil emerges from the same structure and the same chance as the messianic, and if, as Benjamin states clearly in "Critique of Violence," there is no clear way of distinguishing between these two possibilities, then what is to prevent our exposure to the worst? There are three answers to this question, but I believe decision between them was to be left open. The answers are:

---

[21] Derrida, "Force of Law," 51.

First, for the Heidegger of "The Anaximander Fragment," the answer would involve a return to thinking that which cannot be thought and would permit a redetermination of action by that which is not an act *(Gelasshenheit).*

Second, for Benjamin the hatred of law would seem to be as vengeful in its essence as the practice of law itself, and leave at best a hope that, in its revolutionary romanticism, could still claim a distinct temporality.

Third, for Derrida a deliberate and strategic "mixing" promiscuously always partakes of the worst in order to discern its arrival. This last, the one that lacks any hope, would remain to haunt.

Between these three, what choice, and who can choose? These would be the questions of imminent urgency that the past has given us to return to the future.

2
Locating Reason in Culture and Gender

7

Birth and the Powers of Horror: Julia Kristeva on Gender, Religion, and Death

Grace M. Jantzen

> Perhaps a possibility of stretching the borders of the nameable beyond the boundaries set by a discourse of methods and ideas: by transposing into signs not so much the experience of a subject as fulcrum of reason, whitewashed analogue of the creating God, as that of a loving subject, an array of constant presences and absences, a dialectic of losses and fullnesses.
>
> JULIA KRISTEVA

IN THESE WORDS, Julia Kristeva explores the religious sensibility of the seventeenth-century mystic Jeanne Guyon, setting her against Descartes, who completed the foundation of secular modernity by the "subordination of passions to thought."[1] In Kristeva's work, the transformation of the West into a secular symbolic is crucial for understanding the modern subject, who, with the loss of religion, no longer has available the "cathartic power" that was part of the central drama of Christianity.[2] Human subjects, she holds (following Freud and Lacan), are constituted by "a series of splittings . . . birth, weaning, separation, frustration, castration." Such splittings are simultaneously essen-

---

[1] Julia Kristeva, *Tales of Love,* trans. Leon S. Roudiez (New York: Columbia University Press, 1987 [1983]), 297.

[2] Julia Kristeva, *Black Sun: Depression and Melancholia,* trans. Leon S. Roudiez (New York: Columbia University Press, 1989 [1987]), 132.

tial for the development of mature autonomy, intensely painful, and psychically complex: each rupture is at once birth and death.

> Because Christianity set that rupture at the very heart of the absolute subject—Christ; because it represented it as a Passion that was the solidary lining of his Resurrection, his glory, and his eternity, it brought to consciousness the essential dramas that are internal to the becoming of each and every subject. It thus endows itself with tremendous cathartic power.[3]

Kristeva's sensitivity to that power leads her back, time after time, to reconsideration of religious themes and figures. Although she does not suppose that we can leap backward into a premodern religious world, she takes religious themes, especially in relation to birth, death, and gender, deeply seriously.[4] In this concern with religion, Kristeva has much in common with other contemporary Continental writers often lumped together as "postmodern," who find in premodern texts and themes resources for destabilizing the hegemonic power of modernity.

One might expect, therefore, that as the works of these thinkers become widely available in English, Anglo–American philosophers of religion would welcome the opportunity to engage with them. Among analytic philosophers of religion, however, this is emphatically not the case. For the most part, the work of Continental thinkers has been met with hostile silence. Instead, Anglo–American analytic philosophers of religion occupy themselves largely with questions of the coherence and logical implications of religious assertions, and with evidence for or against their truth. From their own perspective, this no doubt appears as a defense of the faith (or an attack upon it) and may be undertaken out of deep commitment.[5]

---

[3] Ibid., 132.

[4] See, for example, her wonderfully rich essay "Stabat Mater" and other essays in *Tales of Love;* her analysis of Holbein's "Dead Christ" in *Black Sun;* her comparison of psychoanalysis and religion in *In the Beginning Was Love: Psychoanalysis and Faith,* trans. Arthur Goldhammer (New York: Columbia University Press, 1987 [1985]); and her discussion of sin, sacrifice, and abjection in *Revolution in Poetic Language,* trans. Margaret Waller (New York: Columbia University Press, 1984 [1974]) and in *Powers of Horror: An Essay on Abjection,* trans. Leon S. Roudiez (New York: Columbia University Press, 1982 [1980]).

[5] Cf. Thomas V. Morris, ed., *God and the Philosophers: The Reconciliation of Faith and Reason* (Oxford: Oxford University Press, 1994).

From a Kristevan perspective, however, such preoccupation with truth-claims is already thoroughly secular, part of the "subordination of passion to thought" that, after Descartes, constitutes secular modernity. Although at one level analytic philosophers of religion may be attempting to defend religious claims, at a deeper level, what is happening is a betrayal of religion itself, reducing it to a set of beliefs and values within the boundaries of the nameable, rather than exploring its cathartic power for the development of a mature, loving subject able to negotiate rupture and loss. Even worse, by their steadfast rejection of the passions in favor of objective and impartial reason, and by their refusal to acknowledge the gendered nature of their stance, analytic philosophers are actually (though of course not intentionally) using religion to block the emergence of such subjects.

An analytic philosopher might reply that a Continental approach simply abandons truth and rationality and is not properly philosophical at all. In response, a thinker from a Continental perspective could show that this reply already assumes the narrow model of rationality and philosophy that is at the heart of secular modernity, which is precisely what is in question.[6]

A central theme for Kristeva, in which she confronts "the borders of the nameable" and often resorts to specifically religious motifs in doing so, is the theme of birth and death and the losses and ruptures that these betoken. Questions about death have, of course, also preoccupied analytic philosophers, who, arguably, have used "the subject as fulcrum of reason" to debate the coherence of and evidence for concepts of immortality, resurrection, and the relation of body and soul. But what would it be to consider birth and death not in terms of evidence for truth-claims, but for the purpose of the emergence of "loving subjects": subjects, moreover, who in virtue of that birth and the social constructions through which they emerge, are always already gendered? In what follows, I want to explore this question with

---

[6] For further discussion of the differences and noncommunication between Continental and Anglo-American philosophers of religion, see my "'What's the Difference?' Knowledge and Gender," in *Religious Studies* 32 (1996); and *Becoming Divine: Towards a Feminist Philosophy of Religion* (Manchester: Manchester University Press, 1998). For an illustration of it in action, see the exchange between Paul Helm and myself in *Religious Studies* 37 (2001).

the help of Kristeva's insights, which I will both commend and critique.

A DEATHLY SYMBOLIC

The Western symbolic has been shaped by a preoccupation with death and other worlds, and has had much less interest in natality than in mortality as constitutive of human persons. This imbalance is shared by analytic and Continental philosophers, though a few of the latter, notably Luce Irigaray, are recognizing the significance of natality as a category of the symbolic as well as an existential reality.[7] In Kristeva's writings also birth sometimes disrupts the deathly symbolic, most strikingly in "Stabat Mater," where the right-hand column of text, a disquisition on Mary at the foot of Jesus' cross, is destabilized by the left-hand column, which is a poetic evocation of Kristeva giving birth to her son. I shall argue, however, that even in Kristeva's writings, death is much more central than birth; and while I shall lift up her insights over against the preoccupations of analytic philosophers, I shall suggest that for the development of loving subjects, the imaginary of natality opens fresh possibilities.

From the time of the Homeric writings, *mortal* has been a synonym for *human:* humankind, in specific contrast to the immortal gods, is defined by death. Moreover, repeatedly in the Western tradition death is portrayed, paradoxically, as the source of life. In Plato, the true philosopher is the one who "makes dying his profession": it is by living "with one foot in the grave," escaping as much as possible the demands and distractions of the body and its senses, that the lover of truth must live.[8] Heidegger, at the end of modernity, is still saturated with a symbolic of death. It is death, he holds, that makes authentic life possible, since it is the

---

[7] Luce Irigaray, *An Ethics of Sexual Difference,* trans. Carolyn Burke and Gillian C. Gill (London: Athlone, 1993 [1984]); and Irigaray, *Sexes and Genealogies,* trans. Gillian C. Gill (New York: Columbia University Press, 1993 [1987]).

[8] Plato, *The Collected Dialogues of Plato,* eds. Edith Hamilton and Huntington Cairns (Princeton: Princeton University Press, 1961), *Phaedo* 67e.

recognition that I will not live forever that frees me from constantly looking over my shoulder worrying about what other people might think about what I do.[9] Humans are beings toward death.

One way of becoming acutely aware of the extent to which preoccupation with death saturates the Western cultural tradition is to take seriously the juxtaposition with birth suggested in Kristeva's essay. Where are the meditations on natality? Virtually every major philosopher in the Western tradition at some point thinks long and hard about death, often in ways that profoundly affect their philosophical position. Yet it is rare indeed to find careful consideration of natality, either as existential reality or as conceptual category, even though, arguably, the fact that we are natals is as significant for our ontology, epistemology, and moral agency as the fact that we are mortals.

In Christendom, too, death has a central place. The death of Jesus is its pivotal event, celebrated in every Eucharist when the broken body and blood of Christ are offered "for eternal life," as the remedy not only for sin but also for mortality. The rite of baptism, by which one enters the church in the first place, is again an enactment of death. To be sure, it is also symbolic of rising to new life; but this new life is not a celebration of our natality, our bodily, gendered connection with this world, but rather its overcoming. The new birth, in Christendom, is a new birth "not of blood nor of the will of the flesh," not from the body of a woman or "of the will of man, but of God" (John 1:13).

This world is regularly portrayed as a place of exile in which we are at best pilgrims seeking a way to a heavenly city; this flesh is to be mortified (literally "put to death") to free the spirit for immortality. It can be argued that this preoccupation with death and other worlds is a travesty of Christian teaching, with its doctrines of creation and incarnation; and certainly alternative voices can be found lifting up life and flourishing. But that Christendom is deeply entangled in a symbolic of death and has enacted that symbolic upon countless bodies can hardly be denied.

---

[9] Martin Heidegger, *Being and Time,* trans. John Macquarrie and Edward Robinson (Oxford: Blackwell, 1962 [1927]), 307.

A GENDERED GENEALOGY

Now, within the Western tradition both secular and religious, death is regularly treated as a biological fact. Full of significance though it is, it is ultimately a matter of physiology. The discourses of psychoanalysis from Freud onward have done much to perpetuate such a naturalization of death. Kristeva herself largely falls in with this notion, as will become clear. Yet already it is possible to recognize, from the thumbnail sketches of philosophers and of Christendom, that death has gone through significant variations in the Western symbolic. Far from being static, the shifts in the contours of the symbolic of death are markers for changes in what can count as human. In this respect, "death" shouts for the same sort of treatment that Foucault gave to "sex." Both appear initially as sheer biological givens. Yet without denying the physical realities of either sex or death, each of them can be shown to have a genealogy: they are social constructions, and the constructions have no fixed essence.

Moreover, as Foucault demonstrated, every genealogical shift is also a reconfiguration of power; and from a feminist perspective it is clear (though Foucault did not make much of it) that such configurations of power are always already gendered. I suggest that taking this Foucauldian perspective on death with the seriousness it deserves changes the way in which we can read the deadly symbolic of the West, in a manner utterly different from the evaluation of truth-claims about immortality that occupy analytic philosophers of religion.

In the Western tradition death is conceptually linked with women, and true manliness is linked with true mastery of death. Thus for example in the Homeric writings, Odysseus achieves immortal fame by conquering the barren sea, the sea that is itself female and that contains the female monsters and mermaids whose seductive pleasures and dangers he must overcome.[10] At the other end of Western culture, Heidegger celebrates the heroic

---

[10] Adriana Cavarero, *In Spite of Plato: A Feminist Rewriting of Ancient Philosophy,* trans. Serena Anderlini-D'Onofris and Áine O'Healey (Cambridge: Polity Press, 1995), 20–21; Seth L. Schein, "Female Representation and Interpreting the Odyssey," in *The Distaff Side: Representing the Female in Homer's Odyssey,* ed. Beth Cohen (Oxford University Press, 1995), 69.

poet who goes out into the abyss, risking its dangers, to recover a trace of the divine;[11] but as Irigaray points out, the abyss, like Plato's cave, is reminiscent of both womb and tomb, so that the manly heroism of the philosopher-poet is the mastery of female-gendered death.[12] And all through the history of the West, the teachings of Christendom inculcate the mortification of the flesh, where "flesh" is symbolically linked with body, reproduction, and sin through Eve, the mother of us all, who introduced sin and death into the world.

The discourse of psychoanalysis, within which Kristeva writes, appropriates and reinforces the symbolic in which women are metonymically constructed as death. Kristeva's own work is ambiguous. On the one hand she accepts and even deepens the Freudian-Lacanian trajectory of death as female; but on the other hand, the eruption of birth, as in the left-hand column of "Stabat Mater," offers resources for thinking otherwise. I shall argue that these resources can be appropriated for the development of loving subjects well beyond that which Kristeva herself does; and that pursuing a logic of natality destabilizes the subject as fulcrum of reason, with its epistemology of empirical objects beloved of analytic philosophers of religion.

DEATH DRIVE, DEATH WORK, DEAD OBJECTS

Within the writings of psychoanalysis, it is, I suggest, important to distinguish between three related aspects of the discussion of death. First there is the death *drive, Thanatos,* contrasted by Freud with *Eros* and elaborated by Lacan in terms of aggressivity. Second, there is death *work,* the work of separation and mourning that is necessary for our own individuation and the losses that we have to bear. Third, there are objects (or, in Kris-

---

[11] Martin Heidegger, *Poetry, Language, Thought,* trans. Albert Hofstadter (New York: Harper and Row, 1971), 131.

[12] Luce Irigaray, *The Forgetting of Air in Martin Heidegger,* trans. Mary Beth Mader (Austin: University of Texas Press, 1999), 37; see also my chapter "'Barely by a Breath . . .': Irigaray on Rethinking Religion," in *The Religious: Blackwell Companion to Postmodern Philosophy,* ed. John D. Caputo (Oxford: Blackwell, 2002).

teva's terms, abjects) that confront us with death and to which we react with revulsion, separating ourselves as much as possible from such indicators of mortality and placing ourselves in a space created by establishing boundaries that keep death away. Yet these three aspects are ambiguous and sometimes work against one another; for example, our revulsion at "dead" objects is simultaneously a fascination with them in the impulses of our own death drive.

Now, in Kristeva's exploration of religion, she finds that it provided a way of dealing with these different aspects of death. She accepts, in broad terms, Freud's account of the foundation of religion in the murder of the father by his sons out of sexual jealousy and then contrition, so that the slaughtered father is set up as a god:[13] like Freud, she omits to ask where the women were in all this and either treats them as passive victims or ignores them altogether. Nevertheless, she affirms with Freud that religion—specifically Christianity—enabled men to deal with their death drive by reenacting it in ritual, thus freeing them to sublimate their aggressive impulses. Moreover, by treating the death of Christ as substitutionary, thereby affecting an imaginary identification, Kristeva holds that it becomes possible to deal with separation, loss, and mourning: in other words, to proceed with the death *work*.

> On the basis of that identification . . . man is provided with a powerful symbolic device that allows him to experience death and resurrection even in his physical body. . . . Here as elsewhere, *death*—that of the old body making room for the new, death to oneself for the sake of glory, death of the old man for the sake of the spiritual body—lies at the centre of the experience. . . . The implicitness of love and consequently of reconciliation and forgiveness . . . [gives] it an aura of glory and unwavering hope for those who believe. Christian faith appears then as an antidote to hiatus and depression.[14]

And finally, in its boundaries between what is pure and impure, good and evil, clean and unclean, religion offers a way to deal

---

[13] Sigmund Freud, "Totem and Taboo," in *The Origins of Religion: The Pelican Freud Library*, vol. 13, trans. James F. Strachey (Harmondsworth, England: Penguin, 1985 [1913]); Kristeva, *Powers of Horror*, 56f.

[14] Kristeva, *Black Sun*, 134.

with abjection, setting up identifications and exclusions whereby one can constitute oneself as a subject.

I shall return to this theme of abjection in a moment; but it is worth pausing to note how different a world this is from that inhabited by analytic philosophers of religion. If they deal with themes of incarnation and atonement at all, they do so in terms of the conceptual coherence of creedal statements, possibly dismissing a psychoanalytic account of religion as reductionist. The ways in which religion works to enable or inhibit subject formation is not taken to be of philosophical interest. Boundaries are drawn around what counts as proper philosophy, in a manner highly reminiscent of the boundaries that exclude the abject, enabling the maintenance of the "clean and proper body."[15] But if that proper body of pure philosophy is constituted by the abjection of the loving subject, how could analytic philosophy possibly be anything other than death dealing in its turn? I shall return to this.

CHRIST'S CORPSE

Kristeva uses the work of Mary Douglas to explain her account of how a subject or a society constitutes itself by designating certain things as unclean, as filth. Defilement is the other side of social rationality, against which the pure can emerge. Thus there are strong social prohibitions against the things that are taken as defiling: in our society, for example, vomit, shit, menstrual blood, corpses. These are kept carefully out of sight and, as much as possible, out of knowledge. We all shit, of course, and between puberty and menopause women menstruate, but to have to talk about these bodily functions, or for signs of them to appear on our clothing, would be highly embarrassing in Western modernity, and their smells are deemed disgusting.

I say "in Western modernity" because there is an important historical dimension to the abject. This is not the place to go into detail, but it is well known to those who study what is often called the "history of manners," or, indeed, to ethnographers of

---

[15] Kristeva, *Powers of Horror*, 65.

so-called primitive cultures, that what we in the West today find revolting has not been found so always and everywhere. In England until the seventeenth century, judging by Pepys's diary, men and women even of the upper classes did not necessarily deem it essential to have privacy for bodily functions such as urinating or defecating. Sexual intercourse would often be in sight and hearing of others: the history of architecture shows how houses gradually changed from having communal sleeping quarters for family, friends, servants, and visitors to the Victorian four-poster, curtained bed in a separate "master" bedroom.

Similar changes can be traced about such matters as using one's own cutlery and crockery rather than reaching fingers into a common pot; and again about dying and giving birth, which regularly occurred at home with family and friends in attendance. The changes that have taken place have often been described as a growth of civilization,[16] but they could perhaps better be seen as a genealogy of the abject. Be that as it may, in our society at least, the corpse, the dead body, is paradigmatically abject, that from which I must be separated in order to be a living subject. The sight and the smell of a corpse fills us with horror and loathing.

But then, how shall we deal with the dead body of Christ? This is the very body with which it was necessary to identify in order to negotiate our death work. Yet it is also utterly abject. If we take it seriously, it will generate revulsion and fear. One response, when we see the implications of this, is to pass quickly over to the resurrection, the teaching that Christ's body did not stay dead. But such a move is obviously inadequate. It is inadequate theologically, because even a theology that holds a doctrine of literal resurrection does not see the death of Jesus as a mistake, quickly overcome by divine intervention. It is inadequate in terms of the Western symbolic, in which the ritual reenactment of the broken body and blood of Christ continues. And it is inadequate in psychoanalytic terms, because our death work cannot be accomplished through denial or evasion.

Kristeva explores the implications of a full encounter with the

---

[16] See Norbert Elias, *The Civilizing Process,* trans. Edmund Jephcott (Oxford: Blackwell, 1974).

cross of Christ in her essay "Holbein's Dead Christ,"[17] in which she takes as her point of reference the painting by Hans Holbein the Younger, "The Body of the Dead Christ in the Tomb."[18] The painting is a long, low rectangle, only twelve inches high. The life-size corpse lies on a cloth-draped slab, rigid, battered, eyes glassy open. This body is utterly dead; there is no suggestion of resurrection or immortality. It lies there "without any prospect toward heaven."[19] The only thing that seems to escape the frame is the right hand, where one long finger stretches forward as if putting down a marker: this is where it ends. The stiff, cold body offers no comfort. It is a chilling, horrific rendition.

Art historians have long discussed why Holbein might have painted the picture as he did, how it fits in with his other work, and how it relates to paintings by other artists and to the wider cultural climate. Kristeva considers it specifically in relation to the Renaissance and its emergent humanism. If Christendom had taught the importance of identification with Christ, here is a vision of what such identification would come to.

> Christ's dereliction is here at its worst: forsaken by the Father, he is apart from all of us. Unless Holbein . . . wanted to include us, humans, foreigners, spectators that we are. . . . Does Holbein forsake us, as Christ, for an instant, had imagined himself forsaken? Or does he, on the contrary, invite us to change the Christly tomb into a living tomb, to participate in the painted death and thus include it in our own life, in order to live with it and make it live?[20]

Kristeva is suggesting how this painting can facilitate our own death work. The life she writes of is a life without illusions or consolations: this death is not going to be canceled out in a happy-ever-after world beyond. Nevertheless, facing the bleakness of this prospect and recognizing it as our own enables a maturity that does not displace our death work on to others in depression or melancholy, but frees us for the tasks of living. Thus Kristeva writes that Holbein's vision is

---

[17] Kristeva, *Black Sun*, 107–38.
[18] The painting was executed in 1522 and is in the possession of the Basel Kunstmuseum.
[19] Kristeva, *Black Sun*, 113.
[20] Ibid.

of man [*sic*] subject to death, man embracing Death, absorbing it into his very being, integrating it not as a condition for glory or as a consequence of a sinful nature but as the ultimate essence of his desacralised reality, which is the foundation of a new dignity. . . . Because he acknowledges his folly and looks death in the face— but perhaps also because he faces his mental risks, the risks of psychic death—man achieves a new dimension. Not necessarily that of atheism but definitely that of a disillusioned, serene, and dignified stance.[21]

The embrace of death as my inevitable end is a precondition for my development as a mature, loving subject.

THE GENDER OF ABJECTION

Kristeva's reflections on Holbein's painting and its implications for what it is to be a mortal subject shows, by contrast, the shallow consolations of analytic philosophy of religion, with its attempts to grasp at evidences for immortality. Kristeva's theory enables us to confront our own end and come to terms with it with dignity, rather than evade it or lash out in violence to others because we cannot deal with this ultimate alterity in ourselves. Whatever our subsequent relation to Christendom, it can hardly be business as usual after an in-depth encounter with our own death, the death of Christ, the death of God. How we will choose to bear the dead God in the world is a further question, to which there can be more than one answer; but it seems to me unlikely that preoccupation with probabilities of immortality will be one of them.

Nevertheless, in Kristeva's account we have yet another re-inscription of the deathly symbolic of Western culture. It is death that gives me my life, confrontation and embrace of death that founds serenity and dignity. What has happened to birth in all this? How is it that it is never mentioned? As important as it is to deal with our mortality, both as philosophical category and as existential reality, what about the fact that we are *natals:* indeed, that our natality is a precondition of everything else about us, not

---

[21] Ibid., 118–19.

excepting death? Moreover, how is it that Kristeva (and many others who use a psychoanalytic approach) assimilates mental or psychic risks to death? Might it be that this assimilation is connected to the omission of birth?

As a way into these questions, I propose to return to Kristeva's understanding of the abject, that which I expel from myself and keep on the far side of a boundary in order to constitute myself as a subject. Kristeva suggests as examples of the abject (in Western culture) things for which we have particular loathing, sometimes unique to an individual—some people cannot bear the skin on custard—but more often general: vomit, sewage, a piece of filth, above all a corpse. But the reason it is abject is not that it is dirty or full of germs (neither of which is true of the skin on custard, for example), but rather because it does not conform to rigid boundaries between what is inside and outside: "It is not lack of cleanliness or health that causes abjection but what disturbs identity, system, order. What does not respect borders, positions, rules. The in-between, the ambiguous, the composite."[22]

Thus the abject both is and is not a part of me: like vomit, it connects with my viscera and is violently expelled. Because the abject is so intimately connected with my self-constitution as a subject, it is simultaneously fascinating and repulsive: we are horrified by the sight and stench of a corpse, and yet we look. In the corpse, "I behold the breaking down of a world that has erased its borders: fainting away. The corpse . . . is the utmost of abjection. It is death infecting life. Abject. It is something rejected from which one does not part, from which one does not protect oneself as from an object. Imaginary uncanniness and real threat, it beckons to us and ends up engulfing us."[23]

Kristeva differentiates between two types of threat to the boundaries of identity: those that threaten from without, and those that threaten from within. At a societal level, examples of the former are "excrement and its equivalents (decay, infection, disease, corpse, etc.)," while menstrual blood is an example of the latter, because "it threatens the relationship between the sexes" and "the identity of each sex in the face of sexual differ-

---

[22] Kristeva, *Powers of Horror,* 4.
[23] Ibid., 4.

ence."[24] Semen, however, though it also belongs "to the borders of the body," Kristeva asserts has "no polluting value."[25]

But here the question shouts for attention: Why not? Why should there be such a distinction between menstrual blood and semen? Kristeva does not say; but, on her own terms, the response must be that menstrual blood is perceived as threatening to identity and semen is not. But then a new question emerges: To *whom* is it threatening (or not)? Exactly whose identity is at stake here? If the abject is repulsive precisely because it threatens to engulf, who is it that feels such fear—probably unconscious—at menstrual blood but not at semen? It is certainly not the bleeding woman. On the contrary, far from her identity as a woman being threatened or put at risk, the onset of her menses actually confirms it, as semen confirms a man's masculinity. What quickly becomes obvious is that it is *men* who are threatened by menstrual blood and not by semen: the abject is thus constituted in Kristeva's writings from a masculinist perspective.[26]

Kristeva closely follows Freud in his social application of the Oedipus complex, in which a boy must separate from his mother and overcome his hatred and jealousy for his father. In her essay "From Filth to Defilement,"[27] there are frequent echoes of "Totem and Taboo" and explicit discussions of Oedipus in the context of abjection. It has been frequently pointed out, starting with Freud himself, that the pattern of struggle as Freud explained it was an account of *male* psychosexual development, and *patriarchal* society. Kristeva takes this over without comment about its gendered nature. She thus represents the splitting and separation from the mother in terms of a masculine subject, without acknowledging that she is doing so.

She briefly considers anthropologists' accounts of various societies: the Gidjingali, the Nuer, the Bemba, and the Enga; but then she moves to generalizations and even uses the first-person

---

[24] Ibid., 71.
[25] Ibid.
[26] See my chapter "'Death, Then, How Could I Yield to It?' Kristeva's Mortal Visions," in Morny Joy et al., eds., *Religion in French Feminism* (London: Routledge, 2001).
[27] Kristeva, *Powers of Horror,* 56–89.

pronoun, *I*, in the description. Since she is, after all, a woman, this compounds the confusion. Thus, for example, she writes that "fear of the archaic mother turns out to be essentially fear of her generative power. It is this power, a dreaded one, that patrilineal filiation has the burden of subduing."[28] As soon as we ask who exactly experiences this fear and dread of generative power, the unacknowledged gender assumptions emerge: it is certainly not girls or women who have this dread. Again, comparing two tribes with different prohibitions, she says:

> Is that parallel sufficient to suggest that defilement reveals, at the same time as an attempt to throttle matrilineality, an attempt at separating the speaking being from his body in order that the latter accede to the status of clean and proper body, that is to say, non-assimilable, uneatable, abject? It is only at such a cost that the body is capable of being defended, protected—and also, eventually, sublimated. Fear of the uncontrollable generative mother repels me from the body; I give up cannibalism because abjection (of the mother) leads me toward respect for body of the other, my fellow man, my brother.[29]

Again, who is this "I" and "me"? If Kristeva is speaking in her own voice, then we have again the implausible scenario of a woman abjecting her own sexual identity in fear of the generative power of women. The suspicion must be that she is ventriloquizing a male voice, taking up a male subject position with her "fellow man."

Whatever may be said of Kristeva's subject position here, it becomes clear that abjection is strongly gendered in her writing. Ultimately it is the female body that is represented as abject: the body that bleeds, the body that gives birth. Moreover, it is the (boy's) separation from his mother's body that is represented as death work: it is violence to his own desire for unity with her, desire that must be overcome and mourned. In psychoanalytic writings, furthermore, it is this separation from the (abject) mother that lies at the root of much male aggressivity and actual violence against women.[30] That this is an accurate description of

---

[28] Ibid., 77.

[29] Ibid., 78–79.

[30] See Martha Reineke, *Sacrificed Lives: Kristeva on Women and Violence* (Bloomington: Indiana University Press, 1997).

much of Western culture is not in doubt. My point, rather, is that Kristeva (like Freud and Lacan) naturalizes and reinscribes this description, whereas it needs to be challenged at its roots. Becoming aware of its implicit gender assumptions opens the way for such a challenge.

In particular, I suggest that there are a series of identifications that need to be brought into the open and disaggregated. First, there is the assimilation of abjection and woman/mother. Second, there is the assimilation of separation with death. The first I have already discussed; the second I will come to in the final section. What I want to emphasize before proceeding, however, is that if these two assimilations are made, then woman is metonymically linked with death. That comes as no surprise in the Western symbolic, where women are conceptually linked with bodies, reproduction, temporality, and the earth; while men are linked with the mind, rationality, the eternal, and God. It is disappointing, however, to find it again in Kristeva, who in many other ways challenges conventions, but in this respect reinforces them. In her efforts toward the development of loving subjects, these linkages, I believe, must be uncoupled. In the final section of this paper, I shall show how taking birth into account offers a shift in this symbolic: not all separations are death, nor is abjection the right category for the maternal, as I shall argue.

RIGID OBJECTS AND SLIMY OBJECTS

First, however, I want to circle back to the abjection at work among analytic philosophers. They do not discuss abjection, of course, but I believe that some of the same assumptions are present, and that it is important that they should be exposed. The crucial starting point is that in relation to epistemology, objects of investigation are, in modernity, thought of as inert, mechanical, lifeless. Even when philosophers and scientists study living things—plants, animals, human bodies, genes—from the late seventeenth century onward, the model of mechanism has taken hold, with the knowing subject accumulating data or evidence about the object of knowledge.[31] This shift into the epistemology of modernity represented a scientific change, but it betokened a religious change as well. The secularisation process was a process of the removal of God from the world. This removal effected changes both in how the world and its objects would henceforth be understood, and in what religion became in modernity. Whereas in the medieval period there had been an organicist conception of nature, "nature as alive, as part of God's domain,"[32] now the objects of the world were increasingly seen as lifeless and mechanical. A favorite model was the Strasbourg clock, which looked alive but inside was filled with cunning springs and coils that worked the mechanism.[33]

God, by contrast, was removed to the heavens, leaving the earth to pursue its own course. The strongest form of this position was known as Deism, but even those who rejected full-scale Deism were willing to let scientific investigation proceed as though that which was under investigation had been mechanical, lifeless. An epistemology based on sympathy was discarded in favor of measurement and calculation; and *enthusiast* (literally "filled with God") became a term of abuse. The world was figured as a world of dead objects, inert, passive, waiting to be mastered by the masculine mind. This model of a roughly Lockian epistemology is in many respects still with us; it is thus highly revealing that many analytic philosophers of religion look to science as their model for knowledge.[34]

These are broad brush strokes, which I have filled in and nuanced elsewhere.[35] What I am after here is the observation that it is precisely when the object is rendered lifeless and mechanical that the abject is rendered fluid. That which calls forth revulsion

[31] See Steven Shapin, *The Scientific Revolution* (Chicago: University of Chicago Press, 1996); Jonathan Sawday, *The Body Emblazoned: Dissection and the Human Body in Renaissance Culture* (London: Routledge, 1995).

[32] Sandra Harding, *The Science Question in Feminism* (Ithaca: Cornell University Press, 1986), 113.

[33] Shapin, *The Scientific Revolution,* 34–36.

[34] See Richard Swinburne, "Intellectual Autobiography," in *Reason and Christian Religion: Essays in Honour of Richard Swinburne,* ed. Alan Padgett (Oxford: Clarendon Press, 1994).

[35] See my article "Before the Rooster Crows: The Betrayal of Knowledge in Modernity," in *Literature and Theology* 15 (1999).

to the point of violence is that which does *not* behave as dead, inert, passive. It seeps and flows; it is like a living thing in its unrefusable demands; it does not have sharp edges and clearly defined boundaries. And yet it is the *abject,* which behaves like a living thing, that is figured as involved with the death work, while the *object,* which is lifeless, is its other. If I am right in suggesting that the genealogy of the abject is reciprocal with the genealogy of the object, then in modernity we have a deep irony: the object is figured as dead, while the abject, whose ultimate instance is the corpse, is lifelike in its fluidity.

Now, this is initially puzzling on several counts. First, as we have seen, the process of abjection is, according to Kristeva, that which enables me to reject or eliminate death from my living self, to do my death work and individuate my own clean and proper body. But now it looks as though that very work of abjection, by rendering the body a bounded, definable, solid object, surreptitiously figures it as dead: the very thing that is most horrifying to this imaginary. Second, the abject, as we have seen, is in modernity symbolically female. Yet it has been frequently and cogently argued that the material world and material objects are, in modernity, *also* figured female, as passive objects for male penetration and mastery.[36] In this symbolic, the solid, hard, rigid object-body corresponds to masculinist self-perception against the leaky, penetrable bodies of women. How shall this be reconciled?

I suggest that from a feminist perspective, these puzzles can be resolved. Throughout the Western tradition, the body and reproduction have been symbolically linked with the female, while the male is linked with mind, spirit, God. The godlike mind is the knower and master of the female/body/object.[37] But of course men also have bodies. Particularly in a virulently homophobic cultural context, however, men must deny the symbolic linkage of their own bodies with those of the female, must constitute

---

[36] Harding, *The Science Question in Feminism;* Val Plumwood, *Feminism and the Mastery of Nature* (London: Routledge, 1993); Carolyn Merchant, *The Death of Nature: Women, Ecology, and the Scientific Revolution* (New York: Harper and Row, 1980).

[37] See my book *Becoming Divine: Towards a Feminist Philosophy of Religion,* ch. 2.

themselves as impenetrable and solid. Thus, in this respect the male body is set as an object in opposition to the female abject. On the other hand, qua body as opposed to mind, the male body takes its place among the other objects of this world, whose passions and "involuntary movements" must be mastered just as the female body must be mastered by the male mind. Only so will the male be a "clean and proper" self. The result is the permanent instability of the male body in a masculinist culture: it is simultaneously (hard) object and (fluid) abject. It is also permanently ambivalent toward death: always already a mechanistic lifeless thing, even while constituting itself as alive, as opposed to a corpse. If this suggestion is anywhere near correct, then it also goes some way toward explaining the intense (male) preoccupation with death in modernity—a preoccupation that, however, is heavily overdetermined and has long historical roots—and its easy eruption into gendered violence. The calculation of the probabilities of immortality can be seen as a surreptitious reassurance of masculinity, even as the horror at Christ's corpse is a signal of its undoing.

Loving Subjects

If this account offers some insight into the implicit symbolic of analytic philosophy of religion and its resistance to Continental and psychoanalytical perspectives, however, it does not yet deal with Kristeva's assimilation of abjection to the maternal, and separation to death. To find a way of thinking otherwise, I suggest that it is important to remember the extent to which Kristeva shares in the deathly symbolic of the West; and as a countermeasure to that deathly symbolic I suggest that we reconsider birth, a concept that has been repressed in Western culture. The point is not to set up yet another binary for the subject as fulcrum of reason, but to listen to what has been silenced and enable the becoming of loving subjects who can recognize both death *and* birth. If we think of the categories in which Kristeva describes the abject, birth would seem a paradigmatic case. Yet it is not. When we see *why* it is not, we also begin to uncouple some of the assimilations of the deathly symbolic and find a starting point for a new imaginary.

Crucial to abjection is the disturbance of identity, the transgression of boundaries and disrespect of the "borders, positions, rules. The in-between, the ambiguous, the composite."[38] What could be a better description of pregnancy? As the months proceed from conception, the pregnant woman has her identity increasingly disturbed: at first she is simply herself with a fertilized ovum, but as the fetus develops through quickening and toward birth she is increasingly composite, ambiguous, herself and not herself. A growing fetus has no respect for borders or positions; it can be counted on to kick and wriggle just when the pregnant woman most needs to rest. From being one, the woman literally becomes two. And yet this is not psychosis. Although pregnancy and having a child produce new psychological states, some of which may be difficult to deal with, the disruption of a woman's identity can, at another level, if the pregnancy and the child are wanted, also be a deep fulfillment of her identity.

My point is not to romanticize motherhood: an unwanted pregnancy can be deeply traumatic, and even a desired one is often troublesome. But what I do want to insist on is that although pregnancy and giving birth to a child literally split the woman in two, this change from a unified self into two separate selves is not abjection. The fetus, and later the baby, is not loathed but loved; there is protectiveness, not revulsion. Birth faces down the powers of horror and uncouples the link between abjection and the maternal.

Moreover, the fluids that Kristeva associates with abjection are much in evidence, from the vomiting of morning sickness through the water and slime and blood and shit of birth, to the dribbling, incontinent, wrinkled little person who arrives covered in mucus and blood—and yet is utterly beloved. Unlike any of the examples of abjection that Kristeva discusses, although associated with and literally covered in many of them, a new baby is, in the best case, welcome and precious. Nor should we think that this is somehow related to the fact that the infant, once washed clean of the slime of birth, is after all a solid object: we can see

---

[38] Kristeva, *Powers of Horror*, 4.

this by considering how different it is from a corpse. A baby is far softer, far less rigid, far less object-like. Yet it is the corpse, not the baby, that evokes the powers of horror.

But if thinking about birth destabilizes the symbolic that connects the female, especially the maternal, with abjection, is that link not reinstated when we consider, from the point of view of the child, the separation from its mother that must take place if it is to become a subject? It is this separation, of course, upon which psychoanalytic theory has focused, the split from the desired mother and the attendant mourning and death work for the child. Again, however, I want to suggest that, while the work of separation is painful, the assimilation of separation to death is one-sided and highly misleading. If all separation is death, then it becomes impossible to distinguish between separations that, though painful, are well done and life-giving, and those that are devastating and destructive in their effects.

And yet in practice, this distinction is enormously important in dealing with children. Parents usually try their best to help them effect the stages of their separation in a way that enables the development of loving subjects; they try not to bang doors shut so that the only way to separate is indeed like death. Not all parents try, and not all who try succeed: again, I don't want to romanticize parenthood. Nevertheless, the separations and losses attendant upon growing up are more likely to produce loving subjects if the separations are *not* horrific or assimilated to death and abjection, and the distinction should not be erased.

The same is true of other separations and losses that we must deal with throughout our lives: the end of a marriage or partnership, the end of analysis or therapy, even the end of a student's degree program involves loss and perhaps pain, yet these are necessary and life-giving endings that can enable new beginnings. They can be destructive and death-dealing, but they need not be: if we make the assumption from the outset that separation is assimilated to death, we foreclose the possibility of conducting these separations in ways that enable the flourishing of loving subjects.

Not only does Kristeva link separation with death, she links it with murder.[39] For her, the paradigm case is again the develop-

---

[39] Again, this linkage is shared by many psychoanalytic writers.

ment of a child into its own subjectivity. She writes, for instance: "For man and for woman the loss of the mother is a biological and psychic necessity, the first step on the way to becoming autonomous. *Matricide is our vital necessity*."[40] In a culture or a family where this is hindered, depression or melancholia is the result, "putting to death of the self . . . instead of matricide."[41] The choice therefore is either murder or suicide, "to kill or to kill oneself."[42]

But surely this is an assimilation too far. Not all separations are deaths, and not all deaths are violent. To characterize the development of autonomy as matricide, with suicide as the only alternative, closes the opportunity to ponder different *ways* of such development, ways that do not include killing or violence, but rather reciprocal generosity and love, changing and maturing the relationship rather than ending it. This may well be difficult and painful, but it need not be uniformly violent.

Of course, it could be retorted that in using the language of death and murder, Kristeva, like other psychoanalytic writers, is using metonymically grounded hyperbole, the better to make her point. But while allowance must be made for this, my suggestion is that such a rhetorical strategy deflects attention from the urgent need to distinguish between death-dealing and life-enhancing *modes* of separation. Yet learning *how* to part, *how* to negotiate our separations and bereavements, even learning how to die is part of our development as loving subjects: violence is not a helpful paradigm, but rather an indication that things have not gone well. I believe that by a one-sided focus on death and violence and a neglect of birth as a philosophical and psychoanalytic category, the creativity, love, potentiality, and capacity for growth and flourishing that are characteristic of new life are ignored rather than encouraged. Yet it is precisely these that foster the development of loving subjects.

And religion? It has been a constant theme of psychoanalytic writers that religion both contains and perpetuates psychic involvement with death, a theme that is strongly reinforced by

---

[40] Kristeva, *Black Sun,* 27 (emphasis mine).
[41] Ibid., 28.
[42] Ibid., 80.

awareness of the investment of Christendom in the deathly symbolic of the West. Certainly the strategies and preoccupations of analytic philosophers of religion offer very little grounds for hope. I believe that if religion is to have a role in the formation of loving subjects, it will need to focus much more on birth, on natality as the source of creativity and potential, not a birth that sets aside our bodily beginnings, but precisely our bodily birth from our mothers, always already sexuate, in community, connected to the web of life and to the earth. Natality, I believe, opens a gap that enables us to think otherwise, to explore new possibilities of thinking and living. It is up to those of us who are trying to find better ways of doing philosophy of religion to lead the way.

8

Ineffable Knowledge and Gender[1]

Pamela Sue Anderson

INTRODUCTION

WHO DOES *Continental* philosophy of religion? The received view is that Anglo-American philosophers do *philosophy of religion.* Yet increasingly, contemporary philosophers and some theologians would reply "Jacques Derrida" to this opening question. What makes Derrida's philosophy Continental? What topic in philosophy of religion does Derrida consider? I hope to give some indirect answers to these questions. Instead of looking directly at Derrida, I choose to focus my attention on the nature of an exchange at the interface of what have been labeled "Continental" and "analytic" philosophies. I will focus on an example that makes a similar distinction, but uses the adjective *conceptual* rather than analytic to describe one Oxford philosopher who endeavors to "argue with Derrida." This change in a label makes an important difference, philosophically, to understanding this particular exchange between contemporary philosophers. My example intends to help us approach Continental philosophy at the margins of its discourse. I also intend to approach my topic—ineffable knowledge—from the edge of the framework of tradi-

---

[1] This title reflects two of the main concerns from my plenary paper, "Desiring Infinitude: Ineffable Knowledge in Continental Perspective," given at the Continental Philosophy of Religion conference, St. Martin's College, Lancaster, England, 19 July 2000. The original was far too long to publish as one article, so I divided the material into two parts. For the other part, see "Gender and the Infinite: On the Aspiration to Be All There Is," *International Journal for Philosophy of Religion* 50 (December 2001): 191–212.

tional philosophy of religion as predominantly practiced in the Anglo-American world.

My own interest in ineffable knowledge derives initially from reflections in May 1999 at the Ratio conference on "Arguing with Derrida." One of the keynote papers was given by A. W. Moore, who is known for his work in analytic philosophy.[2] The title of his paper was also "Arguing with Derrida."[3] Derrida himself was present to give a response.[4] This was an unusual occasion, when Derrida bowed to the generous nature of an Oxford philosopher who had attempted to find points of convergence for their different perspectives. This was momentous, in the light of certain past failures to bridge the philosophical divide between the Continent (or France) and Britain. Derrida alluded to thirty years earlier, when both the idea and the reality of an Oxford philosopher arguing with him had proved impossible.[5]

This change in what is possible appears indicative of new relations and attitudes developing between the French and the British, as well as between the French and the Americans. However, one dimension of this momentous occasion that went without

---

[2] See A. W. Moore, *The Infinite*, 2d ed., with a new preface (London: Routledge, 2001); and *Points of View* (Oxford: Oxford University Press, 1997).

[3] A. W. Moore, "Arguing with Derrida," *Ratio: An International Journal of Analytic Philosophy* 13 (December 2000): 355–81. Special issue, edited by Simon Glendinning.

[4] Jacques Derrida, "Response to Moore," *Ratio* 13 (December 2000): 381–86.

[5] For an account of "the gulf" made explicit between Continental and analytic philosophers by R. M. Hare and Gilbert Ryle thirty years ago, at the time when Derrida published "Différance" (in *Théorie d'ensemble*, coll. Tel Quel, Paris: Editions du Seuil, 1968), see Simon Glendinning, "The Ethics of Exclusion: Incorporating the Continent," in *Questioning Ethics: Contemporary Debates in Philosophy*, eds. Richard Kearney and Mark Dooley (London: Routledge, 2000), 120–31. Glendinning makes reference to two papers from that period confirming this gulf, as well as equating British philosophy with Oxford philosophers. See R. M. Hare, "A School for Philosophers," *Ratio* 2 (1960); Gilbert Ryle, "Phenomenology versus *The Concept of Mind*," reprinted in Gilbert Ryle, *Collected Papers* (London: Hutchinson, 1971). See also the contribution to the special issue on "Arguing with Derrida" by Simon Glendinning, "Inheriting 'Philosophy': The Case of Austin and Derrida Revisited," *Ratio* 13 (December 2000): 307–31. Cf. Jacques Derrida, "Différance" and "Signature, Event, Context," in *Margins of Philosophy*, trans. Alan Bass (Chicago: University of Chicago Press, 1982), 1–28 and 307–30, respectively.

question was that of gender.[6] Arguably it was a gender-exclusive exchange, with an all-male list of six conference speakers with broadly similar material and social backgrounds. I might call the panel of speakers arguing with Derrida "male-neutral": the philosophical assumption may have been one of neutrality, yet the maleness was conspicuous.

So "ineffable knowledge," the first part of my title, builds critically upon Moore's novel reading of ineffability in Derrida. "Gender," the second part, builds upon my reading of feminist philosophy. In assuming the philosophical relevance of Derrida for the question of ineffability and mysticism,[7] I also noticed two different points of view: those of theologians, including certain Christian philosophers of religion,[8] and those of Anglo-American philosophers.[9] I suggest that the overlap of issues from these

---

[6] I assume here that gender cannot be understood on its own as a cultural construction as distinct from a biological or natural given, i.e., sex. Instead, gender should be interpreted in its relations to various material and social variables, including sex, race, class, religion, ethnicity, and sexual orientation. For my early discussion of the sex/gender distinction, see *A Feminist Philosophy of Religion* (Oxford: Blackwell, 1998), 5–13; and "Gender and the Infinite," 194–96.

[7] Amy Hollywood, *The Soul As Virgin Wife: Mechthild of Magdeburg, Marguerite Porete, and Meister Eckhart* (Notre Dame: Notre Dame University Press, 1995); *Sensible Ecstasy: Mysticism, Sexual Difference, and the Demands of History;* and Thomas A. Carlson, *Indiscretion: Finitude and the Naming of God* (Chicago: University of Chicago Press, 1999).

[8] The word *apophatic* is employed by theologians to describe the experience of emptying of (linguistic) content. This experience is often called mystic and associated with negative theology. Alternatively, the mystic might claim an experience of union with a transcendent being or an absolute oneness. Apophatic, or emptying, practice is sometimes contrasted to cataphatic, or filling, practice in meditation and other religious rites. For renewed theological attention to apophatic experience for those women whose language crosses gender boundaries and moves toward ineffability, see Kitty Scoular Datta, "Female Heterologies: Women's Mysticism, Gender-Mixing and the Apophatic," in *Self/Same/Other: Re-visioning the Subject in Literature and Theology,* eds. Heather Walton and Andrew W. Haas (Sheffield, England: Sheffield Academic Press, 2000), 125–36.

[9] For example, see Jantzen, *Power, Gender, and Christian Mysticism,* 101–9, 278–321; and Moore, *Points of View,* xii, 75, 142, 146–56, 164, 166, 200. In addition, for a relevant argument to avoid "negative theology" as a "metaphysics of presence," see Jean-Luc Marion, "In the Name: How to Avoid Speaking of 'Negative Theology,'" in *God, the Gift, and Postmodernism,* eds. John D. Caputo and Michael J. Scanlon (Bloomington: Indiana University Press, 1999), 20–53. Similar to Moore, Marion establishes "the infinite" as a way to talk

perspectives opens up a new area of philosophical debate, offering common ground for theism and atheism, non-naturalism and naturalism. In particular, I will consider how this ground can bring together Anglo-American philosophers of religion and other British and French philosophers, in an exploration of mystic and other religious expressions *as a form of ineffable knowledge.*

The marked difference in the English-speaking world between the philosopher's and the theologian's conceptual frameworks is open to challenge by new debates and (renewed) relations between philosophers. These relations become more complex when the philosopher is analytic and the theologian is informed by cultural theorists, social historians, and psycholinguists. I turn to consider these new perspectives in the next section; this will lead to a discussion of gender in the third section of this paper.

NEW PERSPECTIVES ON INEFFABLE KNOWLEDGE

Anglo-American philosophy, as seen, for example, in Moore on ineffable *knowledge,* can be far more philosophically nuanced and insightful than evident in the criticisms of contemporary philosophy by those Continental (including feminist) critics informed by various other theorists.[10] It is my contention that the

---

without saying something about something, and so without the metaphysical commitment to affirmations and negations of truth. He finds this "third way" in the work of the fifth-century theologian Pseudo-Denys, who is better known as Dionysius. According to Marion, the thought of Dionysius has been wrongly reduced to negative theology. Instead, as Marion argues, Dionysius can be found to "speak divine truth as the experience of incomprehension," and not negation as affirmation of what is not. Marion endeavors to articulate his third way in terms of the pragmatic use of language as "de-nomination" (which Moore might call "showing," or talking nonsense). For both Marion and Moore, a third way does not give up a commitment to truth, but of "saying" or denying (Marion, "In the Name," 28). Marion also describes this de-nomination as a "saturated phenomenon," since there is an excess of intuition, saturating the measure of each and every concept (Marion, "In the Name," 40). Perhaps in the light of such accounts of ineffability, human finitude, and the infinite, we might speculate about a "negative anthropology."

[10] See, for instance, Jantzen's theological criticisms in *Power, Gender and Christian Mysticism* (Cambridge: Cambridge University Press, 1995), 101–9, 278–321, 344–45; and *Becoming Divine: Towards a Feminist Philosophy of Religion* (Manchester: Manchester University Press, 1998), 154–55, 177–78.

conceptual tools of Anglo-American philosophers should not be too quickly rejected by philosophers or cultural theorists because their analytic accounts do not include Michel Foucault, Jacques Lacan, Derrida, or deconstruction. More broadly construed, so-called Continental philosophy has common concerns with, since influencing crucial strands of, analytic philosophy.[11]

I would like to demonstrate that one of these concerns is ineffable knowledge, especially as expressed in "images of infinitude." This phrase is found in Moore, but its significance can be illustrated by considering Luce Irigaray.[12] Irigaray's writings suggest some of the ways in which philosophers make play with images of infinitude, while knowing at some level that this involves prescinding their own limitations or finitude. Moore identifies Derrida's play with images as one broad area of (the unwitting) attempts to put ineffable knowledge into words, which results in nonsense.[13]

By Moore's own admission in "Arguing with Derrida," he does not intend to represent analytic as opposed to Continental philosophy. As already suggested, he demonstrates how philosophically nuanced perspectives, or "styles" of philosophy, can converge. Admittedly there is plenty of resistance to, or misunderstanding of, any play with nonsense.[14] Nevertheless, I suggest that Moore represents not just an exception, but an increasing tendency for philosophical concerns to converge, if at times un-

---

[11] Derrida himself admits to being closer to a conceptual philosopher, as defined by Moore, than to the so-called Continental side. He insists, "there are many misunderstandings of what I am trying to do, and it's perhaps because I am not simply on the 'continental' side," "Response to Moore," 382.

[12] See A. W. Moore, "Ineffability and Religion," Lecture hosted by the Philosophy Programme of the University of London School of Advanced Study in conjunction with the European Forum of Philosophy, 14 March 2001. For further examples of what might constitute these images of infinitude, see Luce Irigaray, *Elemental Passions,* trans. Joanne Collie and Judith Still (London: Athlone Press, 1992), 28–29; and Irigaray, "Place, Interval: A Reading of Aristotle, *Physics* IV," and "Love of the Same, Love of the Other," in *An Ethics of Sexual Difference,* trans. Carolyn Burke and Gillian C. Gill (London: Athlone Press, 1993), 34–58 and 109–10, respectively.

[13] Moore, *Points of View,* 197–203, 216–19.

[14] See, for example, the review of *Points of View* by Jerry Fodor, "Cat's Whiskers," *London Review of Books* (30 October 1997): 16–17; and also the response by Moore, "Cat's Whiskers," *London Review of Books* (27 November 1997): 8.

wittingly, across former divisions. For one thing, there seems to be a greater awareness of the perspectival nature of philosophical thinking. For another, changes in philosophical understandings of science and possibly renewed interest in metaphysical questions (about frameworks of belief, realism, and antirealism) have encouraged a tendency to dialogue across former divides.

In "Arguing with Derrida," Moore deliberately calls himself a "conceptual philosopher." He makes clear that his tasks are not restricted to the ultimate task of the scientist, that is, to produce truth alone. Admittedly both the scientist and the conceptual philosopher are concerned with the affirmation of a true proposition (or its denial). Yet in taking on this label, Moore means to specify the sort of philosophy he attempts to present in the context of his exchange with Derrida. As a conceptual philosopher Moore seeks clarity for increased understanding, and yet like the scientist he aims to produce truth.[15] But take note that Moore would still reject—as impossible—the conception of either a conceptual philosopher or a natural scientist as someone who *only* affirms truth in the sense of representing what is. Insofar as he intends (theoretically) to produce truth, Moore differs from Derrida. Yet agreement is evident in their quests for understanding, however implicit; and even possibly in a certain "commitment" to truth.[16]

Here Moore is willing to engage in a detached way in playing with nonsense. For example, when he puts a word in inverted commas (that is, single quotation marks), the meaning of the word is waived; in this way, a word that is merely mentioned does not have to have a sense, but neither does it entail talking nonsense.[17] My question is whether this use of inverted commas exhibits a significant possibility for debates about ineffable knowledge.

Aiming to clarify his tasks as a conceptual philosopher, Moore offers a definition of ineffable knowledge, in apparent agreement with Derrida, as "what resists expression by any *customary* lin-

---

[15] See Moore, *Points of View*, 2–3, 28–31.

[16] Derrida admits that insofar as this commitment is not a theoretical matter but an "engagement which calls for performative gestures," he also has a commitment to truth, "if only to question the possibility of truth." See "Response to Moore," 382.

[17] Moore, "Arguing with Derrida," 368, 372.

guistic means; and, more particularly and more pertinently, we can say that it is what resists expression by means of the affirmation of truths."[18] Moore stresses that ineffable knowledge is *shown*. Rather crudely, at this stage, I will call this "know-how," or practical knowledge, rather than "knowing that." Following certain feminist epistemologists, I would like to stress that far too much has been excluded from traditional conceptions of knowledge in focusing exclusively upon the latter. In particular, women's practical knowledge has often been dismissed as "old wives' tales."[19] In the words of Vrinda Dalmiya and Linda Alcoff:

> Traditional women's beliefs—about childbearing and rearing, herbal medicines, the secrets of good cooking, and such—are generally characterized as "old wives's tales." These "tales" may be interwoven into the very fabric of our daily lives and may even enjoy a certain amount of respect and deference as a useful secret-sharing among women . . . [yet] fail to get accorded the honorific status of *knowledge.*[20]

> All modes of knowing, according to the traditionalist, can be *said;* we suggest that some knowledge can only be *shown* and other knowledge can only be said in an inherently perspectival language.[21]

Yet the problem is that some (of this) knowledge is in fact knowing how to do certain things that can be shown, but cannot be put into words—or at least not into the words of a particular (privileged) perspective within the dominant conceptual scheme.[22] As I will discuss further below, Moore's reference to what is shown appeals to a distinction between showing and saying worked out in his own writings. A further question is whether this distinction, as employed by Moore, intends to promote a hierarchy of value whereby saying has greater philosophical value than showing. Moore offers a modification, or extension,

---

[18] Ibid., 362.
[19] Vrinda Dalmiya and Linda Alcoff, "Are 'Old Wives' Tales' Justified?" in *Feminist Epistemologies,* eds. Linda Alcoff and Elizabeth Potter (London: Routledge, 1993), 217–41.
[20] Ibid., 217.
[21] Ibid., 241.
[22] Moore, *Points of View,* 156–57.

of the distinction as found in the early work of Ludwig Wittgenstein: his accounts of showing in both *The Infinite* and *Points of View* go beyond Wittgenstein to a point at which, I suggest, he meets Continental philosophers (such as Derrida) on the question of ineffability.[23] In *The Infinite,* Moore explains, "there are certain things that can be known though they cannot be put into words."[24] "[But t]he full-blown saying/showing distinction, whereby there are things that cannot be said at all, emerges only when I pass from consideration of how things are in my field of vision to consideration of how things are, full stop—to consideration, in other words, of the world as a whole."[25]

In this quotation, the implicit account of reality and the finitude of vision also have Kantian overtones.[26] Elsewhere I have explored these overtones by comparing Moore's account with Paul Ricoeur's Kantian account of the finitude of our points of view in *Fallible Man.*[27] But let us consider some related points from Moore's "Arguing with Derrida." Moore himself would seem to produce nonsense in the first sentence below: "What Derrida [in "Différance"] is drawing attention to . . . is something that can never be the subject of any truth. It is that which in some quasi-Kantian way makes possible and precedes the affirmation of any truth. There are clear links here with what each of Frege and Wittgenstein is doing."[28]

Later in this paper, Moore returns to the contradiction in the above assertion that "What Derrida is drawing attention to . . . can never be a subject of any truth."[29] This is nonsense. The assertion is self-stultifying. In recognizing this, he both distinguishes himself from Derrida, in insisting that the affirmation of truth is an ultimate concern, and draws himself into Derrida's

---

[23] Moore, *The Infinite,* 186–200; *Points of View,* xii–xiii, 156–57, 195–213, 277–78.

[24] Moore, *The Infinite,* 186.

[25] Ibid., 190. For the development of Moore's own account of showing and ineffable knowledge, see *Points of View,* 186–94.

[26] Moore, *Points of View,* 203–9, 249–51.

[27] Paul Ricoeur, *Fallible Man,* trans. Charles Kelbley, with an introduction by Walter J. Lowe (New York: Fordham University Press, 1986); and my "Gender and the Infinite," 196–98, 200.

[28] Moore, "Arguing with Derrida," 362.

[29] Ibid., 366.

play with meaning—even if Moore remains detached in his play. Moore asserts that "Derrida's style of philosophy (unlike conceptual philosophy) does not labour under a restricted conception of what linguistic resources are available to it; in particular, it does not treat affirmation of the truth as its sole primary mode of philosophical expression."[30]

This implies that in order to "argue with Derrida," Moore must be willing to play with nonsense, while at pains to avoid self-stultification. He explains how he avoids the latter:

The first task confronting any conceptual philosopher trying to come to terms with the ineffable is to show how it is possible to affirm truths about the ineffable without belying its very ineffability.[31]

A second task for any conceptual philosopher who accepts that some things are ineffable is to say what the term *things* ranges over in this claim.[32]

The only decent way that I can see of discharging either task is to say that the term *things* ranges over objects of knowledge. The claim that some things are ineffable is to be understood as the claim that *some states of knowledge cannot be put into words,* or more strictly, that some states of knowledge *do not have any content* (and therefore *do not share any content with any truth*). The knowledge in question is not knowledge that anything is the case. *It is knowledge how to do certain things. . . .* knowledge *how to handle concepts . . .* there is nothing self-stultifying about discussing somebody's ineffable knowledge how to do something. We can even put into words what is involved in the person's having the knowledge. What we cannot put into words is what the person knows.[33]

So how do I read the extent of his agreement on this with Derrida or, more generally, with Continental philosophers since Kant? For one thing, Moore allows the possibility that Derrida may communicate something ineffable.[34] For another thing, Moore is

---

[30] Ibid., 363.
[31] Ibid., 366.
[32] Ibid., 367.
[33] Ibid. (emphasis added).
[34] Moore claims, "there is no mystery in the idea of somebody's 'communicating' something ineffable. All that is required for this to happen is that the

willing to play with nonsense. Yet he remains fully beholden to the truth and to the ultimate task of *producing* true and meaningful linguistic expressions, whereas Derrida questions the possibility of truth in his play with ineffability.[35] Moreover, Moore is detached in his play with words, whereas Derrida is serious in engaging with the ineffable. Ultimately, Moore concludes:

> What I hope to have done in this essay is to give some indication of how it is possible, first, to appropriate resources highlighted in "Signature, Event, Context," in order, second, to reckon with ineffable insights afforded by *Différance,* while managing at the same time, third, to conform to methodological paradigms of conceptual philosophy. In various senses of the phrase, then . . . this has been an attempt to "argue with Derrida."[36]

Notice the quotation marks around "argue with Derrida." These make clear his detached way of playing with Derrida. Clearly Moore does not aim to produce nonsense or to engage seriously with it. At most he attempts to argue with where the meaning of this verb phrase is not fixed (that is, this does not have *a* sense, but neither is it talking nonsense).

So what will Continental philosophy of religion gain from Moore's attempt? His arguing helps us to understand the different perspectives, by recognizing the common issues of ineffable insight or knowledge—and the infinite—as well as the very different relations to the same issues. Moore would seem to find common ground for his exchange in Derrida's idea of meaning: the meaning of a word is its infinite potential for iterability in new contexts.[37] Meaning appears to be context-dependent. Yet Moore does not give up his commitment to produce something both meaningful and true. In the end, his clear distinctions between his work and Derrida's on ineffability, as well as any overlap, enables my assessment of the role given to gender by philosophers of religion, especially on topics such as the infinite

---

person exploits language—plays with language—in such a way that other people come to share some of his or her ineffable knowledge." (Moore, "Arguing with Derrida," 367).

[35] Moore, "Arguing with Derrida," 366.

[36] Ibid., 372–73; cf. Derrida, "Différance"; and "Signature, Event, Context," in *Margins of Philosophy,* 1–28 and 307–30, respectively.

[37] Moore, "Arguing with Derrida," 364–65, 372.

and ineffable. The latter terms are linked together by Moore, but I will bring in the question of gender in the third section, in order, ultimately, to revisit the idea of ineffable knowledge in the conclusion to this paper. I turn to my next question.

. . . AND GENDER

Sabina Lovibond has explored the association of the unlimited, or infinite, with femaleness beginning in ancient Greek philosophy. From Lovibond, we learn that for Pythagorean and Platonic philosophers, "the infinite" was a term of abuse. It was associated with chaos, matter, and femaleness, while the finite was good and associated with order, form, and maleness.[38] A twentieth-century feminism of difference—informed by Irigaray—proposed a return to the ancient conception of the infinite as female, while reversing its value from bad to good.

Ironically, feminist theologian Grace Jantzen has recently criticised Anglo-American philosophers of religion for, on the one hand, their drive for infinity as a masculine or male obsession and, on the other hand, their association of ineffability and mysticism with private—and so female—experience. This gendering of the infinite and the ineffable as, respectively, masculine and feminine seems confused, if not contradictory.[39] Jantzen concludes that while the urge for limitlessness is a masculine obsession, the ineffable is and should be rejected, except perhaps in "naming" God.[40] She assumes that for masculinists, the ineffable is an untrustworthy source of knowledge and so associated with

---

[38] Sabina Lovibond, "An Ancient Theory of Gender: Plato and the Pythagorean Table," in *Women in Ancient Societies,* eds. Leonie J. Archer, Susan Fischer, and Maria Wyke (London: Macmillan, 1994), 88–101; and "Feminism in Ancient Philosophy: The Feminist Stake in Greek Rationalism," in *The Cambridge Companion to Feminism in Philosophy,* eds. Miranda Fricker and Jennifer Hornsby (Cambridge: Cambridge University Press, 2000), 10–28.

[39] For a clear example of such contradiction, see Jantzen, *Becoming Divine,* 154–56, 266–68. In the former pages Jantzen equates the masculine with the fear of limits; in the latter she presents the Pythagorean table of opposites as representative of the binary thinking of Western philosophy. Yet in the latter the masculine is equated with the limited.

[40] Jantzen, *Becoming Divine;* and *Gender, Power, and Christian Mysticism,* 278–89.

the feminine. For feminists like Jantzen, we must dissociate women from this devaluation.

But does Jantzen make some illegitimate moves between the nuances of terms? She seems to jump from infinity as a powerful drive to the infinite's association with men, from the ineffable as private in the sense of an experience of a subject, to the ineffable as private in the sense of not in the public sphere but in the (woman's) private sphere. If so, her reading of terms is incompatible with the actual readings of philosophers. Here the Pythagoreans serve as one counterexample. If the Pythagoreans did associate both the infinite with women as disorderly (so not philosophical) and the ineffable with women as representing not truth (not the finite but the infinite), then the infinite has not always represented maleness.

And something has gone wrong in Jantzen's argument. Jantzen herself claims to reject the Pythagorean table of opposites as the source of mistaken gender associations: it created a hierarchy of binary oppositions in which the first term in any pair is male and given greater value, for example, finite/infinite, order/disorder.[41] However, in this case Jantzen seems to be rejecting what she wants to uphold: the value of the finite or a "portion of infinity."

Perhaps Jantzen would counter that the problem is that the masculinism in Western philosophy has involved an *unconscious* urge for infinity. I would go so far as to agree that questions of the infinite and of ineffable knowledge are generally ignored by analytic philosophers in the twentieth century; and in its devaluation, the ineffable is associated with women. Yet this is precisely where the common ground with Continental philosophy of religion comes in. Contemporary philosophers, whether Continental, analytic, or conceptual, face issues of gender and ineffability. My contention is that Continental philosophers of religion today cannot ignore the topic of the ineffable. Moreover, insofar as they take seriously the play of language and imagery, Continen-

---

[41] Jantzen, *Becoming Divine,* 266–70. For her critical reflection upon the possibility of any straightforward extension of gender dichotomies, as found in the Pythagorean table, to men and women with a variety of social and class backgrounds, see Michele Le Doeuff, "Long Hair, Short Ideas," in *The Philosophical Imaginary,* trans. Colin Gordon (London: Athlone Press, 1989), 113–14.

tal philosophers are in a most propitious place to reverse a devaluation of feminist concerns and of femaleness.

My philosophical queries about gender come in at the point where conceptual and other post-Kantian philosophers meet. If the infinite cannot be associated strictly with the male or the female, then the philosopher might attempt to argue that the infinite is gender-neutral, especially since it assumes something not limited by the differences of human embodiment. However, this response seems to exhibit a refusal to recognize how embodiment inevitably "genders" perspectives on the infinite. Despite such refusals, the questioning of gender should persist. Is there a conscious or unconscious masculinist drive for infinity, that is, to be all-knowing, all-powerful, omnitemporal, and without a body? Alternatively, is the place of the infinite a female domain? Perhaps the feminist pursuit of knowledge of (the whole framework of) the finite is, ironically, an urge to find a place in the infinite—from which such ineffable knowledge would be gained. And perhaps male philosophers have been exclusively preoccupied with what is far more certain/possible, that is, the finite, order, truth, and "effable" knowledge. It could, then, be argued that the greater practical, yet ineffable knowledge of the process of "knowing how to be finite"[42] has in fact been a domain of female insight—unacknowledged by male philosophers. As Dalmiya and Alcoff assert: "There is nothing embarrassingly limited about the midwife's perspectival (and hence partly exclusionary) knowledge; rather, it ensures a higher level of holistic care by taking into account certain perspectival facts that are necessarily beyond the reach of traditional forms of knowledge. . . . we suggest that some knowledge can only be *shown*."[43]

What can these lines of argument tell us about ineffable knowledge and gender? In contrast with Jantzen, I would like to insist upon the rich complexity of the philosophical question of ineffable knowledge (of what is beyond, or presupposed by, the finite) in its association with gender(s). This complexity renders impossible any straightforward equation of the infinite with either masculinism or maleness. The complexity of gender (associ-

---

[42] Moore, *Points of View,* 277.
[43] Dalmiya and Alcoff, "Are 'Old Wives' Tales' Justified?" 241.

ations) also challenges conceptual and Derridean philosophers alike. They are equally challenged by gender, especially by the lack of its acknowledgement. I would also maintain that contemporary (Continental) philosophers of religion—including feminist philosophers—need not reject either ineffable knowledge as untrustworthy, or its association with a masculinist urge for infinitude as a refusal to accept boundaries.[44]

In asserting this I take a stand against a current trend to (mis)-represent, on the one hand, Anglo-American philosophy as necessarily rejecting the ineffable as a source of knowledge and, on the other hand, Continental philosophy as rejecting ontological or ontotheological questions as a guide to practical knowledge. Instead, I would insist that ineffability and any urge for infinitude—as evident in making play with the infinite—are not merely employed to prescind the limitations of men or exclude and oppress women. To the contrary, they raise all sorts of significant ontological, metaphysical, and epistemological issues. The danger is to misrepresent philosophers, whether this is Derrida, Moore, or other post-Kantian philosophers, in assuming they fit neatly under particular territorial or gender labels. This would inhibit the possible convergence of perspectives that I am at pains to exploit here.

One of my ongoing methodological concerns is to remain open to a fuller picture of so-called Continental philosophy and its influence since Kant on philosophy on both sides of the English Channel. Another concern is to help expose the unacknowledged role of gender in matters such as ineffable knowledge. I have focused upon Moore's conceptual philosophy precisely because he appears to treat the ineffable as a serious (and necessary) question for epistemologists and all those concerned with knowledge-claims. Ineffability is fundamental to discursive practices, that is, knowing how to do something with concepts. It is fundamental to making narrative sense of life—a philosophical concern on both sides of the Channel. Consider the various attempts of Ricoeur and Adriana Cavarero, or of Moore and Alasdair MacIntyre, to understand the need to make narrative sense of our

---

[44] Jantzen, *Becoming Divine,* 154–55.

lives.[45] Moore claims explicitly in *Points of View* that "knowing how *to be finite* is a paradigm of ineffable knowledge."[46]

This is a highly relevant claim for my unraveling of the gendered associations and the value hierarchy of finite/infinite, limited/unlimited, order/disorder, reason/desire, male/female, and so on. It has potentially important implications for those feminist philosophers who claim that the *hubris* of the male philosopher leads to a categorical denial of ineffable (and gendered) knowledge. I do not advocate simply moving gender issues to the domain of the ineffable—but the various associations of gender with an effable/ineffable distinction should be explored further. Undoubtedly certain feminist philosophers will continue to object that ineffable knowledge could only be a contradiction in terms for the masculinist philosopher, and so its association with femaleness would exclude the topic from any serious philosophical debate.

My contention is again to the contrary: the epistemic injustice done to women whose practical knowledge has been devalued can be reversed by recognition of their insight in knowing how to be finite—as the flip side to recognizing a paradigm of ineffable knowledge. This paradigm of knowing how to be finite includes the states of understanding, or practical knowledge, that we each have to various degrees. We might agree that knowing how to employ concepts and to use language to express truth fits the paradigm. But in more narrowly realist terms, ineffable states of knowledge are not representations and (so) do not answer to how things are. Ironically, this paradigm of ineffability appears compatible with Derrida's concerns precisely because it does not affirm or deny truth, that is, insofar as *truth does depend* upon *how things are.*

---

[45] See Alasdair MacIntyre, *After Virtue: A Study in Moral Theory,* 2d ed. (London: Gerald Duckworth and Co., 1985), 204–25; Paul Ricoeur, *Oneself As Another,* trans. Kathleen Blamey (Chicago: University of Chicago Press, 1992), 140–68; Adriana Cavarero, *In Spite of Plato: A Feminist Rewriting of Ancient Philosophy,* trans. Serena Anderlini-D'Onofrio and Aine O'Healy (Cambridge: Polity Press, 1995); and *Relating Narratives: Storytelling and Selfhood,* trans. Paul A. Kottman (New York: Routledge, 2000); cf. Moore, *Points of View,* 220 ff; and "Ineffability and Religion," 6.

[46] Moore, *Points of View,* 277.

EXTENDING THE ARGUMENT: ON A COMMON URGE
TO MAKE PLAY WITH INFINITUDE

Allow me to begin to summarize, as well as to extend slightly my argument here. In "Arguing with Derrida," Moore endeavors to read his own account of ineffable knowledge in relation to Derrida. He reveals a highly important point of contact between the formerly divergent perspectives of Continental and analytic philosophers or, more accurately, between an antirealist and a realist who might both claim to be conceptual philosophers. Derrida's response to Moore confirms this.[47] Derrida goes so far as to apologize for not long ago reading Wittgenstein and, presumably, for not reading philosophers such as Moore, who owe much to Wittgenstein in their perspectives on ineffability and nonsense.[48] Nonsense, as defined by Moore, is the result of putting into words what we are shown.[49] There is a clear convergence of thought in the play with words. Yet is there a more serious common ground between Moore and Continental philosophy of religion?

As already mentioned, Moore appropriates a distinction from Wittgenstein, saying and showing, to develop his accounts in *The Infinite* and *Points of View*.[50] The latter employs the formula "*A* is shown that *x*," as equivalent to *A* has ineffable knowledge, and when an attempt is made to put what *A* knows into words, the result is *x*. Whatever words are put in place of *x* will be nonsense or mere verbiage, because such states of knowledge are not representations; they do not answer to how things are.[51] To quote Moore: "Knowing how to be finite . . . has nothing to answer to. It is knowledge of how to be finite *in accord with our craving for infinitude*. But there is no independent right or wrong about

---

[47] Derrida, "Response to Moore," 381–82.
[48] As an aside, it may be that, ironically, Wittgenstein's relation to the content, or nonsense, of his *Tractatus Logico-Philosophicus* (trans. D. F. Pears and B. F. McGuinness, with an introduction by Bertrand Russell, London: Routledge and Kegan Paul, 1961) is in fact closer to Derrida's engagement with nonsense than to Moore's detached play with infinitude.
[49] Moore, *The Infinite*, 186–200; and *Points of View*, 180 n. 13, 258–59.
[50] Moore, *The Infinite*, 186–200; and *Points of View*, xii–xiii, 156–57, 195–213, 277–78.
[51] Moore, *Points of View*, 156–57.

it."[52] So this knowing how has nothing to answer to. Yet it is in accord with our craving for infinitude. The craving becomes corrupt when we aspire to be infinite, that is, to be all there is.[53] Thus Moore's account of finitude and infinitude, consistent with Kant and post-Kantian philosophy, recognizes a limit to what we (say we) know. Transgression of this limit renders our aspiration(s) vulnerable as both enabling and corrupting power.

Similar to Moore, philosophers on the Continent have also turned to Wittgenstein's saying and showing distinction in order to grasp the limits of their language/world. For example, Maurice Blanchot turns to Wittgenstein to make his point in *Writing of the Disaster:* "Wittgenstein's 'mysticism,' aside from his faith in unity, must come from his believing that one can *show* when one cannot *speak.* But without language, nothing can be shown. And to be silent is still to speak. Silence is impossible. That is why we desire it."[54] So Blanchot reads Wittgenstein as showing what cannot be said. But this is still speaking *(le dire).*

Moore agrees that we desire the impossible: desiring infinitude. And, in Moore's Wittgensteinian terms, any attempt to put this in language results in (speaking) nonsense.[55] In addition, notice the undoing by Blanchot (above) of the distinction of saying and showing in support of mysticism. This connection with mysticism, as I proposed earlier, exists for both the philosopher and the theologian, who focuses on ineffable knowledge or states of knowledge without content. Blanchot makes a connection between philosophy of religion and mysticism by referring to the mystic's unity, or union with the absolute oneness of reality. This comes into his understanding of (our being toward) death.

With the question of death, we are not far from questions of ineffability, religious expressions or rituals, and knowing how to be finite. In both death and mysticism, the object or content of knowledge is never identifiable—hence we see how ineffable

---

[52] Ibid., 277.

[53] Anderson, "Gender and the Infinite," 192–93, 196–99. See also Hollywood, *Sensible Ecstasy,* 113–14, 118–23.

[54] Maurice Blanchot, *Writing of the Disaster*, trans. Ann Smock (Lincoln, Nebraska: University of Nebraska Press, 1986), 10–11. For Wittgenstein's mysticism, see *Tractatus Logico-Philosophicus,* paragraph 7, 151.

[55] Wittgenstein, *Tractatus,* paragraphs 4.12, 5.62, 6.12, and 6.522; cf. Moore, *Points of View,* 149 ff.

knowledge is without truth. Both are states without content.[56] Moreover, the connection with mysticism and the showing that is always still a saying could also come into studies of gender, male and female mystics.

Following, yet also going beyond Moore and Blanchot, I would like to propose that the language of the female subject who attempts to put (certain) ineffable knowledge into words could, in certain instances, be called religious—as in the case of the female mystic. She might, then, speak nonsense yet show practical knowledge. If so, I would have to reject Jantzen's claim that the modern philosophical framework only allows us to associate the female mystic with strictly private experience. I would also have to confront Moore's position more explicitly. Can his formula be employed to assert that the female subject *(A)* is shown that x is equivalent to A has ineffable knowledge, and when an attempt to put what A knows into language, the result is x? According to Moore, x must be nonsense. Yet he admits that one of the things we are shown is that God exists. But then, "God exists" in the phrase "We are shown that God exists" is a piece of nonsense.

Moreover, his admission that this is a piece of nonsense appears in the wider discussion of human aspiration(s). To the latter discussion, I would add that in "tales" about the human finite— especially those evoking a religious dimension such as tales of mystical experience[57]—two aspirations come together.[58] Here we

---

[56] For a study of the analogy between mystical unknowing and the limits of human knowing, negative theology, and negative anthropology, see Carlson, *Indiscretion,* 239–62.

[57] On the use and abuse of women telling tales, see my paper "An Ethics for Women Telling Tales: Creating New Spaces," presented 27 October 2000, Colloque international, "Espaces publics, espaces privés: Enjeux et partages," University of Cergy-Pontoise, France. A French translation of this paper, "Des contes dits au féminin: Pour une éthique des nouveaux espaces," is forthcoming in the Cergy-Pontoise conference proceedings.

[58] Moore, *Points of View,* 277–78. In "Ineffability and Religion," Moore argues that "the language that results from attempting to put our ineffable knowledge into words is very often of a 'religious' kind." This is not to claim that "attempts to put our ineffable knowledge into words result only in such language; nor, for that matter, that such language results only from attempts to put our ineffable knowledge into words. . . . But there is significant overlap." He goes on to sketch some of this significant overlap.

I can only indicate one area of overlap that seems equally relevant to my

can recognize an aspiration both to affirm the divine and to be God. Perhaps this is, after all, what is meant by the mystic's union with the divine.

To recall an important fact, Moore does not intend to produce nonsense. Instead he aspires to produce truth. Yet if these two aspects of this fact are true, does he belie his own gender bias? In contrast, we might find Irigaray willing to produce (what Moore would call) nonsense, in order to gain knowledge of how to be finite. Consider the attempt of Irigaray to mime the texts of female mystics in light of the above discussion of being shown that God exists.[59] To speak the mystic's silence, Irigaray makes play with images of infinitude. She mimes a female subject's desire to bring together two human aspirations (or, in her terms, the union of the sensible transcendental) of affirming divinity and becoming divine.[60] It would seem that Irigaray *shows* ineffable knowledge in images of female desire, of song and dance, and in other creatively subversive expressions.[61] Similar expressions by other feminists or female mystics contribute to a wider conception of the resources now available to philosophers of religion for accounts of ineffable knowledge.[62] New possibilities for "expressing" the ineffable include strategies for exploiting language in the play of images in a mystic's text, art, or dance. This is similar to what Moore says about Derrida's play with words—it is a manner of exploiting language or showing.[63]

---

discussion. In Moore's words: "Because the attempt to put our ineffable knowledge into words involves prescinding from our limitations, there is an area in which we make play with images of unlimitedness and infinitude. These are applied in the first instance to ourselves. But then, when combined with our re-awakened self-consciousness about the very limitations from which we have been prescinding, they are extended to a reality beyond us. Eventually they sustain talk of God."

[59] Luce Irigaray, "La Mysterique," in her *Speculum of the Other Woman,* trans. Gillian C. Gill (Ithaca: Cornell University Press, 1985), 191–202. See also Amy Hollywood, "Beauvoir, Irigaray, and the Mystical," *Hypatia* 9 (Fall 1994): 158–85; and *Sensible Ecstasy,* 192–210.

[60] Irigaray, "An Ethics of Sexual Difference," in *An Ethics of Sexual Difference,* 128–29.

[61] Concerning music as an example of expressing the inexpressible, see Moore, *Points of View,* 201–3.

[62] Jantzen, *Gender, Power, and Christian Mysticism,* 283, 328–29, 344–46. For more historically and hermeneutically nuanced accounts of ineffability, mysticism, and gender, see Hollywood, *Sensible Ecstasy.*

[63] See Moore, "Arguing with Derrida," 365, 367, 372. Here, to be fair, it should be noted that Jantzen also recognizes the importance of stretching lan-

There may be a common core concern in the variety of masculinist, feminist, and other philosophical attempts to show what is ineffable. Certainly if we follow Moore, an urge to orient our finiteness, in knowing how to be finite, exists. However, I would like to exploit this urge in order to establish a (more) common concern: to better orient our finiteness in terms of gender (including gender's integral relations to sex, race, religion, ethnicity, class, and sexual orientation) by understanding the tendencies of women and men to prescind their limitations. The tendency to deny our material and socially specific limitations has political and ethical implications. This denial is especially true of gender relations in philosophy, whether it is a matter of denying the religious, sexual, or other variables of difference.

Very roughly at this point, I would advocate a closer look at Michel Foucault's account of the immanent nature of power. Following Foucault would mean accepting that the political is no longer a position of exteriority with respect to our relationships.[64] Our political positioning would be understood as part of knowing how to be finite: power would be recognized as immanent in our lives, and hence in both the content of our knowledge and in how we process that knowledge. If relations of power are immanent in our lives, then they have a directly productive role to play in everything, especially in our expressions of ineffable knowledge, or words and practices of a religious kind.

I suggest that we begin to reflect with Foucault that power is everywhere. It is necessary to recognize power's intimate connection with both effable and ineffable knowledge. If the gendered relations of power are integral to the paradigm of ineffable knowledge, then they must be expressed in *how* we make play with images of infinitude. Acceptance of this account of power has its advantages and difficulties. One difficulty is confronting the corrupting relations of power in all expressions of knowledge. One advantage is recognizing the possibilities in a transformation of the power immanent in our relations. Positively, the power for rational change, which circulates in the implicit and explicit networks of the relations shaping our lives, is the com-

---

guage to represent the "inexhaustible fecundity" of the divine, and not "frustrated speechlessness." See *Power, Gender, and Christian Mysticism,* 284, 286.

[64] Michel Foucault, *The History of Sexuality,* vol. 1, *An Introduction,* trans. Robert Hurley (Harmondsworth, England: Penguin Books, 1979), 92–94.

mon (yet ironic) feature of every form of passion (whether religious or not), and so in what remains ineffable.

CONCLUSION

We have seen that conceptual and other post-Kantian philosophers confront a common urge or passion and a common problem. They confront an urge to express the inexpressible as ineffable knowledge. I also maintain that this urge shapes practical knowledge as both passive and productive know-how. Attempts to communicate the ineffable in new ways have become part of the productive project of feminist philosophy today. In particular, Irigaray exemplifies this project. Arguably, Irigaray has *shown* that we know we are in-finite.[65] I would agree "that we know we are in-finite" is nonsense, since claiming to be both finite and infinite is self-contradictory. Yet we are shown this ineffable knowledge as we inevitably aspire to be infinite. In other words, our inscrutable desire for infinitude (as finite beings) becomes apparent in, for instance, Irigaray's play with language, but also in claims that we are shown x.[66]

I have attempted to demonstrate that ineffable knowledge and gender raise important sorts of questions concerning language, reality, understanding, truth, and power. These topics offer a rich terrain for philosophical analysis and debate for Continental philosophers of religion, but also between feminist philosophers and other philosophers or theologians. The novelty of this work on

---

[65] Irigaray, *Elemental Passions,* 89.

[66] We are also shown that desire for infinitude is good in motivating us and shaping the *politicized* nature of works of love. Yet there are equally dangers for men and for women in desiring infinitude. On the one hand, the danger is evident in the male aspiration to be infinite. On the other hand, there would seem to be a similar danger in the female aspiration to become divine. Any desire that overwhelms us remains indefinite until embraced *critically.* The fundamental problem lies in the aspiration to be, or become, whether divine men or divine women, *all that is.* In aspiring to be or become all, "the other" and others are eclipsed. A critical embrace of bodies is meant to change our thinking. It should also challenge our physical, sensual, and material relations with the other and others. However, this sort of transformation, as Irigaray intimates so provocatively concerning sexual difference, involves violence and pain. See Irigaray, *Elemental Passions,* 90; and my "Gender and the Infinite," 198–202.

ineffable knowledge and gender rests in recognizing the ironic, yet necessary tension between the enabling and corrupting power immanent in the material, personal, and social relations of men and women.

No critical reflection on language, understanding, and truth can remain content with traditional answers to the philosophical question of ineffable knowledge. These answers are inadequate, insofar as they have failed to acknowledge a necessary tension in our gendered relations to the finite and the infinite, as both corrupting and enabling. I suggest that Continental philosophy of religion as practiced by both those who aspire to produce truth and those who engage seriously with nonsense can overcome this failure: it can acknowledge this tension as the first step toward new ethical and epistemological relations between women themselves, men themselves, and women and men of different material and social perspectives.

3
Locating Reason in Theology and Spirituality

9

Speaking Otherwise: Postmodern Analogy

Graham Ward

I WANT TO ARGUE for the significance of theology to philosophy and the importance today of philosophical theology rather than philosophy of religion. I want to demonstrate how a new space for analogical thinking has been opened up by certain poststructuralist discourses; how this is a space in which we can think again of an analogical world and a cosmological project; but how, left to poststructural critical thinking alone, this worldview can all too easily endorse a culture of sadomasochism, by enjoying and enjoining its own endless victimage. Only a theological account (not, note, foundation), as the necessary supplement to this analogical discourse, makes possible an ethics and a politics.

Enduring the undecidable, I will argue, slakes us of the power to resist: for all resistance is rendered arbitrary and compromised. And if we can agree that there are still things worth resisting and therefore things worth affirming, then this slaking is politically and ethically dangerous. It opens up the very abyss of *laissez-faire* liberalism. It is not in itself nihilism—it is not so essentialized—but while problematizing the secular, it generates endless indeterminacy. What the theological voice provides is an account of the world as created and an account (never pure, always parasitic) of a relation between creation and its uncreated creator. This relation, never grasped in itself but only in its effects, provides an account of divine intention and divine desire with respect to the created orders, such that ambiguity gains the weight of mystery and the undecidable is not the entry to the *en abysme* but a place for the construal of grace, of the singularity of what has been specifically given. But let us proceed more systematically, with the change poststructural thinking has wrought with respect to philosophy of religion: the return to the analogical worldview.

POSTSTRUCTURAL ANALOGY

Toward the end of Derrida's essay "En ce même dans cette oeuvre, me voici," his gift-offering to Levinas, an observation is made with respect to Levinas's work. Derrida observes that what the work forges is "a certain analogy."[1] What has continually struck me about so much postmodern thinking is its desire to construct a new form of analogy. What organizes this desire and necessitates such thinking are the concerns with difference, alterity, the tension of paradox, and the refusal of synthesis. In wishing to subvert the logics of ontotheology in which the univocity of being circles all things within an immanent economy of the same; in wishing to renegotiate the abject, the other, the difference that cannot be totalized, several poststructural thinkers rehearse the classical problematics that led to discussions of analogy. "The logic of the same" is a command to univocity that institutes forms of totality: patriarchalism, logocentrism, ocularcentrism, phallocentrism, and ontology (as circumscribed by phenomenology). The logic and, more importantly, the appearance, of the other installs a difference.

But pure difference, as such, leads to equivocation. And equivocation leads to agnosticism, because there is no mediation or comparison possible whereby what is different might be accessed and assessed. Equivocation does not give itself to communication, for it imposes a nonrelation. Hence several of the prominent poststructural voices seek a mode of discourse in which the communication of the other can be registered, if only as trace or trace of a trace (as in Levinas and Derrida). This leads several thinkers to concerns with transcendence (Levinas), quasi-transcendence (Derrida), and sensible transcendence (Irigaray).

---

[1] Jacques Derrida, *Psyché: Inventions de l'autre* (Paris: Galilée, 1987), 199. Trans. "At This Very Moment in This Work Here I Am," by Rubin Berezdivin, in *Re-reading Levinas,* eds. Robert Bernasconi and Simon Critchley (London: Athlone Press, 1991), 45.

Ana logia is a reasoning or speaking "above." The analogical, to be *ana*-logical, requires a transcendent horizon. Analogy, while not offering direct access to the transcendent, mediates or negotiates that which makes possible and continually infuses the immanent circles of discourse.

Analogy leads, then, to theological concerns. It opens up the discourse to a theological investigation—whether it be of negative theology (Derrida), Talmudic commentary (Levinas), or the Catholic tradition (Irigaray and Kristeva). Concerns with translatability, interdisciplinarity, iteration, quotation, double-coding, double-binding, parody, and pastiche are all related to the irreducible ambiguity of analogical thinking. They are communications of resemblance, hence relational identities, constituted in and through difference. They are reports on an irreducible alienation endemic to communication, such that discourse is figured as bearing within itself, holographically, an altogether other scene. With Derrida, following de Man, the analogical thinking is temporalized, narrativized in terms of allegory: a speaking of one thing while simultaneously speaking of another. This speaking bears the structure of analogy, which, according to Aquinas, distinguishes between its *res significata* and its *modus significandi*.

The concern with this difference, this otherness as it pertains to a certain exteriority, whether of the phenomenological project, the psychoanalytic subject of desire, or representation itself, the concern with the very possibility of offering (or desiring to offer) an account of this alterity, rests upon and reinscribes the analogical. And so one of the hallmarks of poststructural thinking has been the question—never, as far as I am aware, comprehensively foregrounded as such—of analogy.

To talk of analogy is to consider relation. What is relation? Relation *as such?* We have grown accustomed—maybe our Indo-European syntax structure demands it—to think about relation as between two or more terms, two or more people. We ask who or what is related. But to think through analogy is to think through relation *as such,* relation as more primordial than I or thou, I and it, he and she, she and she, and so on. That is, relation that constructs the possibility of I, thou, she, he, we, or it. This is relation before identity, before subject and object, before positioning. To consider relation *as such* is to consider being-in-relation, the nature of that being that is in relation and of what that "in relation" consists.

Whether one thinks of Levinas's "fecundity," Derrida's *différance,* Lyotard's "event," Irigaray's "interval," Kristeva's "transference," Cixous's "love as not-having"—it is relation *as such* that is being thought through, relation refusing dialectical synthesis. And everywhere in postmodern thought, relationality is predicated on desire and alterity, such that reading and writing itself, the production and consumption of texts, is caught up in the dynamics of relation. The essays and books of any one of these thinkers are offered as meditations, performances-in-relation that resist contemporary reading practices of skimming and paraphrasing, of soundbiting and mining for the relevant (that is, convenient) quotes. Their essays and books are exercises-in-relation that cannot be reduced to mere communication.

These exercises-in-relation, I will suggest, compose cosmologies, worldviews. It is the cosmological that is my ultimate concern: how is the world conceived in and through this understanding of the analogical, through this relatedness in and by means of difference? I will return to this. For the moment, analogy, then, as relation is implicated in construals of difference, desire, and dynamics; it involves a certain expenditure, a certain risk. Analogy opens and holds open meaning; it describes the constitution of the webs of relation that makes meaning simultaneously both possible and impossibly stabilized.

Let us explore this further by returning to Derrida's observation about the work in Levinas's writings.

> If I now ask at this very moment where I should return my fault, it is because of a certain analogy: what [Levinas] recalls about the names of God is something one would be tempted to say analogically for every proper name. He would be Pro-noun *[Pro-nom]* or the First name *[Pré-nom]* of every name. Just as there is a resemblance between the face of God and the face of man (even if this resemblance is neither an "ontological mark" of the worker on his work nor a "sign" or "effect" of God), in the same way there would be an analogy between all proper names and the names of God, which are, in their turn, analogous among themselves. Consequently, I transport by analogy to the proper name of man or

woman what is said of the names of God. And of the "fault" on the body of these names.[2]

He adds in the next paragraph a clarifying parenthesis: "[T]he analogy is kept, though not quite in the classical sense."[3] What Derrida understands by "the classical sense," and how Levinas's reworking of analogy differs from this sense, can be ascertained from an observation concerning "the necessity of interrupting that analogy," of "refusing to God any analogy with beings that are certainly unique."[4] Levinas's tracing of an analogical operation, then, strikes through the tradition of the *analogia entis,* analogy in the classical sense, according to Derrida.

Two distinct operations are evident in this passage: the first with respect to Levinas's work, and the second with respect to Derrida's transposition (and iteration) of Levinas's work. First, then: The "movement in which the Same goes towards the Other" (Derrida is quoting Levinas here),[5] the movement in which the other leaves its trace in the tearing of the same, Levinas sketches by means of a negotiation between several sets of contrasts: ego and illeity, distance and proximity, finite and infinite, presence and absence, Saying and said, and so on. These contrasts culminate in the face: the face of God and the face of man. It is in this *en face,* in which absolute difference between the wholly other and the same produces, forces, even requires a "resemblance," that the term *analogy* emerges. We will have to return to that group of verbs *produces, forces, requires* in a moment, for they mark a site of ambivalence I wish to investigate. For we need to examine the basis upon which these two faces can be brought into relation; the basis for their comparison and differentiation.

The second operation consists in Derrida's wish to push this analogical thinking further, maybe beyond Levinas's work: "I should be able to transpose the discourse on the names of God to the discourse on human names,"[6] he says, making more explicit,

---

[2] Derrida, "At This Very Moment in This Work Here I Am," in *Re-reading Levinas,* trans. Rubin Berezdivin, eds. Robert Bernasconi and Simon Critchley (London: Athlone Press, 1991), 44–45.

[3] Ibid., 45.

[4] Ibid.

[5] Ibid., 13.

[6] Ibid., 45.

because less playful and ironic, what we have above: "I transport by analogy to the proper name of man or woman what is said of the names of God." What is playful and ironic is not only employment of the verb *to transport* (which Derrida knows is related to the Greek verb *metaphorein* and, more commonly, to the operation of metaphor), but also that this transportation is done "by analogy." In other words, having invoked the Levinasian tracing of a certain analogical operation between the face of God and the face of man, Derrida will: (a) trace the operation of that which remains wholly other "within the economic immanence of language" (that is, make manifest the economy of différance); and (b) move from Levinas's "discourse on the name of God" (and proper names with respect to that transcendent naming) to "this discourse on human names" *by* analogy. By means of these two steps, Derrida, then, transposes the Levinasian concern with transcendence to the Derridean concern with quasi-transcendence—which, if I interpret correctly the discussions several of us had at Villanova last year with Derrida, is not a critique of transcendence, but out-transcendentalizing Levinasian transcendence.[7]

Again, this is something we will return to. But for the moment, let me clarify a central question about this transposition, which is, in effect, a turn from a theological project (in Levinas) to a philosophical project (in Derrida). The question is this: By whose mode of analogy does Derrida make his own analogical move? Or, more pointedly, can Derrida's transposition "by analogy" be made on the basis of, as a further consequence of, the logic of Levinas's analogical thinking? Or does Derrida's transposition "by analogy" bring into play an operation of analogy that is not the same as Levinas's?

THE ANALOGICAL WORLDVIEW

Let me point up the direction in which I am taking us here. What I wish to show are the forms of analogy in operation in posts-

---

[7] See *Questioning God,* ed. John D. Caputo (Bloomington: Indiana University Press, 2001).

tructural thinking, and the worldviews constituted from the modes of relationality implicit in such analogical thinking. What interests me most is the reestablishment of analogy in postmodernity not as a formal operation of logic, but as a participatory, even (for Levinas) a pedagogical operation, with respect to understanding the relationship between the *subjectum* and the transcendent. What Levinas's work maintains is an analogical thinking that takes us beyond concerns with semantic relationships and lexical comparisons, to responsibilities within material relationships, to existential relations.

As such, I suggest, certain poststructural incursions into analogical thinking constitute for the Christian theologian both a space for the operation of its own tradition-based thinking and a difference that it can only mark as such. In other words—and are we not very close to what Derrida has done with Levinas—"by analogy" Christian thinking can both reexamine its own past thinking about analogical reasoning, *and* in doing so will situate itself with respect to the analogical worldviews opened up by various forms of poststructuralism.

Let us examine more closely Levinas's "certain analogy," noting that Derrida contrasts it with analogy "in the classical sense" (by implication analogia entis), but does not elaborate upon what that classical sense might be. Derrida does not undertake the analysis of analogy as such, and this is a significant limitation of his analysis of Levinas. For the tradition of the analogia entis, analogy in the classical sense, is not one. Furthermore, it makes a vast difference to the analogical worldview that evolves, exactly which version of the analogia entis is being exposited and maintained.

In the late fifteenth century, in a treatise entitled *de Nominum Analogia,* Cajetan bequeathed to us most of the technical language for the discussion of the structure of analogy. Most particularly, with the tradition of the analogy of being we are concerned with analogies of proportion in which the analogates share something that the analogon perfects. The most typical example, culled from Aristotle, is that of substance and quantity, which both share in being proportionally. That is, the nature of substance's "to be" is greater than quantity's "to be." Analogia entis, in creating what Cajetan calls proportional identity and proportional unity, installs a hierarchary based upon priority and degrees of perfection. Being itself, God's being *(Esse in Actu per Se)*, is beyond our comprehension; it is only accessible through a certain abstraction from the analogates. Nevertheless, Esse in Actu per Se constitutes the analogon that makes possible all proportional sharings *(esse ut actus)* by the analogates. This becomes important theologically, as we will see.

For the moment, what is significant with respect to Levinas and Derrida is that at least two major versions of the analogia entis tradition emerged, both basing themselves very firmly on the work of Aristotle. One became known as the analogy of proportion, and the other as the analogy of proportionality. I have not space to go into these traditions in any depth, although I have done so in some recently published work on allegory.[8] Basically, in the *Physics* book I and *Metaphysics* book II, Aristotle seemed to suggest that being as the efficient cause of all things is univocal. Scotus takes up this interpretation, and upon it is founded the ontotheological tradition, "the Great Chain of Being" (as termed by Arthur Lovejoy), and the monisms of modern thinkers from Scotus to Spinoza and, on a certain reading, Hegel. If being is univocal, then all things participate proportionally in this one unitary and simple analogate, being, rather like genus to species. This is the basis for cosmological arguments for the existence of God, in which the many all relate to the one through chains of causes and effects to the *ens realissimum:* God as the maximally excellent being, the first cause. It is this classical mode of the analogia entis that Derrida, quite rightly, understands Levinas's work to counter. For Levinas, the ontological realm is the realm of totality. His concern with the good beyond being and with the face of the other, constituted by an *illeity* that can never feature or be thematized as such, involves a rupturing of the ontological and the ontotheological.

The second mode of the analogia entis also issues from Aristotle, partly from the *Metaphysics* and partly from the *Sophistical Refutations* book II and *Ethics* book I, in which being is aporetic or equivocal. Porphyry accepted this view, Scotus rejected it,

---

[8] See "Allegoria: Reading As a Spiritual Excerise," *Modern Theology* 15, no. 3 (July 1999): 271–96.

Aquinas modified it by repeatedly insisting "that *being* is not prior to the primary analogate and that nothing is prior in concept to God,"[9] and Cajetan systematized it. According to this form of the analogia entis, an ontological difference separates God from being such as we understand it. Nevertheless, God "is" in the way God is (that is, necessary and eternal), and things in the world "are" as things in the world are (that is, contingent). So, explicitly in debate with Scotus, Cajetan states: "[I]n analogy [of proportionality] . . . the definition of one is proportionally the definition of the other."[10] With respect to God's goodness, therefore: "That *good* must be said to be common to separate goodness and other things which are good by participation, not univocally but by proportion."[11]

Proportion is not a matter of degrees of sharing in one univocal identity, but more a matter of saying that human beings are wise as God is wise, but each is wise in proportion to what they are (human beings on the one hand, God on the other). This Cajetan calls proportional identity, and possibly makes his own error in then wishing to demonstrate that "proportional identity is a kind of identity,"[12] and, therefore, there can be "scientific knowledge of the analogous."[13] For this does not clarify, as Aquinas will, the nature of such knowledge. That is, for Thomas such knowledge is theological—it concerns the world as created by and maintained in God. This knowledge is made possible on the basis of revelation. It is not a natural knowledge. We cannot know the content of terms such as *being, wisdom* and *goodness* when they refer to God. The analogous names cannot then give us "scientific knowledge" about God.

For Aquinas, following a line of church fathers such as Augustine, Gregory of Nyssa, and Pseudo-Dionysius, will affirm "God is said to have no name, or to be beyond naming, beause his essence is beyond what we understand of him and the meaning of the names we use."[14] A further corollary follows from this,

---

[9] Cajetan, *de Nominum Analogia*, trans. Edward A. Bushinski (Pittsburgh: Duquesne University Press, 1953), 77.
[10] Ibid., 54.
[11] Ibid., 62.
[12] Ibid., 49.
[13] Ibid., 70.
[14] Thomas Aquinas, *Summa Theologicae* part I, question XIII, article I.

which also qualifies the scientific nature of our knowledge. If our knowledge of existence, wisdom, and goodness is only proportional (human being is to wisdom as God is to wisdom, a is to b as x is to y), then if we cannot know the subject of the primary analogon (y), to what extent can we understand the nature of the subject b with respect to human beings? In other words, analogical thinking for Aquinas involves an ineradicable apophatic element that is, nevertheless, inseparable from certain forms of cataphatic description employing superlative qualification: *perfectissimus, purissa veritas,* and so on. Metga concludes:

> Thus for St. Thomas, we get knowledge of God in most cases by *via remotionis,* which gives us negative predications on God telling us what He is not. . . . [W]hile logically analogy assures man of his capacity to know "that God exists," metaphysically, it enables theological language to play the eschatological role of keeping man in his perpetual and natural desire of attaining the vision of what God really is.[15]

This is highly significant: language plays an eschatological role; a role *per participationem* is the salvation wrought. Language mediates and is therefore propaedeutic with respect to beatification. Scotus, of course, challenged this apophasis—it seemed to turn theology into an impossible task. But for Aquinas, what is significant is not the extent to which the proportion can be accurately calculated—for it cannot be—but the extent to which the analogates participate in the analogon. Without the *secundum participationem,*[16] without the pedagogical operation of coming to an understanding of "existence" or "wisdom" or "goodness" with respect to practicing the faith in God who possesses these attributes as his essence, then there would only be a dark night in which all cows were black.

Gregory of Nyssa puts this better when, in his own work, he emphasizes that "analogy" is proceeded by "anagogy"—being drawn upward towards a participation in divine existence, wisdom, and goodness that enables one to better understand what these attributes of God, evident within creation, might signify.

---

[15] Norbert W. Metga, *Analogy and Theological Language in the Summa Contra Gentiles* (Frankfurt: Peter Lang, 1984), 51–52.
[16] *Summa Contra Gentiles* I 32, 6–7.

Cajetan seems to offer an account of analogy that facilitates epistemology; for Nyssa and Aquinas, what limited epistemological function analogy affords is only possible on the basis of an ontological participation in God (the anagogical in Nyssa's language) that issues from the practice of being faithful to that which is revealed. Not that we understand the ontology as such; only the effective relations that ensue. Analogy here concerns relations, then. These are not simply lexical affinities, but relations between the uncreated creator and creation, in terms of the active communication of divine perfections and the effects of that activity.[17]

THE ANALOGICAL THINKING OF LEVINAS AND DERRIDA

Now let us return to Levinas's work and Derrida's construal of a "certain analogy" clarifying Levinas's analogical reasoning with respect to the second version of the classical tradition, which is an Aristotelian as much as a Christian tradition. It is the operation of the third that is crucial. Only the third as wholly other constitutes the neighbor as "face," marks a Saying that invokes the said of communication and substitution, interrupts presence with a past immemorial and absent, and transgresses the finite with the excesses of the infinite.

The binaries are important, for they structure the space for the operation of the wholly other with respect to the same, so that the immanent sphere of the same can become a theater for the play of traces of transcendence. Without this operation or play, there would be equivocation rather than analogy. Nevertheless, as Derrida points out, "a hierarchizing dissymmetry remains,"[18] and the *tout autre* is never grasped in and of itself. As with Aris-

---

[17] This interpretation of Thomas would run contrary to those of scholars such as Herbert McCabe, who view Aquinas's teaching on analogy as (a) not a way of getting to know God, (b) not related to the structure of the universe, because (c) it is merely a comment on our use of words. Of course, in part, one would wish to know what McCabe means by "getting to know God"—for "knowing" itself is analogical: therefore we only know to the extent that we are known, and even then know only according to what it is for creatures to know.

[18] Jacques Derrida, *Adieu: To Emmanuel Levinas,* trans. Pascale-Anne Brault and Michael Naas (Stanford: University of Stanford Press, 1999), 95.

totle (on a certain aporetic reading) and Aquinas, Levinas is examining here the effects of God, not God's essence as God. As with Aquinas, God's alterity has defining characteristics: pure act, possessing the attributes of goodness, omnipotence, omniscience. These characteristics are not predicates of God, but essential to God being God. God's alterity, then, is fundamentally God's *simpliciter*. Furthermore, in both Aquinas and Levinas, what the operation of the transcendent other initiates is desire for the other and what the other commands: communication, justice, responsibility.[19] The analogy is installed by the other as a cosmological operation in which community becomes possible because covenant is demanded.

Where Levinas's thinking, though, seems to differ from Aquinas's is with respect to language and sacrifice. First of all, language, for Levinas, is always a betrayal; the other is always betrayed in representation, in what is said. This is because the ontological sphere always compromises. Of course, even in betrayal a trace of the infinite Saying occurs, and the tracing of this trace gives Levinas's laboring its *raison d'être* and a pedagogical role. Nevertheless, the *via remotionis* is extended in Levinas so that representation itself only has a pedagogical function by default, by being undermined from within. Language does not participate in the pedagogy. Put in another way, ontology is so divorced from the wholly other that it does not *constitute* the relationship of creator/creation. The tout autre continually withdraws; it is his withdrawal that plays within the sealed-up immanence of the same.

We are drawn into that withdrawal, drawn up into an absence. We desire, but does the other desire us? Is there participation in divine loving by my loving? For it is this participation, as Cajetan understood, that defends *analogia proportionalis* from Scotus's criticism of equivocation. It is this participation in a divine loving that perfects and affirms my loving, which enables me to understand myself not just as hostage, as endlessly being emptied out toward the other, but as beloved, as highly favored one. Yes,

---

[19] Levinas speaks of Aquinas briefly, alluding to the analogy between the infinite God and the finite human being in *Alterity and Transcendence,* trans. Michael B. Smith (London: Althone Press, 1999), 61–62. It is not a critical discussion, unfortunately.

the other gives in Levinas, but Derrida claims (with some justification from Levinas) that what is given is not an "effect" of God. What is given, the trace which restructures all thinking and acting, is given by a withdrawal; the trace is almost an unintentional consequence of the withdrawal. For if it were intentional, then the giving of the trace would be an intelligible effect of the passing of God. Lacking, then, the dynamics of participation that Aquinas follows Aristotle in relating to the four forms of causality, this withdrawal nevertheless facilitates the proximity of self and neighbor, and enables the ego to understand itself in the accusative and as accused for what is absent.

But my question, fundamentally, is whether Levinas's analogical thinking gives rise to a tragic cosmology. Is the face of God forever turned away from me? Does God care—even for the stranger? Can we speak of God caring? Is this turn *à dieu* always only in and as *adieu?* For in the face of the neighbor I do not see the face of God, I perceive the trace of God's withdrawal as tout autre.[20] In an essay entitled "Bad Conscience and the Inexorable" (in French it is the much more Husserlian *La conscience non-intentionelle*), Levinas writes: "The call of God does not establish between me and the One who has spoken to me a *relation.*"[21] If there is no relation established, is an analogy between "the face of God and the face of man" possible? Does God have a face at all that I can recognize as such?

Perhaps this is why Derrida observes a "certain analogy"—for analogy it is, but teetering on the edge of equivocation. An analogy that cannot overcome the dualisms that stage and require it because of a lack of reciprocity between the face of God and the faces of human beings; a lack of reciprocity founded upon the

---

[20] In the eucharistic liturgy of the Eastern Orthodox church, the priest bows to the image of God, the face of God, in each human being. In this, a certain incarnational theology is practiced and affirmed. Levinas's lacks an incarnationalism. This need not be because the Jewish faith rejects Christ as the mediation of God, the second person of the Trinity. For there is a Jewish incarnational theology in Rosenzweig's *The Star of Redemption* (trans. William W. Hallo, Notre Dame: Notre Dame University Press, 1985), for example. In Rosenzweig, as for the Eastern Orthodox church, the sphere for the operation of this incarnationalism is liturgy. His work describes a liturgical cosmology.

[21] Emmanuel Levinas, *Ethics and Infinity,* trans. Richard A. Cohen (Pittsburgh: Duquesne University Press, 1986), 40.

condition for God being God, that he is "uncontaminated by being."[22] Derrida proclaims Levinas's God as a God who loves the stranger. But does God love the familiar one, the one who is not a stranger? Indeed, does God love the stranger or, more simply, estrangement? Is there any movement of God *toward* anyone—stranger or familiar one? Or is the world as Levinas views it only composed of strangers, betrayals, absences, and withdrawals?

This is a fallen, almost Manichean world, in which only the messianic promise traces a utopic horizon. But the messianism is fundamental, it seems to me: it offers the philosophical project a theological supplement. Again, I have written about this elsewhere so I will be brief here. Abraham does not wander into endless exile; substitution, betrayal, and absence come to an end. This "is the *hope* of a science of society, and of a society, which are wholly human. And this hope is to be found in Jerusalem," Levinas writes in *Au delà du verset*.[23] He adds, significantly, "in the earthly Jerusalem." I emphasize this last phrase for if or when the messianic promise is fulfilled, will God still be uncontaminated by being? I cannot answer that—for Levinas, for the kind of Jewish man Levinas was. I leave it suspended, weighted with the silence that collects about it.

I turn instead to Derrida now, and Derrida's analogical negotiations that explicitly reject Levinas's determining messianism: "The same duty to analyse would lead me to dissociate, with all the consequences which might follow, a structural messianicity, an irrecusable and threatening promise, an eschatology without teleology, from every determinate messianism."[24] Ironically, he does see Levinas as pointing the way to this new "structural messanicity" with his discussions of "a revelation of Torah before Sinai."[25] But what I would like to do is follow through "all the consequences which might follow" for analogical thinking from such a rejection. This returns us to the question I raised earlier,

---

[22] Derrida, *Adieu: To Emmanuel Levinas*, 112.
[23] Emmanuel Levinas, *Beyond the Verse*, trans. Gary D. Mole (London: Athlone Press, 1994), 52.
[24] Derrida, *Adieu: To Emmanuel Levinas*, 118–19.
[25] Ibid., 118.

SPEAKING OTHERWISE: POSTMODERN ANALOGY 201

concerning Derrida's transposition of Levinas's analogical reasoning.

In wishing to examine Derrida's analogical transposition, I am going to avoid the well-rehearsed debates concerning deconstruction and negative theology. Only one aspect of analogy concerns negative theology; only one aspect of analogy has its face turned toward apophasis. The fundamental characteristic of analogy, as I have been stressing, is relation. I want to explore, then, Derrida's analogical thinking through his work on political and ethical relations, most particularly his book *Politics of Friendship*. The "aporia of friendship," he writes, "seems doomed to the similar and the dissimilar."[26] With friendship's association with analogy, Derrida is drawn into a conversation between Aristotle and Aquinas.[27]

His essay "En ce moment dans cette oeuvre" is an essay on friendship, insofar as it is a tribute to Levinas and a prolonged negotiation between Derrida's work and Levinas's. It is not a simple negotiation, by any means. For Derrida is aware of what he has already received from Levinas, and that his own work already operates within Levinas's thinking. No straightforward affirmation/critique/reappropiation can structure his response. Furthermore, the question of who is Derrida and who is Levinas, the location of subjectivities in negotiation, is instinctive to the writing that proceeds through several voices engaging and interrupting each other: voices that are gendered but remain, otherwise, insubstantial, unnamed, uncharacterized *dramatis personae*. The essay constitutes an analogical reading of Levinas's work— much more so than either the critique of the earlier "Violence and Metaphysics" or the appreciation of *A-Dieu*. "At This Very Moment" interlaces their voices and their work, paving out the similarities (with the other, representation and substitution), interpellating the differences (of the feminine voice), and arriving at the point where the interlocutor is unsure who is speaking.

---

[26] Jacques Derrida, *The Politics of Friendship*, trans. George Collins (London: Verso, 1997), 7.

[27] This is a complex issue: the co-implication of friendship and analogy as a cosmological relation. Central to understanding the nature of this relation would be an anthropology that would view the human as itself analogical, which, for Aquinas, would relate being human to Christology and sacramentalism.

Fundamental to the economy of différance is a construal of
the analogical relationship between words: differ/defer sets up a
relation between the similar and the dissimilar. Derrida's key
concept with respect to différance is "iteration." This is a close
companion to James Ross's account of linguistic differentiation
and analogy as one mode of such differentiation: "Outside a context a word has no signification at all (nor any detonation) but
has (in its other contexts of occurrence) partly delimited *possibilities* or *ranges* of signification that are adopted, fitted, to context.
The avaricious adoption results are the species of differentiation
(analogy, metaphor, denomination, and mere equivocation)."[28]
As Ross himself recognizes, these principles of iteration and differentiation infer that: "Potentially infinite polysemy is the feature upon which the indefinite expressive capacity of language
rests."[29] Ross is explicitly developing a dynamic and diachronic
version of Wittgenstein's synchronic description of so-called
"family resemblances"; and a number of scholars have observed
the similarities between Wittgenstein's nonfoundational semantics and Derrida's account of a semiotic differing that installs a
semantic deferral.

It is différance that draws Derrida to Levinas's analysis of substitution and what he would call the haunting of the Saying in the
said. And it is différance that leads him to perform the task of
reading Levinas in what is sometimes a baroque and oblique
manner, for "another language comes to disturb the first one.
It doesn't inhabit it, but haunts it."[30] Meticulously tracing the
"negotiation" that "negotiates the nonnegotiable"[31] in Levinas,
the specter of the other, Derrida is also simultaneously negotiat-
ing the general economy of signification with its aporia, intervals, and interlacings. But unlike Ross and more in line with
Levinas, Derrida's analogical operations are not restricted to lexical determinations or nondeterminations. Ross, following in a
line of modern thinkers examining analogy, treats the subject in
terms of "linguistic regularities and without an 'idea-in-the-

---

[28] James Ross, *Portraying Analogy* (Cambridge: Cambridge University Press,
1981), 48.
[29] Ibid., 49.
[30] Derrida, "At This Very Moment," 18.
[31] Ibid., 20.

mind' model for linguistic meaning."[32] In Cajetan's terminology, Ross (as so many moderns) is treating the logic *in actu signato,* without paying any attention to the manner in which the order *(actus)* is realized concretely (or *in actu exercito).*

It is exactly the contribution of poststructuralist thinkers such as Levinas, Derrida, Irigaray, and Kristeva that they have retrieved a premodern account of the analogical imagination, refiguring analogy's relationship to cosmology. We see this with Derrida, who, in his negotiations with Levinas and in his more recent work on the politics and ethics of deconstruction, transposes the economy of différance into an investigation of relationality as such. It is with this account of relationality that I want to open up the analogical worldview in Derrrida's writing.

Like Levinas, Derrida constructs his analogical world on the basis of several binary considerations focused around identity and its loss, around the rupture in reciprocity. Différance itself concerns doubleness, "two times and two voices."[33] This leads to a series of paradoxical tensions sharing a repeated syntagma: relation without relation, community without community, religion without religion, x without x. This is the syntagma that différance shares with apophatic discourse. In *Politics of Friendship,* Derrida investigates these tensions through a sustained meditation upon the possible impossibility of friendship. This investigation is structurally similar to the possible impossibility of the gift in *Given Time* or *The Gift of Death.* The thinking circles about several themes central to analogical thinking: a determined opposition that, in being determined, necessitates a relation that "signifies in me the other who decides and rends";[34] concepts that bear "the phantom of the other";[35] and the maintenance of "an infinite distance within 'good friendship.'"[36]

Friendship, then, is continually called "back to the irreducible

---

[32] Ross, *Portraying Analogy,* 18. If there were time, we could trace this move toward a formal and nonmetaphysical treatment of analogy that began in the late Middle Ages with Ockham and St. John Thomas, moving through Locke, and then through Kant's deployment of analogy in *The Critique of Pure Reason,* to the more explicit work on semantics by John Lyons and Ross.

[33] Derrida, *The Politics of Friendship,* 50.

[34] Ibid., 68.

[35] Ibid., 72.

[36] Ibid., 65.

precedence of the other"[37] in a manner evocative of Levinas's "certain analogy." But what of the worldview that emerges from Derrida's analogical thinking of relation? We can define that worldview more closely by examining the metaphorics that flesh out his movements between univocity and equivocity, identity and loss:

> We could demonstrate . . . that this equiprimodiality of truth and untruth, like that of all the apparently opposite possibilities that are inextricably linked to it, destabilize all the conceptual distinctions that seem to structure the existential analytic, dooming its logic to an *Unheimlichkeit* marking each of its decisive moments. In truth, it undoes, it disidentifies, the identification of every concept. It appeals to a thinking beyond the concept, but *a fortiori* beyond intuition. It surpasses reason, but *a fortiori* the understanding too . . . the word *unheimlich* is not unfamiliar, though it speaks precisely to the stranger, to the intimacy of hearth and familiar lodgings . . . but above all . . . it provides a place, in a troubling way, for a form of welcome in itself that recalls the haunt as much as the home.[38]

The structure of analogy is explicit, as the economy of différance is transposed into existential and metaphysical categories—existential insofar as différance is given a sociological and anthropological mise-en-scène, metaphysical insofar as an appeal is made to that beyond concept, intuition, understanding, and reason.

There are three points I wish to raise with respect to the existential condition portrayed in this analogical thinking. First, analogy makes no appeal to the theological, as with Levinas. Although a certain rational immanentism is ruptured by a transcendental haunting, Derrida's analysis is not of the transcendent as such, but of the haunting. This distinguishes Levinasian analogy from Derridean. Levinas's founding analogy is between God and human beings; Derrida's is between identity and difference (a development of Husserl's project in *Cartesian Meditations*). What is common to both is an "originary" absence. But how do each *recognize* absence as absence? For something or someone

---

[37] Ibid., 63.
[38] Ibid., 58.

to be recognized as absent, one of two accounts has to be given. Either there was a presence that now is no longer, which is the basis of Derrida's "hauntology" and his account of the work of mourning (whether of Marx or Paul de Man), or there is a transcendental deduction from a certain given. We can put this in syllogistic form:

(a) Language is concerned with the communication of meaning.
(b) Meaning is never self-present, for communication of meaning is always caught in the time lag of re-presentation and so always deferred.
(c) Therefore the condition for the possibility of language as the communication of meaning is an impossibility, an absence or lack it cannot convert. Language simultaneously promises and betrays; it is a friend only insofar as also it is an enemy.

Derrida slides between these two accounts of absence, as does Levinas. The difference between them is that ultimately, Levinas's account of what is exterior, the good beyond being, God, is founded upon a revelation received and disseminated through a tradition, a revelation to Moses of God's face. That is, Levinas's account requires an account in the tradition of a past encounter, a relation. Revelation founds the possibility of Levinas's "trace." We can take this further.

It is not insignificant that the passage quoted above weaves Derrida's voice into that of Heidegger and Kant: Heidegger's *Weltanschauung* is analyzed through Kantian categories. Derrida shares and develops the problematic of identity and difference with respect to Heidegger. But Derrida's construal of analogy is thoroughly Kantian. In *The Critique of Pure Reason,* Kant, having outlined the a priori intuitions of space and time, continues in his transcendental schema to argue for the conditions for experience of the world. There are, you will recall, three conditions, or principles: the principle of the permanence of substance; the principle of succession or causality; and the principle of coexistence, or the law of reciprocity and interconnectedness. Kant arrives at these principles through analogical reasoning of a certain kind. He writes:

In philosophy analogies signify something very different from what they represent in mathematics. In the latter they are formulas which express equality to two quantitative relations, and are always *constitutive;* so that if three members of the proportion are given, the fourth is likewise given, that is, can be constructed. But in philosophy the analogy is not the equality of two quantitative but two qualitative relations; and from the third given member we can obtain *a priori* knowledge only of a relation to a fourth, not of the member itself. The relation yields, however, a rule for seeking the fourth member in experience, and a mark whereby it can be detected. An analogy of experience is therefore only a rule according to which a unity of experience may arise from a perception. . . . It is not a principle *constitutive* of the objects, that is, of the appearances, but only *regulative.*[39]

I suggest that Derrida's analogical thinking owes much to Kantian modes of thinking in that, like Kant, the other, the stranger, the enemy, that which disturbs and destabilizes, dwells within and makes possible the familial, the friend, the hosting. Its "reality," its being there at all, is a deduction of specific existential analyses, as in the case of *The Politics of Friendship.* However, one would have to qualify Derrida's kind of existential analysis from Sartre's, say, or Levinas's, for in the line of Heidegger, it proceeds through texts and with reference to economies of signification. Nevertheless, the point I wish to make is that what the analogy provides is not (as with Aquinas and Levinas) a constitutive principle—a God who constitutes knowledge in and about the world, and human beings with respect to that God and each other. Derrida's analogical deduction, his transcendental reasoning provides, like that of Kant, a regulative principle: a principle of hauntology or spectrality. Such a principle, as Kant understood, is necessary for the possibility of knowledge at all, but it renders all knowledge phantasmic, virtual. Being is not a predicate, and so nothing is added to what is known by saying it exists. Its status, both epistemologically and ontologically, is undecidable. To the extent that it is undecidable, then, one could say, as I'm sure Derrida would say, that we cannot therefore decide either whether the principle of analogy is regulative or constitutive. Who could make such a judgment? From what position?

---

[39] Immanuel Kant, *The Critique of Pure Reason,* trans. Norman Kemp Smith (Basingstoke: Macmillan, 1929), 211.

We cannot, then, even identify and delimit this nonprinciple. This is the Derridean inflection of the Kantian problematic. Since it is undecidable, we cannot make the distinction between regulative or constitutive. This has numerous repercussions for the ontological "status" of Derrida's others, strangers and enemies —which, in turn, renders both ethics and politics impossible. That we can still act, that we can still make a decision is not denied. But the impossibility of ever knowing whether we have acted well or acted justly (the impossibility of knowing whether someone is other, a stranger or an enemy, in need or in plenty, a beggar or a thief) renders decision making local and pragmatic.

But let us examine some of the many implications of this for the difference between the analogical worldviews of Levinas and Derrida. For Levinas, the good beyond being continually disrupts the phenomenal world constituting our knowledge of justice and responsibility in a world that (as we have seen) is dark, punctuated with violence, and pervaded with opaque significations (saids in which the Saying is betrayed). For Derrida, analogical relations at times seem to weave gossamer webs of relation across terrifying tracts of absence. Observe the metaphorics in this description:

> The protection of this custody guarantees the truth of friendship, its ambiguous truth, that by which friends protect themselves from the error or the illusion on which friendship is founded—more precisely, the bottomless bottom of friendship, which enables it to resist its own abyss. To resist the vertigo or the revolution that would have it turning around itself. Friendship is founded, in truth, so as to protect itself from the bottom, or the abyssal bottomless depths.[40]

Observe the metaphorics in this description of the fundamental Derridean syntagma "x without x":

> [T]hese warnings turn endlessly. Yes, like searchlights without a coast, they sweep across the dark sky, shut down or disappear at regular intervals and harbour the invisible in their very light. We no longer even know against what dangers of abysses we are forewarned. We avoid one, only to be thrown into one of the others.

---

[40] Derrida, *The Politics of Friendship*, 53.

We no longer even know whether these watchmen are guiding us towards another destination, nor even if the destination remains promised or determined.[41]

This is the worldview made manifest by Derrida's own analogical thinking, in which rafts of illumination travel like starships through the folds of a dark infinity. It is a world in which analogical relations—amphibolous regulative relations, as Kant calls them—are necessarily instituted, like friendships, to conceal the madness of a semiosis that renders both univocity and equivocity meaningless. And yet, as Derrida understands, this too is only one picture, and to decide upon this cosmology would be too determinative of what différance gives us to think. So elsewhere, another conflicting metaphorics comes into play: "[L]ove *in* friendship, lovence beyond love and friendship following their determined figures, beyond all this book's trajectories of reading, beyond all ages, cultures and traditions of loving."[42]

Here the relations are not regulative, but participate in a transcendent and constitutive relationality. The transcendental in both accounts is a horizon: either dark, abyssal, and taut with unseen dangers, or, much less frequently, welcoming and utopic, promising universal reconciliation or what he calls elsewhere a New International. It is an undecidable horizon and, as such, breeds an agnosticism that cannot but make all action and decision agonistic. The culture of deconstructive double bind is sadomasochistic, as Derrida himself articulates it:

What I thus engage in the double constraint of a *double bind* is not only myself, nor my own desire, but the other, the Messiah or the god himself. As if I were calling someone—for example, on the telephone—saying to him or her, in sum: 'I don't want you to wait for my call and become forever dependent upon it; go out on the town, be free not to answer. And to prove it, the next time I call you, don't answer, or I won't see you again. If you answer my call, it's all over.'[43]

It is a culture in which Derrida advises we be patient: "[W]e must be patient at the crossroads and endure this *undecidable*."[44]

[41] Ibid., 81.
[42] Ibid., 69.
[43] Ibid., 174.
[44] Ibid., 123.

Endurance has none of Heidegger's sense of release in "perdurance," nor any of the mystical surrender of Eckhart's *Gelassenheit*. Derrida composes a different world. It is not a god-forsaken world, as Kant's is not a god-forsaken world. But by refusing to think through the theological as that which the collapse of the secular opens up, by stalling at the theological supplement, then Derrida's world seeks to maintain the integrity of secular thinking and even certain Enlightenment ideals—freedom, equality, democracy by consensus—seeks also to maintain an ethics of integrity based upon maintaining itself, even though the basis for that thinking is aporia as such. Even though what ensues is the impossible possibility of these ideals and the integrity of every discourse with respect to them.

And this is what alarms me. For given the competition that I see in contemporary globalism between a commitment to endless ambiguity and the purveyors of strong market ideologies or forceful fundamentalisms, it's quite clear who would win.

At this point, I wish to clarify that I am not making a moral judgement on Levinas's or Derrida's analogical thinking. I am attempting to draw out two poststructural analogical worldviews, and relationality as it issues from the transcendental or the quasi-transcendental relation such thinking installs. In doing this with respect to Levinas and Derrida, I want to point out what the theological supplement actually facilitates both in Levinas's worldview and in a Christian worldview. The theological supplement both creates the space for transformative practices of hope in what is otherwise a culture of sadomasochism, and stalls a certain quietism or maybe paralysis of action that enduring the undecidable seems to suggest.

This is what makes the theological supplement significant. In arguing in this way, I am not attempting to persuade atheists and agnostics to become practitioners of a tradition-based faith. Theological thinking cannot be applied like a poultice to the bodies politic; rather, the bodies politic have to be understood, lived, and acted upon from within the theological tradition. But I am attempting to clarify the social and political implications of different worldviews and, in doing that, to argue for the significance of the theological account of creation. What I am pointing to, with respect to Derrida's work on ethical and political relations,

is a distinct lack of resources within secular postmodern thinking, for providing an account of ethical and political activity that
is not simply pragmatic and arbitrary.

Finally, ideas are not conceived in a vacuum; construals of
analogy have cultural contexts to which hardly any attention has
been paid. Levinas's analogical thinking was born of a different
world—of two world wars, persecution, concentration camps, re-
surgent nationalism, Cold War pessimism, and the demise of so-
cialism. Derrida's analogical thinking is forged in another
crucible that includes some of Levinas's cultural foci, and others
such as the Algerian War, Bosnia, the fall of the Berlin wall, and
the potential threat of depoliticization with developing globalism. Neither Levinas's nor Derrida's world is Aquinas's world,
and the latter is not mine either. Aquinas's world can seem inor-
dinately "sunny" and "harmonious," like those theologies in
stone at Chartres or Ely. Despite the barbarisms and brutalities
evinced by historians, the Middle Ages have, thoughout the nineteenth and twentieth centuries, operated as subliminal back-pro-
jections for the utopian. I am suspicious of this.

What I attempting to do is investigate the ethical, metaphysical, and ultimately theological account of the analogy of "the
face of God and face of man" in Levinas and analyze the profoundly aporetic cosmology of Derrida, in order that I might
begin the task of picturing an analogical worldview from the perspective of contemporary practices in the Christian faith. That is,
I wish to expand in terms of a Christian cosmology the space for
analogical thinking that some poststructural thinkers of difference have opened up. And while taking seriously, I hope, the
profound understanding of kenosis and substitution, withdrawal,
betrayal, and absence, the practice of the Christian faith has to
relate such insights to its own incarnational ones, which emphasize presence and grace, all things as participating in the goodness of God, and, therefore, in themselves, good.

The doctrines of creation (and the triune Godhead enfolding
that ongoing operation of creation), the doctrines of *poeisis*, both
human and divine (and the economy of salvation in and through
and by the historical, carnal, psychological and social), establish
a different world order that offers hope for eschatologically informed practices for today—a hope endlessly deferred in Derrida

and having the structure of a not-yet in Levinas. The work continues. In my book *Cities of God* (London: Routledge, 2000), I sketch what might be possible in a postmodern Christian account of relations, human and divine: a Christian analogical worldview. What this essay attempts to show is why such analogical thinking can again be taken seriously and what, specifically, Christian analogical thinking can contribute to contemporary debates.

10

Apophasis and Askêsis: Contemporary Philosophy and Mystical Theology

Jonathan Ellsworth

THIS MUCH, at least, is clear: we continue to speak of *apophasis.* Studies on the logic and language of apophatic discourse abound,[1] and more are on the way. But why this concern, today, with apophaticism? More specifically, why is it that apophatic theologies are (still? again?) being studied and discussed in certain segments of contemporary philosophy? And to what end? This essay will first hazard a few answers and offer some remarks on contemporary philosophy's ongoing interests in—and appropriations of—apophatic theological language. Attention will then be called to an essential feature of these apophatic texts that many studies neglect, namely the link between *apophasis* and *askêsis:* one rarely finds mystical theologies where the former is employed without the latter. The consequences of our failure to acknowledge this link will be explored, and I will suggest some of the epistemological, hermeneutical, and ethical implications of such an acknowledgment.[2]

I

Across this body of contemporary work on—or in—apophatic theologies, there are a handful of recurring issues that seem to

---

[1] Including works by Jean-Luc Marion, Jacques Derrida, Pierre Hadot, Kevin Hart, David Tracy, John Caputo, Grace Jantzen, Michael Sells, Denys Turner, and Thomas A. Carlson—to name but a few.

[2] Throughout this essay, the terms *apophatic theologies, negative theologies,* and *mystical theologies* are used rather interchangeably, and in the singular or

have fixed our attention. (1) After Nietzsche and Heidegger, many Continental philosopher-theologians have obsessed over the problems and prospects of freeing themselves from a meta-physically constituted theological vocabulary. The idioms employed by apophatic theologies have been looked to as a possible way out.[3] (2) The logic and language of apophatic discourse is finding currency in its concern to cope with both finitude and the speech of finite beings who desire to speak of the infinite—the transcendent—that which is not containable in language. As Jean-Luc Marion has recently put it, "the question is how far we can go to admit the incomprehensible in terms of the rational. How is it possible, within the limits of rationality, to describe the incomprehensible?"[4] (3) Such questions have, of course, inspired attempts to mark the similarities and differences among classical apophasis, deconstruction, and *différance,* as all three would refer to and designate the "other" of language.[5] (4) Furthermore, these issues have been reported to be no mere matter of a provincial curiosity regarding recent German and French philosophy. Rather, what is sometimes singularly named "negative theology" is said to register the desire and dream of us all. While reflecting upon Jacques Derrida's own relationship to negative theology, Jack Caputo writes: "[I]n Derrida's view, what happens in negative theology happens to us all, is of 'general' import. We are all dreaming of the *tout autre,* about which we do not know how not to speak, under many names, so we will all have to learn negative theology, if not in the 'original,' if such a

---

plural. I have chosen to keep all of these terms, rather than to select just one, as a reminder that each is best regarded as a loose *modern* designation for those ancient texts that resort to apophatic techniques in naming God.

[3] For a number of papers relevant to questions of the extent to which apophatic discourses remain inscribed in or wrest free from metaphysical determination, see *God, the Gift, and Postmodernism,* eds. John D. Caputo and Michael J. Scanlon (Bloomington: Indiana University Press, 1999).

[4] Jean-Luc Marion, "Philosophy and Negative Theology," course lecture, University of Chicago, Spring 1999.

[5] See, for example, Rodolphe Gasché, *The Tain of the Mirror: Derrida and the Philosophy of Reflection* (Cambridge: Harvard University Press, 1986); Kevin Hart, *The Trespass of the Sign: Deconstruction, Theology, and Philosophy* (Cambridge: Cambridge University Press, 1991; reprint, with new introduction and appendix, New York: Fordham Press, 2000); and Thomas A. Carlson, *Indiscretion: Finitude and the Naming of God* (Chicago: University of Chicago Press, 1999).

thing exists, at least in translation, in a generalized apophatics."[6] This is to suggest, then, that one of contemporary philosophy's interests in negative theologies stems from a longing to be a discourse *about* the wholly other (tout autre), a longing to discourse *with* the wholly other.[7]

While these four themes certainly do not cover the whole of contemporary interest in mystical theologies, I take it that they may be viewed as representative of some of the more prominent preoccupations in philosophy and philosophical theology. What underlies these themes is an interest in appropriation. Apophatic theologies are being turned to, not only out of academic and historical interest, but because individuals are finding in these texts resources for the fields of philosophy, philosophy of religion, theology, and politics.[8]

But there is a common and extremely important component of these theologies that has made less of an impact on our appropriations of these old books: namely, their constant concern with the training and preparation one must undergo before embarking upon the course of apophatic ascent. Historically, there are rather particular codes of conduct that precede any initiation into apophatic mystical itineraries,[9] and I wish to highlight this intimate relationship between apophatic theologies and askêsis, so as to make clear that negative theologies do not merely suggest a way of talking, but present techniques, philosophical disciplines or spiritual exercises, that aim at a fairly specific telos: uplift to the divine—or, if you prefer, an experience of alterity.

Given this, I think it worthwhile to raise concerns about the apparent divorce of negative theological language from its constitutive practices. Certainly, if our uses of negative theology

---

[6] John D. Caputo, *The Prayers and Tears of Jacques Derrida* (Bloomington: Indiana University Press, 1997), 32.

[7] An interest that has spread from, perhaps especially, the work of Levinas and Derrida.

[8] On the political uses of negative theology, see Derrida's *Sauf le nom* ("on the name"), trans. John Leavey (Stanford: Stanford University Press, 1995); and especially Derrida's remarks on the political motives in bringing together negative theology and phenomenology in *Sauf le nom*, in *God, the Gift, and Postmodernism*, 75–77.

[9] I have in mind the likes of Plotinus, Evagrius Ponticus, Dionysius, Anselm, Bonaventure, Teresa of Avila, etc.

simply enhance our philosophical vocabularies or linguistic theories, we must wonder to what extent our appropriations enact a betrayal of these theologies?[10] Ultimately, this question will lead us to the issues of why and how philosophy—and philosophy of religions—should attend to the notion of askêsis.

I do need to forewarn that for this essay, I have limited the number of historical figures and texts that would serve as supporting evidence. In doing so, I wish to avoid getting hung up on a particularly contestable figure or example. While I want to stress that my primary concern is with a contemporary *appropriation* of these apophatic mystical texts—and therefore I am not now making a strictly historical point about the way things once were—I do believe that my remarks are well supported by the historical studies of, among others, Andrew Louth and Bernard McGinn, and especially McGinn's four-volume history of mysticism.[11] But I also believe that a rigorous examination of the extent to which a particular person or text might be illumined by a focus upon ascetical conditions stands as work that lies ahead of us, not behind us.[12] So my aims for this essay are modest: I only hope here to be suggestive, not conclusive.

II

We turn now to this notion of philosophical askêsis, that is, philosophical disciplines or spiritual exercises undertaken for the sake

---

[10] I do not mean to suggest that every study must devote itself to the ascetical dimensions of apophatic discourse—certainly it is appropriate for some studies to zero in on linguistic issues and idiomatic features. But the charge here is of an undue lack of attention paid to askêsis in philosophical studies of such works.

[11] See Bernard McGinn's four-volume *The Presence of God: A History of Western Christian Mysticism* (New York: Crossroad, 1991–2001); and Andrew Louth, *The Origins of the Christian Mystical Tradition* (Oxford: Clarendon Press, 1983).

[12] I should say too that I will be bracketing the question of whether particular persons actually achieved mystical ascent, or even undertook the constitutive exercises of such an ascent. What is clear in the texts I will mention is that exercises *are* commended, exercises that we are invited to take up ourselves. So questions of whether the practices promoted by certain figures or texts are "experientially based" or are merely "theoretically constructed" will not draw our focus here. See R. T. Wallis, "Nous As Experience," in *The Significance of*

of the transformation of the self and one's mode of being.[13] My own thinking on these matters has been catalyzed by the work of Pierre Hadot, as well as the studies of Michel Foucault on the topic of philosophical askêsis in Greco-Roman antiquity. I have drawn upon the conceptual resources of Hadot and Foucault to construct a general schematic that will undergird our considerations of the aims of apophatic, mystical theologies. It may, unfortunately, still need to be said that Foucault's encounter with Hadot's work was philosophically decisive for his own engagement with these themes. Foucault was quick to acknowledge this debt and spoke very enthusiastically about Hadot, but Hadot remains relatively unknown, and unread, at least in comparison with Foucault.[14]

Foucault's later version of ethics is itself derived from Hadot's work on askêsis and the exercises of the self. And it would be an illuminating exercise to read mystical theologies through the interpretive framework of Foucault's conceptualization of ethics (the four components of what he calls the *rapport à soi,* the care of the self).[15] But for now, I will restrict myself to some remarks

---

Neoplatonism, ed. Baine Harris (Albany: State University of New York Press, 1976), 123.

[13] Cf. Foucault's "The Ethics of the Concern for Self As a Practice of Freedom," in *Ethics: Subjectivity and Truth,* ed. Paul Rabinow (New York: The New Press, 1997), 282.

[14] On the influence of Hadot on Foucault, see *Foucault and His Interlocutors,* ed. Arnold I. Davidson (Chicago: University of Chicago Press, 1997), 199–202. This influence is evident from Foucault's 1981–82 lecture course, *L'Herméneutique du sujet: Cours au Collège de France, 1981–1982,* ed. Frédéric Gros under the direction of F. Ewald and A. Fontana (Paris, Gallimard/Seuil, 2001). Hadot's works include *Plotinus, Or the Simplicity of Vision,* trans. Michael Chase (Chicago: University of Chicago Press, 1993; *Philosophy As a Way of Life: Spiritual Exercises from Socrates to Foucault,* ed. Arnold I. Davidson, trans. Michael Chase (Cambridge, Mass.: Blackwell, 1995); *Qu'est-ce que la philosophie antique* (Paris: Gallimard, 1995); *The Inner Citadel: The Meditations of Marcus Aurelius,* trans. Michael Chase (Cambridge: Harvard University Press, 1998); and *Études de philosophie ancienne* (Paris: Les Belles Lettres, 1998).

[15] The four aspects of the rapport à soi: (1) ethical substance *(substance éthique):* e.g., feelings, intentions, desires, mind/soul; (2) mode of subjection *(mode d'assujettissement):* the way in which one establishes a relation to the rule and recognizes himself as obliged to heed this rule: e.g., as divine dictate, as natural law, as an aesthetically superior ethic; (3) practices of the self/asceticism *(pratique de soi/l'ascétisme):* fasting, contemplation, meditation, etc.; (4) telos *(téléologie):* immortality, purity, mastery of oneself, uplift to the divine

made in a late interview with Paul Rabinow and Hubert Dreyfus, where Foucault offers his most lucid description of the type or function of askêsis with which I am here concerned: the idea that askêsis provides access to the truth, access to new experiences.[16] I then want to interpret this particular notion of askêsis as a means to new experience, through the lens of mystical theology's emphasis on the need to *cultivate* capacities of receptivity.

So first, Foucault's historical characterization of askêsis from the ancient Greeks through the late medieval period. He says:

> Greek philosophy . . . always held that a subject *could not have access to the truth* if he did not *first* operate upon himself a certain work that would make him susceptible to knowing the truth—a work of purification, conversion of the soul by contemplation of the soul. . . . In European culture up to the sixteenth century, the problem remains: What is the work I must effect upon myself so as to be *capable* and *worthy* of acceding to the truth? To put it another way: truth always has a price; *no access* to truth without ascesis. . . . Descartes, I think, broke with this when he said, "To accede to truth, it suffices that I be *any* subject that can see what is *evident.*" Evidence is substituted for ascesis at the point where the relationship to the self intersects the relationship to others and the world. *The relationship to the self no longer needs to be ascetic to get into relation to truth.* . . . Before Descartes, one could not be impure, immoral, and know the truth. With Descartes, direct evidence is enough. After Descartes, we have a nonascetic subject of knowledge.[17]

In this analysis, Foucault associates the separation of askêsis and epistemology with the origin of modern philosophy, and points

---

or mystical experience. See Foucault's "On the Genealogy of Ethics: A Work in Progress," in *Ethics: Subjectivity and Truth*, 262–65; and *The Use of Pleasure*, Robert Hurley's translation of *L'Usage des plaisirs* (New York: Vintage Books, 1985), 25–32. For reasons still unbeknownst to me, Hurley has translated the plural *plaisirs* with the singular "pleasure," a decision that is at odds not only with the French language, but also with Foucault's work to demonstrate the insufficiency of a singular category "pleasure" to encompass the experience of diverse phenomena with diverse origins.

[16] In the various philosophical movements and schools of antiquity, different ascetical practices had different effects that they were to engender in the individual; e.g., assuage fear, decrease the appetites, instill a philosophical doctrine, achieve cosmic consciousness, etc.

[17] Foucault, "On the Genealogy of Ethics: A Work in Progress," *Ethics: Subjectivity and Truth*, 278–79 (emphasis added).

specifically to Descartes's *Meditations* as a philosophical water-shed. Purification and conversion of the soul are devalued as a means of achieving—or receiving—right perception or truth. For now, I will leave aside questions of the adequacy of Foucault's description of Descartes so as to focus upon Foucault's description of askêsis as the condition of possibility for truth, and the suggestion of the need for an individual to cultivate a receptivity to the truth.[18] For it is precisely such prerequisites as purification and conversion of the soul that are so important for the mystical theologians with which we are concerned here.

In speaking of askêsis, then, I do not have in mind the simple rehearsing of truths one has already come to know, though this type or function of askêsis is certainly important. (Epictetus and his teacher Musonius Rufus primarily viewed askêsis as the application of philosophical lessons.[19] For example, if I am a wealthy Roman Stoic, I know that wealth is neither a good nor an ill, but I may wear coarse clothes and eat only a bit of hard bread for a day or two before a great festival—just to reinforce the point.)[20] In addition to this aim of askêsis, the goal of askêsis that we repeatedly find operating in ascetico-mystical theologies is not merely to apply already learned lessons and truths. Rather, the aim of the practices utilized and commended is to permit access to the truth *in the first place*. That is, these ascetical practices put us in a new position of receptivity to philosophical insight, truth, or experience.[21] What is at stake, then, in our coming to terms with these ascetico-mystical texts—what I take to be the

---

[18] It needs to be said, though, that Descartes does employ certain forms of askêsis. It is, after all, a *meditation* with which he presents his readers. And he does undertake a sort of physical *anachôrêsis*, or withdrawal (he holes up in front of the fireplace, and he endeavors to retreat from the senses), which suggests a sort of inflection of the monastic disciplines of separation, solitude, and interiorization.

[19] See James A. Francis, *Subversive Virtue: Asceticism and Authority in the Second-Century Pagan World* (University Park: The Pennsylvania State University Press), 11.

[20] See Seneca, *Epistle XVIII, Epistulae Morales,* vol. I (Oxford: Oxford University Press, 1965), 47–50.

[21] Let me say too that, at least for now, I want to embrace all of these terms: insight, truth, experience, understanding, new orientation—and perhaps other terms too—as signifiers for what it is that we might find ourselves in a position to receive.

challenge of these texts to us—is the claim that certain practices
and disciplines, certain ascetics, can allow us to cultivate certain
capacities of receptivity.

I offer just a few quotations from or about several persons who
can be taken to support this notion. Plutarch, according to J. M.
Dillon,

> plainly holds that knowledge of God is not simply a matter of
> philosophizing in the modern sense, but rather of training and dis-
> ciplining the mind through ascetic practices and the observance
> of ritual. Of course, intellectual philosophizing—the practice of
> dialectic and other Platonic methods—is necessary also, but it will
> not achieve knowledge of God without the observance of a certain
> way of life.[22]

Pierre Hadot alludes to this ascetical cultivation of receptivity in
the Plotinian preparation for the experience of union:

> For Plotinus, abstract teaching could allude to this experience, but
> could not lead to it. Only asceticism and a moral life could truly
> prepare the soul for such a union.[23]

From Plotinus himself, in *Enneads* 6.9.4, we read:

> The One is absent from nothing and from everything. It is present
> only to those who are prepared for it and are able to receive it, to
> enter into harmony with it, to grasp and to touch it by virtue of
> their likeness to it, by virtue of that inner power similar to and
> stemming from the One when it is in that state in which it was
> when it originated from the One. Thus will the One be "seen" as
> far as it can become an object of contemplation.[24]

In the eighth letter of Dionysius the Areopagite, we read:

> Those closest to the true light are more capable of receiving light
> and of passing it on. Do not imagine that the proximity here is

---

[22] J. M. Dillon, "Plutarch and Second Century Platonism," in *Classical Medi-
terranean Spirituality: Egyptian, Greek, Roman,* ed. A. H. Armstrong, trans.
Jane Curran (New York: Crossroad, 1986), 216.

[23] Hadot, "Postscript," *Philosophy As a Way of Life,* 285.

[24] Plotinus, *Enneads,* Loeb Classical Library, vol. 7, trans. A. H. Armstrong
(Cambridge: Harvard University Press, 1988).

physical. Rather, what I mean by nearness is the greatest possible capacity to receive God.[25]

I understand Dionysius to mean that we grow nearer to the incomprehensible when we cultivate our capacity to receive this other. Let me stress this again with a quotation from Dionysius's *Ecclesiastical Hierarchy*, the second chapter:

> Our greatest likeness to and union with God is the goal of our hierarchy. But divine scripture teaches us that we will only obtain this through the most loving observance of the august commandments and by the doing of sacred acts. "He who loves me will keep my word and my father will love him and we will come to him and make our home with him." What, then, is the starting point for the sacred enactment of the most revered commandments? It is this, to dispose our souls to hear the sacred words as receptively as possible, to be open to the divine workings of God . . . and to accept our divine and sacred regeneration.[26]

As Joseph Stiglmayr has noted, the one concept elevated above all others in Dionysius's spirituality is that "the measure of light imparted is determined by the condition of the subject."[27]

III

So what are the ascetical disciplines or practices that are prescribed as conditions of mystical *theoria?* In middle to late Platonic and Christian mystical theologies, a number of practices are similar to and even derived from Stoic and Epicurean ascetical disciplines. Some of these Hellenistic practices include: intense meditation on fundamental dogmas, the ever-renewed awareness

---

[25] *Pseudo-Dionysius: The Complete Works,* trans. Colm Luibheid (New York: Paulist Press, 1987), 274.

[26] Dionysius, *Ecclesiastical Hierarchy, The Complete Works,* 200.

[27] Quoted in Jaroslav Pelikan's *Christianity and Classical Culture* (New Haven: Yale University Press, 1993), 18. Another passage from Dionysius: "If we may trust the superlative wisdom and truth of scripture, the things of God are revealed to each mind in proportion to its capacities" (*Divine Names,* chapter 1.588a, *The Complete Works,* 49).

of the finitude of life, examination of one's conscience,[28] absti-
nences, memorizations, meditations on future evils or accidents
or death, reflections on the past, silence, listening to others, and
the keeping of notebooks *(hupomnêmata)* and other forms of
writing.[29] And these practices were designed to curb appetites,
reduce material wants, overcome false judgments, and engender
other forms of self-mastery.

Practices perhaps somewhat more specific to mystical theologies than to Greco-Roman philosophies include emphasis on the
reading and appropriation of scriptural texts, as advocated by Origen.[30] Evagrius Ponticus considered the realization of *apatheia*
and *agapê* in the soul to be "the necessary precondition for the
pure prayer . . . that is, for essential *gnôsis* of the Trinity."[31]
Following Evagrius, John Cassian's "constant repetition of the
formula of 'unceasing prayer' *(Deus in adiutorium meum in-
tende: Domine ad adiuvandum me festina),*" is intended to engender the pure heart, the *puritas cordis* that could lead to divine
uplift,[32] and Dionysius also commended constant prayer, especially before speaking about God.[33]

Furthermore, Dionysius considers the cultivation of meekness
as a condition of "earning the sight of God,"[34] and insists that
we keep ourselves from becoming "caught up with the things of
the world."[35] And the practice of *anachôrêsis,* "withdrawal"
from the world—either periodically or perpetually—expands
with the desert fathers and is institutionalized in monasticism.
(This is, of course, a mere sampling of examples.)

---

[28] Hadot, "Philosophy As a Way of Life," in *Philosophy As a Way of Life,*
268.

[29] See Foucault's "Self Writing," in *Ethics: Subjectivity and Truth.*

[30] "For Origen, the transformative process by which the fallen soul is trained
in virtue in order to come to contemplative experience takes place in the very
act of reading and appropriating the scriptural text." Bernard McGinn, "Asceticism and Mysticism in Late Antiquity and the Early Middle Ages," in *Asceticism,* eds. Vincent L. Wimbush and Richard Valantasis (New York: Oxford
University Press, 1995), 64.

[31] McGinn, "Asceticism and Mysticism," 67.

[32] Ibid., 68.

[33] Dionysius, *The Divine Names, The Complete Works,* 68–69.

[34] Dionysius, the 8th letter, *The Complete Works,* 269.

[35] Dionysius, *The Mystical Theology, The Complete Works,* 136.

IV

But what I also want to suggest—and this is important for re-thinking contemporary discussions of apophasis—is that in addi-tion to the practices of meditation, silence, withdrawal, and so on, apophasis is itself an askêsis. When apophasis is employed, it is not just a principle, not just the always available platitude that we cannot predicate x if x is incomprehensible. It is a *medi-tatio,* that is, an *exercise* itself. The apophatic exercise is under-taken to remove conceptual obstacles that would preclude the seeker from mystical experience. As Michael Sells summarizes: "The mind, conditioned by the language and logic of entities, moves inexorably toward delimitation, a tendency that must be continually transformed by new acts of apophasis as long as the contemplative gaze remains."[36] Hence, the *performance* of unnameability—or the experience of the contemplative ascent to unnameability—is not the same as the *principle* of unnameabil-ity. Apophasis is an exercise, according to Dionysius, precisely because it is our concepts, our discursive reasoning, that must be overcome; and this overcoming is never presented as a simple or mundane task by either pagan or Christian mystics, but as a task that will involve a complete dedication of mind, body, and spirit.[37]

In his essay "Apophatisme et théologie négative," Pierre Hadot distinguishes between apophasis as a rational, theological method and the actual, "transrational," mystical experience: "La méthode négative est d'ordre rationnel, et l'expérience unitive est transrationnelle. Ces deux démarches sont radicalement dis-tinctes, mais étroitement unies. [The negative method is of the rational order, and the unitive experience is transrational. The two are radically distinct, but intimately united.]"[38] Hadot wishes

---

[36] Michael Sells, *Mystical Languages of Unsaying* (Chicago: University of Chicago Press, 1994), 18.

[37] In his preface to *Pseudo-Dionysius: The Complete Works,* René Roques writes: "More directly, the radical critique and rejection by the intelligence of each of the names that are more or less accessible to it indicate definite steps forward of this same intelligence in the direction of its own divinization," 6.

[38] Pierre Hadot, "Apophatisme et théologie négative," *Exercices spirituels et philosophie antique,* 2d ed. (Paris, 1987), 193.

to make clear that apophatic operations should not be confused with the realization of mystical experience. Nor should it be assumed that these strategies alone have any ability to bring it about.

In general, neither Neoplatonist nor Christian mystics hold that one's own efforts are able to induce this experience. "L'accumulation des négations peut tout au plus provoquer dans l'âme un vide qui la prédispose à l'expérience. [The accumulation of negations can, at most, elicit in the soul a space to predispose it to the experience.]"[39] The apophatic method provides no guarantee that one will encounter or apprehend the other. Rather, it is a technique that aims to foster a disposition of receptivity by way of a clearing.

What is at issue in these mystical theologies, and their movements of naming and unnaming, are indeed matters of logic, epistemology, and metaphysics (how can finite beings speak of the infinite?), and theories of language (what are the possibilities and limits of language and linguistic concepts?). But also, and no less, these are spiritual matters: that is, they are matters of the soul's relation to something other than or beyond itself.

The activity of negation (apophasis) contributes to the process of discarding form, renouncing everything (we renounce attachments to lower concepts and names of the divine), of detaching oneself from everything (in renouncing attachments, we detach ourselves from these concepts and names)—and so I suggest that these negations, like other purifications and the cultivation of virtues, function as significant prerequisites to mystical ascent.[40] One could argue, therefore, that a study claiming to exam-

---

[39] Ibid.

[40] In his essay "Plotinus and Porphyry" (in *Classical Mediteranean Spirituality: Egyptian, Greek, Roman*), Hadot seems to challenge, if not deny, precisely what I am claiming here: that negations play a transformative (ascetical) role in mystical experience. For Plotinus, he states, "the negations tell us something about the Good, but the purifications actually lead us to it" (247), and "we must not confuse these rational methods [methods of abstraction—*aphairesis*—and negation, *apophasis*] with the activity of discarding all forms, of renouncing everything, of detaching oneself from everything, which actually leads us to the One" (247). On this apparent discrepancy, it should be noted that Hadot's remarks are exclusively referring to Plotinus, and my own are not. And so even if one were to accept his claims about the status of *apophasis* in Plotinus, for the reasons I outline above I think that we ought not to take Hadot's circum-

ine the logic and language of mystical theologies is deficient if it ignores the ascetical components of apophatic discourse, since this discourse is dependent upon a prior ascetical cultivation, and since the discourse itself functions as an askêsis.

V

If we are willing to consider the appropriation of certain types of askêsis, then we will want to consider the criteria by which we shall select, reject, or modify these disciplines.[41] After all, it could rightly be charged that some of these old practices were psychologically and physiologically damaging (self-flagellation, for example), and founded upon harmful views about what it means to be embodied and gendered. While admitting these realities, and acknowledging that it is probably impossible to offer too many assurances up-front, I would nevertheless argue that there are good reasons why this should not keep us from searching for salubrious forms of philosophical disciplines. For keeping strictly to our present (more or less reflective) practices and habits may also hinder our health and prevent us from living more fully. Any sort of self-examination and spiritual transformation will involve certain costs and risks, as will a mode of existence guided primarily by current convention. So how shall we evaluate and choose various practices and aims?

Since most of us are not under the direction of a philosophical or spiritual advisor, it seems obvious that the decision to accept certain disciplines will be made on the basis of our own conception of health, broadly understood. Perhaps the traditional categories of mind, body, and soul are still acceptably vague terms

---

scribed remarks as characteristic of mystical theologies in general. Furthermore, in "Apophatisme et théologie négative," as I point out, Hadot acknowledges that negations do have a part in preparing the soul for the mystical experience. This is particularly significant since these comments are also made in reference to Plotinus, and read as something of a shift away from the earlier remarks.

[41] On the historical significance of spiritual exercises in ancient philosophy and their contemporary relevance, see Hadot's *Philosophy As a Way of Life,* especially the essay of the same name (chapter 11) and the brilliant essay "Spiritual Exercises" (chapter 3).

to which we can apply a conception of health. If so, then the question is: What exercises will facilitate physical health? Mental health? Spiritual health? And we might begin with practices we believe to be conducive to an account of flourishing that attends to each of these aspects. (For all of the intellectual discipline of students and professors of philosophy, the common neglect of physical exercise and dietary discipline is stunning. And yet we continue to criticize Descartes for *his* dualism.)

Again, I suggest that ancient attitudes and exercises that we regard as psychologically or physiologically damaging be left aside. We can start elsewhere. But what we will have to be open to is the fact that *if* certain practices were to lead to some sort of transformation (call it spiritual insight), it would be conceivable, even probable, that our conception of health would be transformed as well.

So we begin selection according to our present conceptions of health, and we remain open to the possibility that our conceptions of health and human flourishing may be modified in time.[42] The relationship between practices and our conception of health is dialogical: according to our current aims and needs, we will adopt certain attitudes and exercises to cultivate and practice. But as it is the function of spiritual exercises to transform us, we may come to see new attitudes or shortcomings to foster or address.

VI

If it can be said that Levinas, Derrida, or any number of contemporary philosophers are concerned with the experience of otherness, and if we accept this aim as a suitable description for those who employed classical apophatic discourses, then we may do well to explore the ancient ascetical practices intended to open up the individual to alterity, to expand his or her capacities of receptivity. Does it not befit us, if we are to maintain an interest in apophaticism, to examine and attend to these practices that

---

[42] Underscoring the importance of this openness, Hadot states that it is imperative in every spiritual exercise that "we must *let* ourselves be changed, in our point of view, attitudes, and convictions" ("Spiritual Exercises," 91).

were held to be necessary preconditions for this access? And if we desire to do something more than merely *talk* about welcoming or receiving the other, then we ought to ask: What codes of conduct, what ways of being, must we cultivate?

Of course, the concern to enhance capacities of receptivity is not entirely foreign to contemporary philosophy. Jean-Luc Marion's works "The Saturated Phenomenon" and *Etant donné* display an interest in the issue of how to become a better receiver. But Marion (like most phenomenologists) does not take this concern explicitly in the direction of askêsis. We might say the same of Levinas, whose emphasis on issues of receptivity to the other (for example, in conversation) and responsibility for the other (in the readiness to substitute myself for the other) also seems to call for an elaboration of and dedication to specific ascetical practices.[43]

However, with regard to the notion of the "apprehension of God, or the other," A. H. Armstrong has claimed that

> there is nothing very helpful to be said, because I agree with Plato and many modern religious philosophers in supposing that what it means can only be learnt in practice, *and by each in their own way*. . . . One can only recommend a serious attention to and enjoyment of the world in the hope that those who apply themselves to it, holding in check for a time the desire of power or satisfaction, may become aware of the divine presence.[44]

It seems to me that Armstrong underemphasizes the importance of taking up practices recommended by those individuals, communities, and texts that care to offer instruction on these matters. Starting points are perhaps increasingly important and necessary, since our cultures are capable of placing us at a great remove from even basic principles of spiritually disciplined and attuned

---

[43] Jean-Luc Marion, "The Saturated Phenomenon," trans. Thomas A. Carlson, *Philosophy Today* (Spring 1996): 103–24. *Etant donné: Essai d'une phénoménologie de la donation* (Paris: Presses Universitaires de France, 1997). Emmanuel Levinas, *Totality and Infinity,* trans. Alphonso Lingis (Pittsburgh: Duquesne University Press, 1969), 51. See also Levinas, "Responsibility for the Other," in *Ethics and Infinity,* trans. Richard A. Cohen (Pittsburgh: Duquesne University Press, 1985).

[44] A. H. Armstrong, "The Apprehension of Divinity in the Self and Cosmos in Plotinus," in *The Significance of Neoplatonism,* 188 (emphasis added).

lives. At any rate, what I wish to press is whether we can learn more *from* others *about* others than is suggested in the quote from Armstrong.

On a personal note, I suppose that it is precisely the sense of foreignness and unfashionableness that I get when reading mystical theologies that leaves me unwilling to ignore them. I am reminded of Michel Foucault's intuition about the nature of philosophical activity in general. In *L'Usage des plaisirs,* he writes, "what is philosophy today—philosophical activity . . . in what does it consist, if not in the endeavor to know how and to what extent it might be possible to think differently, instead of legitimating what is already known?"[45]

Assuming that we do not think that to *do* philosophy is simply to do criticism, or merely to study intellectual history, or to invent theories to undergird certain already held beliefs or habits, then it seems worthy and worthwhile to present certain practices and techniques that have been regarded as necessary prerequisites to self-transformation and self-transcendence.

There are also important hermeneutical and pedagogical factors that encourage an attention to the disciplines enlisted by particular authors and texts. By examining these disciplines, we can at least ensure that we understand the conditions that the authors themselves regarded to be necessary for possible understanding, and so reconnect askêsis with hermeneutics. (Consider Anselm's prayer in chapter 1 of the *Proslogion.*) Pedagogically, we can inform students of these disciplines and conditions, and so afford the chance for these students to undertake some of these practices. It would seem, in doing so, that we both permit the occasion to present disciplines of a philosophical way of life, and do justice to the premises that certain authors viewed as essential. This instruction is, then, instruction about reading, thinking, and living philosophically, instruction that I take to be well worth pursuing.[46]

---

[45] Foucault, *The Use of Pleasure,* 8–9.

[46] My thanks to Tom Carlson, Arnold Davidson, Mathew Geiger, Philip Goodchild, Rick Furtak, Regina Schwartz, and David Tracy for their comments on various stages of this essay, and especially for the meaningful conversations on these and related matters.

11

Continental Philosophy, Catholicism, and the Exigencies of Responsibility: The Resources of Maurice Blondel's Works

Gregory B. Sadler

A QUESTION that confronts practicing Roman Catholics engaged in Continental philosophy is the relationship between the practices, tradition, and intellectual resources of the Catholic Church and the boundaries of what is called Continental philosophy. Often the discourses that allow a renewed philosophical boldness in speaking about Christianity are marked by an equally liberating and corrosive temerity that, claiming to speak for none, or perhaps only for the other or the guest, seems to easily to aim to speak for all, to judge for all, to legislate for all. We must ask whether it is true that orthodoxy, one's self-location within a dialogue with a long and deep tradition, amounts to a certain blindness alleviated only by framing our concerns within a seemingly more comprehensive and critical perspective afforded by the works of figures dominant in what is termed Continental philosophy. Or, we should also ask, does orthodoxy provide us with resources that might be lacking, even needed, there? This is a new ramification of what was called in Maurice Blondel's time *le problème religieux*. Is the only choice possible one between a stultifying orthodoxy that is ultimately a ground of irresponsibility, a repository of old errors, and philosophical positions that reappropriate themes right from the heart of Christian tradition and practice but extricate these from their contexts, deracinate them, distance them from the church, from the politics, from the history, teachings, and practices that preserved them, but that irremediably distorted them as well?

This is a false dichotomy, and a hyperbolic formulation of the problem. Still, it is a representative reflection on a historical condition, one present, and one past. In the present there are many criticisms, some transparently inadequate, in certain Catholic circles, of recent Continental philosophy. But likewise, insistence on negative theology, on the violence and distortion inextricable from institutions, traditions, practices, on certain formulations of the problems of responsibility or idolatry, risks erecting a dangerous and irresponsible hermeneutic principle—namely that a philosopher, who remains within and orients him- or herself by orthodoxy and does not take his or her understanding of that position and decision fully from dominant figures in Continental philosophy, is not only a priori in error, but subverts and perverts the possibility of morality and real religion.

Blondel's work is particularly timely, at present, since he played an important role in one of the past episodes of this tension and conflict. His early work, *L'action (1893)* placed him in a position where he was accused by philosophers of having smuggled Catholicism into his philosophical work, and by reactionary Catholics of having rationalized theology, of being a Modernist. One of his aims was to indicate that this was a dispute and dichotomy that denatured both philosophy and theology, that while neither could be reduced to the other, rigorous philosophical analyses eventually led one to the point of having to take a position on the insufficiency of philosophy, of the requirement for transcendence, but furthermore, to take a position with respect to orthodoxy. In two important works that followed, the *Letter on Apologetics* and *History and Dogma,* Blondel clarified his position in response to his critics, and in the process put into play themes that, through later authors, had an important role in the Second Vatican Council. Blondel's own work, not only by its conclusions but by its very existence, provides us with an indication of the illusory and ideological status of a forced decision between recent Continental philosophy of religion and Catholic thought, since if one could not carry out work in terms of the themes, problems, and rigor reemphasized by recent Continental philosophy from a Catholic perspective, Blondel's works would not even exist.

In this paper, I maintain that Maurice Blondel not only engaged with many of the same themes that recent Continental philosophy of religion does, but that he also provides a systematic treatment of the relationship of the philosophical use of these themes and the religious practices, traditions, institutions, texts, and thought that nourish and determine such themes. This paper is divided into three parts. In the first, I indicate certain methodological similarities between Blondel's and Derrida's work. In the second part, I present Blondel's working out of the relationship between philosophy, theology, Christianity, and the Catholic Church. In the third part, I suggest that Blondel's work provides a partial basis for fruitful dialogue and interaction between Continental philosophy and Catholicism.

From the beginning of his published work, Blondel was concerned with the effects of a history of philosophy and Western thought that froze categories of thought and argumentation, that kept one from thinking certain problems and relations, that allowed *parti pris* to take the place of thinking things out to their conclusions. He was concerned that things should not be simply taken for granted. It is for this reason that the largest part of *L'action (1893)* consists in a sequence of interlocking analyses, beginning from the "givens" of modern science, moving then to the level of the body and materiality, to the psyche in relation to materiality and corporeality, through volition and intentionality, from individual action to social action and organization, culminating finally in superstition and religion. Each of these analyses indicates the insufficiency of these various levels and entities, that is, their incapacity to fully suffice onto themselves, to provide their own substantial grounds, which they are often taken, by proponents of one sort of reduction or another, to have. The works of the later metaphysical trilogy, in particular *L'être et les êtres,* likewise repeat and amplify this set of ascending analyses.

Blondel treats these in terms of dynamics of idolatry, the grounds of which we shall return to presently in discussion of the option. Of chief importance here is that Blondel criticizes these in terms of hypostatization of entities, of reification in social processes, of a concealed abrogating of divinity by the subject, and that he sees a practice of philosophical analysis and engagement with these figures of hypostatization as integral to the task to be carried out by philosophy. In *L'action (1893)* and in the *Letter on Apologetics*, he employs what he calls "the method of immanence"[1] in order to undermine these hypostases. In later works, this is formulated as a "philosophy of insufficiency," in which philosophical analyses take the claims of full self-sufficiency regarding given orders of phenomena at their word, work their implications out more fully, and indicate these claims as concealing fundamental insufficiencies.

Blondel's analyses of philosophical positions bear a certain resemblance to Derrida's own textual practices. In *L'action (1893)* and in the *Letter on Apologetics*, Blondel formulated this explicitly in terms of reading through a position and taking it to its full conclusions, precisely to see if it was in fact self-sufficient.[2] This amounts negatively to a refusal to simply accept dominant representatives at their word as having produced definitive works on the subjects and problems, refusing to remain behind the conditions they impose on the discussions.

The philosophical practice of deconstruction does precisely this, in two principal ways. First, one can read an author against or on him- or herself, indicating the hidden, and perhaps inevitable contradictions, in the position and works—Derrida's treatment of Husserl in *Speech and Phenomenon* provides a prime example of this. Second, one can, so to speak, index an author's position against what would be required in order for that position to be true or to work; in other terms, to see what supports and sustains that author's position while unacknowledged or acknowledged, but simply subordinated or negatively valorized in the work.

Sustained criticisms of idealism, naturalism, positivism, and ideological constructs of the person as a completely subsistent, sufficient, and self-possessed being occur throughout Blondel's

---

[1] Maurice Blondel, *The Letter on Apologetics and History and Dogma,* trans. Alexander Dru and Illtyd Trethowan (Grand Rapids, Mich.: Eerdmans, 1964), 158–59.

[2] Blondel, *L'action (1893): Essay on a Critique of Life and a Science of Practice,* trans. Olivia Blanchette (Notre Dame: University of Notre Dame Press, 1984), 12; Blondel, *Letter on Apologetics,* 166.

works. More relevant here in light of Derrida's recent explicit focus of political and religious questions are Blondel's criticisms of hypostatization in social, moral, political, and religious matters. In *Patrie et humanité,* he frames the problem by distinguishing two types of abstraction, one "qui examine des aspects complémentaires et qu'on peut appeller méthodologique [that examines complementary aspects and that one could call methodological]," and another

> qui met les choses en pièces pour refaire, après coup, l'unité brisée, l'abstraction qu'on peut nommer ontologique (puisqu'elle prétend fabriquer le monde et la société humaine avec des atomes et des égoïsmes) [that breaks things down so as to reconstruct the broken unity afterwards, the abstraction that one could call ontological (since it pretends to construct the world and human society from atoms and egoisms)].[3]

It is this second form of abstraction, a widespread type of philosophical practice, that leads to the hypostatization of such entities as nation, race, class, social group, homeland, culture, or society. Blondel considers this problem again in *L'être et les êtres,* where he writes:

> Nous voici donc en face de nouveaux prétendants à l'être. Il convient d'examiner leurs titres, fût-ce dans l'obscurité brutale ou dans les clartés scientifiques dont s'auréolent ces sortes de Léviathans que seraient les nations ou les races. Quelle consistance nous offre cette réalité a trois dégrés dont l'histoire—ancienne ou actuelle— nous présente des types un peu différents, mais qui ont toujours pour caractère commun ce qu'on eût appelé autrefois un millénarisme, la promesse d'un état supérieur et en quelque sorte définitif, une solidité enfin ontologique. [Here we are confronted with new claimants to being. It is advisable to examine the titles of their claims, whether made in brutal obscurity or in the spaces of scientific clarity, with whose halo those sorts of Leviathans, those that would be nations or races, crown themselves. What constancy this reality, three degrees removed, offers, whose history—ancient or current—presents us with slightly different types, but types that always have as a common character what one would in other times

---

[3] Blondel, *Patrie et humanité: Cours professé à la Semaine Sociale de Paris* (Chronique sociale de France: Lyon, 1928), 11–12. All translations, unless otherwise noted, are mine.

have called a millenarianism, the promise of a future and in a certain way definitive state, a solidity, in the end, ontological.][4]

Blondel extends such critique to certain interpretations of Catholic dogma, for instance in *History and Dogma* when he condemns the extrinsicism all too common in Catholic circles at the time, that simply superimposed Catholic dogma schematically, and as a reified product, onto the events of history.[5]

There is a closer connection between Blondel's and Derrida's approaches, one that can be indicated both negatively and positively. Negatively, both of these figures refuse to allow themselves to be caught up in a certain historical problematic, in particular that of a valorized distinction between pre-Modernity and Modernity, namely by assuming a time or epoch in which such systematic hypostatization would not have been completed or would be overcome immanently. Derrida and Blondel recognize that such hypostatization, as well as the violence and injustice that accompany it, has been a problem throughout history, one irresolvable from within horizons bounded by the human that exclude the divine, naturalize it, or force it idolatrously into a simply human perspective.

There is a positive aspect as well; as Derrida has made more clear in recent works such as *Specters of Marx, Aporias,* and the *Gift of Death,* and as Blondel maintained from the start, their philosophical practices are oriented and motivated by historically mediated moral and religious considerations. Hypostatization is critically indicated as such not simply out of a desire to tear down, to denigrate, or to affirm a universalistic and terrorist skepticism, but precisely because it places impediments, traps, stumbling blocks, *skandala*. It represents and replicates practices of scandalization that stand in the way of moral and religious relations, not only of practicing, but of thinking out as a practice the exigencies of justice, of relations to the other, the other other, and the absolute other.[6]

---

[4] Blondel, *L'être et les êtres: Essai d'ontologie concrète et intégrale* (Paris: Alcan, 1935), 108–9.

[5] Blondel, *Letter on Apologetics,* 226–31.

[6] Blondel has a brief but very fruitful treatment of alterity near the conclusion of *L'action (1893),* in which the problematics of the other in relation to *charité* are sketched out (405–6).

Historically, this means that there is no original position, no principles or configuration that could function completely immanently, through metaphysical closure, as a complete foundation and touchstone for ethical, political, and religious thought and action. There is, to use Blondel's terms, no solution to the problem of human destiny fully immanent to human history and society. History remains determinate but open at every point to transcendence, and the task precisely of deconstruction and Blondel's philosophy of insufficiency is to refuse despair in light of this, to continue to think out and to practice what is needed, what is required. This also means, however, that everything continues to remain in play, to have its exigencies, to require a redemption that is not foreclosed by these philosophical practices. Blondel writes in *L'action (1893)*:

> Neither space nor duration, nor scientific symbolism, nor individual life, nor social organism, nor moral order, nor metaphysical constructions, can be erected separately into subsistent realities. . . . Each order of phenomena is equally original as a distinct synthesis, transcendent with regard to those that are its antecedent conditions, irreducible to those it seems subordinate to as its consequents, solidary with all, finding in none its total explanation, having its reality neither in itself nor in any other."[7]

Blondel's focus on action and the will, on the inevitability that one must take absolute positions, what Blondel calls the inescapability of the problem of action, leads us into a discussion of the grounds of such hypostatization, of the sublimization of the self and the domination of the divine. Blondel frames this in

---

In *L'être et les êtres,* Blondel writes: "Difficulté plus insolubile [concentration of self in self-assertion] encore quand nous comprenons qu'il est illégitime, qu'il est impossible de nous centrer en nous-même, de faire tourner l'univers autour de notre égoïsme, de méconnaître que la personalité doit devenir la conscience de l'impersonel et qu'elle vaut, qu'elle croît surtout par le don de soi et par la dévouement à tous. . . . La personne ne peut être seule: elle ne saurait être elle-même que par une sorte d'exode et de générosité [A difficulty still more insoluble when we understand that it is illegitimate, that it is impossible to center ourselves in our selves, to make the universe revolve around our egoism, to misunderstand that the personality must become consciousness of the impersonal and that it has its value, that above all it grows by the gift of itself and by devotion to everyone. The person cannot be alone: it can be itself only by a kind of exodus and generosity]" (101).
[7] Blondel, *L'action (1893)*, 413.

terms of an option between egoism, or selfishness *(égoïsme)* on the one hand, and mortification on the other, a choice between taking something, whether it be the self, a relationship, society, a fetish, a methodology, as the ground of and index of reality and the source of value, and of recognizing the insufficiency, the relativity of all of these to an absolute that cannot be figured fully immanently in their terms.

In all of these cases, there is still a fundamental dynamic of the subject; although the subject cannot suffice fully onto itself, it can will, it can posit, it can attempt imperiously to decide the question of being in this way. It can decide that something other than God is so sufficient. Even though it might appear this is the height of self-abnegation, it is in fact, whether it be in the most virulent and ideological nationalism or religious fundamental-ism, or whether it take the form of an abstentious skepticism or nihilism, a concealed form of self-assertion by the subject,[8] one that, however, founders in this attempt at self-presence.

> To judge that one finds within oneself the truth necessary for one's conscience, the energy of one's action and the success of one's destiny, is not only to deprive oneself of a gratuitous and optional gift which, rejected and disdained, would still not compromise the happiness of an average life; no, it is in truth to give the lie to one's own aspiration and, under the pretext of loving only oneself, to hate and lose oneself.[9]

The other term of the option is not simply a rejection of such hypostatizations and the practices and thought that both engen-ders it and takes place within its framework; instead, it is a recog-

---

[8] In *Patrie et humanité,* following the passage footnoted above, Blondel writes: "Ainsi comprise dans cette même perspective abstraite et artificielle, la nation, elle aussi, facticement constituée en sa notion typique qui confère indû-ment aux particularités de tel ou tel peuple le caractère réservé à ce qui est d'ordre objectif et universel, la nation n'est plus qu'un égoïsme collectif, plus terrible qu'une somme des égoïsmes individuels [So understood in the same abstract and artificial perspective, the nation, it as well, factitiously constituted in its typical notion that unduly confers to the particularities of such and such a people the character reserved for what is of an objective and universal order, the nation is no more than a collective egoism, more terrible than a sum of individual egoisms]" (13). For Blondel's early treatment of skepticism and ni-hilism, see *L'action (1893),* parts 1 and 2.

[9] Blondel, *L'action (1893),* 343.

nition of the orientation of the orders of beings within these frameworks to a "being," a "sole thing necessary," to a God that is not simply yet another reified concept or hypostatized being, but who exceeds all these while allowing them. Orienting the will of the subject toward God, refusing the allure of positing and assenting to easy and final solutions, the glamour of the illusion of complete presence, is, while not a precondition of revelation or the gift, the path that leads to its fullness.

> Mortification, then, is the true metaphysical experiment, the one that touches on being itself. What dies is what hinders from seeing, from doing, from living; what survives is what is already reborn. . . . So many people live as if they were never to die; it is an illusion. We must act as if we were dead; that is reality. As we take this infinite of death into account, how everything changes sign! And how little advanced is the philosophy itself of death! . . . Therein [in mortification] lies the secret of the holy terror which modern consciousness experiences, just as the ancient soul had felt it, at the approach, at the very thought, of the divine. If no one loves God without suffering, no one sees Him without dying. Nothing touches him that is not reborn; for no will is good if it has not gone out of itself, in order to leave the whole place open to the total invasion of His will.[10]

A difficult set of questions remains, however, at this point, one which concerns Blondel as well as recent thinkers. Is philosophy necessarily caught in such egoism, such idolatry? Does the introduction of these themes take us irremediably and irrevocably out of philosophy and into theology? Or is Blondel correct in maintaining that his perspective remains one within philosophy, a philosophy that would attempt to take account of its own insufficiencies here, perhaps as a preparation for faith, perhaps in some other capacity more appropriate to philosophy?

One of Blondel's chief concerns in the *Letter on Apologetics* and *History and Dogma* was to sketch out the historical relationship between philosophy, theology, and the church, motivated particularly by the problems coming to the fore in the Modernist Crisis. The fundamental problem was that both Catholic theology and the philosophy that since the later Middle Ages had emanci-

---

[10] Ibid., 353.

pated itself from the church made absolute and irreconcilable claims, not least because they concerned the most important and fundamental aspects of human life. The danger, as Blondel saw it, was, on the one hand, of modern philosophy that came more and more to pronounce not only on the social function or truth of religion, but on its very conditions of possibility; and on the other hand, a Catholic Church whose discourses, thought, and practice were marked more and more by entrenchment, by refusal to even entertain discussion with opposed positions. The problem raised in this paper, that of the possibility of taking up actively the insights of Continental philosophy of religion and the exigencies of Catholic practice and thought at the same time, is, in certain respects, a modification of the one Blondel faced and engaged himself within. Recent Continental philosophy of religion, although it aims at undoing the hypostatizations spoken of above, in particular by critiques of idolatry, by discourses about secrecy, the guest, alterity, or responsibility, does in fact unavoidably make absolute claims in the process, claims that strike at the very heart of a Catholic tradition and community that must, equally unavoidably, rely to some degree upon texts, teaching, authority, political relationships, and an inevitable claim to provide a grounding locus for the transmission of the divine gift.

Blondel argued that philosophy, in matters of religion and in particular in relation to Christianity, had to come to grasp its own limits. Philosophy must be allowed by theology, in particular the theology of the church, to come freely to its own limits, to realize both its own importance and competency and the conditions, the realities even, that keep it from being able to make absolute and exclusive claims further than that competency.

> Philosophy, in fine, giving up the pretension of containing and controlling *totum et omne de omni et toto* and the contrary but correlative pretension which makes it only a construction of thought or an epiphenomenon on the surface of life, must now precisely define its own competence and scope, including its own dynamism in the whole system of determination which it studies.[11]

---

[11] Blondel, *Letter on Apologetics*, 180.

Philosophy is a practice of autonomy, of working out the conditions of it, and it functions most properly in its own domain when
it comes to realize, as Derrida's recent works indicate, that these
limits are precisely in heteronomy that, far from nullifying the
autonomy of philosophical work, is its ground. Recently this heteronomy has been thought out in terms of the other, responsibility, the gift, the guest, in philosophical reappropriations of what
has been there in the texts that the Catholic Church has considered canonical for millennia. It would be strange if philosophy,
having had pointed out to it the heteronomy imposed upon it by
dealing with Christianity, would then arrogate to itself the function of deciding what the conditions of such a heteronomy would
be for all—ignoring, refusing dialogue with, and excluding other
thinkers on the grounds of reference to philosophical concepts.

The problem posed in this paper is the problem of the relationship between philosophy and Christianity taken to a second level.
The problem of this difficult relationship in relation to the absolute still turns on a double basis that Blondel indicated. First,
there is the question of the relationship of Christianity as a historical phenomenon to philosophy and the human condition. Second, there is the more trenchant question of the role of the church
in its mediative function.

The first is brought out well by both parties here. Both Blondel
and Derrida maintain a radical insufficiency of human being, and
figure it in relation to exigencies transcendent to merely natural
existence. Derrida, in calling for a Christian Europe, in discussing the conditions of the gift, in speaking of *aporiai,* acknowledges more than simply a radical insufficiency of being; the
themes that he draws upon, some of them from Christian sources
and from a history shaped by the phenomena of Christianity, take
a position tentatively that Blondel takes more strongly.

> If Christianity were a belief and a way of life added to our nature
> and our reason as something optional, if we could develop in our
> integrity without this addition and we could refuse deliberately and
> with impunity the crushing weight of the supernatural gift, there
> would be no intelligible connection between these two levels [phi-
> losophy and Christianity], one of which, from the rational point of
> view, might as well not exist. . . . But as soon as this Revelation
> seeks us out, so to speak, on our own ground and pursues us into

our inner fastness, as soon as it regards a neutral or negative attitude as a positive backsliding and a sort of culpable hostility, as soon as the poverty of our limited being can contract a debt which must be paid for in eternity, then the encounter takes place, the difficulty stares us in the face, and the problem is set. For if it is true that the demands of Revelation are well-founded, then we are no longer simply on our own ground; and there must be some trace of this insufficiency, this impotence, this demand in man simply as man, and an echo of it even in the most autonomous philosophy.[12]

The second question is the point at which the most controversy emerges. If one grants that thinking through themes originating in Christian texts, figures, and practices radically changes one's philosophical position, then what is the status of the institution that has mediated them? Is the church merely a necessary but ultimately superfluous evil? Does the fact that it has, always must have, an institutional structure and discourses, that it purports to teach doctrines and dogmas, that it is always already complexly intertwined with political power, mean that from a philosophical position, any collusion with it must be a source of irresponsibility? Or, to the contrary, is the full understanding of the import of these themes somehow dependent on the locus and the tradition in which they have been more than theory and took flesh in practice?

Blondel argues in *History and Dogma* against a philosophical approach to the phenomena of religion that refused, on grounds of rigor, to treat the doctrines, discourses, and practices of Christianity except as deracinated from their contexts, under the rubric of historicism. His criticism there has a much broader scope of application than simply to historicism; it retains its validity as a criticism of claims to grasp more universally and philosophically such phenomena while selectively excluding the voices and concerns, whether on an epistemological, moral, or even religious basis, of those who are substantively engaged in those phenomena.[13] This is to decide the issues in advance:

---

[12] Ibid., 154–55.

[13] Blondel was aware of the structure of moral objections. He writes of those who take exception not necessarily to the exigencies imposed by the divine gift, but to the fact that these come to be mediated historically by the church, which asserts claims to such mediation: "This cruel dilemma is more or less obscurely

By the very fact of having begun by eliminating the problems which may be called realistic. . . . it will be impossible to rediscover anything but a notion . . . of the complex dialectic which controlled the organization of Catholic dogma and discipline. And this kind of knowledge, which has for its sole aspect the external aspect and the intelligible form of Christian facts, can only extract an ideology from them, and ideology in which everything is reduced to an evolution of concepts, indefinitely sublimated, with no other ballast than indefinitely tractable texts.[14]

Philosophy, in recognizing its own limits, does not simply come to a full stop, a blank that it has no relationship to, or an unknowable noumenon. When it overreaches itself, it does create a blindness or forgetting, it ignores phenomena and their exigencies precisely because it has ruled out their possibility beforehand, precisely at the time it congratulates itself on its treatment of them. The fundamental problem with this is, however, not simply a matter of philosophical consistency that would be violated, but the fact that these discourses on ethics, on politics, on religion, the practices and thought determining and determined by them assume, through life, an absolute importance. Philosophy contributes to these most fully precisely by performing its labors of critique, of analysis, of synthesis, while forbearing, for reasons it has itself weighed, from attaching to its results an absolute stature.

One can see in the work carried out in recent Continental philosophy a clear grasp of this realization within philosophy. One of the most important themes has been of maintaining space or time, openness to these problematics, particularly to religious phenomena. The question that still has to be raised however, is whether there is not still a sort of unwarranted exclusion carried out, still a form of dogmatic blindness on the part of philosophers, a dogmatism that would impose exclusions precisely on the grounds that the others are the dogmatists because they are Catholic, because they practice, because they locate themselves

---

felt by men and keeps alive in their hearts a sort of hostile unrest or nagging suspicion as if there were in the heart of Catholicism a repellant harshness against which one should rebel in the name of some new ideal of justice and loving-kindness." *Letter on Apologetics,* 154.

[14] Blondel, *Letter on Apologetics,* 258.

within that church and tradition, because they maintain the need for such an institution, its discourses and practices, in all its complexity.

Philosophy makes use of, and takes seriously, entire arrays of phenomena, texts, interpretations, practices. But there is still a sort of forbearance, a willful drawing away from any engagement in Catholicism, in the church. Blondel's ironic observation retains its force. "It would be strange if it were scientific to study the letter and the spirit of all cults but one."[15] The philosophical reappropriation of religious themes, if it takes the history of those themes responsibly, especially if it aims at extracting something of a moral and political order and value from them, stands to benefit from closer intellectual connection with and critical dialogue with Catholicism, rather than by a peremptory dismissal or a sort of intellectual catharism. Blondel envisioned such philosophical work as finding a sort of confirmation precisely by looking beyond its limits.

> [I]t is legitimate to push our investigation up to the point where we sense that we should desire interiorly something analogous to what dogmas propose from the outside. It is legitimate to consider these dogmas, assuredly not primary as revealed, but as revealing; that is, to confront them with the profound exigencies of the will and to discover in them, if it is there, the image of our real needs and the awaited answer. . . . Perhaps, in considering them thus we would be surprised at the human meaning of a doctrine which many judge unworthy of further examination and which they confuse (opposed reproaches whose very contradiction should provoke a bit of reflexion) with a dry formalism of practices, with an unction of mystical feelings, with a routine of sensible ceremonies, with a casuistic jurisprudence, with a mechanical discipline. We ought at least to interpret its spirit with the care that we would bring to a Sanscrit text or to a Mongol custom.[16]

For Blondel, as we have indicated previously, the question of such engagement was not a neutral one. We inhabit a culture in which the emancipation of philosophy and its continued tangled relation to Catholicism is a historical result but also a question

---

[15] Blondel, *L'action (1893)*, 360.
[16] Ibid.

continually redecided; we inhabit a culture that already prejudices the question by the very ways in which subjectivities are
formed and approach matters through the disciplines.

> [W]ithout prejudging any properly religious question . . . it is nec-
> essary to set aside, through philosophy, the obstacles accumulated,
> wrongly to be sure, by a hostile partisan philosophy, not against
> the content of some dogmatic formula or other, but against the
> very notion of revelation and the possibility, the usefulness, of
> any defined dogma. They want philosophy to have its proper and
> independent domain. Theology wants the same with and for phi-
> losophy. Both the one and the other demand a separation of com-
> petences; they remain distinct from one another, but distinct in
> view of an effective cooperation: *non adjutrix nisi libera: non lib-
> era nisi adjutrix philosophia.* . . . The fullness of philosophy con-
> sists, not in a presumptuous self-sufficiency, but in the study of
> its own powerlessness and of the means which are offered from
> elsewhere to supply for its own powerlessness.[17]

At the same time, the formulations that problems are given, the
critiques carried out, the philosophical positions taken and, inevitably, by the very ways of framing the problems, the necessity,
even when one aims only to speak for oneself, to speak in absolute terms, sometimes seems too harsh, unduly exigent, and even
dismissive of the discourses, practices, and doctrines that we rely
upon, and that are all so very many people have.[18]

> [I]n the simplicity of the most common practices, there is more
> infinite than in the haughtiest speculations or in the most exquisite

---

[17] Blondel, *Letter on Apologetics,* 191.

[18] One focus point for this discussion could be the reading one makes of this
passage: "Why this language, which does not fortuitously resemble that of
negative theology? How to justify the choice of a *negative form (aporia)* to
designate a duty that, through the impossible or the impracticable, nonetheless
announces itself in an affirmative fashion? Because one must avoid good conscience at all costs. . . . To protect the decision or the responsibility by knowledge, by some theoretical assurance, or by the certainty of being right, of being
on the side of science, or consciousness or reason, is to transform this experience into the deployment of a program, into a technical application of a rule or
a norm, or into the subsumption of a determined 'case.' All these are conditions
that must never be abandoned, of course, but that, as such, are only the guardrail
of a responsibility to whose calling they remain radically heterogeneous."
Jacques Derrida, *Aporias,* trans. Thomas Dutoit (Stanford: Stanford University
Press, 1993), 19.

feelings. . . . Who then gives proof of his spiritual fruitfulness, the one with the unction of speech, or the one who even dryly, can do what he could not speak of? Yet it is the dialectician of interior feelings who glories in the abundance of his piety; and it is the one faithful to the letter who is reproached for having a devotion all for show. What is external still, are feelings, thoughts; what is most intimate, what manifests life best and transfigures, are works.[19]

Blondel stresses this requirement of action, of engagement within a community, not only of scholars, nor simply of humble believers, but of a community that historically has incorporated both, that has attempted to think out and practice the exigencies of the gospel message.

"To keep" the word of God means in the first place to do it, to put it into practice; and the deposit of Tradition, which the infidelities of the memory and the narrow limits of the intelligence would inevitably deform if it were handed to us in a purely intellectual form, cannot be transmitted in its entirety, indeed, cannot be used and developed, unless it is confided to the practical obedience of love.[20]

We are continually faced with the task of rethinking out, and of practicing, what it is that others before us have in fact had to practice and think. There is a conservative function to realizing this, to realizing that while nobody has had it all perfectly right, while there is no final and static solution given immanently to us, still we have models, we are not called to radically rethink everything out again from the start. Blondel notes:

[F]aced by intellectual novelties, or exegetical hypotheses, there is an autonomous principle of discernment in the total experience of the Church: in taking account of ideas and facts, traditional faith also takes account of proven ways, of practice confirmed by the fruits of sanctity, of the enlightenment gained through piety, prayer, and mortification. That testimony is not the only one, no doubt, but it has its own inalienable value because it is based at the same time on the collective age-old action of the most human of men and on God's action in them.[21]

---

[19] Blondel, *L'action (1893)*, 376.
[20] Blondel, *Letter on Apologetics*, 274.
[21] Ibid., 274.

The fundamental question that, therefore, has to be continually reopened and reexplored is precisely the one of orthodoxy. Where does one place oneself with respect to the historical phenomena of Christianity, with respect to the communities that supply an uncertain but unbroken ground for these practices, and that prepare the way for the revelation of truth? Does one have debts only to figures of the other, and not to all those others of the past and present? Is the church merely a historical vehicle for the themes of which so many are coming to reassess the importance, or is the relationship more complex, imposing its own exigencies, perhaps not from the perspective of thought abstracted from practice, but certainly within the discipline and ascesis of thought, the response to the gift, the relationship of faith? This is where my paper must end, for this remains an open question, one that has, from Blondel's perspective, to be resolved in the choices we make, the option we choose, which one cannot presume to make for another, nor compel a resolution.

4
Religion inside the Limits of Reason Itself

12

From Neo-Platonism to Souls in Silico: Quests for Immortality

Edith Wyschogrod

"Sɪᴇ ʜᴀʙᴇɴ alle müde Münde/Und helle Seelen ohne Saum [they all have weary mouths/pure souls without a seam]," wrote Rilke longingly.[1] Awe-inspiring and mysterious, humans in their mortality could not hope to attain the enviable purity of the angelic soul. The yearning for soul has become far more complex in postmodernity, in that soul has been rendered moot in modernity's various accounts of mind-body dualism. In its Cartesian version, mind as the ground of certainty came to occupy the void left by the evacuation of soul. With the demise of the modern subject famously described as the ghost in the machine, we may now ask who comes after the subject. According to Jean-Luc Nancy, the question is about "the deconstruction of interiority, of self-presence, of consciousness, of mastery."[2] With the emergence of a new conceptual landscape of dematerialization, the subject is envisioned as an etiolated mathematized body, a string of genes that have become the bearers of immortality.

Consider these words in a popular account of the gene as the agent of natural selection:

> The genetic material in organisms today traces back generation by generation through an unbroken chain of descent (with modification) of ancestral molecules that have copied and replaced themselves ever since the origin of life on earth about 4 billion years ago. . . . Only germline genes are potentially immortal; somatic

---

[1] Rainer Maria Rilke, *Fifty Selected Poems*, trans. C. F. MacIntyre (Berkeley: University of California Press, 1947), 24.

[2] Jean-Luc Nancy, Introduction, *Who Comes after the Subject*, eds. Eduardo Cadava, Peter Connor, Jean-Luc Nancy (London: Routledge, 1991), 4.

entities (ourselves included) are merely ephemeral vessels that evolved as a means of perpetuating DNA.[3]

I hope to show that Neoplatonic configurations of soul arise transgressively in genetic transfiguration. In what might be seen as acts of biological prestidigitation, we are brought back in and as our genes or, in Derridean terms, we re-arise spectrally: "For there to be ghost, there must be a return to the body, but to a body that is more abstract than ever. The spectrogenic process corresponds to a paradoxical *incorporation*." One returns not to the old body but as "an incarnation [of it] in *another artifactual body*, a ghost"[4] that haunts what I call the Pythagorean body. Has Darwin's "dangerous idea," to borrow Daniel C. Dennett's phrase, drawn the specter of soul into the apocalyptic events of our world, or can Pythagorean bodies be read otherwise?

In what follows, I point first to some manifestations of the depersonalized subject. Next I examine the accounts of soul in the Neoplatonist philosophies of Plotinus and Iamblichus, in order to show that the gene-self of evolutionary biology, surprisingly, evokes the Pythagorean soul of Neoplatonic speculation. I go on to describe the recent conceptual shift from the materiality of a visible and tangible body to the soul *in silico*. Finally I consider whether identity, as constructed through invisible gene-links rather than through bodily resemblance, offers an opportunity to break with the twentieth century's nefarious uses of evolutionary biology, or whether it perpetuates the danger.

THE FLIGHT OF THE SUBJECT

By contrast with the ghostly self of postmodernity, the modern self is posited as an individual entity, a body and the perceptual experiences it causes. Such an individual is born, persists in existence for a time, and dies. Consider analytic philosopher P. F. Strawson's by-now canonical mid-century description of the idea

---

[3] John C. Avise, *The Genetic Gods: Evolution and Belief in Human Affairs* (Cambridge: Harvard University Press, 1998), 3–4.

[4] Jacques Derrida, *Specters of Marx: The State of the Debt, the Work of Mourning, and the New International,* trans. Peggy Kamuf (New York: Routledge, 1994), 126 (emphasis in original).

of the person as "the concept of a type of entity such that both predicates ascribing states of consciousness and predicates ascribing corporeal characteristics . . . are equally applicable to a single individual of that single type."[5]

Modernist notions of mind-body continuity, whether materially or linguistically construed, are challenged by depictions of contemporary socio-cultural upheavals. Jean Baudrillard sees a radical shift in the transformation of the play of appearances of the body into genetic code, blurring the boundary between the human and the inhuman. "At the level of genes, the genome and the genotype, the signs distinctive of humanity are fading. . . . immortality [of the soul] has passed into the (biological, genetic) code, the only immortal token which remains."[6] He goes on to ask whether we have not returned to "a (clonal, metastatic) de facto eternity," not in a beyond but in our world.[7] At the same time, and paradoxically, Baudrillard notes a "galloping acceleration, a dizzying whirl of mobility," a hastening of events, a turbulence that does not bring history to a close but results in the swallowing up of events in a "retroversion of history."[8] These retroversions may have swallowed up entitative notions of self but, unnoticed by Baudrillard, the soul remains as an absent presence in a culture in which its meanings have expanded from music to food, as well as in the gene bodies we are thought to be.

In his account of personal identity, analytic philosopher Derek Parfit is more likely to see himself as the heir of Strawson than the friend of Baudrillard. It can, however, be argued that his puzzle cases and the hyperbolic tropes of Baudrillard are not altogether dissimilar. Would a teletransported replica of me still be me? Parfit asks. If certain things happened to me, would I become a different me or would I actually cease to exist? By now a shibboleth (in the everyday non-Derridean sense of the word) is Parfit's claim that although we ordinarily ascribe thought to thinkers, we cannot conclude from the content of our experiences

---

[5] "Persons," in *Essays in Philosophical Psychology,* ed. Donald F. Gustafson (New York: Doubleday and Company, 1964), 388.

[6] Jean Baudrillard, *The Illusion of the End,* trans. Chris Turner (Stanford: Stanford University Press, 1994), 95–96.

[7] Ibid., 99–100.

[8] Ibid., 111–12.

that a thinker is a separately existing entity. To be sure, there is no demarcating a person apart from a brain and body and a chain of physical and mental events. But what matters for Parfit's reductionist view, a phrase he understands honorifically, is that persons are defined by what he calls Relation R, a psychological connectedness/continuity that may be ascribed to any number of causes, for example, brain states.[9] Our thoughts and experiences can be fully described without claiming that they belong to a thinker or to a subject of experiences, and they are better accounted for by "an *impersonal* description."[10]

That the ongoingness of psychological states can be depicted in an impersonal way leads Parfit to envisage a conception of the person that Baudrillard might see as "the simulation of an infinite trajectory."[11] Parfit takes cognizance of Thomas Nagel's term *series person,* by which is meant an r-related series of embodied brains such as might be created by a scanning replicator that annually destroys and then reproduces a person's brain and body, and of which blueprints can be made just in case an individual happens to be destroyed.[12] This sci-fi scenario may well be otiose for Parfit, since the "I" that I am is always already a series-person in that intrinsic to the criterion of identity is the connectedness of my multiple psychic states, which may be ascribed to any cause.

If my continuous experiences constitute who I am, death is a mere break with these experiences, so that, for Parfit, the possibility of my death as tragic in any classical sense is precluded. Baudrillard becomes Parfit's odd bedfellow when he asserts that a celebratory death too must be ruled out. Yet for both, there is solace for the demise of the subject: the appeal to imaginative creation, a surprisingly modernist solution. Baudrillard does not, as might be expected, counterpose the impersonal play of illusions and phantasms, of simulacra that refer to nothing other than themselves or to "electronic encephalization" as having consoling power.[13] Instead he urges transposing language games on to

---

[9] Derek Parfit, *Reasons and Persons* (New York: Oxford, 1986), 215.

[10] Ibid., 225 (emphasis in original).

[11] Baudrillard, *Illusion of the End,* 2.

[12] Ibid., 290.

[13] Jean Baudrillard, *The Ecstasy of Communication,* trans. Bernard and Caroline Schutz (New York: Semiotext[e], 1988), 17.

social and historical phenomena, "the heteroclite tropes which are the delight of a vulgar imagination."[14] Despite the reductionist view of self that Parfit espouses, like Baudrillard he proclaims: "We may want our lives to have greater unity in the way that an artist can create a unified work." It is up to us, he contends, "to express or fulfill our particular values or beliefs."[15]

Such reversions to modernist accounts reflect a flight from the Pythagorean body, one that in its postmodern genetic guise can be viewed as a re/disfiguring of Neoplatonic descriptions of the soul's nonmateriality, rationality, control of behavior, and immortality. I shall argue first that soul enters into the mathematical algorithms used by evolutionary biologists and artifical life theorists not as a gesture of nostalgia, but as the object of a quest for what Neoplatonists claimed to have found in the Pythagorean conception of soul as number, a standing against death that must remain, as for Heidegger, the unthought standard of the measure of that which cannot be fathomed.

I shall not treat the story of the gene as the grand narrative of evolutionary biology, but as a tale fissured transgressively by another tale, that of the soul. Far from reflecting a will to enumerate, to calculate, I argue that in the mathematized models of soul in antiquity, soul is itself divine number and, as such, enters errantly into postmodern accounts of the gene as the agent of replication. In considering the relation of soul to number, I shall attempt to follow Heidegger's path of thinking: attending to what was thought as presaging the thinking that is to come.[16]

THE SOUL IN PAGAN NEOPLATONISM

Speaking of early and later thinking, Heidegger says of Anaximander's philosophy of nature and Nietzsche's will to power that "[they] bring the Same to language, but what they say is not identical. [When] we can speak of the Same in terms of things

---

[14] Baudrillard, *Illusion of the End,* 122.

[15] Parfit, *Reasons and Persons,* 446.

[16] Martin Heidegger, *Early Greek Thinking: The Dawn of Western Philosophy,* trans. David Farrell Krell and Frank A. Capuzzi (San Fransisco: Harper and Row, 1984), 16.

that are not identical, the fundamental condition of a thoughtful dialogue between recent and early times is automatically fulfilled."[17] While it must be conceded that quantitative thinking has eventuated in planning and ordering, so long as we do not lose sight of the *Seinsfrage* there can be, for Heidegger, "[a] historic dialogue between thinkers." One need not speak only of degeneracy, but of being "adrift in errancy" toward that which is Greek, and of this errancy as the "space in which history unfolds."[18]

To be sure, Heidegger decries the principle of *nihil est sine ratione* ("nothing is without reason") that expresses the being of calculation. On this view, a thing can be said to exist "when and only when it has been established as a calculable object for cognition."[19] Although being and reason are primordially inseparable, being has become *ratio:* "The differentiation into being and ground/reason remains concealed."[20] Like the bifurcated tree (in old German known as *Zweisel*), Heidegger sees ratio as a forked growth, such that ratio and that upon which it rests are not severed.[21]

When ratio, however, is seen as numeration and as being, it cannot exhibit the requisite mode of togetherness. With Aristotle, reason is unmoored because number is envisaged as bound up with time as the now such that: "The now is number, not limit, not *peras* but *arithmos.*" Limit must be one with the being that it limits, whereas "[n]umber is not bound to what it numbers. Number can determine something without itself being dependent . . . on the content and mode of being of what is counted."[22]

The accounts of soul to which I shall turn elude this difficulty. In the belonging-together of number and soul, number is no longer a measure that is applied to an entity or to a motion, but is itself both measure and the being that is measured. Thus (to borrow Heidegger's distinction), soul is the same but not identi-

---

[17] Ibid., 23.

[18] Ibid., 26.

[19] Martin Heidegger, *The Principle of Reason,* trans. Reginald Lilly (Bloomington: Indiana University Press, 1991), 120.

[20] Ibid., 108.

[21] Ibid., 104.

[22] Martin Heidegger, *Basic Problems of Phenomenology,* trans. Albert Hofstadter (Bloomington: Indiana University Press, 1982), 249.

cal with number, an identity in difference not unlike the bifurcated tree, the Zweisel.

It goes without saying that there is a sea of commentary about
the nature of soul in Neoplatonic philosophies. Nevertheless, to
track the lineage of the Pythagorean body, some remarks about
what is revealed and concealed by the proper names Plotinus and
Iamblichus are required. For Plotinus, ultimate reality, "the
one," is seen as a hierarchy of degrees of unity. Each of three
hypostases, the one, intellect (*nous* or mind), and soul, are organized in order of dependence, each being a diminution of the
power of the preceding level and requiring additional faculties
for its support. This descent is depicted as the participation of a
lower stratum in a higher and, in a manner distinctive to Plotinus,
as emanation, a flowing or streaming forth.[23]

The emanation doctrine implies that entities disseminate their
perfections, thus helping to explain how spiritual principles exercise causality. The energy or power of agency is not reduced by
the activity of the divine hypostases, which must not be evisaged
as creative agents, but rather as imbricated in a process that is
always already fully determined. The self-dissemination of the
one is sometimes interpreted as governed by the principle of
plenitude, the need to exemplify every kind of being. Evolutionary biologists, however, reject the principle in that it is not a
plethora of types of genetic material, but rather appropriately
adaptive forms of DNA that are needed for the creation of new
species.[24]

For Plotinus, receiving a shape is not the result of creative
agency, but of a being's imitation of its source. Beings have a
desire to rise, to return to their causes. In its unrealizable striving
to attain a perfect vision of that which is higher, intellect, the
first hypostasis, is compelled to splinter its vision into a world of
individual forms,[25] a path that ends in materialization. Just as the

---

[23] Stephen Gersh, *From Iamblichus to Eriugena: An Investigation of the Prehistory and Evolution of the Pseudo-Dionysian Tradition* (Leiden, The Netherlands: E. J. Brill, 1978), 17–18.

[24] Daniel C. Dennett, *Darwin's Dangerous Idea: Evolution and the Meaning
of Life* (New York: Simon and Schuster, 1995), 115.

[25] R. T. Wallis, *Neoplatonism* (London: Gerald Duckworth and Co., 1972),
65–66.

gene may be seen as coded instruction in contrast to its apparent expression as phenotype, for Plotinus, the visible manifestation of an entity, its image, requires correction and dematerialization accompanied by de-spatialization.[26]

It is crucial to recall that beyond individual souls, soul as such is a hypostatic plane that flows from the intelligible or divine mind that contains it. As one and without distinction, soul lends itself to division, a division that is manifested as entry into a body. At the hypostatic level, soul possesses the vision of a superior condition and, thus understood, is not the soul either of any particular existent or even of the cosmos.[27] Plotinus's account is worth citing at length:

> The nature which is at once visible and indivisible, which we affirm to be soul, has not the unity of an extended thing: it does not consist of separate sections; its divisibility lies in its presence at every point of the recipient, but it is indivisible as dwelling entire in the total and entire in any part. . . .
>
> Itself devoid of mass, it is present to all mass . . . it has never known partition . . . but remains a self-gathered integral, and is parted among bodies [in that] bodies cannot receive it except in some partitive mode; the partition, in other words, is an occurrence in body, not in soul.[28]

The types of soul must be distinguished as the soul that remains in the intelligible realm but is somehow different from it: the world-soul that rules the cosmos as cosmic agency that initiates change while itself remaining unchanged, and individual souls. In a dense analysis in the manner of Deleuze, Eric Alliez attributes the fall of the soul not to its intrinsic nature or as dependent upon intelligence from which it derives in the manner of the cosmic hypostases, but to its own initiative that he calls the soul's audacity, its move from "undivided multiplicity" to real division. "Henceforth the lower potentiality ceases to tend toward the higher."[29] The move is one from a cosmic to a temporal

[26] Ibid., 61.

[27] Plotinus, *The Enneads,* trans. Stephen MacKenna (New York: Pantheon Books, n.d.), IV:1, 1, 255.

[28] Ibid., IV.1.1, 257.

[29] Eric Alliez, *Capital Times: Tales from the Conquest of Time,* trans. George Van Den Abbeele (Minneapolis: University of Minnesota Press, 1996), 48–49.

image, disconnecting time from the quantifiable order of the cosmos to that of soul. In a less subjectivized reading, Eyjolfur Kjalar Emilsson holds: "As immanent in the cosmos, soul is a set of instructions," and, in that regard, like a genetic code or computer program.[30] I make a stronger and essentially different claim: that codes and programs can be seen as transgressive expressions of soul in the culture of postmodernity.

Plotinus's odd view of the relation of soul and body is pertinent to the analysis of the computational modeling of the gene that I shall consider shortly. Unlike Aristotle, for whom the soul is the actuality of the body, inseparable from it, Plotinus sees the connection as that of a compound, as both conceptually and actually separable. Still, Plotinus maintains that soul cannot be in body or in space as in a container, since such claims presuppose that the soul is itself a body.[31] Nor is the soul present as form in matter in that these are inseparable. We imagine the soul to be in the body because the body is visibly animate, and from this we infer that it is ensouled.[32] Rejecting the analogy of helmsman to ship or even of the skill of the helmsman to the steering of the ship, Plotinus finds a more satisfactory analogy in the relation of light to air: "The light is the stable thing, the air flows in and out; when the air passes beyond the lit area it is dark; under the light it is lit."[33]

Plotinus comes to the astonishing conclusion that he has found a genuine parallel to the body-soul relation in the claim that "the air is in the light rather than the light in the air."[34] Plotinus thus confirms Plato's view of the all, in that Plato puts the body in the soul and not the soul in the body *Timaeus* 34B.[35] That the body is in the soul as the air flows in and out of the light can be seen spectrally in the claim of evolutionary biologists that the visible body is, *in nuce,* in the genes, the latter outlasting observable

---

[30] Eyjolfur K. Emilsson, *Plotinus on Sense-Perception: A Philosophical Study* (Cambridge: Cambridge University Press, 1988), 24.

[31] Plotinus, *Enneads,* IV.3.20, 277.

[32] Ibid., IV, 3:20, 277.

[33] Ibid., IV, 3:22, 278.

[34] Ibid., IV, 3:22, 278.

[35] In other contexts, Plotinus reverses this order and refers to soul as in the body. See Emilsson, *Plotinus on Sense Perception,* 34–35.

corporeality, a ghost or *Spuk* of the soul's incorporation of body.[36]

The nature of the soul as deathless is wedded to Plotinus's view of the good such that, as in Plato's *Republic,* the good "exist[s] beyond and above Being . . . beyond and above the intellectual principle and all Intellection."[37] If soul is turned toward the intellectual principle, it may come to possess the good. What is more, soul possesses life, and "life is the Good to the living."[38] Not unaware of the worm in the apple, Plotinus contends: "If life is a good, is there good for all that lives? No: in the vile, life limps: it is like the eye to the dim-sighted; it fails of its task."[39] Yet even if mingled with evil, life is still a good. Is death then an evil? No, for in what is by now a familiar apothegm of Platonism, if the soul can continue to attend to its proper functions after death, "then death will be no evil but a good."[40] The notion that life in the body can be considered an evil, and that even in this life the soul must separate itself from evil and pursue the good,[41] re-arises spectrally in the envisaging of genes. Traits that enable individuals of a given species to act for the good of others, thus to pursue a good, are borne by genes.

THE NUMBERS GAME

In his analysis of mathematics in Neoplatonism, Dominic O'Meara argues that to see the soul as number, one must turn from Plotinus to Iamblichus, who sought to lay down an older and more authentic Platonism that reflected Pythagorean notions.[42] In conformity with Aristotle, Plotinus had identified

[36] Jacques Derrida, *Of Spirit: Heidegger and the Question,* trans. Geoffrey Bennington and Rachel Bowlby (Chicago: University of Chicago Press, 1989), 112.
[37] Plotinus, *Enneads,* I.7.1, 65.
[38] Ibid., I.7.2, 65.
[39] Ibid., I.7.3, 65.
[40] Ibid., I.7.3, 66.
[41] Ibid., I.7.3, 66.
[42] "La question de l'être et de non-être des objets mathématiques chez Platon et Jamblique," in *The Structure of Being and the Search for the Good: Essays on Ancient and Early Medieval Platonism,* ed. Dominic O'Meara (Brookfield, Vt.: Ashgate Publishing Co., 1998), 406. See chap. 15.

number with the category of quantity. At the same time, he saw numbers themselves as substances distinguishable from quantitative measure applied by the soul to sensible things. Plotinus could not see how numbers in themselves could be substances, while numbers inhering in objects did not exist, but were measures.[43]

This sticking point is pondered by Iamblichus. By positing a multilayered participational doctrine of forms, he is able to transcend a purely quantitative view of number. On his account, there is a transcendent form, a universal form or form that is immanent in objects, and finally the formed material particular. All these are levels he designates respectively as unparticipated, participated, and participant forms.[44] Similarly, mathematical objects are arranged hierarchically as physical numbers, intelligible numbers, and divine numbers that transcend the intelligible.[45] Rejecting the suggestion that numbers are merely incidental to the things that they measure, Iamblichus is home free: numbers exist in things like other immanent forms and are not merely accompanying attributes.

Mathematical objects are not the result of abstracting from matter but are self-existent, superior in being to sensible things, ontological algorithms, as it were. Iamblichus calls the number in which sensible things participate "physical number" and makes the striking claim that number includes all other principles responsible for the structure of sensible things. Thus O'Meara comments:

> What is the difference between physical number and the other principles responsible for the physical structuration of sensible things? In the treatise on Pythagoreanism, Iamblichus does not seem to envisage such a distinction. Physical number includes all the principles of sensible things. Or rather, the objects studied by the mathematician contain in a paradigmatic way whatever is responsible for the organization of sensible objects. Iamblichus has

---

[43] Plotinus, *Enneads*, VI.I.4, 445–46.

[44] Wallis, *Neo-Platonism*, 126–27.

[45] For a comparable use of numbers in Neoplatonism generally, see Stephen Gersh, *From Iamblichus to Eriugena: An Investigation of the Prehistory and Evolution of the Pseudo-Dionysian Tradition* (Leiden, The Netherlands: E. J. Brill, 1978), 139–41.

a tendency to lead back all the constitutive principles of the world to mathematical principles.[46]

In considering the inseparability of soul and number, it should be noted that letters, characters, and numbers are used by some Neoplatonists in formulating a thaumaturgical theory of soul premonitory of later kabbalistic speculation. Theodorus of Asine appeals to letters, characters, and numbers to account for the nature of the soul. Although Iamblichus insists that the soul is number, he rebukes Theodorus on the grounds that even if the soul were number, this idea and other metaphysical principles cannot be derived through arbitrary numerological manipulation.[47]

What, then, is the precise relation of individual souls to number for Iamblichus? Recall that for Plotinus, even an embodied soul remains purely in itself, but when the soul acts it goes outside itself and undergoes change. Although subject to alteration, the soul does not become totally transitory, in that it must persist through many lives. Thus, the soul is intermediate between permanence and change.[48] In his commentary on Neoplatonic doctrines of soul, Carlos Steel maintains that its intermediate status forces the soul to create its own order of reason, "mathematical forms that at the same time are intelligible forms and models of sensible things."[49] Mathematical discourse is precisely this plenitude or fullness of the rational.

Iamblichus considers the soul as the intertwining of geometric figure, as number and as a harmony bringing disconnected things into proportion. In his treatise *On General Mathematical Science,* he attributes extraordinary generative power to the mathematicals:

---

[46] O'Meara, *The Structure of Being and the Search for the Good,* 414, chap. 15. Translation mine.

[47] See Iamblichus, *The Exhortation to Philosophy, Including the Letters of Iamblichus and Proclus' Commentary on the Chaldean Oracles,* trans. Thomas S. Johnson (Grand Rapids, Mich.: Phanes Press, 1988), 30–31. For a detailed account of this controversy, see Gersh, *From Iamblichus to Eriugena,* 289–304.

[48] See Carlos G. Steel, *The Changing Self, A Study on the Soul in Later Neoplatonism: Iamblichus, Damascius, and Priscianus* (Brussels: Verhandelingen van de Koninklijke Academie, Weternschappen, Letteren en Schone Kunsten van Belgie, 1978), 58–59.

[49] Carlos G. Steel, "*L'âme, modèle, et image:* Philosopher and Man of Gods," in *The Divine Iamblichus: Philosopher and Man of Gods,* eds. H. J. Blumenthal and E. G. Clark (London: Bristol Classical Press, 1993), 21. Translation mine.

The soul exists in ratios common with all mathematicals, possessing on the one hand the power of discerning them, and on the
other hand the power of generating and producing the incorporeal
measure themselves, and with these measures the soul has the capacity to fit together the generation and completion of forms in
matter by means of images, proceeding from the invisible to the
visible, and joining together the things outside with those
inside. . . . In brief the definition of the soul contains in itself the
sum-total of mathematical reality.[50]

This description is cut to fit the gene, allowing for signficant
terminological changes. Although evolutionary biologists and artificial life theorists may not believe that genes contain the whole
of mathematical reality, the generative power of calculative models is likely to be endorsed. Could the genome, as the collection
of genes of an organism, not be seen as a writing under erasure
of "that actuality of [soul]" described by Iamblichus to which
"the power of reason belongs?"[51] Can we say, then, that both
soul and gene are codes of iterability, of repeatable traces engaged in a Derridean play of difference?

This play is discernible yet again in the mode of temporalization of each. Consider first Plotinus's claim that in the divine
realm, all is eternal presence. "Life—instantaneously entire,
complete, at no point broken into period or part—which belongs
to the authentic existent by its very existence . . . this is eternity,"
he maintains.[52] By contrast, generated things exist in time and
can expect "the annulment of [their] futurity."[53] For Plotinus,
there was a time when time was other than transiency, when it
was at rest within the authentic existent, until stirred by an active
principle, the all-soul.[54]

But how could time have been at rest? For Plotinus, eternity is
not itself repose but merely a participant in repose, and therefore
eternity can be fissured by difference, by time: "[Eternity is]
something in the nature of unity, yet compact of diversity. Where

[50] Gregory Shaw, *Theurgy and the Soul: The Neoplatonism of Iamblichus*
(University Park: The Pennsylvania State University Press, 1995), 192–93.
[51] Iamblichus, *The Exhortation to Philosophy,* 78.
[52] Plotinus, *Enneads,* III.7.3, 225.
[53] Ibid., III.7.4, 225.
[54] Ibid., III.7.11, 234.

we see life we think of it as movement, where all is self-identity
we call it Repose; and we know it as, at once, Difference and
Identity when we recognize that all is unity with variety."[55] What
is more: "Time put[s] forth its energy in a constant progress of
novelty . . . while the ceaseless forward movement of Life brings
with it unending Time," an endless futurity that is inconceivable
apart from soul.[56]

Must we not acknowledge that there is in soul and in Darwin's
dangerous idea (the forward movement of life) the same efferent
play of difference? Is this "constant progress of novelty," this
"ceaseless forward movement of life" not borne by replicant
genes, the Spuk or ghost of soul?

Whose Life Is It, Anyway?

When evolutionary biology considers the body as code, what is
envisaged is not the dissolution of the body as phenotype, the
bodily expression of genes in interaction with the environment,
but rather the demotion of the body's privileged status. The organism's form is severed from what counts as the individual biological entity, the gene that is said to be the "real" agent and
recipient of heritable action. Thus Richard Dawkins, who famously refers to the selfishness of genes, offers no disclaimer to
the view that "any animal form can be transformed into a related
form by a mathematical transformation although . . . the translation may not be a simple one."[57] The gene's eye view sees evolution as taking place not on behalf of the organism as the
indivisible unit of biological individuality in accordance with
older accounts, but rather in the interest of the gene, "that little
bit of chromosome that lasts for many generations."[58]

Dawkins's endorsement of the self-organizing propensities of

---

[55] Ibid., III.7.3, 224.

[56] Ibid., III.7.11, 234.

[57] The view is that of D'Arcy Thompson cited in Richard Dawkins, *The Extended Phenotype: The Gene As the Unit of Selection* (Oxford: W. H. Freeman
and Company, 1982), 2.

[58] Richard Dawkins, *The Selfish Gene* (Oxford: Oxford University Press,
1976), 33.

genes and his denial of higher purposiveness as governing the process are effectively expressed in Daniel Dennett's metaphor of cranes and skyhooks. Mindlike accounts of evolutionary change are referred to as skyhooks that function like the *deus ex machina* of classical drama, while cranes do the actual everyday work of lifting without appeal to mental causes. Thus:

> A skyhook is a mind-first force or power or process, an exception to the principle that all design and apparent design is ultimately the result of mindless, motiveless mechanicity. A crane . . . is a subprocessor special feature of a design process that can be demonstrated to speed up the basic, slow process of natural selection . . . and is demonstrably a product of the process."[59]

For Dennett there are only cranes and no skyhooks. To be sure, neither Dennett nor Dawkins denies the significance of organisms. What is perceived as radical in Dawkins's description of the phenotype is his expansion of standard accounts to include not only the organism's perceptible attributes, but the outcomes of gene activity that lie outside the bodies in which the genes are lodged.[60]

To make sense of the contention that gene activity can be outside the body, it is crucial to see the centrality of replication in Dawkins's account. For Dawkins, a replicator is anything of which copies can be made. Information-bearing DNA molecules, gene strings are replicators, active when their effects lead to their being copied, passive when they die out. The gene is the "unit of heredity" that is to be retained in the evolutionary process. Only those likely to be copied survive, while passive replicators become extinct.[61] Difference does not disappear, since each gene is defined in relation to its alternative forms of the gene, alleles, a difference within the same. It is still genes that are the units that labor in the interest of self-replication, genes all the way down.

Although the phenotype continues to be "the all important instrument of preservation; it is not that which is preserved,"[62] or, as Dawkins avers more graphically: "A body is the gene's way of

---

[59] Dennett, *Darwin's Dangerous Idea,* 76.
[60] Dawkins, *The Extended Phenotype,* 292.
[61] Ibid., 83–85.
[62] Ibid., 47.

preserving the genes unaltered."[63] To be sure, Dawkins concedes, genes are strung together along chromosomes that, in turn, enter into more complex forms and finally into organisms. Yet he insists upon an "atomistic" account of the gene as the unit of selection that actually survives, a Pythagorean entity, a soul-like vehicle of its own immortality.

In his Gifford lectures, Holmes Rolston III, departing from Dawkins, insists that the organism is more than an aggregate of selfish genes. It is far better to begin with the whole organism as a synthesis that "codes its morphologies and behaviors in the genes which are analytic units of that synthesis, each gene, a cybernetic bit of the program that codes the specific form of life."[64] Although this claim is embedded in his larger theological program, it is still possible to consider Rolston's claim for the organism apart from this framework. Appealing to the language of computer science, he asserts that "the integrated knowledge of the whole organism is 'discharged' level by level as one goes down through the organ, cell, organelle, enzyme, protein molecule, DNA coding,"[65] replicating Iamblichus in top-down or descending order of forms as well as numbers.

Just as the soul, for Iamblichus, is seen as the bearer of value, the gene is viewed by some evolutionary biologists as a carrier of ethical norms. It must be recalled, however, that even if genes provide the means for the emergence of self-sacrificial acts on the part of individual animals, such altruistic acts are undertaken in the ultimate interest of gene replication. Genes may be value-coded, but the realization of value is measured in terms of reproductive success. In a by-now classical formulation, E. O. Wilson defines evolutionary altruism as "enhancing the personal genetic fitness of others at the cost of genetic fitness on the part of the altruist; either reduc[ing] its own survival capacity or curtail[ing] its own reproduction or both."[66] Evolutionary biologists largely

---

[63] Dawkins, *The Selfish Gene*, 22.

[64] Holmes Rolston III, *Genes, Genesis, and God: Values and Their Origins in Natural and Human History* (Cambridge: Cambridge University Press, 1999), 79.

[65] Ibid., 80.

[66] Edward O. Wilson, "Biological and Social Bases of Altruism and Sympathy," in *Altruism, Sympathy, and Helping: Psychological and Sociological Principles*, ed. Lauren Wispe (New York: Academic Press, 1978), 11.

agree that altruistic traits are acquired in the interest of self-pres-
ervation, and that genetically anchored rules are rules of pru-
dence. Plotinus's narrative of the relation of the soul's desire
for the good is re/disfigured as gene activity that allows for the
replication of a particular good, so that this good is not lost.

A New Heaven on a New Earth?

The interpretation of the body as code lends itself readily to the
modeling of life that is humanly contrived through the use of
computational prototypes, thus advancing the pervasiveness of
Pythagorean design. In turning to computational paradigms for
understanding biological life, Christopher Langton asserts that
life is not a property of matter, but rather of its organization, for
which computational models are eminently suited, so that now
research can be directed away from "the mechanics of life to the
logic of life."[67]

It could be argued that the creation of artificial life would be
served most effectively by relying upon the organic chemicals
of carbon-chain chemistry. Apart from the practical difficulties
inherent in such an effort, Langton contends that more can be
learned from the "creation of life *in silico,*" in that it opens up
the "space of *possible* life."[68]

Dennett makes a more modest claim for artificial life. The development of genetic algorithms indeed enables us to simulate
and manipulate evolutionary processes, but, despite the flexibil-
ity of the program, its parameters are set. Nevertheless, such programs afford the opportunity to "'rewind the tape of life' and
replay it again and again in many variations."[69] What is mimed
is the genotype as "a bag of instructions," a procreative artifice
that specifies behaviors or modifies structures. In essence, what
Langton seeks is the generating of behavior through the creation

---

[67] Christopher G. Langton, "Artificial Life," *The Philosophy of Artificial Life,*
ed. Margaret A. Boden (New York: Oxford University Press, 1996), 47.

[68] Ibid., 50.

[69] Dennett, *Darwin's Dangerous Idea,* 212.

of computational automata.[70] Now the human agent steps out of the picture as breeder and allows the computer to engage in the process of selection.

In some recent simulation systems, even the earlier proxies for the human agent, the algorithmic breeding agents, are eliminated. The computer programs themselves compete for computer processing unit (CPU) time and memory space. Langton maintains: "The programs reproduce themselves and the ones that are better at this task take over the population."[71] In Baudrillardian fashion, Thomas S. Ray, the developer of one such program, the Tierra, contends: "There is no connection between the Tierran world and the real physical world. I have created a virtual universe that is self-contained."[72] Computers are now seen to transcend the instructions of their programs and to generate mutations, or novel behavior. If sufficiently powerful, they are unpredictable. Langton declares: "It is impossible to determine any non-trivial property of the future behavior of a sufficiently powerful computer from a mere inspection of its program and its initial state."[73] The only way to determine changes is to run the program.

WHO ARE WE, AFTER ALL?

Dawkins's account of gene evolution is not archeologically but eschatologically driven: the tape does not run backward, but forward. The purpose of reproduction is neither the perpetuation of the species nor of the individual organism as the unit of natural selection, but rather the conservation of the active germ replicator, the "ancestor of an indefinitely long line of descendents." Although some germ lines may die out, "any germ line replicator is potentially immortal."[74]

---

[70] Ibid., 42–47. For an additional account of humanoid automata, see Jean Claude Beaune, "The Classical Age of Automata: An Impressionistic Survey from the Sixteenth to the Nineteenth Century," in *Fragments for the History of the Human Body*, part 1, eds. Michel Feher, Ramona Nadoff, and Nadia Tazzi (New York: Zone Books, 1990), 431–80.

[71] Ibid., 88.

[72] See his "An Approach to the Synthesis of Life," in Boden, ed., *The Philosophy of Artificial Life*, 136.

[73] Langton, "Artificial Life," 58.

[74] Dawkins, *The Extended Phenotype*, 83.

From these claims, it is possible to infer that the germ line poses a challenge to the identity of the individual as phenotype and, as such, to the *genos* or *ethnos* to which she or he belongs. But what is meant by appearance, by resemblance? In analyzing the concept of resemblance, Derrida considers the resemblance of Socrates to the tribe of poets, contending that if Socrates resembles them, it does not mean he is their fellow. Yet he is also like them, both speaking and not speaking from the place from which they speak, and playing on the spatiality of place as "a political place and a habitation."[75] Is Socrates the one he seems, the same, speaking from the same place as the others, or is he other than the others?

Consider now another text, another place: the Levitical consecration of Aaron and his sons as priests for all generations: "And you shall command the people of Israel that they bring to you pure beaten oil for the light, that a lamp may be set up to burn continually. In the tent of meeting outside the veil which is before the testimony, Aaron and his sons shall tend it from evening to morning before the Lord. It shall be a statute forever to be observed through their generations."[76]

For traditional Judaism, this command wends its way forward in post-exilic form. Those who now claim patrilineal descent from the priestly caste as determined through oral transmission may, upon the occasion of the pilgrim festivals, engage in the practice of blessing the congregation. Standing before the assembled congregants, they drape their prayer shawls around head and body. With outspread fingers, their hands having earlier been washed by those who claim descent from the Levites, the "descendents of Aaron," they then turn to the congregation and recite a blessing. Because the divine presence is now said to rest upon them, the congregation must avert its eyes from the performers.

How does the "fact" of priestly descent re-arise in a postmodern culture of virtualized multiple identities? Those claiming priestly origin and belonging to groups historically identified as

<hr>

[75] Jacques Derrida, *On the Name,* trans. David Wood, John P. Leavey Jr., and Ian McLeod (Stanford: Stanford University Press, 1995), 108.
[76] Lev. 27:20.

of Israelite descent have been seen as providing an interesting gene pool for scientific inquiry. After genetic testing, an identical gene borne on the y, or male, chromosome was found to be present in 10 percent of those claiming such descent, and absent in other members of the larger group. Recently it came to media attention that the Lemba people of southern Africa claim that they are Israelites and that approximately the same proportion of the male population have the requisite gene, a claim borne out by genetic testing. The phenotypical bodies of the heretofore recognized groups and of the Lemba are now bearers of a newly minted gene-borne identity, an identity determined not by virtue of manifest characteristics, but by genetic similarity in a new-old relation of same and other, identity and difference.

Are narratives of genetic likeness simply descriptions of a technologically contrived functional immortality, as Baudrillard would have it, or might they be entering wedges into reconstructing accounts of authochthony as based upon physical resemblances? Is the description of the gene-self a narrative of continuity that can be told and untold in the Plotinian language of soul as that which is "devoid of all mass . . . a self-gathered integral, . . . parted among bodies [in that] bodies cannot receive it except in some partitive mode; the partition, in other words, is an occurrence in body, not in soul."[77]

Do body and soul, gene and visible body, each remain other to the other, or does what is other re-arise spectrally? Speaking of *Geist,* Derrida warns that "the entirely other announces itself in the path of the most rigorous repetition. And this repetition is also the most vertiginous and the most abyssal."[78] Did not soul, as an absent presence unmentioned in the narrative of natural selection, give rise in the last century to apocalyptic political consummations? Is the gene as that which is computationally modelled, a Spuk or specter of soul, likely to undergo the previous fate of Darwin's dangerous idea? Or can genes wander errantly through bodies that differ, undermining invidious destinctions to become nomads of a differentiated same—in Plotinus's words, like soul, "a choral dance under the rule of number?"[79]

---

[77] Plotinus, *Enneads,* V.4, 318.
[78] Derrida, *Of Spirit,* 113.
[79] Plotinus, *Enneads,* V.4, 318.

13

Gilles Deleuze and the Sublime Fold of Religion

Clayton Crockett

INTRODUCTION

IN MANY WAYS, the possibilities for contemporary philosophical and theological thinking have been determined by Kant. Whether explicitly or implicitly, religion has been thought consistently either within, along, or beyond the limits legislated by classical modern reason. At the same time, its status has remained problematic, because it was left out of the fundamental sources of human knowledge according to Kant's critique. Although he essentially appended religion onto morality, since that time, religion has flirted with and been skirted by scientific theoretical knowledge, ethics, and aesthetics. In his *Theology of Culture,* Paul Tillich has eloquently described this dilemma, and his solution is to locate religion as the "depth" of each of these three realms of knowing, or culture. Tillich narrates "the story of how religion goes from one spiritual function to the other to find a home, and is either rejected or swallowed by them."[1] Homeless in relation to morals, art, feeling, and technical knowledge, "religion suddenly realizes that it does not need such a place. . . . Religion is the depth dimension in all of them."[2] Tillich utilizes a metaphorics of depth in order to articulate a theology centered around an understanding of religion as ultimate concern. Now, having set up religion as a problem in relation to Kant, I want to set religion as such aside, in order to return to it at the end of this

---

[1] Paul Tillich, *Theology of Culture* (New York: Oxford University Press, 1959), 6.

[2] Ibid., 7.

chapter. For the key to Kant's thinking, which is determinative for modern and postmodern philosophy and theology, is the question of the sublime. Here, contrary to a simple-minded reading of the *Critique of Judgment,* and unraveled in part by later thinkers, there are at least three distinct versions of the Kantian sublime.

First, there is the dynamical sublime. Although in the third *Critique* Kant spends more time elucidating the mathematical sublime, the dynamical sublime has proved (over)determinative for our understandings of religion. Kant's presentation of the dynamical sublime relies in part on his description of the mathematical sublime, and in both cases the sublime emerges from an interaction among human faculties, rather than primarily as an object of nature. He writes, "true sublimity must be sought only in the mind of the judging person, not in the natural object the judging of which prompts this mental attunement."[3]

The dynamical sublime is fundamentally distinguished by the notion of elevation. In the dynamical sublime, nature prompts the mind to reflect upon nature's power or might, its ability to overwhelm the human person. At the same time, however, the very notion of the sublime provides a moral elevation that raises the human being, in her spiritual value, above nature. "Hence nature is here called sublime *[erhaben]* merely because it elevates *[erhabt]* our imagination, making it exhibit those cases where the mind can come to feel its own sublimity, which lies in its vocation and elevates it even above nature."[4]

This elevation underlies the Hegelian concept of *Aufhebung,* which Hegel modifies by allowing the concept to include both a lifting up and a preserving at a higher level. In the *Science of Logic,* Hegel explains:

> ['T]o sublate *[aufheben]*' has a twofold meaning in the language: on the one hand it means to preserve, to maintain, and equally it

---

[3] Immanuel Kant, *Critique of Judgment,* trans. Werner Pluhar (Indianapolis: Hackett, 1987), 113.
[4] Ibid., 121.

also means to cause to cease, to put an end to. . . . Thus what is sublated is at the same time preserved; it has lost its immediacy but is not on that account annihilated. . . . The double meaning of the Latin *tollere* does not go so far; its affirmative determination signifies only a lifting up.[5]

The notion of sublation essentially involves elevation, even though Hegel expands the definition of tollere to include both a canceling and a preservation. The notion of Aufhebung derives from the elevation characterized by the dynamical sublime, because it is the sublime feeling or judgment that elevates the human being (spirit) above nature, overcoming the negativity of immediate nature while at the same time preserving its mediated essence.

In a different way, Freud also relies on the dynamical sublime for his conception of sublimation. In *Civilization and Its Discontents,* Freud explains that sublimation involves a refined expression of a libidinal drive at a higher level:

[S]ublimation of the instincts lends its assistance. One gains the most if one can sufficiently heighten the yield of pleasure from the sources of physical and intellectual work. When that is so, fate can do little against one. A satisfaction of this kind, such as the artist's joy in creating, in giving his phantasies body, or a scientist's in solving problems or discovering truths, . . . [yields a pleasure which] has a special quality . . . [such] that such satisfactions seem 'finer and higher.' But their intensity is mild compared with that derived from the sating of crude and primary instinctual impulses.[6]

In contrast with Hegel, Freud claims that the instinct or drive loses its essential intensity in this movement of elevation, which is less primally satisfying. Here nature is only partially overcome, and yet the promise of civilization rests upon the ability to sublimate, or rise above, the brutal anti-social nature of the drives. Elevation is the key to sublimation, even though Freud remains pessimistic about its long-term success. One may value the relation between a lower material base and a higher spiritual

---

[5] G. W. F. Hegel, *The Science of Logic,* trans. A. V. Miller (London: George Allen and Unwin, 1969), 107.

[6] Sigmund Freud, *Civilization and Its Discontents,* trans. J. Strachey (New York: W. W. Norton, 1960), 30.

level in different ways, even though the same logic of (dynamical) sublimation is at work in these opposing viewpoints: one
view may assert the primacy of the spiritual sublime over a crude
material base in a quasi-Hegelian way, and the other may assert
the credibility and reality of material nature in opposition to an
idealizing spiritual illusion, which is more Freudian. Despite
their divergent evaluations, Freud and Hegel share a similar understanding of the sublime in its dynamical or elevating mode,
and many of their acknowledged and unacknowledged heirs follow this understanding in their interpretations of religion.

Second, there is the mathematical sublime; although Kant introduces it first in the *Critique of Judgment,* I present it second
because it is less explicitly recognized than the dynamical sublime. The mathematical sublime occurs when the imagination is
prompted to progress toward an infinite apprehension, and reason
intervenes to force imagination to present or comprehend this
apprehension in one temporal presentation, which is impossible
for imagination to do, and which inflicts a profound wound upon
imagination and human thinking itself. Kant explains that "reason demands comprehension in *one* intuition, and *exhibition* of
all the members of a progressively increasing numerical series,
and it exempts from this demand not even the infinite (space and
past time)," but this task is impossible for the imagination.[7] The
resulting conflict occurs:

> In presenting the sublime in nature the mind feels agitated, while
> in an aesthetic judgment about the beautiful in nature it is in restful
> contemplation. This agitation . . . can be compared with a vibration
> *[Erschütterung],* i.e. a rapid alternation of repulsion-from, and at-
> traction to, one and the same object. If a thing is excessive for
> the imagination and the imagination is driven to such excess as it
> apprehends the thing in intuition, then the thing is, as it were, an
> abyss in which the imagination is afraid to lose itself.[8]

The mathematical sublime brings human thinking to the edge of
an abyss, which is an estrangement or dislocation from itself that
results from the effort of conceptualizing the mathematical sublime. For Kant, reason declares victory because it has the power

---

[7] Kant, *Critique of Judgment,* 111.
[8] Ibid., 115.

to force imagination to wound itself, but this raises profound problems for later thinkers less confident in the power of human reason. In Freud, the mathematical sublime resembles the uncanny, which is the déjà vu experience in which human consciousness experiences a profound disorientation at the deepest depths of the self, in a dizzying confrontation with the unconscious. Jacques Lacan has elaborated the mathematical sublime into a psychoanalytical theory with profound implications for theology, with his contention that "God is unconscious."[9] Tracing the mathematical sublime from Kant to Freud and Lacan raises important and potentially disturbing questions about human subjectivity and religious belief.[10]

In its critique of Kantian "modern sublimity," the theology of Radical Orthodoxy primarily attacks the negative implications of the mathematical sublime, although it relies on a version of the dynamical sublime in order to sublate autonomous reason and secular modernity with Christian faith. As Phillip Blond characterizes modern sublimity in *Post-Secular Philosophy,*

> The peculiar though understandable result of all this is that God becomes unknowable and yet deeply feared . . . a self-sufficient finitude denies itself any relationship with infinity. . . . This situation has produced in all subsequent secular thought a relationship with the higher which can perhaps only be described as sublime. . . . The sublime is, in reality, not an encounter with the truly transcendent but an error of subreption, a reflex of finite thought which can only project the beyond as a negative image of its own (self) limitation. . . . The sublime delivers what is taken to be, for modernity, the transcendent experience *par excellence,* the congruence of terror and vacuity.[11]

In *The Word Made Strange,* John Milbank echoes this conclusion with his critique of Kantian philosophy, where he contrasts a substantial theology of the good, associated with Aquinas, with

---

[9] See Jacques Lacan, *The Four Fundamental Concepts of Psychoanalysis,* trans. Alan Sheridan (New York: W. W. Norton, 1977), 59.

[10] See my detailed interpretation of the mathematical sublime, and its significance for theological thinking, in *A Theology of the Sublime* (London: Routledge, 2001).

[11] Phillip Blond, Introduction, *Post-Secular Philosophy* (London: Routledge, 1998), 15–16.

a formal and empty theology of right. Milbank claims that because of the intrinsic unknowability of things in themselves,
"Kant's entire philosophy is in a sense an aesthetic of the sublime in which one is brought up against the margin of organized,
formal, 'beautiful' experience, and at this margin becomes overwhelmed by the intimation of the materially formless, and infinitely total."[12] In this way, secular modernity separates divine
love from omnipotent power, because the materially formless
and infinitely total testifies to an incomprehensible might.

Milbank locates the source of this modern sublimity in Duns
Scotus, because Duns Scotus developed the category of neutral,
univocal being, which logically precedes any positive or negative
(moral) determination. Milbank argues that to leave room for any
autonomous, disinterested philosophy is to remain trapped within
metaphysics, so theology must *sublimate* philosophy: "[P]hilos-
ophy as spiritual discipline . . . can indeed be embraced and con-
summated in a Christian version by theology."[13] The only way
to overcome modern sublimity, then, is for theology to "entirely
evacuate philosophy, which is metaphysics, leaving it nothing
(outside imaginary worlds, logical implications or the isolation
of *aporias*) to do or see."[14] Despite Milbank's impressive erudi-
tion, he remains trapped within a Kantian problematic, because
he is relying on a logic of sublimation or sublation (Milbank's
teacher, Rowan Williams, is a Hegelian theologian), which is a
variant of the dynamical sublime, in order to overcome the negativity implied by the mathematical sublime.

What Milbank, Blond, and the rest of the theologians of Radical Orthodoxy overlook, however, is the third version of the Kantian sublime, the Deleuzian or Baroque sublime. The Deleuzian
sublime is a fold, and it involves a stretching or folding of form
in human thinking and material being that evades the critique of
Radical Orthodoxy, because being is thought in terms of a fold
rather than a break, hole, or gap. With his conception of the Baroque sublime, Deleuze rolls Kant back toward Leibniz in order
to develop a constructive metaphysics that is neo-Baroque.

---

[12] John Milbank, *The Word Made Strange: Theology, Language, Culture* (Oxford: Blackwell, 1997), 10.
[13] Ibid., 49–50.
[14] Ibid., 50.

THE BAROQUE SUBLIME

In one of his last works, *The Fold,* Deleuze develops a metaphysics of the fold by way of an encounter with Leibniz. In order to understand *The Fold,* however, it is necessary to go back to Deleuze's earlier work in *Kant's Critical Philosophy* and *Difference and Repetition.* The key to Deleuze's understanding of the fold lies in his interpretation of Heidegger in a brief interlude of *Difference and Repetition.* In opposition to the predominant interpretation of Heidegger's ontological difference between being and beings as a gap or break, which occurs fundamentally in Sartre, Deleuze reads the ontological difference more profoundly as a fold between being and beings.

In his "Note on Heidegger's Philosophy of Difference," Deleuze claims that Sartre developed the Heideggerian "Not" into a "discovery of the negative and negativity." On the other hand, Merleau-Ponty "undoubtedly followed a more thoroughly Heideggerian inspiration in speaking of 'folds' and 'pleating.'"[15] Deleuze then makes two important assertions, which are necessary to demonstrate the continuity of his philosophy of difference with Heidegger. First, he claims that "the *not* expresses not the negative but the difference between Being and being." Second, the ontological difference "is not 'between' in the ordinary sense of the word. It is the Fold, the *Zwiefalt.*"[16] Here ontological difference is understood as a fold, which is elaborated more fully in *The Fold,* where Deleuze claims that "the ideal fold is the *Zwiefalt,* a fold that differentiates and is differentiated."[17]

The second notion that is necessary in order to read *The Fold* is the idea of the Kantian sublime that Deleuze develops in *Kant's Critical Philosophy,* especially the retrospective preface. Deleuze reads Kant's three critiques panoramically, in order to ask in each three books how the faculties of reason, understanding, and imagination are interrelated. In the third *Critique,* which is char-

---

[15] Gilles Deleuze, *Difference and Repetition,* trans. Paul Patton (New York: Columbia University Press, 1994), 64. I owe many of these insights into Deleuze and the Baroque sublime to the influence of Gregg Lambert.

[16] Deleuze, *Difference and Repetition,* 64–65.

[17] Gilles Deleuze, *The Fold: Leibniz and the Baroque,* trans. Tom Conley (Minneapolis: University of Minnesota Press, 1993), 30.

acterized by Rimbaud's formula "a disorder of all the senses," Deleuze's reading of the sublime becomes the basis for a concept of discordant accord, which is the root of Deleuzian harmony. In the *Critique of Judgment:*

> The various faculties enter into an accord which is no longer determined by any one of them. . . . The Sublime goes even further in this direction: it brings the various faculties into play in such a way that they struggle against one another, the one pushing the other towards its maximum or limit, the other reacting by pushing the first towards an inspiration it would not have had alone. . . . It is a terrible struggle between imagination and reason, and also between understanding and inner sense. . . . It is a tempest in the depths of a chasm opened up in the subject. The faculties confront one another, each stretched to its own limit, and find their accord in a fundamental discord: a discordant accord is the great discovery of the *Critique of Judgment,* the final Kantian reversal.[18]

The sublime paradigmatically illustrates a discordant accord, because the desperate struggle between reason and imagination nevertheless produces a felt sense of purposiveness amid the disorientation or purposivelessness. The sublime becomes the basis of a Deleuzian harmony, and provides the tension necessary for the activity of folding.

In *The Fold,* Deleuze elaborates a Baroque sublime. Here,

> the Baroque refers not to an essence but to an operative function, to a trait. It endlessly produces folds. . . . Yet the Baroque trait twists and turns in its folds, pushing them to infinity, fold over fold, one upon the other. The Baroque fold unfurls all the way to infinity. First, the Baroque differentiates its folds in two ways, by moving along two infinities, as if infinity were composed of two stages or floors: the pleats of matter, and the folds in the soul.[19]

The two modes of the fold, the pleats of matter and the folds in the soul, can be correlated with the two forms of the sublime, the mathematical (pleats of matter) and dynamical (folds of the soul), so that in a sense Deleuze encompasses both forms of the

---

[18] Gilles Deleuze, *Kant's Critical Philosophy,* trans. Hugh Tomlinson and Barbara Habberjam (Minneapolis: University of Minnesota Press, 1984), xii–xiii.

[19] Deleuze, *The Fold,* 3.

Kantian sublime within the Baroque sublime. Although Deleuze distinguishes between two levels or floors of the Baroque architecture, this should be read minimally rather than maximally. The two levels are distinguished in order to articulate harmony. "What makes the new harmony possible," he writes, "is first, the distinction between two levels or floors, which resolves tension or allots the division."[20] This harmony follows the model of the discordant accord, or the Kantian sublime, because a major key is overlaid upon a minor key, which is the reverse of a piano or an organ. For Deleuze, the minor key, or the discord, is primary, and the major or accordant key arises out of the layering or folding of key on key, form on form. The reason this discordant or conflictual relationship can be harmonious is that the tension between the two keys or faculties in their striving forms a fold, or a layering that allows creative becomings and thoughts to unfurl.

Deleuze folds Kant back into the infinite possibilities of Leibniz, but without the overarching pre-established harmony by which God synchronizes monads. For this reason, the fold is *neo-Baroque*, as Deleuze explains. For Leibniz, worlds are incompossible with each other, and God chooses the best possible world, which allows the most creativity to take place. For Whitehead, whom Deleuze reads as a twentieth-century Leibniz, incompossible worlds can coexist in a relationship of discordant accord, and God is not separate from the play of existence. Here God "becomes Process, a process that at once affirms incompossibilities and passes through them."[21]

In the sublime, solutions pass through discords, or incompossibles, which means that harmony is predicated upon disharmony without ceasing to be harmonious. This is how the Kantian sublime transforms Leibniz, even as Leibniz allows Deleuze to evade some of the negativities of the Kantian antinomies. For Deleuze, "solutions no longer pass through accords. It is because the conditions of the problem itself have changed: we have a new Baroque and a neo-Leibnizianism."[22] Harmony arises fundamentally out of the minor discords, or dis-chords.

---

[20] Ibid., 29.
[21] Ibid., 81.
[22] Ibid., 136.

THEOLOGY, MORALITY, AESTHETICS

This harmony is reflected in Deleuze's explication of Leibniz's theology. According to Deleuze, "Leibniz's morality is a morality of progress" because morality "consists in this for each individual: to attempt each time to extend its region of clear expression . . . so as to produce a free act that expresses the most possible in one given condition or another."[23] God's role is to reconcile individual morality with worldly progress, which makes damnation necessary. This is similar to Calvinism, where God is glorified by the contrast of damnation and election, but in Leibniz damnation is not only necessary in order to have the best of all possible worlds, but also freely chosen, which is the opposite of Calvinist predestination. Deleuze writes: "Leibniz's optimism is based on the infinity of the damned as the foundation of the best of all worlds: *they liberate an infinite quantity of possible progress.*"[24]

In Leibniz, the damned liberate an infinite quantity of possible progress for the others, the saved. This is accomplished by means of rage, by which the damned damn themselves "when they renounce their own clarity."[25] For Deleuze, however, a world that is Whiteheadian and neo-Baroque implies that damnation and salvation do not take place among different monads, but remain a continual possibility within each person, according to which becomings are expressed and which folds are unfurled. Harmony involves a modulation in which infinite possibility, "salvation," or accord is predicated upon damnation or discord (the minor key), which is always already a fold, one that stubbornly refuses to unfurl in order to allow other (un)foldings. These becomings and unfoldings make up and exceed the autonomous subject, or monad, but this does not preclude the possibility of harmony, or progress, or morality.

The reasons for Deleuze to turn to Leibniz for "solutions" are at once epistemological, ethical, and aesthetic, and Deleuze's in-

---

[23] Ibid., 73.
[24] Ibid., 74 (emphasis in original).
[25] Ibid., 74.

terest in Leibniz can be expressed in explicitly aesthetic terms. In Leibniz, Deleuze locates a chiaroscuro, or a harmonious mixture of light and shadow, which places Leibniz between the darkness implied by an irreducible conflict of antinomies in Kant on the one hand, and the pure light of Spinoza on the other, whom Deleuze (along with Guattari) calls the "Christ of the philosophers."[26] In an essay on Spinoza, Deleuze claims that "if Spinoza differs essentially from Leibniz, it is because the latter, under a baroque inspiration, saw the Dark . . . as a matrix or premise, from which chiaroscuro, colors and even light emerge."[27] Although Deleuze has long championed Spinoza as the model of a philosopher, Spinoza's exemplary singularity forces Deleuze to doubt whether he can actually be imitated. Spinoza is the "infinite becoming-philosopher" who thought the "impossible"—the "best" plane of immanence—once, "as Christ was incarnated once, in order to show the possibility of the impossible."[28] The turn to Leibniz is a way to recast that (im)possibility, and to demonstrate it as more possible, even if as incompossible.

This resolution echoes the problem set up by Lacan at the end of *The Four Fundamental Concepts of Psychoanalysis,* where Lacan juxtaposes "the dark God" glimpsed in the horrors of Nazism and the Holocaust with the *amor intellectualis dei* (intellectual love of God) of Spinoza. Lacan claims that the dark God is a legacy of Kantianism, which as the moral law of pure desire culminates in "the sacrifice . . . of everything that is the object of love in one's human tendencies." Lacan idealizes Spinoza, but declares that "this position is not tenable for us," and that "experience shows us that Kant is more true."[29] Lacan exaggerates the negativity of a Kant read "*avec* Sade," but he frames a dilemma for other thinkers, including Deleuze, who ultimately uses Kantian tools to exploit a Leibnizian possibility.

---

[26] See Gilles Deleuze and Félix Guattari, *What Is Philosophy?* trans. Hugh Tomlinson and Graham Burchell (New York: Columbia University Press, 1994), 60.

[27] Gilles Deleuze, "Spinoza and the Three Ethics," in *Essays Critical and Clinical,* trans. Daniel W. Smith and Michael A. Greco (Minneapolis: University of Minnesota Press, 1997), 141.

[28] Deleuze and Guattari, *What Is Philosophy?* 60.

[29] Lacan, *Four Fundamental Concepts,* 275.

CONCLUSION

The Deleuzian sublime is a fold, which occurs when two or more faculties strive against each other, and in their striving they form an accord, which takes the form of a fold, or an unfolding. Similarly, Kantian form consists in the production of a fold, a folding that occurs not only in the *Critique of Judgment* but also in the *Critique of Pure Reason.* There is a formally sublime moment to all thinking, which occurs in the act of trying to reflexively account for the act of thinking, a folding of thought back upon itself in an attempt to comprehend the source of thinking. This sublimity of the transcendental imagination disrupts the objective workings of the Kantian understanding, but it is the stretching and folding of the productive imagination, or *Einbildungskraft,* that generates form and meaning.[30]

The sublime represents the paradigmatic case of a conflict of the faculties, which strive for a higher form in Kant's *Critical Philosophy,* which ultimately constitutes a fold. For Deleuze, the interrelationship of Kantian faculties generates higher forms of knowledge, desire, and feeling. For Tillich in the *Theology of Culture,* religion is the depth aspect of knowledge, desire, and feeling that is characterized as "ultimate concern." Although Deleuze uses a metaphorics of height as opposed to Tillich's metaphorics of depth, to think Tillich along with Deleuze is to think religion itself as a fold, that is, as the sublime par excellence.

Rather than a break or limit within human experience, religion can be understood as a folding of a determinate form (either a form of culture or a form of human knowing) back upon itself in an attempt to present the unpresentable, that is, the sublime, or the very process of folding itself. The Deleuzian sublime stretches and folds in its proliferation of folds, which challenges the dictates of classical human reason, or what Tillich calls technical reason, but which evades the misdirected criticisms of Radical Orthodoxy. The only way to think beyond the limits of classical reason is to really grapple with and understand modern

---

[30] On the notion of *Einbildungskraft,* or the pure productive transcendental imagination, and its centrality to the *Critique of Pure Reason,* see Martin Heidegger, *Kant and the Problem of Metaphysics,* trans. Richard Taft (Bloomington: Indiana University Press, 1990).

reason, and particularly Kant, which is an encounter Radical Orthodoxy refuses but which has decisively marked Deleuze and his entire philosophical endeavor.

AFTERWORD: ON CINEMA AND BELIEF

If religion is thought as a sublime fold, what, if anything, does that imply for faith or belief? Despite some postmodern attempts to critique or problematize the notion of belief, Deleuze attempts an ambitious transformation of belief itself.[31] In *Cinema 2: The Time-Image,* Deleuze articulates what is fundamentally at stake when he argues that the challenge for contemporary cinema (and, one might add, no less for philosophy and theology) is "to produce belief in a relation between man [sic] and the world." For Deleuze, "the modern fact is that we no longer believe in this world."[32] Our experience of the world is intolerable; "the intolerable is no longer a serious injustice, but the permanent state of a daily banality." Since the link between humanity and the world is broken, "this link must become an object of belief: it is the impossible which can only be restored within a faith."[33]

But this faith, and this belief, does not refer to another world, or even to a world transformed by either human or divine agency. Even though Deleuze explains the problem in relation to cinema, his definition of cinema is extremely broad and includes what we consider philosophy, and what I would call a secular theology.[34] Cinema refers not primarily to the movies we watch, but to the ways in which our perceptions and conceptions are inherently cinematic, and philosophically this is explicated in reference to Bergson in the cinema books. According to Deleuze:

> Restoring our belief in the world—this is the power of modern cinema (when it stops being bad). Whether we are Christians or

[31] See Amy Hollywood, "Deconstructing Belief: Irigaray and the Philosophy of Religion," *The Journal of Religion* 78, no. 2 (April 1998): 230–45.

[32] Gilles Deleuze, *Cinema 2: The Time-Image,* trans. Hugh Tomlinson and Robert Galeta (Minneapolis: University of Minnesota Press, 1989), 171.

[33] Ibid., 171–72.

[34] See *Secular Theology: American Radical Theological Thought,* ed. Clayton Crockett (London: Routledge, 2001).

atheists, in our universal schizophrenia, we need reasons to believe in this world. It is a whole transformation of belief. It was already a great turning-point in philosophy, from Pascal to Nietzsche: to replace the model of knowledge with belief. But belief replaces knowledge only when it becomes belief in this world, as it is.[35]

To think religion differently involves thinking the fold; however, the stakes of this Continental philosophy of religion concerns the possibility of relinking humanity and the world. Here the task is not simply to trace or unfold a line of thinking out of sheer indifference, but to create theological concepts that produce belief in this world, as it is, while not disavowing the impossibility of this very task due to the intolerability of contemporary life.

---

[35] Ibid., 172. On Deleuze and cinema, and its importance for theoretical thinking, see Gregg Lambert's essay "Cinema and the Outside," in *The Brain Is the Screen: Deleuze and the Philosophy of Cinema,* ed. Gregory Flaxman (Minneapolis: University of Minnesota Press, 2000), 253–92.

5
Reason within the Limits
of Religion Alone

14

Schelling, Bloch, and the Continental Philosophy of Religion

Wayne Hudson

> Positive philosophy is historical philosophy.
>
> SCHELLING

> Religion in the mind is not credulity and the practice is not forms. It is a life. . . . It is not something *else to be got,* to be *added,* but is a new life of those faculties you have.
>
> RALPH WALDO EMERSON

INTRODUCTION

IN THIS ESSAY I discuss in part I some aspects of the approach to religion that Schelling developed in his late "positive philosophy." In part II, I explain how these ideas were taken up and reworked by Ernst Bloch. In part III, I interpret the implications of these developments for the contemporary Continental philosophy of religion. The first two parts of the essay are fairly conventional; the third part is not.

I

Since at least the seventeenth century, there have been attempts to challenge "stasis thinking" in the West. The most important challenge to stasis thought, however, occurred in the work of the German philosopher F. W. J. Schelling (1775–1854).[1] Recently Schelling has been elevated to the status of a postmodern thinker, the teacher of Heidegger, a radical metaphysician who anticipated Lacan in proposing "an economy of difference" characterized by irreducible differentiality.[2] Moreover, many commentators now read Schelling as responding to the failure of the philosophy of reflection and the discovery of the unreliability of the subject.[3] This is an advance on the older literature, which focused on the number and character of Schelling's various phases,[4] but it still tends to reduce Schelling to a disciple of other philosophers, whereas Schelling is a major philosopher whose work needs to be grasped in its own terms.

Today Schelling can be seen as a thinker of historical process who attempted to grasp reality as coming into being, rather than as already finished or pre-given. In his late philosophy, Schelling envisaged "the absolute," or, in modern language, the whole, as changing in the course of the historical-natural process. Accordingly, he attempted to develop a historical metaphysics for which

---

[1] For most of the nineteenth century, Schelling was neglected in the Anglophone world because he was seen as a reactionary idealist; most of his major works were untranslated, and what was available gave no idea of why Hegel and Fichte regarded him as an astonishing genius. In German countries his standing was more secure, and a very telling list of thinkers—Heidegger, Jaspers, Ricoeur, Tillich, Bloch, and Habermas—were profoundly indebted to his ideas. For excellent recent literature on Schelling, see in German Axel Hutter, *Geschichtliche Vernunft die Weiterführung der Kantischen Vernunftkritik in der Spätphilosophie Schellings* (Frankfurt am Main: Suhrkamp, 1996); and Christian Iber, *Subjektivität, Vernunft und ihre Kritik* (Frankfurt am Main.: Suhrkamp, 1999). For scholarly resources on Schelling's late philosophy, see Manfred Frank, ed., *Schelling Philosophie der Offenbarung 1841–42* (Frankfurt: Suhrkamp, 1977).

[2] Slavoj Žižek, *The Indivisible Remainder: Essays on Schelling and Related Matters* (London: Verso, 1997); and Thomas Pfau, *Idealism and the Endgame of Theory: Three Essays by F.W.J. Schelling* (Albany: State University of New York Press, 1994).

[3] Andrew Bowie, *Schelling and Modern European Philosophy* (London: Routledge, 1993); Pfau, *Idealism and the Endgame of Theory*.

[4] Xavier Tillette, *Schelling: Une philosophie en devenir* (Paris: Vrin, 1970); Walter Kasper, *Das Absolute in der Geschichte: Philosophie und Theologie der Geschichte in der Spätphilosophie Schellings* (Mainz: Matthias-Grünewald, 1965); Horst Fuhrmans, *Schellings letzte Philosophie* (Berlin: Junker and Dünnhaupt, 1940).

human freedom and decision making changed how reality came to be.

Schelling's breakthrough here turns on his radical rethinking of the traditional concept of "the ground." According to Schelling, modern rationalism cannot generate an adequate ontology because the ground of the world is not reason but a real ground, which is itself a void or darkness, and the failure to develop an account of the actual as opposed to a purely conceptual ground is the key to the failure of modern philosophy.[5]

In a major anticipation of Heidegger's distinction between the ontic and the ontological, Schelling insisted that a distinction needed to be made between "existence" and "ground" in every being. He rejected the Greek conception that what a thing became was already given in its ground, or reason, or concept. Instead, he emphasized that the "subject" of the world was "that which can be" *(Seinkönnen),* where this changed radically in the course of history and could not be encompassed within a world of ahistorical essences. As Manfred Frank and John Sallis have argued, Schelling's position here is a major development in philosophy, although one only now beginning to be widely understood.[6] Schelling himself used his notion of a real unground *(Ungrund)* to develop an ontology of human freedom and the notion of positive philosophy.

In his Berlin lectures *On the Philosophy of Revelation and Mythology,* running to some 2,100 pages in German, Schelling set out to supplement a negative philosophy, arrived at from reason, with a positive philosophy, arrived at from the contingent facts of history, including the history of world religions, states, and art. This positive philosophy was based on Schelling's claim that the facticity of existence cannot be understood by reference to concepts. For Schelling the fact *that* something is has to be grasped independently of *what* it is. Schelling used this insight to invert the traditional proof of the existence of God. Instead of

---

[5] Schelling, *On the History of Modern Philosophy,* trans. Andrew Bowie (Cambridge: Cambridge University Press, 1994).

[6] Manfred Frank, *Der unendliche Mangel an Sein: Schellings Hegelkritik und die Anfänge der Marxschen Dialektik* (Frankfurt am Main: Suhrkamp, 1975); John Sallis, *Delimitations: Phenomenology and the End of Metaphysics* (Bloomington: Indiana University Press, 1995), ch. 18.

trying to prove that God exists, he studied the realm of facticity and tried to show that God's existence and activity emerge a posteriori as an appropriate explanation of the whole system of the world. Nonetheless, to show this from the facticity of existence was not possible by deductive argument. Instead, reason had to go outside itself, enter into *ecstasis,* and affirm the divine existence as an act of faith, hope, will.

Against this background, Schelling developed a highly distinctive approach to religion, including a concept of postreligion that went beyond the utopia of a religion of reason that he shared as a young man with Hegel. It is not necessary for my purposes here to follow Schelling's unusual and distinctive treatments of God, creation, the fall, and the incarnation. It is enough to explore his thesis that the study of actual mythologies and religions of all kinds can be used to generate a philosophical religion that goes beyond both natural religious consciousness and revealed religion, not only because it is produced by them, but because it addresses the possibilities that arise by both necessity and contingency in reality itself. This thesis even today provides a program of possible research.

Schelling rejected the rationalist approaches of the Enlightenment, including Kant's critical philosophy of religion, and denied that an adequate philosophy of religion could be derived from the purely internal relations of reason. Instead it was necessary, he argued, to study the history of the actual religions that have appeared. Schelling alleged that a decisive advance could be made by studying the history of mythology as a process of the dialectical development of potencies *(Potenzendialektik),* by studying revealed religion as a process of the mediation of "free religion," and by grasping the immanent possibility of "philosophical religion," when this did not yet exist.

For Schelling, mythology and religion are neither purely imaginary nor simply reflections of existing social forms. Nor are they falsehoods that die out with the birth of reason, as the Enlightenment tended to believe. Nor are they the rational in pictorial form, as in Hegel. For Schelling, mythology is not an unproblematic representation of religious truth, but the result of oppositions between latent cognitive drives, the product of unconscious desires and fears, the result of subterranean psychic stresses. Moreover, for Schelling mythology is not decisively critiqued from outside; it critiques and overcomes itself. Schelling argues that the history of mythology is the history of the real potencies that rose up in the depths of the unconscious, that is, of an actual becoming of God in human cultural history: "*Objectively* considered, mythology is what it claims to be: 'a *real theogony*, a real history of the gods. But since only those gods are real who have God as their ground, it follows that the final content of the history of the gods is that of the generation (the birth, the bringing forth) of *God,* a real becoming of *God,* in consciousness.'"[7]

Consciousness does not choose or invent the representations found in mythology:

> Since consciousness chooses or invents neither the representations themselves nor their expression, mythology arises just *as such* and possesses no other meaning than the one expressed. As a result of the necessity with which the *content* of the representations is produced, mythology possesses from the very beginning a *real* and therefore a *doctrinal* meaning. As a result of the necessity with which the *form* arises, its meaning is completely literal *(durchaus eigentlich)*, i.e. everything in it is to be understood just as it is stated, and we are not to look for implicit or disguised meanings. Mythology is not *allegorical,* it is *tautegorical* (the term is borrowed from Coleridge). For mythology, the gods are beings who really exist. They are not something else, and they do not *mean* something else. They mean *only* what they are.[8]

And again:

> In the mythological process, man is not dealing with things at all, but with *powers that rise up in the depths of consciousness—* powers by which consciousness is moved. The theogonic process which gives birth to mythology is a *subjective* process for as much as it unfolds in *consciousness* and manifests itself in the formation of representations. But the causes and also the objects of these

---

[7] Victor C. Hayes, ed., *Schelling's Philosophy of Mythology and Revelation* (Armidale, NSW: Australian Association for the Study of Religions, 1995), 113–14. For ease of reference, quotations from Schelling are taken from Hayes. However, the reader should be aware that the interpretation of Schelling's technical positions, as well as their translation, is often highly contested. I have ignored these issues for the purposes of this essay.

[8] Hayes, *Schelling's Philosophy of Mythology and Revelation,* 112–13.

representations, are the real theogonic powers *as such*. . . . It is not the mere *representations* of the potencies but the *potencies themselves* which form the content of the process.[9]

Hence, according to Schelling, mythology is a necessary theogonic process in which God brings himself into being by means of the historically actual birth of the gods, that is, the manifestation of diverse and conflicting powers that emerge from the depths of the unconscious to grasp human beings. Schelling also argues that the history of religion and mythology reveals that the unconscious changed in the course of history. And human beings have an actual and real relation to God in mythological religion, because God intervenes in world history to reveal himself sequentially in mythological forms.

Similarly, Schelling deals with revelation as a real historical process that cannot be derived from reason: a process in which "free religion" emerges and comes to replace mythology or unfree natural religion; here his emphasis falls on the sheer fact of revelation, whenever it occurs. Accordingly, he draws a sharp distinction between mythology and revelation:

> The representations of Mythology are the products of a *necessary* process, a movement of the natural consciousness, left merely to itself, on which . . . no free cause *outside* of consciousness can have any further influence. Revelation, however, is expressly conceived as something which presupposes an *Actus* outside of consciousness, and a relation which the most free cause, God, grants or has granted to the human consciousness not out of necessity but in complete freedom.[10]

Schelling then went further, and outlined a conception of philosophical religion. According to Schelling, the mediation of natural and revealed religion led to a philosophical religion for all humanity. This religion would be faith become intelligible and mundane, a synthesis of church and world. It would be free from external authority, and all would access it by their own volition. Indeed, Schelling envisaged a free association of all peoples and religions. The philosophical religion would be both philosophy

---

[9] Ibid., 115.
[10] Ibid., 207.

and religion,[11] but it would not be philosophy in the sense of naturalism: "Reason does not lead to religion, just as Kant's theoretical result shows that there can be no rational religion. That we *know* nothing of God, is the inevitable conclusion of every authentic rationalism, every rationalism which understands itself."[12] Rather, philosophical religion was the result of comprehending the actual religions of humanity: "Without philosophical religion it is impossible to comprehend the real religions—Mythological and Revealed—or to interpret and give an account of them."[13]

However, by interpreting these two religions in the light of philosophical religion, one could perceive that philosophical religion had "nothing in common" with rational religion. For philosophical religion implied the rational interpretation of actual facts, not theses that could be derived from reason without them. Schelling did not suggest that philosophical religion would replace Christianity. On the contrary, consistent with his emphasis on actual contingent historical developments that could not be duplicated by the internal relations of reason, Schelling envisaged a Johannine Christianity that became universal:

> Christianity will then no longer be the old, narrow, stunted, puny Christianity of the prevailing dogmatic schools, and still less a Christianity thinly confined to miserable formulas which shun the light, nor will it be whittled down to an exclusively personal kind of Christianity. Instead, it will be a truly public religion . . . the religion of all mankind in which mankind will, at the same time, find the supreme knowledge.[14]

Schelling's claims here are obscure, subject to different interpretations, and widely criticized in the German secondary literature.[15] In the context of Continental philosophy, however, the crucial point is that Schelling directed attention to the history of actual religions and away from a priori reasoning. Moreover, he

---

[11] Ibid., 334.
[12] Ibid., 197.
[13] Ibid.
[14] Ibid., 334.
[15] Dietrich Korsch, *Der Grund der Freiheit: Eine Untersuchung zur Problemgeschichte der positiven Philosophie und zur Systemfunktion des Christentums im Spätwerk F. W. J. Schellings* (Munich: Chr. Kaiser Verlag, 1980).

treated "religion" as radically historical and as in no way something pious or good. Schelling grasped that the study of actual religions might support a very harsh view of the historical process as one in which advances occurred in the context of brutal struggles and cruel deceptions, as the potencies fought among themselves for supremacy. In positing the horizon of philosophical religion, Schelling was not offering an escape from the agony of the world. He was mapping a new advance that he believed was already emerging as a result of the self-critique of the processes of mythology and revelation. Of course, a contemporary reader may reject Schelling's account of actual religions as based on a speculative production by dialectic and as too teleological. Schelling does not prove that his potencies actually operate, and his treatments of actual religions are often high-handed. Nonetheless, he does signal that the Kantian project of "religion within the limits of reason" is naïve, both because reason is historical and because actual religions involve irrational elements.

Later Continental philosophy was profoundly influenced by Kierkegaard, who, of course, was decisively influenced by Schelling. It is arguable, however, that the Continental philosophical tradition placed too much emphasis on Kant and then submitted to Kierkegaard's pieties. As a result, "religion" was never translated into actual religions that themselves were the products of dangerous and irrational forces. Schelling's revolutionary turn to the fact *that* something is was not taken up, and Schelling's own followers, including Paul Tillich, largely buried his discoveries in theologies of our own intensities.

II

Schelling's legacy was taken up and extended in a nontheological form, however, in the work of the German Jewish philosopher Ernst Bloch (1885–1975). Bloch's work is of great interest, now that it can be reread without his own imbrication in Marxism, because his philosophy of the future modernized and reset ideas latent in Schelling's late philosophy. These ideas included the notion that the future can be built by taking an active approach to history and working up models that can then be tested and corrected. Bloch broke with all "stasis ontology," including the remnants of this ontology in Schelling,[16] and developed a process philosophy in which reality was theorized as an open system able to be built in the course of social and natural history. He rejected the classical philosophical conception of the identity of thought and being (panlogism), and instead hypothesized a process in which "the existing" and "the logical" were mediated with each other over time. For Bloch, this process could be transformed by human agency in the form of theory-praxis.

Bloch set out this radical conception of the world in a master work (still untranslated), *Experimentum Mundi* (1975), in which he gave an account of a historicized theory of categories. As with Schelling, the historical-natural world is "unfinished" and needs to be thematized in ways that leave room for radically new contents still to come. It is a world of risk and contingency, albeit with a stable structure *(Realdialektik)*. Bloch's approach here assumes a form of *process realism,* such that forward imagination that grasps the tendency-latency of the process, and not simply the reified "facts" at hand, can outline what things can become as a result of human labor *(Fortbildung).*[17] This process realism combines both reflection and production based on an active co-knowledge *(Mitwissenheit)* of the unfolding course of the world. It can do so because consciousness is "causally affected," in Kant's famous phrase, by the possibility-content of the world even when it is substantially "not yet."

For Bloch, human imagination is informed by the object.[18] Here he refunctions the ancient Stoic doctrine of *phantasia kataleptike,* according to which subject and object "embrace" in the act of knowledge in such a way that there is a productive bridge between the subjective-ideal judgment and its objective-real correlate.[19] For Bloch, integrating process realism and human imagi-

---

[16] Although Habermas dubbed him, with some truth, "a Marxist Schelling," Bloch also integrated into his philosophy the work of Eduard von Hartmann, the philosopher of the unconscious; and the work of Jakob Frohschammer, the philosopher of the imagination.

[17] Ernst Bloch, *Experimentum Mundi,* in *Gesamtausgabe,* vol. 15 (Frankfurt am Main: Suhrkamp, 1975), ch. 13; cf. Bloch, *Tübinger Einleitung in die Philosophie,* in *Gesamtausgabe,* vol. 13, ch. 17.

[18] Bloch, *Experimentum Mundi,* 54–56.

[19] Ibid., 63–65.

nation provides elements of a method that can be used in working to bring about the good future. The future can be built by taking an active approach to history and working up models that can then be tested and corrected. Hence he seeks to uncover the *uto-pian surplus* in cultural materials, and to actively inherit this uto-pian surplus as potentially constitutive of future developments.[20]

In his open system, Bloch integrated Marx's emphasis on the detectivistic study of political and economic processes with the warm stream of the utopian surplus of the whole of world culture. His work included a remarkable articulation of a concept of "metareligion." Bloch expounded this concept in one of his most interesting books, *Atheism in Christianity* (1972).[21] Like Marx, Bloch assumed that religion in the sense of a literal belief in supernatural powers had been discredited by the Enlightenment. Unlike Marx, however, Bloch believed that it was possible to inherit the hope content and the wish mysteriums of religion at precisely the points where they seemed to confront commonsen-sical, mundane, and disillusioned views of reality. Metareligion, in Bloch's sense, is an afterlife of religion, in the sense of a continuing assertion of counterfactual hope. Superstition and su-pernaturalism disappear, together with the "binding back" of re-ligion. "Binding" here is a matter of social logical organization, and can characterize formations of personal identity, institutions, and organizational forms, where in particular empirical cases these may be different and conflict. For Bloch, metareligion in this sense amounts to a positive inheritance of religion: to what religion can still be in the context of an illusion-free atheistic world outlook that occupies rather than abandons the work ter-rain of religion.

Ultimately, it is not clear that Bloch avoided the trap famously identified by his teacher, Georg Simmel. Long before his con-temporaries, Simmel saw that the modernist impulse in the arts would be applied to metaphysics and religion as well, and that bids to destroy old forms and to gesture toward new forms at a

---

[20] Ibid., 409–17.
[21] Ernst Bloch, *Atheism in Christianity: The Religion of the Exodus and the Kingdom,* trans. J. T. Swann (New York: Herder and Herder, 1972).

time when no new forms were available would not be enough.[22] Bloch's attempt to theorize metareligion as a form of *religion after religion* was both voluntarist and over-optimistic. It also privileged the link between traditional religion and binding back, without studying the alternatives.

Nonetheless, Bloch's model of a form of religion after religion that can be produced by human historical action on the basis of utopian surplus, or the objective imagination found in the history of religion worldwide, remains a powerful project that may be able to be reworked in more contemporary terms. Of course, to overcome Simmel's objection, Bloch would have to work with the old forms, as he failed to do, and to theorize their potential as transitional organizational arrangements. But this was precisely a possibility that could be read from Schelling's turn to the history of actual religions. Like Schelling, however, Bloch was imprisoned in a dialectical thought that concealed from him the radical implications of the materials that he discussed.

III

I now turn to the implications of these ideas for the contemporary Continental philosophy of religion. First, there is a clear implication that philosophy of religion needs to take account of historically positive data about religious traditions, actual mythologies, and particular esoterisms, and not only be about Kantian *aporias* based on ahistorical notions of religion, reason, or language. This implies that work on the philosophy of religion that is ethnocentric and unhistorical may require substantial qualification.

Second, these ideas imply that historically productive forms of critique relevant to future constellations of spiritual experience will be found in actual religious traditions and esoteric movements, not only in secular or quasi-secular critiques of them. Again this is controversial, and it implies that recent develop-

---

[22] See Georg Simmel, "The Change in Cultural Forms," in *Simmel on Culture: Selected Writings,* eds. David Frisby and Mike Featherstone (London: Sage, 1997), 103–7.

ments in Buddhism, Hinduism, and Islam could be as important in principle as Parisian celebrations of alterity and difference. But the contemporary Continental philosophy of religion has only begun to address these developments, and then not in detail.

Third, Schelling interprets the empirical record of actual mythologies and religions in conflictualist terms that do not imply preexisting perfection or support any super-ego moralism. The ideas of Schelling and Bloch challenge the more idealizing strands in the Continental philosophy of religion, especially the work of Levinas. For Schelling, unreason is involved in real-world states of affairs, and spirituality itself emerges through forms of egotism. There is also the implication that the real history behind pious surfaces is sometimes monstrous and anti-theodic.[23] And for Bloch, philosophy of all kinds needs to be studied as socially conditioned semblance, rather than as a master discourse that can itself provide the grids by which religious data can be explained.

Fourth, the work of Schelling and Bloch suggests that contemporary Continental philosophy of religion lacks an adequate theory of historical reason,[24] let alone a historical sociology for which reason begins "outside itself" and comes to play a role in the process as a result of dialectical developments.

Fifth, Schelling's development of an ontology of freedom calls into question the possibility of a rationalist philosophy of religion and, in particular, the possibility of developing a rationalist theory of God that will be consistent with the actual contingent facticity of world history.

Sixth, both Schelling and Bloch challenge contemporary Continental philosophy of religion to come to terms with naturalism. It cannot be emphasized too strongly that Schelling's voluntarism both about God and about being is integrated with a dynam-

---

[23] Nonetheless, Schelling is not Lacan, let alone Žižek. There are also strong theological elements in the late Schelling that radically challenge secular consciousness. For Schelling there is a real "Lord of being" who cannot be comprehended in the old philosophy, a real "World of Ideas" (*Ideenwelt*) in which the characters of things are determined, and a protemporal order. Moreover, the universe as a whole is to be understood by reference to a God in the process of becoming.

[24] Cf. Hutter, *Geschichtliche Vernunft: Die Weiterführung der Kantischen Vernunftkritik in der Spätphilosophie Schellings.*

icist naturalism for which the human being and its freedom arises on the basis of nature and remain part of it. Schelling's naturalism here implies that no absolute separation is possible between the organizational character of nature and the organizational character of mind. Schelling located the human subject and its freedom *inside nature*. In effect, he replaced the subject of German idealism with the claim that we ourselves are always located in nature, in something that already exists. Further, according to Schelling, the life of the human being gives access to the structure of the universe:

> Just as man, according to the old and nearly threadbare saying, is the world on a small scale, so the processes of human life from the utmost depths to its highest consummation must agree with the processes of universal life. It is certain that whoever could write the history of his own life from its very ground, would thereby have grasped in a brief conspectus the history of the universe.[25]

Finally, both Schelling and Bloch challenge contemporary Continental philosophy of religion to clarify its ontology of freedom in the context of a possible religion after religion. Schelling's unfinished world opened to risk does not clarify the role of human agency in the determination of the future in detail, and he is remarkably vague about exactly how his philosophical religion is to be brought about. Bloch supplements Schelling at this decisive point, by making metareligion an outcome of a philosophy of the future based on anticipation and objective imagination. But Bloch also fails to provide a coherent account of individual freedom, and his wider speculations about freedom in a socialist society do not remedy these gaps at crucial points. Hence metareligion is to be an advance in human freedom, but how this will be achieved in precise institutional terms is left vague.

Contemporary Continental philosophy of religion has not really entered this challenging terrain, despite Jean Luc-Nancy's important work on a post-Heideggerian philosophy of freedom.[26] Indeed, it has barely started to take proper account of either the

---

[25] Frederick De W. Bolman, *Schelling: The Ages of the World* (New York: Columbia University Press, 1942), 93–94.

[26] Jean-Luc Nancy, *The Experience of Freedom,* trans. Bridget McDonald (Stanford: Stanford University Press, 1993).

radical facticity and contingency of the human historical world
or individual freedom as a fact of nature. It is even less ready for
the program of a utopian heuristics of world historical experience
announced by Schelling and rendered practicable by Bloch.
These are challenges that, arguably, need to be taken up.

15

Politics and Experience: Bergsonism beyond Transcendence and Immanence

Philip Goodchild

THE SOCIAL FUNCTION OF RELIGION

THIS PAPER ASSUMES a political vision that, not being widely shared, requires explicit statement. The fundamental human relations that determine the shape of ecological, social, and personal worlds are not governed by legal, contractual, or institutional principles, but by constitutive practices. At present, the dominant constitutive practice of contemporary social relations is the global market. Production, distribution, and consumption are constituted for the purposes either of making money or of providing "value for money"—that is, a value subject to public measurement. These economic principles, by giving a public and social representation of diverse needs and impulses, usurp the place of the constitutive practices that they may or may not measure: ecological sustainability, subsistence, social welfare, education, personal fulfillment, and spirituality. The result of the contemporary global market's inability to distribute production in accordance with such needs and impulses results in the threat of an imminent triple apocalypse, epitomized by the consequences of an anticipated average global temperature rise this century of between 1.5 and 5.5 degrees: ecological catastrophe, social breakdown, and personal suffering. What is most urgently required, and should therefore be the primary focus of intellectual endeavor, is an alternative practice of social constitution.

Prior to the globalization of modernity, religions were the effective practices of social constitution and cohesion. In a global context, they become necessarily limited in this role. On the one hand, religion has the function of producing social cohesion; on the other hand, the history of religions is characterized by an increasing proliferation of modes of religious life. These two dimensions of religion, the synchronic and the diachronic, are necessarily in tension: cohesion and diversification are incompatible. Moreover, the modes of social cohesion that have existed have often been morally ambivalent, never far removed from violence, conflict, domination, and suppression. On what basis, then, may we think and create an ethical mode of social cohesion?

One remarkable period in this history of tensions between cohesion and diversification, one that has come to have world-historical significance, is the history of England in the sixteenth and seventeenth centuries. It is here that a nonreligious basis was sought for social cohesion, at the same time as "religion" and the "religions" became objects of rational reflection. For England passed through changes in religious orientation with its successive monarchs; it allowed considerable freedom of religious expression; and, through overseas explorations in the New World and the Pacific, it came into contact with other histories and cultures.[1] Such awareness of diversity allowed the religions to become an object of reflection.[2] Moreover, religion itself became reified as an object of rational reflection. For England was heavily influenced by a form of Calvinism where faith was understood as assenting to creeds and propositions, as well as by the Arminian response to Calvinist predestination, which allowed people to contribute to their own salvation by making a profession of faith.[3]

The result was a shift in belief: what was revealed in Christianity was no longer God's self-revelation but "saving knowledge,"

---

[1] Peter Harrison, "Religion" and the Religions in the English Enlightenment (Cambridge: Cambridge University Press, 1990), 3.

[2] Harrison cites Richard Hooker (1593) as the first to use the phrase the religions, and Edward Brerewood (1613) as the first to subject them to systematic analysis. Harrison, "Religion" and the Religions in the English Enlightenment, 39.

[3] Harrison, "Religion" and the Religions in the English Enlightenment, 19–23.

an "objective religion," a doctrine of salvation.[4] Thus in the later seventeenth century, hundreds of pamphlets and tracts appeared claiming to present in propositional form the essence of true religion, the minimum required for salvation (and social cohesion).[5] As a result, the conflict between differing Christian sects became projected onto the world as the problem of religious pluralism: the existence of contradictory, competing belief systems.[6] Religion failed to achieve its social function.

It was within the English context that the idea of a secular nation-state was forged as an alternative principle of social cohesion.[7] Such a secular principle of social cohesion required a discourse that would criticize religious claims to authority that functioned as political rivals. This discourse, a critical evaluation of religion that was not based within religion, one that posited a purely "natural" religion in its place, became the philosophy of religion. It became part of a broader enterprise that wished to set social cohesion on a rational basis.

If attempts to establish a natural religion were to founder by the end of the eighteenth century, two principal alternative directions emerged. In the first place, the broader project of establishing social cohesion on a rational basis has continued until this day. Indeed, following Immanuel Kant's turn to practical reason in order to set religion within the limits of reason alone and remove clerical authority, the philosophy of religion has continued, particularly within the Continental tradition, as part of the attempt to set social cohesion on a rational basis. History shows that reason has little aptitude for this role. In the second place, David Hume's assessment that reason is merely a slave to the passions led to the development within Britain of a utilitarian

---

[4] Ibid., 24.

[5] Ibid., 25.

[6] Of course, many forms of conflict were present, and this justified the projection. Yet conflict has been exacerbated by the introjection of exclusive forms of identity construction in the colonial and postcolonial worlds.

[7] The principal distinction is that made by John Locke between the Commonwealth, "a society of men constituted only for the procuring, preserving and advancing of their own civil interests"—these being life, liberty, health, leisure, and possessions—and a church, "a voluntary society for the public worship of God," this being in such a manner as they judge effective for the eventual salvation of their souls. "Letter on Toleration," in *The Locke Reader,* ed. John W. Yolton (Cambridge: Cambridge University Press, 1977), 245, 248.

philosophy grounded on the organization of passions and interests, and the subsequent ideology of a free market for regulating
interests.

If a secular form of social cohesion has become dominant, it
is trade: economic globalization harnesses competing interests
and makes them interdependent. Only alongside a harmonization
of interests does it become possible to affirm the liberty and
rights of persons in the market of life. Yet if practical reason is
purely regulative, it is not constitutive: the right to be protected
from violence, and to have liberty to enter into contracts, does
not guarantee the availability of contracts that will advance one's
civil interests. Thus legislative and contractual relations do not
effectively generate social cohesion.

Recent French philosophy has sought to reformulate reason so
that it is better suited for its practical functions. For example
Emmanuel Levinas, by proclaiming ethics as first philosophy,
fractured the identity of any ego or group by the primordial demand of the other; Gilles Deleuze, by constructing a philosophy
of immanence, has attempted to immerse reason in desire as a
utopian principle of social cohesion.[8] Both have a critical assessment of the emancipatory prospects of reason and religion in
general, yet Levinas maintains a most rigorous conception of divine transcendence in line with his Jewish tradition, while Deleuze may be situated in a Spinozist pantheist-atheist tradition.

Critique emerges from these commitments: Levinas and Deleuze are thus exemplars of trends to take philosophies of transcendence and immanence to their highest degree of purity, so as
to purge thought of all traces of domination. Each concept is
accompanied by a corresponding mode of social existence: the
affirmation of transcendence is characterized by what we might

---

[8] Deleuze's philosophy has rarely been recognized as an ethics, in spite of
Michel Foucault's preface to the English translation of *Anti-Oedipus,* trans.
Robert Hurley, Mark Seem, and Helen R. Lane (London: Athlone, 1984), xiii.
The secondary literature that best draws this aspect out includes my book *De-
leuze and Guattari: An Introduction to the Politics of Desire* (London: Sage,
1996); my article "Deleuzean Ethics," *Theory, Culture, and Society* 14, no. 2
(May 1997): 39–50; and Daniel W. Smith's "The Place of Ethics in Deleuze's
Philosophy: Three Questions of Immanence," in Eleanor Kaufman and Kevin
Jon Heller, eds., *Deleuze and Guattari: New Mappings in Politics, Philosophy,
and Culture* (Minneapolis: University of Minnesota Press, 1998), 251–69.

call a "methodological respect," whether this is manifested in the form of trust, of prioritizing a particular narrative or tradition as a hermeneutic framework, of worship, or, in Levinas's case, of obligation. The affirmation of immanence is characterized by a "methodological suspicion," which attempts to remove all traces of transcendent authority, whether these are thought to inhibit access to truth, morality, social production, satisfaction of interests, or, in Deleuze's case, desire. Contemporary concepts of transcendence and immanence thus capture, respectively, the essence of respectful traditions and suspicious modernity.

Within modern thought, concepts of transcendence and immanence have been important in differentiating theological from secular thought, traditional theism from feminist religiosity, and religious worldviews of Semitic or Greek origin from those of Indian or Chinese origin. Yet in order to differentiate between transcendence and immanence, the meaning of *difference* itself must be conceived here, perhaps as a pure exteriority (in terms of transcendence) or as an internal self-differentiation (in terms of immanence). Thus explorations of the relations between differing religious philosophies begin after taking up a stance in relation to this issue. One must situate oneself in relation to the religions and modernity in order to begin to address the problem of social cohesion within contemporary pluralism.

The initial postulation of the relation between concepts of transcendence and immanence may be crucial for determining the future cohesion between religious philosophies and perspectives that are specific to traditions, cultures, or genders, as well as for determining the place of religion for critical thought. The fundamental importance of Levinas and Deleuze for philosophy of religion is that they each enable us to address plurality from a situation beyond particular traditions, as well as beyond the universal pretensions of modernity.

Now, it is somewhat striking that the criteria for absolute transcendence and absolute immanence should be indiscernible from each other: all pretenders must be removed from the role of the absolute.[9] It is also striking that these two should acknowledge a

---

[9] Levinas notes this: "The 'unknown' God does not take shape in a theme, and is exposed, through this very transcendence—through this very nonpresence—to the denials of atheism." *Time and the Other* (Pittsburgh: Duquesne University Press, 1987), 117.

major influence in common who has been relatively neglected in the reception of French philosophy outside France: Henri Bergson (1859–1941). Deleuze's intellectual debt to Bergson is clear: his 1956 essay "La conception de la différence chez Bergson"[10] sets out the research program for Deleuze's masterwork, *Difference and Repetition.*[11] Similarly, Levinas singles out Bergson's doctoral dissertation, *Time and Free Will,* as one of the five finest books in the history of philosophy, placing it alongside the *Phaedrus,* the *Critique of Pure Reason,* the *Phenomenology of Spirit,* and *Being and Time.*[12] Levinas indicates the way in which Bergson foreshadows and enables his own philosophy: "With the advent of Bergson—in opposition to the entire tradition, issuing from the Greeks, of reason isolating and identifying the categories of being—it is the human, free time of duration that is declared to be first philosophy."[13] Levinas underlines the importance of Bergson for the "entire problematic of contemporary philosophy": Bergson "puts into question the ontological confines of spirituality."[14] In order to explore the difference between philosophies of transcendence and immanence, we may thus do well to turn back to Bergson—noting that any recollection of his thought must also be a critical reappropriation.

Henri Bergson's will, dated 1937, states: "I would have become a convert [to the Catholic Church], had I not seen in preparation for years the formidable wave of anti-Semitism which is to break upon the world. I wanted to remain among those who

---

[10] *Les études bergsoniennes* 4 (1956): 77–112; translated by Melissa McMahon as "Bergson's Conception of Difference," in *The New Bergson,* ed. John Mullarkey (Manchester: Manchester University Press, 1999), 42–65.

[11] This influence of Bergson is emphasized in recent studies: Keith Ansell Pearson, *Germinal Life* (London: Routledge, 1999); Dorothea Olkowski, *The Ruin of Representation* (Berkeley and Los Angeles: University of California Press, 1999); Eric Alliez, "Sur le bergsonisme de Deleuze," in *Gilles Deleuze: Une vie philosophique,* ed. Eric Alliez (Le Plessis-Robinson: Synthélabo, 1998), 243–64; and Alain Badiou, *Deleuze: The Clamor of Being* (Minneapolis: University of Minnesota Press, 2000).

[12] Emmanuel Levinas, *Ethics and Infinity,* trans. Richard A. Cohen, (Pittsburgh: Duquesne University Press, 1985), 37.

[13] Emmanuel Levinas, "Vladimir Jankélévitch," in *Outside the Subject* (London: Athlone, 1993), 87.

[14] Levinas, "The Old and the New," *Time and the Other,* 132.

tomorrow will be persecuted."[15] This moral gesture, as Jewish as it was Catholic, proved prophetic: Bergson died in 1941 from pneumonia contracted from having stood for hours in a queue of Parisian Jews registering with the Nazi government. This image of an old man left out in the cold by a closed society organized purely for war resonates with the fate of Bergson's philosophy in academic circles beyond France (until recently): briefly celebrated, then marginalized, excluded, forgotten. Where mentioned, neglect of Bergson's philosophy is justified by misrepresentation and abuse—means that amount to repression, a failure to think it through properly. What is it about Bergson's philosophy that is unbearable for modern thought?

Bergson describes our own civilization as a "closed society": one whose essential characteristic is to include a certain number of individuals and to exclude others.[16] Social cohesion composes us for discipline in the face of the enemy; peace is a preparation for war. In a time of war, normal duties toward humanity are regrettably suspended.[17] Thus if war has been declared on Bergson's philosophy in the form of a suspension of the rational procedures of respect and measured argument, this is because the circumstances are exceptional.[18] Bergson, in praising an "open society" extending love "to animals, to plants, to all nature," values the exception and undermines the cohesion based on exclusion.[19] Yet espousal of such values is not uncommon. In what way is Bergson's philosophy exceptional?

Bergson's social theory also contrasts two historical tendencies at work in society: the tendency toward invention and comfort that industrial civilization takes to its extreme, and the

---

[15] Quoted in Frederick Burwick and Paul Douglass, eds., *The Crisis in Modernism: Bergson and the Vitalist Controversy* (Cambridge: Cambridge University Press, 1992), 6. In fact Bergson's father was a Polish Jew, while his mother was an Irish Catholic.

[16] Henri Bergson, *The Two Sources of Morality and Religion,* trans. R. Ashley Audra and Cloudesley Brereton (Notre Dame: University of Notre Dame Press, 1977), 30.

[17] Ibid., 31.

[18] Julien Benda is reported to have said that he would have joyfully killed Bergson if in that way his influence could have been arrested. See Burwick and Douglass, *The Crisis in Modernism,* 2–3.

[19] Bergson, *The Two Sources of Morality and Religion,* 38.

tendency toward asceticism that predominated in the Middle Ages. In our society, artificial needs are created by the senses constantly being aroused by the imagination, and such artificial needs guide the spirit of invention to manufacture for the sake of selling. Bergson's reproach against capitalism is that it has created a mass of new needs without taking care to see that old needs are satisfied; it has widened the gap between capital and labor. Bergson's own socialist preference, to see a central organizing intelligence coordinate industry and agriculture, reflects the countervailing ascetic tendency: the exclusive habits of capitalism must be counterbalanced by the socialist drive to set industry and agriculture to work for the sake of those at the periphery.[20]

Bergson, therefore, envisages raising the form of social cohesion from the sphere of instinct to that of intelligence. If war results from the competition of instincts for limited resources,[21] the extraordinary genius of capitalism lies in harnessing the vices of ambition, luxury, avarice, and lust and organizing their disparate drives to work for the common good of the production of wealth, mediating instinct and fulfillment through the production and expenditure of wealth, so replacing conflict with cooperation. Thus, in capitalism social cohesion is motivated by instinct. Intelligence alone, however, cannot provide any motivation for social cohesion. Bergson points out that moral philosophy is impotent here: "Never, in our hours of temptation, should we sacrifice to the mere need for logical consistency our interest, our passion, our vanity." Intelligence is like the fly wheel rather than the driving machinery; if society is an organization, implying a coordination and subordination of elements, such an organization cannot be formed by reason alone.[22] Instead, powerful motives of instinct, obligation, and emotion construct society.

In *The Two Sources of Morality and Religion,* Bergson makes a frequent contrast between two understandings of society: one is based on an abstract concept of human nature and the philosophical ideal of respect for this abstract concept; the other results from the practice of "moral pioneers" and "great mystics"

---

[20] Ibid., 298–307.
[21] Ibid., 284.
[22] Ibid., 23, 27.

who found communities to spread the creative emotion of love for and to all beings. This differentiation of two sources of society is a strategy within a critique of practical reason. Instead of subjecting morality to reason, Bergson subjects reason to morality: practical reason itself must express creative emotion. Instead of subjecting practical reason to abstract logic or transcendent obligation, practical reason attains freedom when it is driven by intuition of a creative emotion that, overtaking interests, passions, and vanity, gives new forms to thought.

In contrast to capitalism, Bergson's ascetic construction of society is motivated by the common drive of creative emotion inspired by saints. Where people intuit the moral sensibilities of the saints and mystics, the mystics themselves directly intuit the love of God, and build their vision of the open society through the mediation of the love of God.[23] It is this religious source for society that entails a different nature for an open society in contrast to a closed one. Yet there is nothing radical in appealing to utopian impulses. Bergson's philosophy will only be exceptional if, in addition to appealing to a religious impulse, he constructs a different form of intelligence together with a different form of social cohesion on this basis. Bergson makes no such claim for intelligence, but he does for intuition. If intuition implies an exceptional operation of intelligence that no longer serves the needs of capitalist society, then this explains the need to obliterate memory of this thought.

TIME AND SYMBOLS

Bergson's famous distinction is between time that can be counted and time that is lived. Countable time is the time of Aristotle, Kant, physics, laboratories, clocks, factories, labor: a number may symbolize and substitute for it, just as hourly wages are paid. Bergson shows that this is an abstraction, for the essence of time is to pass:[24] once an event has happened, it does not recur

---

[23] Ibid., 53.
[24] Henri Bergson, "La pensée et le mouvant," *Oeuvres* (Paris: Presses Universitaires de France, 1953), 1253.

again. Thus durations, episodes of real time, are not superposable upon each other, so that one may be measured or counted by the other. For this to occur, real time must be replaced by an abstraction that has eliminated the essential: change. Measurable, homogeneous time is an abstraction where nothing takes place: the living is measured insofar as it conforms to the behavior of inanimate clocks. Bergson shows how this conception of time is in fact based on a conception of space: for in counting, one disregards individual differences and counts units that are assumed to be qualitatively identical, yet differentiated from each other in an ideal space.[25]

The idea of number is based on an intuition of homogeneous space; thus, when we count separate moments in time, we do so by some process of symbolical representation in an imaginary space.[26] Where what "properly belongs to the mind is the indivisible process by which it concentrates attention successively on the different parts of a given space," space is "what enables us to distinguish a number of identical and simultaneous sensations from one another."[27] Experienced time, the distribution of attention, is modified to conform to space.

A confusion of time and space is evident in Kant's description of his conception of time: "We represent the time-sequence by a line progressing to infinity, in which the manifold constitutes a series of one-dimension only; and we reason from the properties of this line to all the properties of time, with this one exception, that while the parts of the line are simultaneous the parts of time are always successive."[28] Omitting to explain succession, Kant omits time itself from its concept.[29] For "time is not a line along which one can pass again."[30]

[25] Henri Bergson, *Time and Free Will,* trans. F. L. Pogson (London: Swan Sonnenschein, 1910), 77.

[26] Ibid., 86.

[27] Ibid., 84, 95.

[28] Immanuel Kant, *Critique of Pure Reason,* trans. Norman Kemp Smith (Basingstoke: Macmillan, 1933), 77.

[29] In practice, Kant adopts this conception of time where nothing happens, so that the passage of events in relation to time, numbered in succession, and the passage of time in relation to events as an experience of duration, are indistinguishable and convertible. Certainty, derived through schematization of the categories in a time that happens all at once, is gained at the cost of experience.

[30] Bergson, *Time and Free Will,* 181.

For Bergson, by contrast, externality is distinct from succession: for externality is the distinguishing mark of things that occupy space, while succession in time involves the coinherence of the past in the present as memory, such as when one hears individual notes as a tune. Succession involves "a mutual penetration, an interconnexion and organization of elements."[31] This Bergsonian dichotomy may prove essential in analyzing contemporary cultural atomism as deriving from the subjection of life to representation in terms of space, and in suggesting possibilities for cohesion.

There is already a conflict here with Levinas, who suggests that Bergson replaces alterity with confusion and coincidence.[32] By drawing on the kinetic image of a flow,[33] Bergson overemphasizes continuity against alterity, missing what Levinas calls the "crispation and isolation of subjectivity,"[34] and with it absolute novelty in time whereby the future is surprising. Bergson's method of immanence makes creation the attribute of the creature, overlooking the mystery presupposed by the opening of time.[35]

In response, a Bergsonian may claim that Levinas relies on a spatial image of alterity and exteriority,[36] evident in that the ethical imperative is *signified,* and signification rests on a spatial image of discontinuity and rupture. For if persons and objects are not merely external to each other in space, but co-endure in time, where time is differentiated from spatial exteriority, then there is some degree of interpenetration. If persons are individuated by experience, then they are composed of all the events that affect them, prior to a spatial distinction of interiority and exteriority. The issue will hinge on epistemology, on the nature of experience, and to this we will return.

---

[31] Ibid., 101.

[32] Levinas, *Time and the Other,* 133.

[33] Ibid., 119. Note that Bergson repudiates the image of duration as a bottomless, bankless river. See Bergson, *Introduction to Metaphysics,* trans. T. E. Hulme (London: Macmillan and Co., 1913), 53.

[34] Ibid., 92.

[35] Ibid., 80.

[36] Levinas explicitly denies this, yet his concept of signification evokes a spatial exteriority. See Emmanuel Levinas, *Totality and Infinity: An Essay on Exteriority,* trans. Alphonso Lingis (Dordrecht, The Netherlands: Kluwer, 1991), 175.

Bergson extends his critique of spatialization to the dialectical formation of concepts: language normally requires us to establish between our ideas the same sharp and precise distinctions as between material objects.[37] Thus: "Consciousness, goaded by an insatiable desire to separate, substitutes the symbol for the reality, or perceives the reality only through the symbol. As the self thus refracted, and thereby broken to pieces, is much better adapted to the requirements of social life in general and language in particular, consciousness prefers it, and gradually loses sight of the fundamental self."[38]

For "there is no common measure between the mind and language."[39] It is possible to invert Bergson's analysis: instead of treating the idea of extension as given a priori, one may regard it as being composed from superposition itself: an act of substitution or exchange treating measuring and measured as equivalents. For Bergson indicates that "the intuition of a homogeneous space is already a step towards social life":[40] it is a principle of organization and coordination of elements. The materiality of matter, extended in space, is merely the distribution of a "discontinuous multiplicity of elements, inert and juxtaposed."[41] In such an analysis, duration, mobility, impetus—in short, life itself—is eliminated from matter.

Bergson defines the objective by substitutability,[42] and thus by the sacrifice of the changing and living in the real. "For we contrive to find resemblances between things in spite of their diversity, and to take a stable view of them in spite of their instability; in this way we obtain ideas which we can control, whereas the actual things may elude our grasp."[43]

What social form is enacted when a group of thinkers treat their concepts as a stockpile of elements, inert and juxtaposed, prepared for substitution and exchange? Modern reason is the marketplace of thought where, lacking trust in each others' expe-

---

[37] Ibid., xix.

[38] Ibid., 128.

[39] Ibid., 164–65.

[40] Ibid., 138.

[41] Henri Bergson, *Matter and Memory*, trans. Nancy Margaret Paul and W. Scott Palmer (London: George Allen and Unwin, 1911), 171.

[42] Ibid., 83.

[43] Bergson, *The Two Sources of Morality and Religion*, 242.

riences of thinking, we require guarantees of value from the goods themselves. Yet insofar as reality is delimited to the measurable, the superposable, and the substitutable, all that remains is the "superficial skin,"[44] and philosophy cannot get beyond the symbol, forever nostalgic for the absolute, "the gold coin for which we never seem able to stop giving small change."[45] Thus technological reason substitutes its own symbols for the realities of life: "*Thinking* usually consists in passing from concepts to things, and not from things to concepts. . . . To try to fit a concept on an object is simply to ask what we can do with the object, and what it can do for us."[46]

In brief, the representation of reality in both science and metaphysics is a *commodification,* replacing the thing with a quantifiable symbol fashioned for the purpose of exchange. A symbol may contain a trace, but does not preserve the memory of the birth and life of its object.[47] As Spinoza says, the concept of a dog does not bark. It is hardly surprising that such an operation of the intelligence is in accord with capitalism: capitalist materialism must exclude memory so that it can constitute its illusion of a material world for the satisfaction of instincts.

More than this, Bergson's critique is relevant to the entire history of Western philosophy. For, from Plato onward, philosophy is haunted by a nostalgia for a "transcendental signified," a commodity to be traded within thought that has now become an irrecoverable memory. Abstract conceptual thought can only represent objects in sterile abstraction, independently of their own fecundity, self-expression, and becoming. Thought, then, functions as a medium of exchange like money, exchanging itself for a variety of real objects by means of representing them in imagination, but rendering them in a sterile, conceptual form, where they are deprived of any use. Ultimately, the relations between objects established by rational thought express the social relations between thinkers in the fantastic form of a relation between things. Just as Marx suggests that commodity fetishism

---

[44] Bergson, *Matter and Memory,* 28.
[45] Bergson, *Introduction to Metaphysics,* 6.
[46] Bergson, *Introduction to Metaphysics,* 34, 35.
[47] As Marx says, we cannot tell from the taste of wheat who grew it. Marx, *Capital,* vol. 1., trans. Ben Fowkes (Harmondsworth, England: Penguin, 1976), 211.

may be described by analogy with religion—"there the products
of the human brain appear as autonomous figures endowed with
a life of their own, which enter into relations both with each
other and with the human race"—concept fetishism gives rise to
the illusion of the religious.[48] For here a play of symbols, an
illusion or shadow, seems to take on a determining role.

Nietzsche explained the power of religious illusions as follows:

> If one shifts the centre of gravity of life *out* of life into the "Be-
> yond"—into *nothingness*—one has deprived life as such of its cen-
> tre of gravity. The great lie of personal immortality destroys all
> rationality, all naturalness of instinct—all that is salutary, all that
> is life-furthering, all that holds a guarantee of the future in the
> instincts henceforth excites mistrust. *So* to live that there is no
> longer any *meaning* in living: *that* now becomes the "meaning"
> of life.[49]

It matters little whether one is concerned here with religious or
conceptual illusions. For to live in relation to something outside
life is to forfeit the meaning of one's own life. Then one continues to exist under an indefinite reprieve, a stay in execution,
where unlimited demands and obligations can be made. Moreover, once concepts take on a life of their own and enter into
relations with one another of substitution and exchange, then the
principal concept will be the general equivalent, the concept of
truth, which gives meaning to all other concepts. Thought becomes a quest for truth, a relation to being, in order to give value
to all one's other thoughts.

Yet such a concept is merely a concept of a concept; it is an
effect of the organization of thought. As such, a pure "exteriority" enters the heart of subjectivity and exerts its mastery over
the subject; it capitalizes on thought. This is not the mastery of
domination, but the mastery of infinite debt: in order to coordinate one's thoughts with those of others, one has to translate
them into symbols that can be exchanged and taken as valid.
Thus "truth," understood in practice as the validity of thought

[48] Marx, *Capital,* vol. 1, 165.
[49] Nietzsche, *The Anti-Christ,* trans. R. J. Hollingdale (Harmondsworth,
England: Penguin, 1990), 165–66, §43.

on an open market, becomes the primary value that must be sought above all others.

Far from reason being a condition of autonomy, then, reason itself may be entirely heteronomous. Reason may be an obligation required of us by an illusory god that invades our very souls. Philosophy, in its desire for reality, attempts to conjure the lost object of desire and thought that has been murdered by symbolic thinking. Yet in every nostalgic gesture aimed at recovery, symbolic thinking is again used, so the sacrificial gesture is repeated. Metaphysics is thus essentially theological, is ontotheology, not simply insofar as it involves the idea of a creator God determining the meaning of being as causal making, but insofar as it worships the spirit of a transcendental signified as compensation for the primal murder of the commodity of thought.

Moreover, when symbolic thinking takes itself as its own object, then it sacrifices itself, forever deferring the presence of its own meaning. In any attempt to reconstitute transcendence from the trace of the absent contents of thought, such transcendence remains pure, unthinkable, impossible. Such transcendence has no priority, but is merely a determinate effect produced by a certain strategy of thinking.

Indeed, to the extent that language is able to designate, to apply a rule to a case or a sign to an object, to name this object as this object, then it is inseparable from a certain tracing of borders, an incision into the flux of reality, by which *this* is distinguished from *not-this*. In all representation one finds the phenomenon of the border, which is merely the spatialization of time, an abstraction from the flux of reality. Such a spatialization of time depends on its commodification, its rendering in countable units, its abstraction from its own life. Determination itself is determination by death. Thus Derrida is essentially right in identifying death as the meaning of bordering as such, as the principle that both traces and ruins the borders; for death makes borders possible, while itself evading all borders.[50]

Indeed, to the extent that death makes thinking in terms of limits possible, while death itself is the impossible transgression

---

[50] Jacques Derrida, *Aporias,* trans. Thomas Dutoit (Stanford: Stanford University Press, 1993), 73–4.

of the limit of the possible, a crossing of the border, then "transcendence" can only be thought in terms of death. Moreover, to the extent that the concept of immanence is defined in opposition to transcendence, as that which "does not hand itself over to the transcendent or restore any transcendent," and life is defined as resistance to death, then this conceptual piety is still repeated.[51]

Death is never encountered in experience: if others die, we can only diagnose this from symptoms;[52] if I die, then I am no more.[53] Then, as Derrida says, "fundamentally, one knows perhaps neither the meaning nor the referent of this word."[54] Death is purely symbolic: like a repressed or unconscious signifier, death only acquires its meaning from the terms it relates—the reciprocal relations and obligations it produces between people, or within a person. On the one hand, time imposes itself upon us: moments pass, and so long as temporality is thought in terms of perishing, then death is given transcendentally; on the other hand, so long as death is thought of as a limit to time, then death itself is only given through time itself.[55] The two concepts are constructed in reciprocal presupposition. As Derrida himself speculates: "Who will guarantee . . . that language is not precisely the origin of the nontruth of death, and of the other?"[56]

Then could the gestures of postulating concepts of time and death, and consequently transcendence and immanence, be the generation of transcendental illusions, or false problems? Bergson shows how false problems arise when there is a confusion of the "more" and the "less": so, for example, the idea of nothing contains more than the idea of being: it includes the idea of being, a generalized operation of negation, and the psychological motive for negation. Thus the problem of why there is something

[51] Gilles Deleuze and Félix Guattari, *What Is Philosophy?* trans. Hugh Tomlinson and Graham Burchell (London: Verso, 1994), 60.

[52] In regard to the death of others, Martin Heidegger writes: "The dying of Others is not something we experience in a genuine sense." *Being and Time,* trans. John Macquarrie and Edward Robinson (Oxford: Blackwell, 1962), 282.

[53] In regard to the death of the self, see Maurice Blanchot, *L'espace littéraire* (Paris: Gallimard, 1955), 103–209.

[54] Derrida, *Aporias,* 22.

[55] Martin Heidegger, *On Time and Being,* trans. Joan Stambaugh (New York: Harper Colophon, 1977), 3.

[56] Derrida, *Aporias,* 76.

rather than nothing rests on a false problem. Similarly, the conception of an empty homogeneous medium is not simple, but extraordinary, being a kind of reaction against the heterogeneity that is the ground of our experience.[57] Furthermore, the idea of spontaneity is simpler than that of inertia, since inertia can be understood only by means of spontaneity. In his method of intuition, Bergson begins with the experience of thinking rather than what is represented in thought. Bergson applies this method to eliminate the problem of free will, which "has sprung from a misunderstanding":[58] for if experience in time cannot be conceived in terms of space, then recurrence is impossible,[59] and so the principle of determination, that "the same causes produce the same effects," has no possible application to experience in time.[60] Instead, Bergson suggests that we have immediate knowledge of "free spontaneity."[61]

Bergson's method of intuition breaks with the epistemologies of Descartes, Locke, and Kant. Bergson attacks the doctrine, common to materialism and spiritualism, that perception is formed miraculously in the brain: as though consciousness were inexplicably added to physical movement here.[62] Bergson explains how this requires a "transformation scene from fairyland":

> The material world which surrounds the body, the body which shelters the brain, the brain in which we distinguish centres, he [the materialist or idealist] abruptly dismisses; and, as by a magician's wand, he conjures up, as a thing entirely new the representation of what he began by postulating. This representation he drives out of space, so that it may have nothing in common with the matter from which he started.[63]

Instead, the perceived object, the rays of light it reflects, the retina, the nerves affected, and the brain all form a single whole.[64]

---

[57] Bergson, *Time and Free Will*, 97.

[58] Ibid., 240.

[59] Ibid., 130.

[60] Ibid., 201.

[61] Ibid., 142.

[62] Bergson, *Matter and Memory*, 79–80.

[63] Ibid., 32–33.

[64] Ibid., 37–38. Bergson thus challenges modern dualism of separate systems for science and for consciousness: "How is it that the same image can belong

The radical force of Bergson's theory derives from his insight "that it is really in [the perceived point] P, and not elsewhere, that the image of P is formed and perceived."[65]

Perception overflows the material boundaries of the body in space. For if existence in space is defined by mutual separation, rendering action at a distance inexplicable for Newtonian dynamics, existence in time implies some degree of "mutual penetration, an interconnexion and organization of elements."[66] That an object endures in time, and does not merely exist in space, allows at once that it may be conditioned by perception and recollection. The possibility that we grasp the very object, "that we perceive it in itself and not in us,"[67] overthrows the necessary force of most of modern philosophy, and not merely that of Cartesian

---

at the same time to two different systems, the one in which each image varies for itself and in the well-defined measure that it is patient of the real action of surrounding images, the other in which all change for a single image, and in varying measure that they reflect the eventual action of this privileged image?" (p. 13). Although Bergson states that neither of these systems is implied in the other, this is not immediately true, unless it is further stated that the privileged image is capable of self-determination, of initiating its own movement. Similarly, when Bergson argues that the brain functions like a telephone exchange, relaying or delaying movement (p. 19), and then moves on to suggest that it allows choice, it symbolizes indetermination (p. 21), and finally implies indetermination (p. 23), he lulls us into thinking that an argument has taken place. In practice, Bergson starts "from this indetermination as from the true principle" (p. 21), and has every right to do so based on the reintroduction of duration and freedom in *Time and Free Will*. Yet having allowed memory and choice from the beginning of his analysis of perception, sociobiological assumptions of the ultimately technical nature of intelligence are not well-founded.

We may, therefore, amend the emphasis of Bergson's analysis. The brain, itself biologically determined, does not introduce any interval, any indetermination, between perception and action. Action, in response to a perceived promise or threat, takes time, however; and in the interval between promise and fulfillment (p. 23), the interval of action itself, there is a duration. Duration allows for recollection from different layers of memory; it allows choice and freedom. Memory may act directly on the body: it tends "to urge the body to action, and to impress upon it . . . movements and attitudes" (p. 168). Bergson therefore only seems to posit an absolute difference in kind between matter and memory (p. 81), suggesting that the "past is only idea, the present is ideo-motor" (p. 74), for he himself suggests that memories "spontaneously go to meet the perception" (p. 119). Instead of defining the present merely by actuality or activity (p. 74), he suggests that "the present is simply *what is being made*" (p. 193).

[65] Bergson, *Matter and Memory*, 38.
[66] Bergson, *Time and Free Will*, 101.
[67] Bergson, *Matter and Memory*, 38.

dualism. Instead of starting with the perceiving mind, Bergson, following an open operation of intelligence, travels from the periphery to the center.[68] Gone is the transcendental aesthetic; gone is the Kantian critique of metaphysics;[69] gone is the inaccessibility of the "thing-in-itself": on Bergson's hypothesis, "an ever-deepening knowledge of matter becomes possible."[70]

The heritage of empiricism, transcendental idealism, phenomenology, hermeneutics, structuralism, and poststructuralism is only relevant for a comprehension of a commodified symbol, a substitute for the perceived object, by adding a medium through which the symbol can be organized and comprehended. Moreover, empiricist, Kantian, and positivist critiques of arguments for the existence of God become squabbles against dogmatic philosophy; nothing may be decided in advance about what may be known by intuition.[71]

INTUITION AND TENDENCY

Bergson's scandalous notion of intuition is the key to whether his work offers any prospects for an ethical or religious mode of social thought. At first sight these prospects seem dim, following the linguistic and deconstructive turns. Yet it is precisely such turns that Bergsonism militates against by returning to "naturalism" through direct experience of objects. For Bergson, all division of matter into independent bodies with absolutely determined outlines is an artificial division.[72] Elsewhere, Bergson suggests that if our body is the matter to which our consciousness applies itself, then it comprises all we perceive: in addition to our small body, we also have a "huge, inorganic body."[73] An example of such perception would be telepathy, which Bergson explains as follows: "Our bodies are external to one another in space; and our minds, in so far as they are attached to those

---

[68] Ibid., 44–45.

[69] Bergson, *An Introduction to Metaphysics,* 69–75.

[70] Bergson, *Matter and Memory,* 48.

[71] Bergson, *The Two Sources of Morality and Religion,* 240–52.

[72] Bergson, *Matter and Memory,* 259.

[73] Bergson, *The Two Sources of Morality and Religion,* 258.

bodies, are separated by intervals. But if the mind is attached to the body only by a part of itself, we may conjecture that for the other part of the mind there is a reciprocal encroachment."[74] Furthermore, if the past is preserved like a cone, where only the apex fits into matter, then the realm of reciprocal encroachment may be called the "spirit."[75] Such encroachment is the basis of an open society.

The possibility of perception in the object grounds Bergson's method of intuition. For by "intuition is meant the kind of *intellectual sympathy* by which one places oneself within an object in order to coincide with what is unique in it and consequently inexpressible."[76] This is a process of "intellectual auscultation" by which one searches deeply into the life of an object and feels the "throbbings of its soul."[77] Such a process would remain incomprehensible if perception were not in the object itself. Metaphysics dispenses with symbols,[78] which function as so many concealing veils over both the object itself and the inner life.[79] Instead of perceiving objects in space, intuition bears on interior duration:

> C'est la vision directe de l'esprit par l'esprit [it is the direct vision of mind by mind]. . . . Intuition signifie donc d'abord conscience, mais conscience immédiate, vision qui se distingue à peine de l'objet vu, connaissance qui est contact et même coïncidence [intuition therefore signifies consciousness, but immediate consciousness, awareness that is hardly distinguishable from the object, knowledge that is contact and even coincidence].[80]

Bergson thus breaches a taboo of modern thought: he hypothesizes access to the inner life of persons and things outside of us. Bypassing symbolic mediation, he bypasses the labor of the modern intellect, with all its interests and investments. Philoso-

---

[74] Henri Bergson, *Mind Energy,* trans. H. Wildon Carr (London: Macmillan, 1920), 78.

[75] Bergson, *The Two Sources of Morality and Religion,* 263.

[76] Bergson, *Introduction to Metaphysics,* 6.

[77] Ibid., 31.

[78] Ibid., 8.

[79] Bergson, *Matter and Memory,* 48.

[80] Henri Bergson, *La pensée et le mouvant* (Paris: Presses Universitaires de France, 1947), 27.

phizing becomes a simple act.[81] It is such a challenge to vested interests that requires swift suppression. But Bergson warns that metaphysics "must abstain from converting intuition into symbols";[82] it is doubtful whether the work of intuition is able to manifest itself at all in the modern public sphere, where thought is mediated by language. Does intuition enact its own self-censorship, rendering itself sterile and harmless?[83] Moreover, telepa-

---

[81] Ibid., 139.

[82] Bergson, *Introduction to Metaphysics,* 43.

[83] In the phenomena of evolution, however, Bergson finds a way of rescuing and expanding intuition, and, to my mind, this is an unfortunate compromise. Bergson finds definite directions followed in evolution: theories of chance evolution, like theories of a pre-existing model, cannot explain how a complex, coordinated organ such as an eye came to be formed (Henri Bergson, *L'évolution créatrice,* Paris: Presses Universitaires de France, 1957, 89). Moreover, since there is no evidence for the Lamarckian inheritance of acquired characteristics, Bergson posits the *élan vital* as an inward impulse passing from germ to germ down generations of individuals (p. 88). Since nothing can be added in experience to that original impulse, it proceeds by differentiating and complicating the successive stages of individuals that it creates; it is a "faculty of resolving problems," it "divides what it defines" (*The Two Sources of Morality and Religion,* 113–14).

Now, since the whole of the élan vital is in us, in our germ, we have only to introspect to discover our unity with other living forms. It is in this way that intuition of other living forms becomes possible: we share the same élan vital in germ. To help us in our work of introspection to distinguish between nature and culture, we may observe the following point: "[I]f along each of these lines [of evolution] an essential characteristic develops more and more, we may conjecture that the vital impetus began by possessing these characteristics in a state of reciprocal implication" (p. 115). Thus if one distinguishes the tendencies, say, of instinct and intelligence, then one may find a "virtual instinct" operating inside us. This is the method often applied in *The Two Sources of Morality and Religion.*

Yet this method is conjecture, not intuition. There are a number of problems here: first, intuition is reduced to taxonomy. "Lines of fact" are identified by the same principle as that which they are intended to demonstrate; however many such lines may appear to "meet," the procedure is purely ideological, confirming a point of view already chosen. Moreover, Bergson does not adequately show how one can distinguish between creative characteristics such as instinct and intelligence, properties of the élan vital, and created characteristics, such as "tool-making intelligence." Most significantly, in abiding by neo-Darwinian orthodoxy, which prohibits the Lamarckian inheritance of acquired characteristics, Bergson removes any role for memory. Yet if memory is not a mere idea but a principle of action, memory may affect what is being made without itself being found in the body, leaving traces for positive science. Thus Bergson's theory of an élan vital, while it may operationalize memory in a general sense, does not take advantage of specific memories.

thy and access to the memories of others seem to be comparatively rare phenomena, not accessible by will or technique. What, realistically, does intuition offer as a method, apart from introspection and conjecture? What can we discover of the interior life of things?

We do not intuit objects as objects; nor do we intuit as subjects. We can only intuit shared temporal life, the tendencies in other beings that are also manifested in us. If, as Bergson tells us, "metaphysics is the science which claims to dispense with symbols,"[84] or at least it frees itself from ready-made concepts in order to create "supple, mobile and almost fluid representations, always ready to mould themselves on the fleeting forms of intuition,"[85] then such concepts are created by the tendencies intuited.

It is this tendency of Bergsonism that has been taken the furthest by Deleuze. Intuition is the determination of differences in nature: not exteriority in space, but tendencies toward self-differentiation.[86] The creation of concepts becomes a process of making distinctions,[87] of following and intensifying a tendency. A concept is no longer a representation, for concepts "are indeed things, but things in a free and wild state."[88] The uncivilized freedom of the concept lends it a double power: on the one hand, thought is liberated to mime the gestures of the forces that form thought—"Life will no longer be made to appear before the categories of thought; thought will be thrown into the categories of life";[89] on the other hand, the concept is not limited by laws of nature, by subjective presuppositions, nor by historical conditioning. Instead, it shapes the boundaries through which nature, the subject, and history can be understood—it marks the significant thresholds. The transcendental freedom of the concept lends it an ethical and political import: it is not concerned with what things are, with what they mean and where and when they can

---

[84] Bergson, *Introduction to Metaphysics,* 8.

[85] Ibid., 18.

[86] Deleuze, "Bergson's Conception of Difference," 43–44.

[87] Deleuze interview, *Le Monde,* 6 October 1983, p. 1.

[88] Gilles Deleuze, *Difference and Repetition,* trans. Paul Patton (London: Athlone, 1994), xx.

[89] Gilles Deleuze, *Cinema 2: The Time-Image,* trans. Hugh Tomlinson and Robert Galeta (London: Athlone, 1989), 189.

be found, but with what happens,[90] what we do,[91] or what it enables us to think and do.[92]

Tendencies, for Deleuze, are at the same time the conditions of real experience and an "experienced foundation"; at the same time "the pure and the lived, the living and the lived, the absolute and the lived."[93] Moreover, a tendency, as an alteration, differentiates itself from itself: "[T]he thing differs from itself *in the first place, immediately.*"[94] Indeed, the tendency defining a thing is distinguished as that which alters from that which does not. Yet Deleuze draws Bergson toward monism, for a tendency splits into tendencies, one of which is the principle of the divisible.[95] Nevertheless, in describing a virtual tendency as "simple, pure," as "a thing, a substance,"[96] despite the initial shock of this paradoxical formulation, Deleuze is in danger of reintroducing essentialist, spatialized thought back into metaphysics. For Deleuze as for Bergson, virtual tendencies are distributed in an imaginary *space,* even if it is a space of memory.

One cannot help fearing that Deleuze, like Bergson himself, falls short of Bergson's fundamental insight insofar as he passes over experience.[97] For if a thing differs from itself in the first place, it does so not only as being both actual and virtual, differentiated and self-differentiating, as altering in time, but it also does so insofar as the actual waits for the event to take place—in an experience of duration. Experience is separated from its conditions. Yet it may maintain a relation to them in such a way that it affects those conditions themselves. The practice of intu-

---

[90] Gilles Deleuze and Félix Guattari, *A Thousand Plateaus,* trans. Brian Massumi (London: Athlone, 1988), 192.

[91] Gilles Deleuze, *Empiricism and Subjectivity,* trans. Constantin V. Boundas (New York: Columbia University Press, 1991), 14.

[92] Gilles Deleuze and Félix Guattari, *What Is Philosophy?* 34.

[93] Deleuze, "Bergson's Conception of Difference," 46.

[94] Ibid., 53.

[95] Ibid., 49.

[96] Ibid., 45, 53.

[97] This is less an oversight than an inherent difficulty in conceiving experience. At times Deleuze does give central importance to experience, e.g. Deleuze and Guattari, *Anti-Oedipus,* 19; Deleuze's final verdict, however, is that the transcendental field is not defined by pure immediate consciousness, for there is nothing that can reveal it. See Gilles Deleuze, "Immanence: A Life . . ." *Theory, Culture and Society* 14, no. 2 (May 1997): 3–7.

ition—as a disciplining of attention—affects the experiences one has. For Bergson and Deleuze, the virtual is separated, absolved of a relation with the actual, and immanence is rendered absolute, insofar as "phenotype" does not determine the "genotype," that is, the germ remains absolute.[98] It is on this basis that Bergson's concept of the *élan vital* arises;[99] it is also on this basis that Bergson distinguishes between "static" and "dynamic" religion, between "crass superstition" and direct mystical intuition of the divine. Yet religious practice, insofar as it attends to memory, to spiritual powers, to virtual tendencies, may influence and affect them, may offer conditions for their actualization.

Let us summarize: modern thought, in its sacrifice of experience to the concept, places thinkers as strangers in a marketplace where they encounter each other with mutual suspicion, trusting only in the hard currency of the concepts exchanged. Modern reason cannot reconstitute the broken cohesion that it destroys in its own practice. Furthermore, it makes little difference whether one conceives difference in terms of transcendence or immanence, the alterity of the stranger or the self-differentiating tendency shared with the colleague. In both cases, experience will be determined from without, whether by imperative or impulse. The meaning of difference omitted in each is that made by the direct intuition of the virtual conditions of experience. Premodern religious thought, by contrast, for all its errors and superstitions, offered at least the social conditions of trust and complicity in which experience itself could be trusted and shaped, apart from its value in a sale.

While one may not wish to abandon any of the liberations effected by critical thought, premodern thought can still have value in teaching us about the distribution of attention, about self-determination, and about spirituality. If it does so without unity or universality, transcendence or immanence, then this is no great loss. The limits to possible experience are not given by reason alone; they can only be determined by experiment in experience.

---

[98] The importance of neo-Darwinism for Bergson and Deleuze is emphasized persuasively, in spite of rather scant textual evidence, by Keith Ansell Pearson, in *Germinal Life.*

[99] Bergson, *The Two Sources of Morality and Religion,* 113–14.

RELIGION AND MEMORY

Bergson's argument for freedom can be reformulated as an argument for the religious as an excess in temporal experience over any determination. The concepts of time, experience, and spontaneity here are not clear, for they merely express an excess over all determination—experience is not found in the concept of experience, but in experience itself. This is the source of the antimonies of pure reason, and of debates in philosophy: concepts are born from the sacrifice of experience; it is thus easy for an opponent to point out the absence of the referent in the concept.[100]

The concept of transcendence, whether based on analogy, ontology, revelation, or alterity, simply does not transcend—thinking the concept (in modern thought) remains forever divorced from the reference of the concept. It is thus easy for opponents of transcendence to point out the absence of transcendence in the concept, whether these are secular opponents of Christian theology or Buddhist opponents of Upanisadic metaphysics. For the transcendent, the ultimate measure of values, has already disappeared when the question of its own value is raised. If such debates rest on a false problem, then can we think otherwise?

Religion may interpenetrate the field of experience. The concept of experience here merely has a unity as a symptom—it is the pain that a living thought feels on being sacrificed to a symbolic representation. Experience is the tendency of memory, or other dimensions of time, to reassert themselves: the tendency to direct attention in a particular direction. Instead of experience being an object or commodity of thought to be subordinated to some useful purpose, experience itself thinks, is interpenetrated with thought. To borrow a slogan from Marx, "Life is not determined by consciousness, but consciousness by life."[101]

To situate a philosophy of religion within experience is to directly oppose the modern reason epitomized by Kant's call to

---

[100] Bergson applies this principle to debates between rationalism and empiricism. See *Introduction to Metaphysics,* 28.

[101] Karl Marx, *The German Ideology,* ed. C. J. Arthur (London: Lawrence and Wishart, 1970), 47.

banish inward and external experience, sudden enlightening, and interaction with the supernatural, from religion within the limits of reason alone.[102] For since repeatability and substitutability are the preconditions for conceptual symbolization, modern reason can only grasp religion insofar as it is translatable into an object of history, sociology, linguistics, anthropology, cultural studies, or comparative religion. Theories and descriptions of religion have been unable to grasp religion in its excess. For to the extent that religion can be explained, that reasons can be given for its occurrence; or to the extent that it can be described, that other concepts may be substituted for its own, it is brought back into the sphere of economy. Where rationality is economical, religion, like nature, is lavish. To the extent that religion is a way of interacting with the excessive and exceptional, then it will exceed rational critique in its present form.

Religion itself is excessive: in its pervasiveness, variety, complexity, and irreducibility of forms, religion exceeds rational description and definition. There is no necessity for religion. Religion is supererogatory; it is pure gift. The only explanation for the variety of religion is that there is no sufficient reason. Furthermore, religion is irrational in the ways in which it deploys and "wastes" its excess. The amount of time, energy, and resources that humanity dedicates to religious activities such as offerings, prayer, worship, and renunciation is inestimable. In each case, the product of such human labor is withdrawn from circulation; all religion is sacrifice. Similarly, the amount of intellectual activity squandered in the repetition of dull and questionable beliefs, dogmas, and clichés is also immense; it prevents the application of human intelligence to the transformation of conditions of existence in creative praxis.

Yet religious practice, unlike modern reason, does not sacrifice all memory: its strategies of repetition may be regarded as attempts to make the traditional, the past, even if it has never been present, live again in the present. Chants, mantras, drumming, invocations, liturgies, rituals, festivals, pilgrimages, dances,

---

[102] Immanuel Kant, *Religion within the Limits of Reason Alone,* trans. Theodore M. Greene and Hoyt H. Hudson (New York: Harper and Brothers, 1960), 48.

songs, storytelling, veneration of ancestors, preservation of traditions, recitation of doctrines, and observance of laws—repetition
is to be found throughout the experience of religion. Such experience involves the giving of due attention and honor to the ancestors, who in return give the ritual by which they are honored. On
the one hand, following the ways of the ancestors means that the
ancestors give ritual behavior itself; they give order and shape to
life. But on the other hand, the living return honor to the ancestors by repeating such rituals. Such an exchange between the
living and the dead takes place in one and the same practice:
ritual is given as order and returned as honor. One gets what one
gives, and gives what one gets. Tradition, insofar as it is repeated,
is experienced as a gift.

Ritual repetition, however, is extremely precarious: there is the
danger that the stereotypical gesture will be simply repeated,
substituting for the relation to the ancestors. As most religious
practitioners recognize, practice does not simply aim at repetition, but at a relation with the ancestors and gods. There is an
element of uncertainty and indeterminacy in all ritual: one does
not know in advance that the being-given of the ritual will be
given. This anxiety over a relation to the asignifiable manifests
itself in three ways. First, one may attempt to resolve the uncertainty by repeating the ritual; time becomes punctuated by
rhythm and order. Second, one may wait for signs of divine favor
to be manifested in the events of life, so that time becomes history, punctuated by differentiated events expressing the acts of
the gods. Third, the anxieties of sacred ritual and historical faith
may be realized in an "experience": there is an extravagant and
irrational dimension of religion, bordering on the phenomenology of psychosis, filled with visions, voices, insights, convictions, withdrawals from the world, and powerful emotions. Even
though it is more feared than desired, it is difficult to overestimate the influence of such singular events in the history of
religion, events that are not repeatable, generalizable, or substitutable—and to overestimate the influence of delusions arising
from taking such events as repeatable, generalizable, or substitutable.

Bergson himself came to place what he called mysticism—
direct intuition of the creative love of God—at the heart of his

philosophy of religion.[103] While his execution of this move now seems deeply problematic, the direction in which he points is clear.[104] When Bergson points out how the mystics have tended to found religious orders, it is a spiritual society for the preservation and transmission of inspiration that he has in mind.[105] And it is to music that Bergson turns when he wishes to show how the encroachment of inspiration operates:

> We feel, while we listen, as though we could not desire anything else but what the music is suggesting to us, and that that is just as we should naturally and necessarily act did we not refrain from action to listen. Let the music express joy or grief, pity or love, every moment we are what it expresses. Not only ourselves, but many others, nay, all the others, too. When music weeps, all humanity, all nature, weeps with it. In point of fact it does not introduce these feelings into us; it introduces us into them, as passersby are forced into a street dance. Thus do pioneers in morality proceed.[106]

For Bergson, there are two kinds of emotion: there is the emotion that is a disturbance resulting from a representation, and there is the emotion that precedes, causes, and exceeds the idea.[107] If dynamic religion is primarily a creative emotion, then any critique of religious morality and metaphysics is irrelevant to the truth of its inspiration.[108] Moreover, by bypassing the significance of morality and metaphysics, Bergson's open society is merely an emotion or contagious atmosphere; it avoids the dangers of an oppressive universalism that is blind to the particular.

For Bergson, mystical morality is immensely simple: the mys-

---

[103] Bergson, *The Two Sources of Morality and Religion,* passim.

[104] Bergson's study of mysticism, heavily influenced by Vivekananda, Evelyn Underhill, and Rudolf Otto, cannot stand in the contemporary field of the comparative study of mysticism: such mysticism is largely a cultural construct, an ideology of the superiority of his own Catholic faith. There is little unity among the few figures he cites, let alone those he does not. Moreover, Bergson establishes no clear identity between the élan vital, which knows nothing of death and constitutes humanity for violence, and the divine love that is understood in the Christian faith as sharing in human suffering and death.

[105] Bergson, *The Two Sources of Morality and Religion,* 236.

[106] Ibid., 40.

[107] Ibid., 252.

[108] Ibid., 49.

tic does not recognize any problems. All that is required is affirmation:

> True mystics simply open their souls to the oncoming wave. Sure of themselves, because they feel within them something better than themselves, they prove to be great [wo]men of action. . . . That which they have allowed to flow into them is a stream flowing down and seeking through them to reach their fellow-men; the necessity to spread around them what they have received affects them like an onslaught of love.[109]

Bergson thus does not feel the need to address the question: What is to be done? For the fixed forms of morality and metaphysics may be judged according to good or bad, true or false, included or excluded; yet creative emotions may be openly affirmed.[110] There remains the question, however, of how such emotions are to be associated, coordinated, and subordinated: the social cohesion of creative emotions. This question requires an alternative operation of intelligence.

Moreover, Bergson suggests that intuition is difficult; it requires working against the natural operation of our intelligence, which consists in "attention to life." But intuition itself is attention to life; it merely exercises a degree of freedom in how such attention should be distributed. Indeed, the distribution of attention quickly takes on the forms of habit and obligation; it becomes a social memory in the form of honor—the degree of value, that is, the degree of attention that ought to be paid to someone. One may suspect that such a difficulty is cultural rather than natural: as Bergson himself points out, memory appears to diminish with intellect, due to the growing organization of recollections with acts.[111] In fact, it is our faculty of recollection that diminishes when it is constantly organized to coordinate with purposeful action.

Our civilization's style of life, whether saturated with media

---

[109] Ibid., 99. Bergson actually names very few mystics, and gives no explicit discussion of their individual lives, teachings, and writings: only St. Paul, St. Teresa, St. Catherine of Siena, St. Francis, and St. Joan of Arc are mentioned explicitly. Bergson, *The Two Sources of Morality and Religion,* 228.

[110] Given the doubts we have raised about the existence and goodness of the élan vital, it is questionable whether we can repeat this simple affirmation.

[111] Bergson, *Matter and Memory,* 199.

images or not, tends to diminish recollection. Memory does not only work spontaneously; it requires an active effort of recollection. The difficulty in practicing intuition is less that it operates against any "natural" intelligence than that it is difficult to stimulate appropriate recollections. Whereas in "dynamic" religion creative emotion imposes itself upon our attention, in so-called "static" religion one has to adopt techniques to engage in recollection. Indeed, it "sometimes happens that well-nigh empty formulae, the veriest magical incantations, contrive to summon up here and there the spirit capable of imparting substance to them."[112] If one allows the role of memory in so-called static religion, then a sharp distinction in kind between the static and the dynamic, the superstitious and the mystic, falls away. Such techniques, from a modern perspective, seem unprofitable: they waste time. But this presupposes that the value of values is already determined. By contrast, the distribution of attention, the intelligent operation of intuition, creates values in the way it chooses to spend time.

From a modern perspective, "life," its duration and quality, becomes the objective measure of values: it is life that demands attention. Where money measures value in circulation, and labor time measures value in production, life time measures value in consumption. Indeed, this is a way of giving attention to time: on the one hand, labor time is regarded as a countable stock, a linear quantity; on the other hand, life time has a quality and duration. In ritual, however, attention is paid to that which lies outside of the experience of time. For alongside the sphere of the distribution of value, there is also a sphere of the distribution of attention. By giving attention to fantastic images, the myth-making function generates the idleness, the nonproductivity, in which recollection can occur. Recollection here is the action of a region of the past in the present: it is the spontaneous arrival of memory. Since the blessings of the gods are uncertain and fortuitous, they cannot be subjected to scientific investigation through repetition. Ritual is conducted, therefore, in an atmosphere of hope and fear, interest and anxiety.

The uncertainty of ritual has two consequences: first, it gener-

---

[112] Bergson, *The Two Sources of Morality and Religion,* 215.

ates a closed society, for the gods are immune to economic obligation. On the one hand, one attempts to rationalize worship with a principle such as: The gods bless those who perform worship correctly. On the other hand, when blessing is not received, then someone must be to blame for impiety. One who is impious, or who is marked by misfortune, is not to be trusted: his or her place is forfeited in a community of trust, generosity, honor, and attention. Second, however, ritual time is neither labor time nor lived time: it is given time. Such a time is not quantifiable, nor can it be said to pass. Instead, it can only be given. The gods watch the ritual. They have an interest, a share in the sacrifice. For watching is not purely passive: one gives time.

While people glorify the gods by offering the sacrifice, the gods glorify people by taking an interest in them, attending to them, giving time to them. There is therefore a commerce with the gods, but it is not a commerce of commodities. It is a commerce of attention, interest, giving time. Of course everything is uncertain here, even the very existence of the gods. What is given in ritual, however, is a way of attending to time, which, not passing, is immune to life and death: it is an eternity that coexists with a short duration. It is a collective memory that gives social cohesion, apart from representation.

The difference between cultic and mystic religion consists in a different relation to the eternal. The melody of each develops the same theme. Yet for cultic religion, the eternal, the given time of ritual, is always past or future: it is either about to be given or is yet to come. In practice, hope and fear are coextensive with ritual practice. Such hope and fear consist in the very attention to time and eternity that is found in ritual. The mystic, by contrast—no longer understood as a religious type, but as a conceptual persona, a mode of philosophical experience—remembers: instead of approaching the sacred via the symbol, the symbol is approached via the sacred. This excess over the symbolic is manifested first of all as chaos: the mystic is stripped of all belief, all ritual, and given a new mode of existence in eternity, where there is no attachment to life nor fear of death.

This chaotic excess over the symbolic order requires that the insights of the mystic be excluded, insofar as they cannot be recuperated. Of course, the mystic continues to endure in labor time and life time, but a new source for the distribution of values, and the distribution of attention has been given. Instead of attention being turned to the fantastic images of the myth-making function, attention is turned to the being-given of reality itself, where all reality is coextensive with cultic time. Thus mystic religion founds the open society. Such universal affirmation is enhanced by the desire to spread the power to intuit existence *sub specie durationis.*

Bergson's so-called "active" mystic is not merely one who succeeds in uniting technical and mystical tendencies. The active mystic attends to all reality, but attends to such reality on the basis of the "love of God": here, one is driven by creative emotion to an ethical confrontation with the whole of reality. God is manifested as neither an object alongside the mystic nor a recollection, but simply as the very mode of existence of the mystic, a coordination of values, a distribution of attention. God is the repetition of repetition, unlimited harmony, infinite resonance. Then if religion may shed any light on problems of social cohesion and intelligence, it will do so through the cohesion it constructs via the distribution of mutual attention to the inner life.

CONCLUSION

In modern thought and life, reason and aspiration are conducted in relation to transcendentals that are never fully given in experience, whether these are concepts of space and time, energy and information, or whether they are death, birth, obligation, wealth, pleasure, desire, or meaning. In practice, such transcendentals can only be preserved and communicated by the modes of thinking and conduct that they support; that is to say, such transcendentals are produced by our modes of thinking and living. In modern life, if nothing is more certain than death and money, then God may be dead but religion is not, for irrespective of our personal beliefs, transcendent sources of meaning and value force themselves upon our conditions of existence. We may not believe in the newly dominant gods, but our thoughts and bodies believe for us in the attention and time they give to death and money.

Yet our concepts of time and money, death and birth, transcendence and immanence, difference and repetition, do not allow us to recollect the spiritual powers that actually determine our ways of thinking, valuing, and acting, for they are separated from the processes by which they are generated. A philosophy of religion directed toward the intuition of experience subordinates economic reason, characterized by sacrifice of experience, to rituals of recollection, anticipation, and even singular experience. This is no longer religion subordinated to critical reason, but critical reason as a dimension of religious practice. Only as such can we welcome, name, honor, but also render finite, the influence of the spiritual powers that govern our lives. Critical thought remains essential for distinguishing thought and practice from experience itself—it expresses an ascetic spirituality, a long series of reflections and analyses aimed at removing delusions and prejudices one by one. What remains of religious thought, after the work of a critical philosophy of religion, is experience itself—as a tendency to direct attention, thought, and conduct in a particular direction. It is a way of giving time.

In such an ethical practice of thought, responsibility for the other and intensification of life in the living become inseparable, predicated on neither lack nor plenitude, death nor birth, transcendence nor immanence, but on the intensity of experience of which we are capable. So Nietzsche described a philosopher as one "who constantly experiences, sees, hears, suspects, hopes, dreams extraordinary things; who is struck by his own thoughts as if from without, as if from above and below, as by *his* kind of events and thunder-claps; who is himself perhaps a storm and pregnant with new lightnings."[113]

---

[113] Friedrich Nietzsche, *Beyond Good and Evil,* trans. R. J. Hollingdale (Harmondsworth, England: Penguin, 1973), 198, §292.

NOTES ON CONTRIBUTORS

Pamela Sue Anderson is Fellow in Philosophy and Christian Ethics, Regent's Park College, Oxford University, England. She is the author of *Ricoeur and Kant: Philosophy of the Will* (1993); *A Feminist Philosophy of Religion: The Myths and Rationality of Belief* (1998); as well as various articles in Continental philosophy, ethics, and philosophy of religion. She has a forthcoming book, *Revisioning Gender in Philosophy of Religion: The Ethics and Epistemology of Belief,* and has started a project on "an ethics of memory."

Gary Banham is Research Fellow in Transcendental Philosophy at Manchester Metropolitan University, England. He is the author of *Kant and the Ends of Aesthetics* (2000) and co-editor of *Evil Spirits: Nihilism and the Fate of Modernity* (2000). He has recently co-edited a special issue of *Tekhnema: Journal of Philosophy and Technology,* on teleology, and is editor of a special issue of *Angelaki: Journal of the Theoretical Humanities,* on aesthetics and the ends of art. He is the series editor for the new Palgrave series *Renewing Philosophy* and is currently writing a book on Kant's practical philosophy.

Bettina Bergo is Assistant Professor of Philosophy at Loyola College (Maryland). She is the author of *Levinas between Ethics and Politics: For the Beauty That Adorns the Earth* (1999). She has translated Levinas's *Of God Who Comes to Mind* (1998) and *God, Death, and Time* (2001). She is co-editor with Diane Perpich of *Levinas's Contribution to Contemporary Philosophy,* a special issue of the New School for Social Research Graduate Faculty Philosophy Journal. She is the author of numerous essays on Levinas and contemporary French philosophy and was, in academic year 2001–2002, a fellow at the Radcliffe Institute for Advanced Study at Harvard.

John D. Caputo holds the David R. Cook Chair of Philosophy at Villanova University. His most recent publications include *On Religion* (2001); *Blackwell Readings in Continental Philosophy: The Religious* (editor, 2001); *More Radical Hermeneutics: On Not Knowing Who We Are* (2000); *God, the Gift, and Postmodernism* (co-editor, 1999); *The Prayers and Tears of Jacques Derrida: Religion without Religion* (1997); *Deconstruction in a Nutshell: A Conversation with Jacques Derrida* (1997).

Clayton Crockett is the author of *A Theology of the Sublime* (2001) and editor of *Secular Theology: American Radical Theological Thought* (2001). He is also managing editor of the online *Journal for Cultural and Religious Theory* (*www.jcrt.org*). He teaches religion and philosophy at Wesley College in Dover, Delaware.

Jonathan Ellsworth lives and studies philosophy in Chicago. He has recently taught seminars in the philosophy department at Wheaton College on the history of philosophical *askêsis,* and on Henry David Thoreau.

Philip Goodchild is Senior Lecturer in Religious Studies at the University of Nottingham, England. He is the author of *Gilles Deleuze and the Question of Philosophy* (1996); *Deleuze and Guattari: An Introduction to the Politics of Desire* (1996); and *Capitalism and Religion: The Price of Piety* (2002). He initiated and organized the conference on "Continental Philosophy of Religion" at Lancaster, England, upon which this collection is based.

Matthew Halteman is a candidate for the Ph.D. in philosophy at the University of Notre Damé. He is writing a thesis on the problem of transcendence in hermeneutic phenomenology, especially in the work of Martin Heidegger and Jacques Derrida.

Wayne Hudson is Professor of History and Philosophy and Director of the Centre for Advanced Studies in the Humanities at Griffith University, Brisbane, Australia. He is a world authority on the German philosopher Ernst Bloch. Recent publications include *Creating Australia: Changing Australian History* (1997); and *Rethinking Australian Citizenship* (2000).

Grace Jantzen is Research Professor of Religion, Culture, and Gender in the Department of Religions and Theology, University of Manchester, England. She is the author of many articles and books, most recently *Power, Gender and Christian Mysticism* (1995); and *Becoming Divine: Towards a Feminist Philosophy of Religion* (1998). She is currently at work on a large project provisionally entitled "Death and the Displacement of Beauty."

Donna Jowett is an Assistant Professor of Philosophy at Nipissing University in Ontario, Canada, where she teaches in the areas of history of philosophy, phenomenology, hermeneutics, and deconstruction. Her primary research focus is ethical experience as informed by the thought of Emmanuel Levinas.

Gregory B. Sadler is a Ph.D. candidate at Southern Illinois University at Carbondale, working on a dissertation on "Maurice Blondel, Catholicism, and Modernity." He has published articles on Blondel, Hegel, and Adorno, and is the publisher and reviews editor of *Catholic Horizons,* a new journal devoted to Catholic engagement with modernity and postmodernity.

Graham Ward is Professor of Contextual Theology and Ethics at the University of Manchester. He is the editor of several volumes, including *The Postmodern God* (1997) and the *Blackwell Companion to Postmodern Theology* (2001). He is author of *Barth, Derrida, and the Language of Theology* (1995), *Theology and Contemporary Critical Theory* (1996), *Balthasar at the End of Modernity* (forthcoming), and *Cities of God* (2000), and is executive editor of the journal *Literature and Theology.*

Edith Wyschogrod is the J. Newton Rayzor Professor of Philosophy and Religious Thought at Rice University. Her books include *Saints and Postmodernism: Revisioning Moral Philosophy* (1990); *An Ethics of Remembering: History, Heterology and the Nameless Others* (1998); and *Emmanuel Levinas: The Problem of Ethical Metaphysics* (rev. ed. 2000).

INDEX